READING A NEW TESTAMENT
DOCUMENT ETHICALLY

Society of Biblical Literature

Academia Biblica

Saul M. Olyan,
Old Testament Editor

Mark Allan Powell,
New Testament Editor

Number 1

Reading a New Testament
Document Ethically

Reading a New Testament Document Ethically

Elna Mouton

Society of Biblical Literature
Atlanta

READING A NEW TESTAMENT
DOCUMENT ETHICALLY

Copyright © 2002 by the Society of Biblical Literature

Library of Congress Cataloging-in-Publication Data

Mouton, Elna, 1952–
Reading a New Testament document ethically / by Elna
    Mouton.
      p. cm. — (Academia Biblica ; 1)
    Includes bibliographical references.
    ISBN 1-58983-028-8 (pbk. : alk. paper)
    1. Bible. N.T. Ephesians—Socio-rhetorical criticism. 2. Ethics
in the Bible. 3. Christian ethics—Biblical teaching. I. Title.
II. Series: Academia Biblica (Series) ; 1

BS2695.6.E8M68 2002
227'.506—dc 21

2002008200

07 06 05 04 03 02   5 4 3 2 1

© Quotation from the Greek New Testament, 3rd edition, 1975, with permission of the United Bible Societies,
© Quotation from the new International Version of the New Testament and Psalms, 1989, with permission of the International Bible Society.

Printed in the United States of America
on acid-free paper

To my extended (and potential) family in
Christ, and finally

Τῷ δὲ δυναμένῳ ὑπὲρ πάντα ποιῆσαι
ὑπερεκπερισσοῦ ὧν αἰτούμεθα ἢ νοοῦμεν
κατὰ τὴν δύναμιν τὴν ἐνεργουμένην ἐν
ἡμῖν, αὐτῷ ἡ δόξα ἐν τῇ ἐκκλησίᾳ καὶ ἐν
Χριστῷ Ἰησοῦ εἰς πάσας τὰς γενεὰς τοῦ
αἰῶνος τῶν αἰώνων, ἀμήν.
(Eph. 3:20-21)

TABLE OF CONTENTS

ACKNOWLEDGMENTS

This book is a slightly revised version of my doctoral dissertation, which was accepted by the Faculty of Religion and Theology at the University of the Western Cape (South Africa), and conferred in September 1995. It was titled *Reading a New Testament document ethically: Toward an accountable use of Scripture in Christian ethics, through analysing the transformative potential of the Ephesians epistle.*

A project of this nature is essentially a team effort. I therefore admire everyone who (in)directly contributed to its enrichment and final completion. Firstly, I would like to thank Professor Mark Allan Powell, editor of the Society of Biblical Literature New Testament Dissertation Series, for including the book in this fine series, as well as managing editor Leigh Andersen for her meticulous care and kind assistance during the publication process. I also thank Felicity Grové from the Faculty of Theology at Stellenbosch most sincerely for performing miracles in preparing the camera-ready copy for publication.

Professors Dirk J. Smit and Bernard C. Lategan acted as promoters. For their academic excellence and integrity, and personal ethos and wisdom, I offer them a profound word of appreciation and respect. They challenged my interests and style of scholarship in numerous ways. Yet, while their influence may be obvious from the book, I take full responsibility for the final product and for any unworthy use of their notions. I also wish to thank Doctor Jacques Rousseau for his scholarly expertise and dedication as supervisor during the initial stages of the project.

The original study was financially supported by a grant from the Centre for Science Development at the (South African) Human Sciences Research Council (currently the National Research Foundation), which I thankfully acknowledge.

My gratitude goes to the University of Port Elizabeth for their financial assistance in terms of annual research funds, and for granting me sabbatical leave during 1994 and 1999 (the latter as visiting scholar at Princeton Theological Seminary, New Jersey, during the fall semester), which allowed me to complete the initial study, and rework it for publication. I am also appreciative of the encouragement and moral support of my colleagues Piet Naudé, Martin Oosthuizen, Helena Glanville, Lionel Hendricks, Gerrit Loots, Helen Efthimiadis (now Efthimiadis-Keith) and Japie Havemann in the Department of Biblical and Religion Studies, as well as the creative role of many students who provided me with the opportunity to articulate my thoughts.

I can never adequately thank those people in the scholarly community who inspired me, and introduced me to other scholars and new ways of thinking. Among others, I single out the following South African scholars with whom I could discuss various aspects of the project, and who gave valuable advice: Johnnie H. Roberts and Johannes N. Vorster (UNISA), Piet J. Jonas (Huguenot College), Johan C. Thom and Jan Botha (US), and G. Francois Wessels (UWC); as well as the following international scholars: J. Wentzel van Huyssteen (Princeton Theological Seminary), Wayne A. Meeks and Abraham J. Malherbe (Yale

Divinity School, New Haven), Phyllis Bird (Garrett-Evangelical Theological Seminary, Evanston, Illinois) and Tom Olbricht (Pepperdine University, Malibu). Professors Roberts, Vorster, Naudé, Dr. Havemann and Ms Efthimiadis willingly read through parts of earlier drafts of the document and gave constructive comments.

The names and works mentioned in the list of works cited are representative of a large range of academic and church traditions. For being my conversation partners over the past years, I thank them. Some became kindred souls though we never met personally.

I acknowledge my great debt to research assistants André Agenbag, Jalize Uys, Sue Welman, Franziska Andrag-Meyer and Karin Hattingh at the Universities of Port Elizabeth and Stellenbosch, with whom I spent precious times in discussing the subject, and who assisted with the tedious task of proof-reading. A word of thanks to Sister Carmel Honeywill and Beth Botha who patiently scrutinized the original script to edit my English.

How does one thank family and friends for their lifelong inspiration, prayers and concern? To my dear parents Appie and Joey, and brothers Carel, Johan, Braam, Theo and their families, I express genuine thanks for their indispensable role in providing the love, warmth and humor to keep me going. I owe a special thank you to my friends Willemien Appel and Jans Scholtz who encircled me with their prayers and other forms of substantial support. Willemien devoted much of her time and energy to create the ideal working environment at home. For the treasured gift of commitment I sincerely honor her.

I gladly dedicate the book to my extended and potential family in Christ, to whom I owe a lot of the motivation and inspiration for the project. It was *only* in communion with Christian believers from various traditions that I could define my identity as a human being. Finally, I am in awe, and overwhelmed by the countless blessings which I experienced along the way. For such a reward I can only witness to the immeasurable greatness and mercy of the God of our Lord Jesus Christ who continues to honor us with the life-giving presence of the Spirit.

ELNA MOUTON
Stellenbosch
Heritage Day, 24 September 2001

INTRODUCTION

For me, this project unfolded as a stock-taking venture of a lifetime's exposure to, and use of the Bible. It has particularly developed from thirty years of practical experience in different church ministries, alternated by full- and part-time training and teaching in biblical studies. However, the journey started much earlier in my childhood, with decisive influences from my parents and four brothers, *Kinderkrans*, Sunday School, catechism and day school teachers, other religious leaders and friends, and especially the *Afrikaanse Christen-Studentevereniging* (Afrikaans Student Christian Association) in my high school and undergraduate years. During all these phases the Scriptures played a major formative and transformative role in my life.

After completing my undergraduate studies at the University of Stellenbosch (South Africa) in the early seventies, and a three year Diploma in Christian Ministries at the Huguenot College of the *Dutch Reformed Church* (DRC), I worked for four years as an ecclesial-social worker in the Canzibe congregation of the *DRC in Africa* in the previously independent state of Transkei (Eastern Cape). In this context the Bible functions in a particular way, *inter alia* as the result of decades of missionary work by different churches. Guided by the local church board, my major responsibilities were to teach the Bible to children in Sunday School, to train Sunday School teachers, organize youth camps, do house and hospital visiting as part of the moral equipment and pastoral care programs of the congregation, and to assist with religious education in primary and secondary day schools in the Ngqeleni district. This experience challenged me with the complexities involved in the interpretation and appropriation of the Bible in a cross-cultural situation.

Looking back on this period, I remember how deeply moved I was by the total commitment and dedication of many adults and children—most of them deprived of proper educational and other infrastructural facilities. For one thing, in this environment the Bible is highly regarded by many people as the normative "Word of God"—which very often means that it is applied almost literally as moral direction in every time and place. This further occurs within a cultural system essentially characterized by values such as patriarchy, gender stereotyping and social stratification. These values necessarily obscure the role and talent of women and children, and impede their participation in social institutions—particularly the church. As for my role—as a Reformed, Afrikaans woman in a traditionally African-animistic, patriarchal, Xhosa-speaking society, I soon learned to respect both its limitations and potential. My role, as I gradually understood it, was in the first instance to *listen* with all my senses, and to *learn* as much as humanly possible of the foreign—mainly oral—culture and language, before I could even think of teaching effectively. Although I gradually shared some very basic Bible-reading skills with them, I realized that the process of hermeneutic appropriation in that specific (and any other) context would finally depend on a continuing ecumenical dialogue among Christians from different church and cultural traditions—which indeed is quite a normal practice in those surroundings.

Thereafter I moved to the city of Port Elizabeth (also in the Eastern Cape) where I was called by the previous *Sinodale Sendingkommissie* and *Vroue-sendingbond* of the DRC to serve in the Livingstone Hospital and industrial ministries in the northern and north-eastern urban areas. Within the contexts of these inter-denominational, multi-cultural ministries, I was *inter alia* responsible for training people (the majority having no formal theological training) to serve as volunteers in visiting the sick, in conducting Bible-study groups during lunch and tea breaks, and to be available as pastoral workers on the factory floor. For six years I could participate in, and observe how people use the Bible in various situations—from seeking guidance and comfort in (sometimes extremely tense) labor relations, to wrestling with God's will under circumstances of severe physical, emotional, social and spiritual pain, financial misery, political and other forms of disillusionment and despair. Once again, I was confronted with many ways in which the Bible functioned in cultural and church traditions significantly different from my own. The point is that—in spite of, or perhaps because of all the affliction—the Bible plays a pivotal role in the lives of many of these people, functioning as a living source of hope, comfort and consolation, encouragement and strengthening of faith.

In the Livingstone Hospital ministry I was particularly blessed by the spirituality of staff members and patients who often worked, lived and persevered under difficult and even dangerous circumstances. In the process I learned to appreciate the empowering, transforming media of not only Bible-reading, prayers, sermons and songs, but also dreams, visions and dancing. Which often reminded me of the popular saying: *In Africa theology is not thought out but danced out.* In the industrial world I was often embarrassed by the enormous economical, political, relational, mechanical and electronic powers which daily determine the quality of people's lives—forces which appeared to be too mighty to be influenced by (individualistic) human intervention. As far as the role of the church in the market place, the public square, was concerned at that stage, its proclamation (in spite of hopeful signs) too often only concentrated on the personal relation between God and individuals, without being complemented by the full, concrete, prophetic implications of such a relation in that context—also with regard to oppressing structures and powers. The marginalized and often exploited role of women and *black* people, for instance, was and still is more often addressed by trade unions and other secular institutions than by the Christian church. These observations convinced me that it would at least take a concerted effort by many motivated, informed Christians in the workplace to bring about any significant change—in terms of sound and righteous economic principles, fair labor practice, and respect for human dignity. However, to what extent Christians are equipped by the churches to effectively fulfil such a trans-formative role, was and remains a serious and urgent question.

Subsequently, I was responsible for administering an outreach of the Eastern Cape Synod of the DRC to thousands of Christian women, and to give some guidance with regard to their encompassing role in church and society, and particularly in the moral formation of their families. A major challenge which surfaced during this period, was to approach the widely felt need for a gradual shift from *activity* and *issue*-based programs in the churches, to the nurturing of *people* in "communities of character" (Hauerwas 1981), where the formation of moral agency with regard to various family and societal *relations* would be the focus. In the process, a major handicap was the traditional attitude toward, and— worst of all—the biblical justification of the subservient role of women in the church and society. Whereas the latter was at that stage rapidly changing, the former remains in many respects a sensitive issue. For example, in the higher meetings of the DRC, official agreement on the issue of women in the offices of deacon, elder and minister was only reached in the eighties. It did not however (immediately) change the practical situation, language and attitude toward wo- men in many individual congregations, which emphasizes the continuing need for a proper understanding of Christian identity and ethos. I once again became con- vinced that any system of gender or other form of stereotyping needlessly hobbles social institutions, and *especially the church as an alternative community.*

As a general observation, it struck me time and again that most Christians involved in the abovementioned spheres of life (including my own approach during a pre-critical phase), use the Bible in a *one-sided mode,* that is, *only* with regard to its "theological"—often narrowly referred to as its "spiritual"—dimen- sion. With a one-sided approach to Scripture, biblical "truths" or specifically selected verses are often absolutized and treated as casuistic laws and principles, or even worse, as direct imperatives from God, applicable in the same way at all times and under all circumstances. Although I would never question the sincerity of such readers/audiences, I find this approach entirely unsatisfactory and *ethical- ly irresponsible,* because it does not (always) take the concrete circumstances of people seriously, and therefore does not (always) adequately account for the in- tended functions or pragmatic effects of the biblical documents. A sensitivity for the linguistic, literary and socio-historical aspects of these documents is often totally absent. In this way the dynamic and complex, multi-faceted nature of the Bible is either ignored or underplayed, while critical discussion is often immun- ized. Ironically, this was and is still happening in spite of various paradigm shifts occurring in the broad scholarly field of biblical studies, Christian ethics, and missiology since the Reformation, and particularly during the twentieth century.

Twelve years ago I moved into yet another phase of involvement with the Bible, namely that of the formal training in biblical and religion studies of students in theology and education in the Faculty of Arts at the University of Port Elizabeth (UPE), and recently as the first full-time female professor (in its existence of 141 years) in the Faculty of Theology at the University of Stellen- bosch (Western Cape). During the former period I was also invited to serve as an elder in a dominantly Afrikaans-speaking DRC congregation, with the special task of training people in Bible reading. However broader in scope, the bifocal vision on the two spheres of the church and the academy confirmed my previous observations. Although the context of a university is essentially different from that of the church, the enormous challenge with regard to an accountable use of Scripture in the moral formation of *people*, with a view to the transformation of a moral and civil *society*, and the information of moral *decision-making* and *action*, remains the greatest common factor among all institutions involved in Christian religious education (such as family, church, school, college, university).

For me, these observations irrevocably brought the *integrity*, *credibility*, *relevance* and *authority* of the churches and biblical studies to the fore, and consequently urged me to critically question the nature and shape of all forms of formal and informal religious and theological training and education. More than ever I became convinced of one thing: How people read and are guided to read the Bible, constructs and decisively determines their patterns of thinking, speaking and acting—including their understanding of who they are, and of their position and role in the church and society. I therefore believe that a *broadening and refining of people's interpretive skills could, accordingly, deepen their ability to appropriate the Bible in an ethically responsible way.*

This conviction surfaced through one of the most dramatic experiences of my life, namely the gradual confrontation with a *multi-dimensional* approach to Scripture. This process was especially stimulated while I was studying for a master's degree at the UPE, and participated in postgraduate seminars which were attended by students from various church and cultural traditions. A multi-dimensional approach did not only articulate why I often felt uncomfortable and dissatisfied with a one-sided approach to the Bible, but also offered a meaningful way out of that dilemma. The impact of the experience on my own thinking was of such a manner that I always longed for an opportunity to work through the consequences and psychological processes implied by it. The present study provided that opportunity, for which I am extremely grateful.

This is—for me the most significant part of—the story of my life....

The main aim of the book is not to provide answers to specific moral questions, but rather to create or foster a certain sensitivity for the variegated complexities involved in the process of understanding the Bible with respect to present contexts. For this reason it is basically *descriptive* in nature. It is meant to encourage those who sincerely wrestle to know God's will for their lives, but also to challenge those who—often unconsciously—disrespect the full textuality of the Bible, while underestimating the contextuality and creative potential of contemporary readers. As far as the scholarly community is concerned, it wishes to invite and stimulate an ongoing dialogue, a reading "in communion" (Fowl & Jones 1991), among various interpretive communities of the New Testament, particularly between biblical scholars and Christian ethicists.

Chapter one maps the methodological contours of the study by inquiring into the interpretive processes of which readers implicitly and often unconsciously form part when they claim to validate their faith utterances and religious experiences from the Bible. Drawing on notions from scholars in various disciplines, the intriguing and thorny issue regarding *the ethics of interpretation* is discussed. This pertains to the creative tension in the process of understanding between the free, imaginative role of readers or listeners and their contexts, and the inherent nature and constraints of the biblical texts. Because biblical scholars approach their subject from different angles, they are obliged to give proper account of their interpretive acts, and especially with regard to the pragmatic effect of those acts.

As a case study, *chapter two* wishes to take the textuality of one New Testament document—the Ephesians epistle—seriously by reading it from the three perspectives of its linguistic-literariness, its socio-historicity and its rhetoricity. The shape and thrust of the document emerges as the implied author's focus on the (mainly Gentile) recipients' identity and ethos in their relation to the living God, Jesus Christ and the Spirit. Their radically new identity *in Christ*, and corresponding ethos of love, compassion, righteousness and holiness, are intrinsically related to the paradoxical power of Christ's sacrificial death, resurrection and exaltation. In the end all the syntactic, dynamic, and dialectic elements of the document converge in its christological and ecclesial orientation. It has to be noted that exclusively masculine terms are used in reference to God and humanity throughout chapters two and three. It is done in concurrence with the male-dominated God and human language of the original Ephesians text. For this reason the *New International Version* of the English Bible is used alongside the Greek text instead of—for instance—the *New Revised Standard Version* which uses human inclusive language. This is a deliberate choice in order to illustrate the dangers of a one-sided literal approach toward biblical understanding. I will argue, however, that the very thrust of the Ephesians epistle requires that gender-sensitive language be used by later interpreters.

Chapter three explores strategic rhetorical devices, or the transformative potential of Ephesians in more detail. It concludes by saying, in Ricoeurian terms, that the communicative power of the document is its ability to disclose—through the metaphorical processes of identification, estrangement and reorientation—*an alternative moral world*, or to open up *a new way of looking at reality*. In this way Ephesians invites subsequent readers (via the textual construct of its "implied readers") to adopt and appropriate its christological and ecclesial vision in ever changing circumstances.

Chapter four travels the long road from the Ephesians text to the needs and contexts of contemporary Christian ethos and ethics. It first takes a look at some implications of the dynamic, metaphorical, complex, christological and communal nature of Ephesians and its authority for Christian ethics. Secondly, the Ephesians response to different moral paradigms, which developed during the history of (Christian) ethics, is investigated through inquiring into its potential role in the formation of moral *people*, the transformation of a moral *society*, and the information of moral *decision-making* and *action*. The book concludes by suggesting revisionary criteria for an ethical reading of the New Testament, which collectively characterize hermeneutic appropriation as "an integrative act of imagination" (Hays 1990).

Four excursions (one in chapter two and three in chapter four) are included to elaborate on specific subsections of the study. From a methodological point of view it has to be noted that, although these are presented in brackets and in a slightly smaller print, their function is to support and strengthen the main argument of the book.

CHAPTER ONE

READING A NEW TESTAMENT DOCUMENT ETHICALLY: TOWARD DEFINING THE CHALLENGES FOR CREDIBLE TEXTUAL COMMUNICATION

(The) ethos (of biblical scholarship) is the shared intellectual space of freely accepted obligations and traditions as well as the praxial space of discourse and action. Since ethos shapes our scholarly behavior and attitudes, it needs to be explored more explicitly in terms of its rhetorical aims, which seek to affect a common orientation among its practitioners.

(Elisabeth Schüssler Fiorenza 1988:9; 1999:22)

An "ethical" reading of the New Testament may refer to a wide range of issues. The subject of "ethics" may, likewise, be approached from various legitimate perspectives. For the purpose of this study, the focus will be on an ethical reading which concerns three closely related, yet distinguishable, subjects:

- *the ethics of responsible New Testament interpretation*; and—as a logical consequence or expression thereof—

- the *intended ethical, pragmatic,* or *rhetorical effects* of the New Testament documents; and

- their *use* or, rather, *functioning and appropriation in contemporary Christian ethos and ethics.*

By exploring these aspects, the book links up with and hopes to stimulate and contribute toward the urgent and cumulative discussion on the relation between biblical studies (in general, and New Testament science in particular) and Christian ethics (cf. Ogletree 1983; Spohn 1984; Verhey 1984a; 1984b; Gustafson 1984a; 1984b; Curran 1984; Birch & Rasmussen 1989; Fowl & Jones 1991; Smit 1992). It is *not* its purpose to deal with a specific *ethical theme* in the New Testament, though the development and variety in the understanding of particular concepts may form an important aspect of the ethics of biblical reading (cf. Hays 1990:44–47; Furnish 1968:112–206, 212–224). However, the focus will be on the reading and intended ethical effect of *one document*, representative of the multi-vocal canon of the New Testament, namely the epistle to the Ephesians. Its distinctiveness for this purpose is related to its explicit focus on the re-interpretation of power and its exigence of a deeply divided society as a possible analogy for the challenges facing South African churches at the moment. How to (re)interpret, translate and appropriate its implied moral effect in terms of the changing needs of later (Christian) readers, as a modest illustration of how the Bible could be used in Christian ethics, is indeed the main methodological challenge of the study.[1]

---

[1] *Christian* ethics—as the dynamic and creative reinterpretation of biblical

Recent developments in the fields of literary theory, philosophy of science and biblical studies reveal a remarkable interest in *the ethics of interpretation.* This coincides with a major shift in hermeneutical discussions in general, and biblical studies in particular.[2] This namely represents a shift from (a) an emphasis on origins and *text production,* focusing on the historical nature of biblical texts (broadly speaking from the seventeenth to the early twentieth centuries), via (b) *text preservation and mediation,* emphasizing the structural facet (from the 1970s to the 80s), to (c) *text reception and interpretation,* highlighting the rhetorical and pragmatic aspects of textual communication (since the 1980s, with special reference to the creative, critical role of readers—Lategan 1978; 1984a; 1986b; 1987; 1989a; 1991a; 1991b; 1991c; 1992a; 1992b; 1992c; 1994a; Combrink 1986;

---

perspectives by subsequent readers, in different socio-historical circumstances—has to be distinguished from *biblical* ethics or, rather, the implied ethos of each biblical document as understood in its particular context (cf. Verhey 1984a:159–160, 169–197; Gustafson 1984b:151–154; Curran 1984:187–194; Birch & Rasmussen 1989:11–14; Botha 1994a: 36–42). As a matter of fact, the present study was prompted by the striking similarities, and yet, radical differences between *biblical* and *Christian* ethos and ethics. While sharing a basic faith commitment with those early Christian communities, contemporary readers of the Bible in general, and the New Testament in particular, are obviously confronted and shaped by different moral issues, stories and historical forces (cf. 4.3.3 n.27).

[2] Hermeneutics—as a general philosophical enterprise—basically refers to *the theory of interpretation.* As such it embraces *the art and science of understanding,* which implies that it should simultaneously be seen as a (so-called) right *and* left brain function—calling for the acknowledgement and co-operation of both faith, intuitive, imaginative, poetic, aesthetic, emotional *and* logic, rational, cognitive human capacities (cf. Cuthbertson 1992; Ricoeur 1977:80; Lategan 1994b:131). New Testament hermeneutics—as a specialized form of hermeneutics—is the science which deals with the theoretical foundation and presuppositions of methods of New Testament interpretation—presuppositions being principles assumed as precondition for whatever else one believes, but which themselves may remain unexamined and uncriticized throughout an argument (cf. Combrink 1986:213–217; Berger 1988; Jeanrond 1991:1–11, 159–182; Lategan 1992b; Solomon 1990:324). "Insofar as biblical texts form part of a dynamic communication process, their essential hermeneutical nature is undeniable. Interpretation is essential to discerning the will of God" (Lategan 1992b:150). In the communication of written texts, the process of understanding is characterized by a dialectic between the direction of thought opened up by those texts and its appropriation by contemporary readers. "To appropriate or to make one's own what was considered previously alien or foreign is without doubt the purpose of all hermeneutics" (Hartin 1994:515, cf. 521; 1992:67–68; Ricoeur 1976:91). The challenge of interpretation can also be phrased in terms of the famous concept of the twentieth century German philosopher Hans-Georg Gadamer as the *Horizontverschmelzung,* the "fusion of the horizons" between past and present, between sender (speaker or written text) and receiver (audience, readers, interpreters)—see Thiselton 1977; 1980:10–17, 24–47, 293–314; 1992:313–330; Combrink 1986:213–14; Lategan 1992b:149–150, 152. This "fusion" does not exclude critical distance and tension though (Thiselton 1980:307–308, 313–19).

1988; Hester 1994; Botha 1994c:291–293). With regard to the last phase, the emphasis on readers and their contextuality refers to "an awareness that the actual circumstances in which a text is read and interpreted, have a direct effect on any such interpretation. A contextual approach to texts acknowledges this effect and attempts to make it part of the methodological reflection on interpretation" (Lategan 1991c:1; cf. Combrink 1986:212–218). Although these phases or paradigms cannot be separated neatly, it is helpful to understand how the focus on the context of readers developed:

> Each of the three waves was set in motion by the discovery of an important feature of texts and their interpretation. This feature became the dominant consideration and even assumed absolutistic dimensions. Inevitably, as insights in the nature of interpretation progressed, this dominant consideration was deabsolutized and superseded by other aspects (Lategan 1991c:1).[3]

The shift from the context of the *author* to the *text*, and then to the context of the *readers*, seems natural enough, but in actual fact forms part of a much wider and growing interest in the pragmatic effect of language (Lategan 1991c:4; cf. 1984a:4–7, 10–14; 1987:112–114; 1992c:625–626). This encouraged the development of reception theories and reader response criticism, which made it "abundantly clear to what extent the reader plays a constituent part in assigning meaning to texts" (Lategan 1991c:4; cf. 1987; 1989a; 1992a:4–7; 1992c; Thiselton 1992:516–555). At the same time, these developments coincide with recent trends in (Christian) ethics, which focus on notions such as contemporary readers' creative role with respect to responsibility and relationality, public discourse, narrative and postmodern thinking (cf. 4.4.1.4).

The current emphasis on the role and context of readers in the process of understanding may possibly be ascribed to a whole range of factors, such as socio-political developments on a global scale, distinct epistemological shifts in the human sciences, and the intellectual, philosophical and socio-economical climate of the late twentieth century. In the case of biblical scholarship, the emergence of liberationist, black, feminist, womanist, male and fundamentalist theologies, for instance, concurs with the call for a more *contextual* exegesis and hermeneutics, or *local* theology (cf. Botha 1991:1, 5[4]; Berg 1991:227–300;

---

[3] To speak about "phases" is perhaps not the best explanation of the process of interpretation, because it gives the impression of consecutive periods replacing each other in the course of history. We should rather speak of historical "paradigms," for in many aspects of social history today, *all* these phases are simultaneously prevalent and influential. Most of the time we live in all these paradigms at the same time. In epistemology, the theory of science or knowledge, a paradigm refers to "the complex of convictions, values, and worldview shared by a scientific community which provides its philosophical framework for valid academic inquiry" (Deist 1990:185; cf. Van Huyssteen 1986:7).

[4] References to South African New Testament scholar Jan Botha's doctoral thesis

Lategan 1990; 1991c:4; 1992b:153; Thiselton 1992:410–470; R. M. Naudé 1993: 148–150; Deist 1989c).

It is against this background that the use or functioning of the Bible in Christian ethics has become an issue of serious moral concern. Whatever the causes for the current interest in the ethics of interpretation may be, it is clear that *the identity, ethos, integrity, credibility and relevance of biblical scholarship and theological education* is at stake (cf. Smit 1988b; 1992; 1993b; 1993c; 1994b; 1994d; Du Toit 1981; Van Huyssteen 1987:3; Van Huyssteen & Du Toit 1989:1–4; Fowl & Jones 1991:4–21; Thiselton 1992:1–30, 611–619).[5] In this regard Anthony C. Thiselton (1992:2), authoritative British biblical scholar, rightly remarks: "How we read, understand, interpret, and use biblical texts relates to the very identity of Christian faith and stands at the heart of Christian theology."

My first concern will therefore be to define what is meant by "an ethical reading of the New Testament." I hope to develop and illustrate my own specific understanding of an ethics of interpretation within the wider context of the scientific interpretation of the New Testament. Since the proof of the pudding is in the eating thereof, I shall also deal with the issue on a practical level by reading Ephesians from the perspective of its three main textual dimensions, namely its structural or linguistic-literary facet; its socio-cultural or historical aspect; and its theological, conceptual, rhetorical or transformative aspect (cf. Lategan 1982:50–52; 1985a:5–6; 1991c:2–5; Rousseau 1986; Thiselton 1992:8–10).

1.1 THE ETHICS OF INTERPRETATION

Why start with "an ethics of interpretation" while the concrete needs of people—now, in South Africa, Africa and further—seem to be the real issue? Why not start with something like "a biblical perspective on violence and injustice, or the HIV/AIDS pandemic?" The answer is simply because such a (so-called) biblical foundation in itself would be no guarantee that what followed would be more biblical than if such critical reflection were absent. One primary reason for that is that we all involuntarily read from within a specific socio-historical context, and then project our own convictions back into the Bible (Bosch 1980:43). "It is true," says Gerald West (1991a:6), South African biblical scholar, "that the point, and, indeed, the cry in South Africa, is not to interpret the world but to *change*

(1991) only occur where original thoughts have been reworked substantially or left out in its published version, *Subject to Whose Authority? Multiple Readings of Romans 13* (1994b).

    [5] Dirk J. Smit, respected South African systematic theologian and ethicist, consistently challenges biblical scholars by pleading for some kind of integration or organization of interpretive methods and reading strategies into a "responsible hermeneutics." He emphasizes that, "after the methods of interpretation have had their day, the results must be organized in some way so that people can believe, hope and act—and someone must do the job" (Smit 1988b:478).

it." Then he quotes David Tracy, acclaimed North American systematic theologian: "But, we will change too little, and that probably too late, if we do not *at the same time change our understanding of what we mean when we so easily claim to interpret the world"* (emphasis mine).

It was especially J. Hillis Miller—in the context of literary studies, and from a deconstructionist perspective—who claimed that the *ethics* of reading is of fundamental importance for any literary study (Miller 1987a:3; cf. Botha 1991:2).[6] To describe the reading process as particularly *ethical*, basically refers to the wide range of *choices* readers continually have to make: Why read this particular text and not another? How do we consider this text to hold answers for our personal and social needs? On whose behalf are we reading it? What do we expect from it? Why use this method of reading and not another one? Do we not (more often unconsciously) project our own fears, hopes, desires and interests onto the text even before we start reading? Or, do we allow it to continuously surprise us, to speak for itself in its "otherness?" (cf. Tracy 1991:96; Thiselton 1992:611–619).[7]

Thus: How *are* people using the biblical texts—confessed by Christian believers to contain God's inspired will for their lives—to transform and/or justify their beliefs and practices? What are the creative processes involved in moving from "here" and "now" (the context of contemporary readers) to "there" and "then" (the multi-vocal texts of the Bible), and back to "now" (determining its

---

[6] Contrary to conventional literary theory, the term "deconstruction" reflects the conviction that a *text* is not an independent entity making meaningful impressions on a subject, but an intertextual network (cf. Jeanrond 1991:84–86; Thiselton 1992:80–141). "Thus the interplay between a reader and a 'text' (both forming part of an intertextual world) immediately constitutes a new 'text.' This triggers a chain reaction involving new texts with their own intertextual worlds, the meaning of each new 'text' being modified in the process. Consequently, 'meaning'—as something intrinsic to and deducible from a text— is replaced by 'dissemination' (free intertextual play of meanings) and 'deferment' (when the meaning of a term/text is superseded by the function it acquires in the free play of intertextuality)" (Deist 1990:65). The same applies to the concept of "Scripture." David H. Kelsey's perceptive work, *The Uses of Scripture in Recent Theology* (1975), rests on the premise that "there is in actual theological practice no one standard concept 'scripture.' 'Scripture' is not something objective that different theologians simply use differently. In actual practice it is concretely construed in irreducibly different ways" (Kelsey 1975:2).

[7] In their discussion of the (Christian) moral life, Birch and Rasmussen (1989:35–65) refer to the concept "moral" as a particularly *human* consciousness, an awareness of the difference between *is* and *ought*, the difference "of what presently exists from a world which could be better than it is. 'Moral' consciousness resides in this distinction of 'is' from 'ought' and this *capacity to choose* a different world.... (M)oral creatures live with a conscious sense of both right and wrong, better and worse" (Birch & Rasmussen 1989:36; emphasis mine). However, this does not mean that every choice is necessarily a *moral* choice. Deciding whether to buy a red or a grey car, might be a matter of *aesthetics*, whereas deciding whether to buy a car worth $20, 000 or $200, 000 may become a *moral* choice (cf. Birch & Rasmussen 1989:37).

appeal in a current situation)?[8]

A second round of questions could include the following: How are the biblical writings *supposed to* be used by later readers—in order to account for their specific *nature* and *purpose*? What *are* their nature and intentions? What attitudes, dispositions and perspectives are presupposed for a proper understanding? What kind of questions may be expected to be answered by the Bible, and what not? What is its epistemological status (authority) for our theological and ethical explanations (supposed to be)? And if we identify with its perspective and intention as the original documents, the authoritative canon of the Christian faith, what role *should* it play in understanding others and ourselves, in viewing personal and societal problems and their solutions? (cf. Lategan 1992a). *How* does it supply us with valid criteria for character formation and problem solving? And even more seriously: Should we still use these texts (as embedded in its androcentric and patriarchal first century Mediterranean socio-cultural settings) to encourage, comfort and empower Christians in the critical and democratizing context of a postmodern society, and if so, *how* should we do it? And finally: What are the implications of these choices for the church's preaching, teaching and pastoral work, and for religious education in general (i.e., communicating the results of the reading process)?

These actions—as well as their intended or unintended consequences—can be responsible or irresponsible, and are therefore matters for ethical reflection and evaluation. While the Bible provides for different legitimate modes and methods of reading, the *choices of people* regarding these methods of interpretation, or how people *use* such methods—that is their interpretive acts—are subject to moral reflection:

> (O)ne aspect of the ethics of interpretation is the insistence that people should take responsibility and accept public accountability for their acts of reading and interpretation.... The method of reading as such is not ethical or unethical. Only *people* can act ethically or unethically (Botha 1994b:4; cf. 1994a:43).

The great diversity which currently characterizes the methodology of New Testament interpretation (cf. Marshall 1977; Lategan 1982; 1984a; 1985a; 1988;

---

[8] Influential South African New Testament scholar Bernard C. Lategan (1987:114–115; 1989a:5–7; 1992c:626–627), in various discussions on aspects of reader-oriented research, and with reference to differences between theoretical and empirical approaches, makes a useful distinction between categories of readers with regard to biblical texts: *first readers* (of whose readings very little evidence exist), *past readers* (whose successive readings constitute the reception history of these texts), and *contemporary readers*. "By far the most accessible are *contemporary readers* of the Bible, who offer examples of a wide variety of readings" (Lategan 1989a:6). To these categories of "historical or real readers" (outside the text) may be added the theoretical or textual construct of the "implied reader" (inside the text)—see 1.6.1 n.33.

Rousseau 1986:4–28; Mack 1990:13–14; Berg 1991:39–454; Botha 1991:3–5), indeed makes the ethical evaluation of different acts of interpretation necessary and urgent. For example,

> If an interpretive community uses methods of interpretation in such a way that it remains an esoteric 'pure' academic endeavor, isolated from life, or if an interpretive community tolerates such practices, it becomes an ethical problem. Thus, the ethics of interpretation asks (i) *who* (that is, which individual or group) reads (ii) *which* Bible (that is, what view of the text does the interpretive community hold, what authority does it grant the text) (iii) *how* (that is, using which methods) and (iv) *why* (that is, whose interests are at stake, what does the interpretive community want to achieve with their acts of interpretation)? (Botha 1994b:4–5; cf. 1994a:43; Smit 1991b).

Further, if we consider the act of reading to be an *ethical choice, decision* or *responsibility*, what kind of responsibility are we talking about—responsibility to whom or to what? (cf. Miller 1987a:4). Who or what decides what is valid and what not? To whose authority is the act of reading and interpretation subject? (Botha 1994b). "When is my act of reading responsible—responsible *both* to the community in which I live *and* to the nature of the material with which I work, namely ancient written texts?" (Botha 1991:2). Further, how do we respond to the methodological challenge of the paradox between the constraints of a text and the freedom of its readers, and the possibilities of subjectivism and relativism opened by that freedom (Lategan 1987:116; 1992c:627; Van Huyssteen & Du Toit 1989: 6, 37; Jonker 1991)?

These questions form part of the choices readers always and necessarily make, whether consciously and deliberately or not—before, during and after the reading process. This recognition forces biblical scholars to consider and give account of the basis for their choices. As a point of departure, account has to be given of the reality that any discussion on the ethics of interpretation is embedded within a particular socio-historical situation, which in turn is decisively determined by the history of New Testament hermeneutics. Without going into any detail, I take a look at major *challenges* arising from the inheritance of previous interpretations, and at how these add to, and help to define the complex issue of ethically responsible interpretations of the New Testament.

1.2 MORAL CHALLENGES ARISING FROM THE HISTORY OF NEW TESTAMENT HERMENEUTICS

The documents of the New Testament are read and appropriated today against the background of a long and rich research history (see, among others, Bruce 1977; Grant & Tracy 1984; Lategan 1970; 1982; 1984a; 1991c; 1992b; Mouton 1987: 12–25; Jeanrond 1991:12–92; Burrows & Roren 1991; Thiselton 1992; Kaiser 1994; Silva 1994b). This history reveals a large variety of ways in which the

Bible has been used in concrete, practical situations through the centuries.[9] How people read their own and others' contexts, or interpret the history of research, will probably be influenced by the same perspectives and presuppositions from which they interpret the Bible. Accounting for these perspectives, therefore, forms part of an ethics of interpretation.

Positively, we are today deeply indebted to many individual and groups of scholars from different periods of history, during which a variety of emphases contributed toward a growing understanding of the complex nature of the biblical writings. These emphases were *inter alia* stimulated and influenced by many different existential needs and questions, historical and philosophical phases or paradigms, models of rationality, interests, (social, political, religious, academic) contexts, personalities, abilities, and views of the Bible (cf. Lategan 1982:53–68; Birch & Rasmussen 1989:74–81).

Among other aspects, the process of ongoing interpretation highlighted the reality—which is of crucial importance for the purpose of this study—that the biblical documents function on different complementing levels or dimensions, at least with regard to a structural, historical and rhetorical level. They may therefore be approached from different legitimate angles, which means that a great variety of questions can be put to them (cf. Lategan 1982:48).[10] Although the importance of each of these dimensions cannot be underestimated, none of them offers an exclusive key to textual understanding. The different emphases rather brought the need for a more *integrated* approach to the fore, which resulted in various socio-communicative theories during and since the 1980s (cf. Lategan 1984a:4–12; 1994b:134; Rousseau 1986:40–41).

However, the variety of perspectives and questions has another side to it. The history of biblical research has often also been characterized by misunderstanding and divergence, by "conflicting and confusing" ways of interpretation

---

[9] See, among others, MacIntyre 1966:110–145; Furnish 1968:279; Mott 1982; Hartin 1987; 1991; Oosthuizen 1988; 1993; Roberts 1990; Botha 1991:12–17; 1994b:1–2; Thiselton 1992; Glanville 1992:15–21; Layman 1991; Wogaman 1993. For a recent example of the role of Scripture in public worship in South Africa, see the informative articles by Smit 1989, and Müller & Smit 1994.

[10] The historical-critical research of the biblical writings (1600–1920), for instance, helped us—in spite of some dangerous results—to realize that the Bible is a book with its own unique *nature* (origin, background and composition) and *intention* (stimulating a faith relationship between God and humankind—cf. Lategan 1991c:2; Rousseau 1985a:4; Mouton 1987:22). Likewise, the emphasis on literary theories, linguistics and literary science (1960–1980), and reception aesthetics (1980s) made us aware of the literary and structural aspects of the biblical documents, as well as the determining role of their readers (cf. Lategan 1982; 1985a; 1991c; Eagleton 1983). The application of insights from communication theories in the twentieth century (with regard to sender, medium, and receiver) further confirmed and refined the major results of research done by biblical scholars of previous centuries.

(cf. Lategan 1982; 1985a; Rousseau 1984; 1986:4–5, 33–34). Like the *enrichment* of various emphases, the *confusion* was also caused by the influence of different philosophical paradigms on the hermeneutic process during the course of history. These frames of thinking, together with the personal preferences, perspectives, dispositions[11], in short: the *ethos* of individual scholars, schools or (sub)disciplines, often led to an over- and/or underexposure, to the absolutization and/or neglect, of one or more dimension(s) of the biblical texts:

> The 'theological dimension' of the Bible was so overemphasized, especially in the middle ages, but also more recently in orthodox and fundamentalistic circles, that it was seen as a timeless, heaven-produced truth which failed to take the classical and metaphorical nature of the Bible into account. The 'historical dimension' was highlighted to such an extent from the seventeenth to the twentieth century (especially in the more radical historico-critical approaches) that the Bible was often reduced to being seen as just another ancient book among many—another corpse for 'scientific' dissection! The overexposure of the 'linguistic' and 'literary' dimensions which came to the fore in certain circles of a structuralist and literary-science approach during the second half of the twentieth century, tended to neglect the socio-cultural and traditio-historical dimensions of the Bible (Rousseau 1989b:2).

The over- and/or underexposure of certain dimensions of the biblical texts consequently brought about divergent results which in turn often caused misunderstanding, conflict and even bloodshed.[12] In the process the church and its

---

[11] Birch and Rasmussen (1989:79–81) define "dispositions" as persisting, recurring, consistent, engraved attitudes, those character traits people possess over a long enough time that they become part of their temperament. Such attitudes are the habits of heart and mind, the customary patterns which influence people to act and make decisions almost reflexively. As such, they give expression to people's basic perspectives.

[12] Numerous examples can be mentioned here. I single out a tragic period in the recent history of my own country and church tradition, namely the theological justification of apartheid by the Dutch Reformed Church (and other churches) in South Africa—cf. De Gruchy & Villa-Vicencio 1983; Kinghorn 1986; Loubser 1987; Bosch 1991b; Fowl & Jones 1991:96–99; Hartin 1992:65–66; Deist 1994; Müller & Smit 1994:396–399. At the same time, liberation theologians often used the Bible to justify violence in the struggle against apartheid. For concrete instances of such exclusive relations between group interests and theological justification in South Africa, see De Gruchy 1979; Vorster 1979; Smit 1986; Deist 1989a, and the important Human Sciences Research Council (HSRC) report on religion and intergroup relations: Oosthuizen, G. C., Coetzee, J. K., De Gruchy, J. W., Hofmeyr, J. H., & Lategan, B. C. 1985. *Religion, intergroup relations and social change*. Pretoria: HSRC (cf. Lategan 1986a).

In this respect it needs to be remembered that the enlightening role of God's Spirit has consistently been implied in history as the ultimate prerequisite for understanding the Scriptures (Mouton 1987:26–28, 157–158). No biblical scholar would (hopefully) ever deny this. It therefore remains an enormous challenge to account for the dilemma of

officials—including biblical scholars—use the Bible as a normative conscience-binding instrument "with the intent of exerting control over the communicational environment" (Rousseau 1985b:92, quoting R. W. Budd & B. D. Ruben). This makes the use of Scripture in Christian ethics a *moral* issue (Rousseau 1984:50–52; 1985b:92–94; 1986:19–24; Smit 1991a; 1991b; 1992).

In order to understand something of our moral inheritance, and the endless number of spheres and contexts of Christian ethics within which the Bible played an important role, some of the most important historical phases in the development of ethics will be dealt with in chapter 4.4.1. This includes the traditions of *Christian* moral thinking, which were decisively influenced by the former. All these trends may help to construct a picture of the complexities involved in New Testament hermeneutics, and to sensitize contemporary readers accordingly—particularly with regard to its functioning in Christian ethics.

A crucially important implication from such a historical overview for the purpose of the book, is that the Bible has been used in Christian ethics during the past twenty centuries, and continues to be used, in many different ways—*depending on the question(s) being put to it*. If people want to use the Bible in finding answers and making decisions with regard to particular moral *issues*, they will use it in a specific way. If they want to use the Bible to *educate their children* and to *form communities of character* where people learn to adopt and live specific virtues, they will use it in other ways. If they want to use the Bible to tell how the *world* and *society* should be, they will use it in yet another way. Without realizing it, people approach the Bible from radically different historical paradigms and sets of questions, and consequently get different answers, and come to different conclusions. These are some of the challenges which emerge from the history of New Testament interpretation, and which prompt the ethics of interpretation.

1.3 HERMENEUTICS AND THE ETHICS OF INTERPRETATION REPHRASED IN TERMS OF COMMUNICATION PROCESSES

An ethics of interpretation is thus concerned with and wishes to account for the delicate network of relations and choices involved in processes of understanding. We have seen that, since the 1980s, a new recognition for the active and creative role of audiences or readers emerged in biblical scholarship, specifically against the background of different personal and cultural contexts (cf. Lategan 1984a; 1989a). This process has emphasized anew that biblical hermeneutics does not only pertain to the understanding of *God* (albeit partial and provisional), but also includes the understanding of *humankind* and *reality* as a whole—before, during,

---

diverging or *conflicting* verbal and non-verbal interpretations of the Bible. For a detailed discussion of this matter, see the D.Th. thesis of Jan C. Woest (University of the Western Cape, 1993), titled "Heilige hermeneutiek?: 'n Sistematies-teologiese ondersoek na die rol wat in die Christelike tradisie aan die Heilige Gees toegeken word rondom die verstaan van die Bybel en die moontlikheid van 'n legitieme *Hermeneutica Sacra*."

and since the New Testament times (cf. Rousseau 1989b). This necessarily leads to the recognition that New Testament hermeneutics—in accordance with its nature—calls for *an inter-disciplinary, relational and dialogical approach* (cf. J. Botha 1992:191–193; 1994b:3–4). This forms an important premise of the present study.

It has been indicated that the ethical choices readers continually make when reading texts—including biblical texts, during the centuries and today—are influenced by many, many factors. Since the influential work of philosophers of science (such as Thomas Kuhn and Karl Popper during the second half of the twentieth century) paved dramatic changes in the understanding and explanation of knowledge and experience (cf. Van Huyssteen 1986:37–46, 63–87), also the experience of faith from any specific paradigm is recognized to be *relational* in nature. This includes people's relation to their personal and cultural-historical environment, to themselves, to one another, to the earth, to history, to God, to the original documents of their faith—in short: to their practical everyday reality.[13]

Because this observation is of vital importance for understanding the nature of the Bible and consequently for its use in Christian ethics, the *relational* aspect of interpretation needs some further discussion. I shall therefore take a brief look into the nature of these relations, which—in typical twentieth century language—may be defined in terms of the static, dynamic and dialectic elements of *communication* (cf. 1.6).

Accounting for various *relations* necessarily leads to the exploration of different *communication processes* involved in those relations.[14] This forms an

---

[13] A "critical realist" perspective on rationality locates human knowing of every sort between the extremes of positivism (in which the subject is lost) and phenomenalism (in which the object is lost—cf. Van Huyssteen 1986:151–214; 1987:19–23; Wright 1992:31–37). Being opposed to positions of naive realism, such as fundamentalism and biblical literalism, scholars working from the epistemological principle of critical realism recognize "that there is no uninterpreted access to reality" (Van Huyssteen 1987:24). We therefore realize that everything we have to say about the religious experiences of the biblical authors and their first readers, as well as our own understanding of the text as subsequent readers (cf. Lategan 1985b:68–70), is "provisional, inadequate and partial, but—on the other hand—also necessary as the *only* way of referring to the reality that is God, and the reality of God's relation to humanity" (Van Huyssteen 1987:24, cf. 24–31; Combrink 1986:215).

[14] The fundamental characteristic of any "meaningful" relation is the art of genuine, honest and open—in the sense of critical, creative, interested, imaginative—*communication* (cf. 1.1 n.6). From a Christian perspective, this includes communication with other human beings (in the process of understanding), and with the living God (as understood in relation to the biblical texts, their history of interpretation, and God's presence in contemporary situations). It also necessarily involves the important role of metaphorical *language* and ultimate *commitment* in faith utterances (cf. Van Huyssteen 1986:151–163, 169–214; 1987:24–31; Rousseau 1986:51, 65–66; Mouton 1987:49–50, 69; Glanville 1992:129–142).

essential notion right through the book. If we as subsequent readers of the biblical documents continuously use them to justify our ethos, faith utterances and solutions for the world, our primary methodological responsibility would therefore be to *account for* the numerous relations and processes involved in our acts of interpretation. To give account of our appeal to the Bible as warrant for our beliefs and practices, is essential for different reasons. An unnuanced, direct appeal to Scripture (as if it holds "eternal" truths, applicable in the same way to all times and places) would be suspect in at least two important ways. Firstly, the Bible itself contains a large variety of viewpoints, related to individuals' and faith communities' experiences and understanding of God's will under different circumstances. Secondly, it has become clear that diverse interpretive methods and paradigms can yield diverse readings of any given text (Hays 1990:42). We have seen that, although this refers to the wealth of different complementing perspectives, it may also be seen as a moral problem of diverging interpretations (cf. Rousseau 1985b:92–94; 1986:4–5)—a crisis which has become most acutely embarrassing with regard to ethical questions.

Thus, bearing in mind that a text has inexhaustible hermeneutic potential, we realize that there is no easy escape from the imperative to interpret the Bible in an ethically responsible and sound way. In a nutshell, this asks for an *explanation* of the complex hermeneutical journeys which we by implication undertake when we choose the Bible as canon or norm for our lives. These include the journeys

• from—our understanding of—the historical situation of which we form part (i.e. the *context, moral world, perspective, presuppositions, etc.* of contemporary readers);

• to the *biblical documents* and—our understanding of—their *nature* and *intention*, the communication processes represented by them, and their embeddedness within a specific socio-cultural *context* and *moral world*;

• and eventually, back from "there" and "then" to "here" and "now," appropriating the Bible as *criterion* for the formation of moral people, for acting morally, for making responsible decisions, for solving problems, for building a good and moral society.

As a theoretical point of departure in the development of an ethics of responsible reading, the hypothesis of this study is to take the *texts* of the New Testament and their "textuality" seriously, and to read them with the full sophistication offered by present-day strategies of reading.[15] According to the above-

---

[15] To choose the text as starting-point or gateway in the communication process (Rousseau 1986:41–43; Birch & Rasmussen 1989:16; Jeanrond 1991:112–113), is simply a methodological or theoretical choice. In reality reading always occurs within and from a particular context. Mott (1982:viii) rightly explains that "(t)he interpretation of Scripture begins in the life experience of listening in faith as the Word of God is read and taught and

mentioned vision, this necessarily has to be followed by, or go along with, an analysis or "reading" of the *context* within which those texts are being read today, and within which they are expected to communicate hope (cf. Botha 1994c:296–306).

Reading a New Testament document ethically would further include a serious rendering of the intended moral effect or transformative potential of that document. In the case of the epistolary *genre* (to which Ephesians probably belongs), the intended effect was—generally speaking—to respond to the needs or exigencies of particular individuals or communities, and to persuade them to bring about a change of attitude and behavior in their situation (cf. Malherbe 1986:79–85; Stowers 1986). This is referred to as the *intended pragmatic or ethical effect* of a document, and necessarily forms part of the ethics of interpretation.

One may agree with Botha (1991:8; 1992:185–193) and Rousseau (1986:42) that such an act of serious reading should *precede* any claims about text-extrinsic relations made on the basis of the text—be they ancient or postmodern matters of history, society or the self. At the same time, responsible interpretation cannot stop there while remaining aloof from the reality of contemporary readers. If the Bible is primarily concerned with a dynamic relationship between the living God and humankind within the concrete reality of everyday life (Swanepoel 1989:76; cf. Birch & Rasmussen 1989:13–14), it calls—in accordance with its very *nature*

---

of obedient conduct guided by this Word." One could therefore argue that the hermeneutic process naturally, unconsciously and technically starts with the existential needs of readers within a specific historical situation. In that case we would have to account for the readers' presuppositions and needs *before* we start reading a text. Bearing in mind that understanding functions like a "circle" (according to the hermeneutical theory developed by German theologian Friedrich Schleiermacher, 1768–1834, and German existentialist Martin Heidegger, 1884–1976; cf. Lategan 1992b:149, 151; Thiselton 1980:104, 143–204; 1992: 1–30, 204–236; Jeanrond 1991:5–6), it is almost impossible to pinpoint a specific starting-point. In the ongoing hermeneutical circle, or sometimes redefined as a hermeneutic "spiral" (a more open-ended metaphor for the progressive process of understanding—cf. Thiselton 1980:104), the role of readers can even change from that of senders to recipients, while the role of the text can be either that of recipient, medium or sender. This encompassing understanding of the hermeneutic spiral finds its fullest expression in the works of Gadamer (cf. Thiselton 1992:222, 313–330). With regard to the "contextualization" of the Bible (which will be discussed further in chapter four), one may ask: Who or what encourages the hermeneutic leap from the needs of contemporary readers to the biblical text, or *vice versa*? Does the text itself (and, e.g., the Christ event) open up new possibilities of reinterpretation? Or does the process necessarily involve a combination of both? The basic hypothesis of this study is that the hermeneutical processes involved in the understanding of the New Testament today include both these journeys in constant interaction with each other. The dynamic *nature* and *intention* of the biblical documents, as well as the Christian faith, are of such a kind that it always brings new insights, and demands a new actualization in every new situation (cf. Lategan 1982; 1984a:13).

and *intention*—for "an interpretation with a view to life" (Botha 1994b:4). This is confirmed and substantiated by the threefold critical task which Hays (1990:43–46) suggests for the use of the New Testament in Christian ethics, namely a *descriptive, synthetic* and *hermeneutical* task.[16] The latter will be the focus of the last chapter.

In my own search for some kind of balanced integration of the numerous aspects of biblical interpretation, I have been informed and influenced by many scholars from different traditions and historical periods, but also by many wise, "ordinary" people (in the sense used by West 1991a:142–163). Most of these are reflected by the diversity of voices represented in the list of works cited at the end

---

[16] The *descriptive* task is fundamentally exegetical in character. "The first thing we must do in order to understand the ethics of the New Testament is to explicate in detail the message of the individual writings in the canon." He then nuances the exegetical task in an important way: "Our descriptive work cannot be confined, however, to the explicit moral teachings of the New Testament texts; the church's moral world is manifested not only in such teachings but also in the stories, symbols, social structures, and practices that shape the community's ethos" (Hays 1990:44). The *synthetic* task that Hays proposes, entails the search for a possible coherent ethical perspective within the diversity of the canon (cf. Van Huyssteen & Du Toit 1989:36–40). To keep readers honest by insuring that their synthetic proposals respect rather than erode the texts though, he suggests that the full range of canonical witnesses be confronted, and that particular intra-canonical tensions not be harmonized prematurely or forcefully (Hays 1990:44–47). In other words, readers have to allow themselves the freedom to discover the intentions of the text and be surprised by it (cf. Miller 1989; Fiorenza 1988). Hays goes on to say that such tensions as referred to here can be handled only "if they can be located within a comprehensive characterization of the New Testament's moral concerns or themes. What we need, in short, is a cluster of master (*sic*) images to govern our construal of New Testament ethics. The unifying images must be derived from the texts themselves, rather than superimposed artificially, and they must be capable of providing an interpretive framework that links and illumines the individual writings" (Hays 1990:45). I concur with this step as an essential aspect of an ethics of New Testament interpretation, although it is not my purpose to construe such a broad interpretive framework for Christian ethics here. For examples of such an approach, see Ogletree 1983; Verhey 1984a; Breytenbach & Lategan 1992; Schrage 1988; Marxsen 1993; Ramsey 1993.

The last critical phase is the *hermeneutical* task—bridging the chasm between the New Testament writings and successive readers, appropriating its message "as a word addressed to us.... This task of hermeneutic appropriation requires *an integrative act of imagination....*" (Hays 1990:45; cf. 1989:25–29; Lategan 1994b:134).

In conclusion Hays (1990:46) remarks that "the pivotal choices for New Testament ethics as a theological discipline are made, whether consciously or unconsciously, in our working methods for performing the synthetic and hermeneutic tasks." (This confirms the importance of the descriptive exegetical task as prerequisite for any Christian ethical discussion). Hays then suggests useful guidelines for the synthetic and hermeneutical tasks of a church that seeks to be a "Scripture-shaped community" (1990:46–55).

of the book. The rest of this chapter is an attempt to account for these influences, as methodological premise for the chapters to follow.

1.4 AN INTEGRATED ETHICS OF READING AND ACCOUNTABILITY

In the context of biblical scholarship at large, questions regarding an ethics of interpretation—and therefore the integrity of biblical scholarship—were most pertinently asked by Elisabeth Schüssler Fiorenza (1988; 1999:1–102; cf. J. Botha 1992:170–174).[17] In a discussion of her challenging and now influential 1988 article, Smit (1990a:16–28) surveys the contributions of three other scholars who recently emphasized the need for a shift in the ethos of scholarly interpretation, namely Anthony Thiselton and David Tracy who both work from a hermeneutic tradition, and Wilhelm Wuellner, reintroducing or reinventing rhetorical criticism (cf. Hester 1994). I limit my discussion at this point to Fiorenza's contribution.[18]

She defines the ethics of interpretation as a reading which respects the rights of the text, and assumes that the text being interpreted "may say something different from what one wants or expects it to say" (1988:5; cf. Hays 1990:46). At the same time, with respect to the ethics of biblical scholarship as an institu-

---

[17] These suggestions were made during and since her presidential address at the Annual Meeting of the *Society of Biblical Literature* (SBL) in Boston, December 1987. For some of the American and South African responses to Fiorenza's provocative address, see Smit 1990a; 1990b; J. Botha 1992:174–184; Craffert 1996. Fiorenza developed these suggestions further through various publications, especially in her major 1999 book *Rhetoric and Ethic: The Politics of Biblical Studies* (Minneapolis: Fortress).

[18] The impact of her suggestions has to be understood against the backdrop of the SBL's ethos at that stage (1987). She refers to the society's 1908 presidential address in which Frank Porter charted *three shifts* in the then dominant ethos of biblical scholarship. After the first stage, during which the Bible was imposed upon the present as an external authority, the period of historical science followed (through which biblical scholarship was passing in 1908). This brought deliverance from dogmatic bondage, and treated biblical history like all other histories. However, Porter already envisaged a third phase during which, while the rights and achievements of historical criticism would be freely accepted, the power of the Bible would once more be felt (Fiorenza 1988:3; cf. Wuellner 1989a).

Fiorenza (1988:4–5) reckons that much of what has been done in biblical studies during the fifteen years preceding her address (particularly in the adoption of insights and methods of literary studies and philosophical hermeneutics), has followed Porter's lead. This has brought about that the Bible is (now) read like any other great book, the greatness of which does not consist in its accuracy as biographical record of facts, but relies on *its symbolic power to transfigure human experience and reality*. However, this third (literary-hermeneutic) paradigm seems to be in the process of decentering into a fourth paradigm, promising to inaugurate a rhetorical-ethical return. For Fiorenza, this last paradigm relies on the analytical and practical tradition of classical and modern rhetoric in order to insist on the *public responsibility* of biblical scholarship (cf. Fiorenza 1999:31–102).

tionalized academic practice, she maintains that "biblical interpretation, like all other scholarly inquiry, is a communicative practice that involves interests, values, and visions" (1988:4; cf. Fowl 1988). These interests and values, however, do not always reflect the perspectives of the biblical texts. The thrust of her argument is therefore a plea for a redefinition of "true scholarship." Her vision firstly entails a *decentering* of the dominant scientist ethos of biblical scholarship in the SBL, and secondly its *recentering to include the context of all readers* (especially women), and to become a *critical interpretive praxis for liberation*:

> Ethos is the shared intellectual space of freely accepted obligations and traditions as well as the praxial space of discourse and action. Since ethos shapes our scholarly behavior and attitudes, it needs to be explored more explicitly in terms of its rhetorical aims, which seek to affect a common orientation among its practitioners (Fiorenza 1988:8; 1999:22).

Contrary to the tendency in twentieth century formalist literary criticism to emphasize a text at the expense of its context, a critical theory of *rhetoric* insists that context is as important as text, and that one's social location or rhetorical context is decisive for how one sees the world, "reads the context" (Botha 1994c), constructs reality, or interprets biblical texts. "What we see depends on where we stand" (Fiorenza 1988:5; cf. Loubser 1986; Fowl & Jones 1991:13–14). If biblical scholars, theologians and ethicists assume responsibility for the relevance of their interpretive task in relation to the context of contemporary readers, questions such as the following become central: Who is involved in the reading process? On whose behalf is the text being read? What sparks the interest in, and reaction to the text? Whose—which individual or group—interests are served? What kind of world is envisioned? What roles, duties, and values are advocated? What happens between reading a text, and its understanding as practical ethos or change of behavior? What social effects are our theological activities supposed to have (cf. Smit 1993c)? These questions, Fiorenza (1988: 14–15; 1999:26–30) argues, require a double ethics, an ethics of *historical reading* and an ethics of *accountability*, an ethics which respects both the "textuality" of a text and its readers (cf. McDonald 1993:163–246).

1.4.1 *AN ETHICS OF (HISTORICAL) READING*

An ethics of *historical reading* asks what kind of reading can do justice to the text in its socio-cultural context. Of particular importance is her emphasis that a historical reading will allow us, through contextualization, to relativize the values and authority claims of the biblical texts, and to assess and evaluate them critically (Fiorenza 1988:14; cf. J. Botha 1992:185). This would obviously have important implications for the use of the Bible in Christian ethics (cf. Birch & Rasmussen 1989:78–79, 160).

Botha (1992:185–193) broadens Fiorenza's notion of historical reading to *an ethics of reading* (cf. Thiselton 1992:471–555), which ties up with Miller's vision for an ethics of reading. In his MLA (Modern Language Association of America) presidential address in 1986, Miller (1987b:284) emphasizes that respect for a text should be the reader's first responsibility: "I have been working lately on what I call 'the ethics of reading.' If that phrase means anything, it must have something to do with respecting any text discussed, with accepting an obligation to read—to read carefully, patiently, and scrupulously, under the elementary assumption that the text being read may say something different from what one wants it to say or from what received opinion says" (cf. Fiorenza 1988: 5). What a text says can never be taken for granted, "not even after that text has been overlaid by generations of commentary" (Miller 1989:91).[19]

Miller (1989:82) emphasizes the serious reading of any text—not in the positivistic sense of a "close reading" though—as a non-negotiable prerequisite for saying something about the relation of a text to external matters.[20] Botha (1992: 190) endorses this notion: "(W)ithout a preceding rhetorical study of literature, allowing for and trying to understand its nature, how it works, what it can do, we cannot understand the role that the New Testament literature may have in society, history, the church, and individual life." For a *rhetorical* study of literature and its communicative power, Botha (1994b) uses Miller's idea of respect for the "textuality" of a text as it manifests itself in its linguisticality, literariness, historicity and rhetoricity. The text must first of all be read with all methodological sophistication and rigor. "It would be ethically irresponsible to treat the text lightly and to over-simplify the reading process only to make all sorts of claims about possible implications of biblical material for modern social and ecclesiastical contexts" (J. Botha 1992:185). In this sense Botha broadens Fiorenza's concept of an ethics of historical reading to an ethics of *reading* (see also Jeanrond 1991: 116–119; Thiselton 1992:471–555).

---

[19] This is to an even greater extent true of the text of the New Testament. Smit (1994f), with reference to four voices from diverse backgrounds (Gerald Graff from literary theory, Robert Fowler from reader-response criticism, Bernard Lategan from contextual hermeneutics, and Francis Schüssler Fiorenza from systematic theology), discusses the presuppositions of readers about texts as "the (un)official interpretive culture" mediating their experience of those texts. For instance, the influence of mass media over many years, the attendance of numerous sermons, Sunday School classes, and youth camps, make it possible that readers (even New Testament scholars) "know" so much about these documents *before* they read them, that they often do not need to read them seriously in order to be able to talk fluently about them, and even to write about them! And in almost all these encounters with the New Testament some ethical imperative is derived from it (cf. J. Botha 1992:189).

[20] Positivism is a philosophical and methodological position (dominant from the 1920s to the 1970s), holding that only what one is able to perceive through one's senses, can form the basis of knowledge. Accordingly, no metaphysical knowledge can be verifiable (cf. Deist 1990:196; Van Huyssteen 1986:15–22; 1987:20–23).

1.4.2 *AN ETHICS OF ACCOUNTABILITY*

An ethics of *accountability*, on the other hand, holds biblical interpreters responsible not only for the choice of theoretical interpretive models, but also for the *ethical consequences* of the biblical texts and their meanings. Giving account of the intended ethical consequences and political functions of biblical texts in their Mediterranean socio-cultural settings, as well as the contemporary situation within which they are read and acted out, form part of the task of the responsible biblical scholar. This includes a sensitivity for the ideological, religious and material factors influencing the reading process (cf. Wuellner 1989b).[21] In order to answer the question *What is the language of the biblical documents supposed to "do" to readers who submit to their worlds or vision?*, Fiorenza (1988:15; 1999:29) concludes that "the careful reading of biblical texts and the appropriate construction of their historical worlds and of their symbolic universes need to be complemented by *a theological ('theo-ethical' in the 1999 version) discussion of the contemporary religious functions of biblical texts* which claim scriptural authority today in biblical communities of faith" (emphasis mine; cf. Thiselton 1992:4–8).

While Botha also takes the challenge of public accountability seriously, it is at this specific point where his way parts from Miller's notion of serious reading (J. Botha 1992:190–191). Miller's "hard" deconstructionist view of language (1989:92) is that "there is no ascertainable *logos* outside the chain of signs, above, below, before, or after, which can be shown determining its meaning." Botha (1992:190–191) summarizes Miller's position as follows: For him (Miller) "to study the rhetoric of the text is to uncover the ways in which the text's language becomes undecidable. Consequently, to observe the ethics of reading is to respect the undecidability of the text. Paradoxically then, to infer ethical imperatives from the reading of a literary text is to violate the ethics of reading as an activity. For Miller such inferences always and of necessity fail to respect the otherness of the text."

Botha (1992:191) then modifies Miller's position: "Granted that texts are undecidable and ethical imperatives can therefore not be derived from texts and granted that the ethics of reading is precisely to respect this linguisticality of the text, I would still hold that ethical imperatives can be reached, but then located in

---

[21] Fiorenza thus recognizes a methodological compatibility between theology and rhetoric (cf. Cunningham 1990:55–62), as approached from the field of biblical interpretation: "A rhetorical hermeneutic does not assume that the text is a window to historical reality, nor does it operate with a correspondence theory of truth. It does not understand historical sources as data and evidence but sees them as perspectival discourse constructing their worlds and symbolic universes.... Not detached value-neutrality but an explicit articulation of one's rhetorical strategies, interested perspectives, ethical criteria, theoretical frameworks, religious presuppositions, and sociopolitical locations for critical public discussion are appropriate in such a rhetorical paradigm of biblical scholarship" (Fiorenza 1988:13–14; 1999:26–27).

the *interpretive community and the whole process of interaction* taking place in the reading process, and not purely in the text" (cf. Rousseau 1986:2–3, 75–77; Van Huyssteen 1986:169–215; Lategan 1989b; Thiselton 1992:499–508). By this is meant an active dialogical intertextual discourse not only between texts and readers, but rather as a "polyphonic discourse" in and around the text, in which also "non-lingual" texts can contribute to meaning (J. Botha 1992:191–193, drawing on ideas from South African literary theorist Heilna du Plooy). This notion will play an important role in the further discussion on the use of the Bible in Christian ethics (cf. 4.3.5).

My own understanding of an ethics of responsible interpretation wishes to pay due respect to both facets proposed by Fiorenza: the "otherness" of biblical documents and the contexts of contemporary readers, as well as the conversational relationship between the two (cf. Tracy 1991:96; Rousseau 1986:390–424).[22]

This is the vision, but how do we get there—step by step as it were? Which methods, strategies or attitudes would be appropriate to meet such enormous challenges—at this point in time? I hesitate.... Yet, somehow I am deeply challenged by the dilemma, and—realizing that *one other voice* would not necessarily change the world—hope to pray, think and discuss my way through at least some of the complexities and divergence of views on the subject, and by doing that, to "stitch my part of the quilt carefully."[23]

1.5 SUMMARIZING SCIENTIFIC CHALLENGES FOR AN INTEGRATED EXEGETIC-HERMENEUTICAL APPROACH TO THE BIBLICAL DOCUMENTS

A growing awareness of the multi-dimensional nature of textual communication during the second half of the twentieth century stimulated the urge for some kind of an integrating, organizing, comprehensive, all-encompassing approach toward the biblical documents. Lategan has repeatedly argued that a convincing exegetic method has to account adequately for *all* such dimensions (1978:28–29; 1985b:5–6; 1988:69; cf. 1982; 1984a; 1992b:153–154). It should be noted, however, that the mere integration of methods does not necessarily lead to a multi-dimensional methodology:

> Integration normally means that the epistemological presuppositions of
> a particular method function as framework within which procedures of

---

[22] This challenge has indeed been taken up by many New Testament scholars, albeit with different emphases (cf. Rousseau 1986; Botha 1994b; Lategan 1985b:3–7; 1988:69; Smit 1992).

[23] Sallie McFague, North American systematic theologian and respected for her work on metaphorical theology, used this expression in a panel discussion of her award-winning book *Models of God: Theology for an Ecological, Nuclear Age* (Minneapolis: Augsburg-Fortress, 1987) during the Annual Meeting of the SBL/AAR in Washington DC, 20–23 Nov. 1993.

another method are then incorporated. The danger then exists that the presuppositions of the second method are ignored or misrepresented. A multidimensional methodology, on the contrary, takes seriously the presuppositions of each method, and endeavours to interrelate these methods on another level (Jonker 1993:111).

Although Botha—a former student of Lategan—considers the search for methodological integration of importance, he does not undertake the difficult task of developing such a method or model of interpretation. In fact, he doubts whether such a model is attainable (Botha 1991:9). Rather, the contribution of his inter-disciplinary mode of analysis lies in bringing various disciplinary strategies and results into dialogue with one another (Botha 1992; 1994b). In the meantime, however, it is evident by the moral scars of our society that an interrelated, inter-disciplinary, relevant approach has eluded biblical exegetes for too long (cf. Lategan 1985a:3–7; 1988:69; Smit 1988b; 1992).

In terms of the three hermeneutical journeys mentioned above (1.3), it seems that the main *scientific challenges* with regard to such an interrelated, multi-dimensional methodology—as an essential part of an ethics of New Testament interpretation—can be phrased as the search for

- a sufficient *hermeneutical theory and practice*, which would account for human needs and the role of readers in the process of first century and later interpretation; as well as

- (an) adequate *exegetical method(s)*, which would do justice to the multi-facetedness of the biblical texts, and thus respect their unique nature and purpose (cf. Rousseau 1986:19–28).

The urgent need is to develop these approaches *in tandem*, and to somehow hold them together "in creative tension" (Hays 1989:27). Hays (1990:43) explains why this is crucial: "Indeed, careful exegesis heightens our awareness of the theological diversity within Scripture and of our historical distance from the original communities.... to whom these texts were addressed. In other words, critical exegesis exacerbates the hermeneutical problem rather than solving it.... Unless we can give a coherent account of our methods for moving between text and normative ethical judgements, appeals to the authority of Scripture will be hollow and unconvincing" (cf. Lategan 1978:19; Gottwald 1993, with reference to a social class analysis of the biblical world).

While wrestling with these challenges, I do not intend to develop a new method of interpretation. As a theoretical point of departure, I shall use some basic insights from different communication theories and models, and try to integrate them in accordance with the multi-dimensional nature of textual communication and reality as a whole (cf. Lategan 1988:69). In this respect, I found South African New Testament scholar Jacques Rousseau's model for the communication of ancient canonized texts (1986; 1988a; 1988b; 1989b) particularly helpful. One does not necessarily have to concur with all the fine detail of this comprehensive (and rather complicated) model to be able to appreciate its usefulness. While it is primarily a serious and innovative attempt to *integrate* different methods of interpretation, it is at the same time sensitive to the risks attached to such an "integrative" endeavor—particularly with respect to the powerful and often dangerous influence of the presuppositions underlying those methods. It further accounts for the abovementioned hermeneutical journeys in a responsible way, and honors the creative dialogical relationship between texts and readers (cf. Rousseau 1986:388–432). It therefore broadens the process of reading to include hermeneutical issues about understanding, knowledge, communication, and truth. As a "model" it remains open-ended and flexible while functioning within the dynamics of an ongoing hermeneutic spiral.

In the next section I briefly articulate what I consider to be a "coherent account" (Hays 1990:43) of my methods and theories—as a possible framework within which the implied ethical effect of a New Testament document may be pursued further. In order to substantiate the bifocal vision of text and readers, I shall relate the results of a communication theory (as exegetical method) to recent trends in Christian ethics (as hermeneutic praxis) in the final chapter of the book.

1.6 AN INTEGRATED APPROACH TOWARD UNDERSTANDING THE NEW TESTAMENT

New Testament scholars today owe a lot to disciplines such as communication science, linguistics, literary science, social science, reception aesthetics and others, for many new insights into the documents of the New Testament, which—like any oral or written text—form part of a communication process. Although these disciplines may have different philosophical points of departure, I believe that they can be utilized effectively within a multi-dimensional approach toward biblical texts (cf. Rousseau 1986; 1988a; 1989b; Hays 1989; J. N. Vorster 1990; 1991; Jonker 1991; 1993).

Since Lasswell's simple linear model initiated communication science in 1948, the full complexity of communication has come to be acknowledged (Rousseau 1986:35–38). Primarily, communication science made us aware of three basic elements involved in any communication event, namely the *sender* (communicator or source), *message*, and *receiver* (cf. Lategan 1982:50–52; 1985b:67–75; Rousseau 1986:35–43; Mouton 1987:51–54). Should any of these be absent, no communication can take place. With reference to the *medium* by which a message is conveyed, the German linguist Heinrich F. Plett (referred to by Rousseau 1986:36) further distinguished between the *code* (verbal and non-verbal language) and *channel* (written, visual or acoustic).[24]

It is indeed no easy task to combine the intricate relations among these

---

[24] Each of these elements can also be referred to in terms of *static*, *dynamic* and *dialectic* categories (Patte 1976:21–25; cf. Ricoeur 1976:26–37; Rousseau 1986:36; Jonker 1991; 1993:106–112).

elements into one definition. From a structuralist point of view, communication is understood as "a process whereby a sender encodes a certain message in terms of a specific code (e.g. language) and sends it through as specific medium (e.g. written signs) to a receiver who decodes the message in terms of the agreed code" (Lategan 1978:23–28; cf. 1984a:3). From a pragmatic point of view, R. L. Kelley's concise yet descriptive attempt (1977:9, cf. 2–17) may be helpful in accounting for the active role of readers/recipients in processes of understanding: "Communication occurs whenever we create meaning from our interaction with the world."[25]

We have seen in 1.2 that the long history of New Testament research led to the realization that these writings function in terms of three levels or dimensions, namely a structural, historical, and faith level (cf. Lategan 1982:50–52; 1985a:5–6; Rousseau 1986:41–43). These dimensions are applicable to the network of relations among the basic elements in any communication process: the *static* structural or textual level is represented by the written words and medium by means of which a message is conveyed, the *dynamic* historical level by the language of the text and its reference as well as the persons and worlds of the senders and receivers, while the *dialectic* ideological or faith level pertains to the senders' strategies to persuade their receivers, and the receivers' openness to be persuaded by the strategies and perspectives of the text.[26]

Further distinctions can however be made within these dimensions of textual communication. According to Rousseau (1986:47–48), C. W. Morris developed a semiotic model in 1938 by means of which he identified three grammatical *modes* expressed in all written texts (cf. Jeanrond 1991:84–86):

- the *syntactic* mode (which describes the relation between written language signs);

- the *semantic* mode (which focuses on the relation between the signs and that to which they refer, i.e. the "meaning" of words, phrases, sentences and larger literary units);

- and the *pragmatic* mode (with reference to the relation between the signs and their interpreters).

---

[25] Rousseau (1986:39–40) notices an interesting parallel between Kelley's definition of communication in general and the aim of New Testament hermeneutics in particular. Communication science and New Testament hermeneutics are both engaged in the scientific search for the "meaning" of people's existence in interaction with their environment. In terms of *structure* (sender, medium, receiver) and *function* (understanding as the search for and/or creation of meaning) these two sciences have much in common. For this reason, a communicative approach toward understanding the ancient canonized writings of the New Testament seems promising in many ways.

[26] Although "message" is conveyed in the form of a static text, it has to be acknowledged as *seen and interpreted from the readers' perspective* (cf. 1.1 n.6).

Plett combined these distinctions with his text theory, which Rousseau (1986:70–72) subsequently built into his integrated multi-dimensional model for exegesis and hermeneutics. Rousseau did not only discover that Morris' distinctions of syntactics, semantics and pragmatics respectively coincide with the structural, historical and dialectic levels of communication, but that all three semiotic modes function simultaneously in each of the three textual dimensions (cf. Mouton 1987:57).[27] Although I hope to bear these semiotic modes in mind, I will not necessarily distinguish between them in my analysis of Ephesians. My main concern is the *pragmatic function* of each dimension in the communication of the Ephesians text.

To my mind, one of the most useful results of Rousseau's work is his valuable insight into the *focal point* of the network of relations in each dimension (Rousseau 1986:48–51; cf. Mouton 1987:67–74). He summarizes the delicate interrelation of the mutual static, dynamic and dialectic qualities of both the textual dimensions and semiotic modes by means of three main categories, namely:

- the "static *thrust*" (which is the culmination of the linguistic-structural dimension and the syntactic mode);

- the "dynamic cosmological *perspective*" (which combines the interrelation between the author's ultimate commitment and socio-cultural world with the semantic mode;

- and finally, the "dialectic *strategy*" (which reveals a combination of the communicative, persuasive power of the text with the pragmatic mode).

According to Rousseau, all these categories represent the *end result* of the analyses of every level of communication, which finally comes to the fore in the decisive dialectic phase (cf. Lategan 1992b:154).[28] The focus of this study will indeed be on this "final" phase of textual communication, and particularly on the implied ethical impact of the communicative, rhetorical power of Ephesians.[29]

---

[27] For a detailed discussion of Rousseau's model, and its potential application to biblical texts, see Rousseau 1986:41–72; 1988a; 1989b; Mouton 1987:46–74.

[28] Although the term "dialectic" may refer to a wide range of issues—particularly with regard to the approach and method used by the two influential German philosophers G. W. Friedrich Hegel (1770–1831) and Karl Marx (1818–1883), and of which the origins are to be found in ancient Greek philosophy (cf. Solomon 1990:viii, 113, 317; Deist 1990: 70–71)—I am using it here as describing a critical, conversational, dialogical process between the needs, moods, questions and presuppositions of readers and the "responses" of a text.

[29] It needs to be borne in mind that the different dimensions of communication naturally function simultaneously. They are distinguished and analyzed only for the sake of scientific clarity. The application of any model has therefore to be left as open and flexible as possible. The researcher's sensitivity for the inherent complexities of any communication event calls for a humble and provisional attitude toward the interpretation and appropriation of a text. Fully aware of the limitations and relativity of all our methods, we

The *functions* of the three main categories of thrust, perspective and strategy in Rousseau's model are of vital importance for its appropriation. The function of the *thrust* is to reveal pointers in the text, and to *provide relief* in the communication process. *Perspective* (life and world view, or frame of reference) refers to the implied author and recipients' interpretation of their world, and thus serves to *orientate* the reader. The function of the *strategy* is to *persuade* the reader toward the author's perspective, and to bring about effective communication (Rousseau 1986:52–69, 244–260; cf. Mouton 1987:58–59).[30]

According to Rousseau (1986:423–424; 1988c:21–31; 1989a:34–60), New Testament texts thrust (in accordance with their nature and intention) the following basic questions to the fore, which successive readers need to ask in relation to the various dimensions of textual communication:

- *what* is the relief of the most important words, phrases, sentences, symbols, and people involved in the particular text (a *what/who* question)?

- *around what* do the text, symbols, and people *revolve*, that is, what orientates the text, symbols, people (a *how* question)?

- what is the *purpose* or *function* of the specific text, symbols and people involved (a *why* question)?

Attending to these aspects carefully and patiently, while honoring the process in its totality and interrelatedness, forms the heart of an ethics of textual interpretation.

1.6.1   *THE RELIEF-PROVIDING THRUST OF THE STRUCTURAL DIMENSION: IDENTIFYING LINGUISTIC AND LITERARY ASPECTS OF A TEXT*

While we acknowledge the relational role of readers in the reading process, we do have to find a way out of the danger of total relativism where any interpretation is acceptable. In the next chapter I shall explore the three interrelated notions of *thrust*, *perspective*, and *strategy* with regard to Ephesians—as an attempt to respect and obey the pointers, reader instructions, constraints and movement within it, while reckoning with the creative, interpretive role of its readers in every phase.

It has been argued why a document itself could/should be considered as the

---

can only remain involved in the risk and creative tension of understanding God's word in relation to our situation—wholly, responsibly, honestly (cf. Bosch 1980:43–45).

[30] According to this approach, it is especially the author's perspective or ultimate commitment which represents the "inspiration" behind textual communication, and which "determines" the thrust and strategy of a document (Rousseau 1986:50–51; cf. n.37 below). An important challenge for later readers would therefore be to account for their own commitments, and to allow the perspective of the particular text to determine the reading process.

gateway toward understanding the implied communication event reflected by it (cf. Rousseau 1986:42; Botha 1991:8; 1.3 n.15). From this point of view, an analysis of its linguistic-literary dimension will be the first step in the exegetical process. This level refers to text-immanent elements, as revealed in the document's *language structure* and *actantial roles*.[31] Within the scope of this study, I shall concentrate on textual facets in Ephesians which open alternative possibilities of moral identity and behavior—essential elements within all religious texts.

A *linguistic* analysis concentrates on the available information within a text, as the encoded author's construction of her/his "world" (cf. Ricoeur 1976:34–37)[32], as well as that of the "implied readers" as understood by the "author."[33] Although the text was handed over in a frozen static form (cf. Patte 1976:6), it nevertheless reveals a specific *hierarchy* or *relief* of main figures, structural markers and pivotal points (cf. Rousseau 1986:52–56, 99–104; 1988c:23–26).

Since the New Testament was written in the everyday *koine*-Greek of the first century, the Greek grammar, vocabulary and structure will always form the

---

[31] "Actantial roles" are basic logical categories of story-telling that underlie narratives. Occurring in sets of opposed pairs, these actants represent the basic functions fulfilled by different actors in a story (Deist 1990:4). See 2.1.3 n.23 with regard to a possible actantial analysis of the Ephesians text.

[32] Ricoeur (1976:37) describes the term "world" by means of what "we all understand when we say of a new born child that he (*sic*) has come into the world. For me, the world is the ensemble of references opened up by every kind of text, descriptive or poetic, that I have read, understood, and loved. And to understand a text is to interpolate among the predicates of our situation all the signification that makes a *Welt* out of our *Umwelt*. It is this enlarging of our horizon of existence that permits us to speak of the references opened up by the text or of the world opened up by the referential claims of most texts" (cf. Lategan 1987:115; 1992c:627).

[33] Because I am mainly concerned with the Ephesians author and addressees as enscriptured or *rhetorical*—and not necessarily *historical*—categories (cf. 2.1, 2.3), "author" and "readers" will henceforth refer to the *encoded or implied author and readers* (Wolfgang Iser's terms), except when indicated otherwise. It should be borne in mind however that in the case of an ancient text such as Ephesians—originating essentially from within an *oral* culture—the category of implied "audience" or "recipients" would be more appropriate than "readers", even though letter writing was a common form of communication in the cultural setting of the first century Mediterranean world. I use these as interchangeable terms throughout the book. The literary categories of implied author and recipients or readers concentrate on the inside of a text, and are not in the first instance concerned with real readers of flesh and blood, but with how readers are *anticipated* by and in the text. "It is interested in all that can be gleaned from the text in the form of instructions given to, and presuppositions shared by the potential reader of the text.... From all the information gathered in this way, an image of the intended reader can be reconstructed or envisaged.... *The implied reader is a device to engage the real reader by offering a role to be played or an attitude to be assumed*" (Lategan 1989a:7, 10; emphasis mine; cf. Lategan 1987:114–115; 1992c:626–627; Vorster 1989; Deist 1990:123).

basis for the analysis of these writings. Sophisticated methods like *structural and discourse analyses* can be used to identify the logical and chronological way in which an author selected and arranged available material (cf. Lemmer 1988: addendum; Rousseau 1986:455–511; Mouton 1987:76–89), although this is not the aim of the book. The processes of selection and arrangement reveal the *thrust* or *direction* of a text as an author's attempt to guide the readers' thoughts and actions toward a certain goal.

The *recurrence* of specific themes, metaphors, traditional material and actants, as well as their underlying coherence and reference, forms part of the researcher's task in determining the thrust of a document. The recurrence of strategic words, themes, roles and perspectives may serve as a "foregrounding device," aimed at focusing the readers' attention on major aspects of the message and—eventually—at transforming them toward the position where the text would like them to be.[34] By identifying such metaphors, interpersonal roles and traditional material, one can to a large extent construct the author's view of the readers' moral world, as well as the alternative world s/he wished to communicate (cf. Rousseau 1986:246).

To account for the thrust of a text finally involves the implied *function* or *purpose* of different linguistic techniques or structural elements. This means inquiring into the *literary or pragmatic effect* intended or brought about by different linguistic devices employed by the author. The major question here is *what* the author wants to communicate (i.e. what effect s/he wishes to facilitate) and *how* s/he does that through the specific choice of *genre*, and the selection and arrangement of material. In the case of Ephesians, the letter or epistolary *genre* leaves room for a combination of different techniques, such as narrative and argumentative elements (which could appeal to the emotional *and* cognitive senses of its readers—cf. Cuthbertson 1992; Lategan 1994b:132).

1.6.2 *THE ORIENTING PERSPECTIVE OF THE HISTORICAL DIMENSION: UNDERSTANDING THE MORAL WORLD OF A TEXT*

The next dimension in the communication of written texts represents the interrelated roles of the sender, medium and receiver. In the historical analysis the focus is on the relation among the different text-internal elements of a document (identified in the structural phase), its relation to other texts, as well as the socio-

---

[34] With reference to the variety of textual roles and perspectives offered to readers, e.g. that of the narrator, the characters, plot and implied readers (as expressions of the mediating potential of a text, and which Iser calls the "wandering viewpoint" of the reader), Lategan (1992c:627; 1987:115) describes the function of "foregrounding" as follows: "In moving backwards and forwards between these perspectives, the reader will find that different segments of the text are brought into the foreground, while others become marginal. In presenting these different options to the reader, the text is in fact mediating between the reader's position and where the text would like the reader to be."

cultural or "moral world" to which it refers.[35] Its intention is therefore to construct a particular document's intra-, inter- and extra-textual *frames of reference*
(cf. Rousseau 1986:57–63, 277–287; Lategan 1985b; 1994b). "The words, the
expressions, forming the explicit textbase are the *windows* through which we
have to look in order to recognize parts of those frames which suit the text"
(Breytenbach 1990:257).[36]

For many reasons, which will not be discussed here, historical considerations remain inevitable within the purview of New Testament scholarship.
Historical interpretation of the New Testament writings is necessitated by their
very nature as historical documents (Botha 1994b:143; cf. Rousseau 1986:263–
385; Lategan 1978:19–23, 28–29; 1982:50–52; 1985a:7–12; Mouton 1987:102–
154). "Historical interpretation of the New Testament is necessary to provide information for setting the parameters of valid readings of the New Testament.
Such an interpretation serves the purpose of alienation between reader and text
and enables the interpreter to ask critical questions about the communicability
and relevance of these texts" (Vorster 1984:104; cf. Fiorenza 1988:14; J. Botha
1992:185; Thiselton 1992:8–10).

The biblical texts are the result of a dynamic process of human experience
and interpretation from a particular faith perspective. The documents of the New

---

[35] The term "moral world" refers to the collective moral network of a group or
society in terms of customs, rules, taboos, traditions, i.e. the world which they construct
for themselves to live in, the world which has been internalized in their thoughts and deeds
(cf. Meeks 1986b:11–17; Smit 1991b:56).

[36] As in the case of a rhetorical hermeneutic, this approach does not assume that the
text is a window to historical reality, or that it operates with a correspondence theory of
faith (cf. Fiorenza 1988:13). With respect to the problem of textual reference in literary
criticism, scholars such as Norman R. Petersen and Willem S. Vorster tend to speak of
texts as "mirrors" rather than "windows" (Lategan 1994b:122). However, the *integrative*
nature of this process leaves room for the appropriation of both these metaphors to
reference. We do not have to choose, but we need to differentiate in order to allow the free
and full flow of the text in communicating different aspects of reference *behind* the text, *in*
the text, and *in front of* the text. "*Reference behind* the text would.... normally include
allusions, indirect and explicit referrals to the historical background of the text, its time of
origin, historical figures, events, social and political structures of the time, but also of preceding times and normally anything that has to do with the historical dimension of the text.
This type of reference would be extra-textual by nature. *Reference in* would be referrals
which function inside the world of the text, within the narrative or the argument of the text
and is therefore intra-textual by nature. *Reference in front of* the text has to do with what
the text suggests, opens up, makes possible, leads to, produces, achieves and is by nature
again extra-textual" (Lategan 1994b:127). All aspects of textual reference function together as an *integrative symbiotic process* to create meaning (cf. R. M. Naudé 1993:161–
163). Reference in front of the text is not the abolishment of other forms of reference, but
is in fact built on these forms and dependent on them for success (Lategan 1994b:126–128,
134; 1994c:14–15; 1992b:153–154; cf. West 1991a; 1991b; Rousseau 1986:64–69).

Testament specifically reveal the early Christian communities' response to the historical Jesus of Nazareth (cf. Johnson 1999). However, what we have today, is not a photocopy of what happened, but different "faith"-ful human reproductions and interpretations of those events—depending on the authors' degree of involvement, perspective, attitude and frame of reference (cf. Van Huyssteen & Du Toit 1989:28–35).

It is especially in the historical dimension that the *dynamic perspective or life orientation* of the New Testament authors crystallizes—not in a positivistic sense though—as the *ultimate commitment* from which they selected, arranged, reinterpreted and appropriated traditions and other metaphors from their environment.[37] A historical analysis of a text therefore wishes to indicate how an author integrated her/his faith commitment with her/his everyday world (Mouton 1987: 103; cf. Rossouw 1980:23). *The identification of an encoded author's perspective is of vital importance for the reinterpretation and appropriation of a text by subsequent readers, and forms part of an ethics of interpretation.*

The historical nature of the New Testament writings presents itself in a variety of facets, namely a traditio- or text-historical, socio-cultural, and historical-literary facet. The exploration of these would have far-reaching implications for the understanding of the New Testament in general (cf. Rousseau 1989a:16–27), and the formation of the early Christian communities' identity awareness and ethos in particular. Where the text-historical analysis is meant to sensitize readers for the circumstances wherein those texts originated and functioned, the cultural-historical analysis wants to create understanding for the totally different socio-cultural world of the early Christians. The historical-literary aspect involves the history of the formation of the New Testament canon (Du Toit 1989:91–272), as well as its ongoing interpretation (*Wirkungsgeschichte*).

The methods used to explore the historical dimension of communication fall under the rubric "historical method(s)," or in the case of written texts, "historical criticism" (cf. Botha 1994b:142). A plurality of methods have been used in the past to investigate the historical nature of biblical texts. It is well-known that critical New Testament scholarship since the *Aufklärung* has been dominated by the historical paradigm,[38] and in particular the sub-disciplines of the German

---

[37] According to Rousseau (1986:51, 57–65, 246–252, 280–286), the ultimate commitment, perspective or ethos of the author is especially reflected by the dynamic inter-relatedness of the semantic mode of both the structural and historical dimensions on the micro- and macro-levels of a particular text. In the case of the New Testament, this process reveals how the authors selected—from a wide range of possible oral and written sources available, and from their particular perspectives—that which was relevant to their purposes, and edited their documents accordingly (cf. Mouton 1987:69–71, 102).

[38] "Historical paradigm" is a broad and general term for the presuppositions, values, beliefs, techniques and historical methods used to provide perspective on the data of events, people and phenomena of the past (Botha 1994b:142). For its possibilities and limitations, see Vorster 1984.

Historische Kritik.[39]

It is particularly with respect to the extra-textual reference of New Testament documents, that the historical dimension of textual reality challenges later readers with the responsibility of examining the (for them foreign) Mediterranean socio-cultural world of the first centuries C.E.[40] The Bible reflects a socio-cultural world (a "moral world"—Meeks 1986a; 1986b) with its own peculiar idiom, symbols, metaphors, and ethos. This world represents the ways of thinking and behavior to which the *language* (concepts, philosophies, events) and *actants* (persons, roles) of these texts refer, and in which they were embedded (cf. Rousseau 1986:64–69; Nida 1964:4–5). Essentially, the New Testament writings reflect the dynamic interaction between the first Christians and the main cultural-historical streams of that period, namely Judaism and Hellenism.

Written texts are also historically determined in the sense that they originated with the aim to convey a specific message between a historical author or authors and readers within a specific historical situation (cf. Rousseau 1986:57, 264, 413)—though this aspect will not receive major attention in the present study. To explore and understand this dynamic interaction, as well as its rhetorical impact within the cultural-historical setting of the text, is especially important in the case of texts which are time- and culture-wise far removed from successive readers (cf. Nida 1964:4–5, 147–149). The necessity of some kind of validation for a subsequent reception becomes even more imperative when ancient texts are used as *canonized* texts (Rousseau 1986:57).

As far as the historical macro-context of the Ephesians epistle is concerned, it would be important to establish (albeit provisionally) whether it formed part of the Pauline proclamation (the first written phase of the early church's interpretation of the Jesus event—cf. Roberts 1991:13; 1993b; Barth 1974a:10–12), or

---

[39] These sub-disciplines have become known as *Literary (Source) Criticism, Form Criticism, Traditionsgeschichte,* and *Redaction Criticism* (cf. Marshall 1977:126–195; Rousseau 1986:270–295; Mouton 1987:118–122 for the criteria and purposes of each sub-discipline). In spite of the limitations and dangers of this paradigm and its presuppositions, the potential of the different methods cannot be denied (cf. Rousseau 1986:267–269). With regard to the socio-cultural aspect, the results of the developing social sciences and socio-rhetorical approaches toward biblical texts (a redefining and broadening of the historical-critical method) has already shown great potential for a better understanding of the biblical world (cf. De Villiers 1984; Elliott 1986; Botha 1989; 1994b:189–218; Robbins 1990; 1996a; 1996b; Craffert 1991; Domeris 1993; Malina 1981; 1994a; 1994b). For an in-depth social-scientific analysis of a New Testament document, see Elliott, J. H. 1981. *A Home for the Homeless: A Sociological Exegesis of 1 Peter, Its Situation and Strategy*. Philadelphia: Fortress.

[40] New Testament hermeneutics today is especially challenged to account for the Middle-Eastern ways of thinking and living, particularly because the interpretation of the Bible has often in the past been determined by a one-sided Western rationalistic approach. Reading the New Testament in contemporary societies would thus inevitably involve an *inter-cultural* approach.

whether it belonged to the general proclamation of a deutero-Pauline period (cf. Rousseau 1986:284; Lincoln 1990:xxxv–lxxiii; Schnackenburg 1991:24), in which case the designation of the author as "Paul" (1:1; 3:1) might be a rhetorical device.[41]

.1 The (Re)orienting Potential of Metaphor

It has been indicated that *metaphors*, among other literary elements, are important—albeit often hazy—windows through which the moral world of a document can be investigated. Biblical and theological language (as the description of religious experience) is today widely recognized as primarily *metaphorical* in nature (cf. Van Huyssteen 1986:151–168; McFague 1982:42–54).[42]

Our interest in metaphors particularly lies in their *referential* and *relational* nature (cf. Nida 1964:31, 32, 70; Lategan 1985b; 1986b; 1994b; 1994c; Van Huyssteen 1987). Lategan (1994b:134) rightly claims that a "better understanding of the function of reference in all its forms holds the key to unlock the transformative potential of (biblical) texts in contemporary situations." According to the authoritative philosopher, theologian and linguist, Paul Ricoeur (1975; 1976: 89–95; 1977:216–256; 1980:26; cf. Thiselton 1992:351–372; Lategan 1992b:154; 1994b:131–133; 1994c), the referential, communicative or transformative power of a text lies *in its ability to suggest, to open up, to redescribe, to facilitate, to mediate, to make possible, to produce a world in front of it—a "proposed world" which readers may adopt or inhabit.* In this way it discloses a possible new way of looking at things (cf. Fowl & Jones 1991:31; Hauerwas 1981:57).

Metaphors, parables, and models are heuristic fictions or devices, instru-

---

[41] This brings the important yet complex issue concerning the relation between the "historical" and "rhetorical situation" of a text to the fore (cf. 2.3.3; J. N. Vorster 1991; Botha 1994b:141–148). Both are literary constructs of the encoded author—which does not however negate the reality of an "objective" extra-textual situation, and the necessity to explore as much as possible of it via scientific methods of socio-historical research (cf. Botha 1994b:141; Lategan 1985b:75–85; Kennedy 1984:34–35). Historical and rhetorical studies nevertheless represent totally different approaches to a text (cf. 2.2, 2.3). Within the broader context of this study, the focus will be on *rhetorical* elements in the Ephesians epistle. How fundamentally important the historical frame of reference might be for the understanding of a text (as an essential element of an ethics of interpretation), will a detailed analysis take us beyond the immediate scope of the book. I shall therefore mainly (though not exclusively) concentrate on text-internal information and the reader competence presumed by the Ephesians author. This will serve as basis for a construct of the "rhetorical situation" of the text (chapter two). A rhetorical approach—an equally important element of the ethics of interpretation—wishes to respect the text and its particular internal frame of reference.

[42] Since the recognition of the relational nature of all human language and knowledge, the study of metaphorical language became the focus of both the human and natural sciences (cf. Van Huyssteen 1986:158–163).

ments for the redescription of reality or lived experience, which break up inadequate interpretations of the world and open the way to new, more adequate, interpretations (Ricoeur 1977:216–256; Berger 1988:342–357, 430–438; Lategan 1993:404–407; 1994a:21; 1994b:131–133; 1994c).[43] Metaphor can thus help people to see things otherwise by changing the (meaning of the) language they use. As regards religious language, the dynamic reference of metaphors applies to the supernatural world of God on the one hand, and the socio-cultural and moral world of human thought and living on the other. From the biblical authors' perspective, this "world" was continuously redefined in terms of their relation to God (cf. Du Toit 1984a:17; Mouton 1987:124). Their use of metaphors is thus a reflection of how they experienced, substantiated and explained their faith in God within their everyday world. This would also apply to the understanding and explanation of God and reality in contemporary situations. There is no other way by which later readers can interpret and integrate new insights, than by doing it in terms of what is known, that is, by means of metaphorical language (cf. Hays 1990:45–46, 48–50). In this way metaphor permits people to see new connections in things, or as Ricoeur (1980:26) puts it, to "decode the traces of God's presence in history."

In her influential book, *Metaphorical Theology: Models of God in Religious Language*, Sallie McFague (1982:14–29) claims that a metaphorical theology is appropriate and necessary for two reasons: Metaphor is the way people think, and it is the way the parables—as a central form of expression in the New Testament—work. In chapter two of the book, she substantiates this claim by inquiring into the nature and function of metaphor, parable and Scripture, which concern the heart of biblical hermeneutics. In concurrence with other scholars, McFague

---

[43] Reference as redescription, which forms an essential part of interpretation, is *per se* a dynamic and *imaginative* enterprise. Positively, the concept of "imagination" refers to the constructive, creative and innovative role of readers in making sense of texts. However, the issue of imagination also often raised suspicion and even provoked resistance during the history of interpretation, especially in circles where it was viewed as opposed to historical evidence, facts, or data. Lategan (1996) discusses the role of imagination in interpretation in a nuanced way, with special reference to the functioning of the concept in Ricoeur's later work. The seventh study in Ricoeur's seminal *The Rule of Metaphor* (1977: 216–256) is devoted specifically to the relationship between metaphor and reference. Lategan focuses on three aspects of Ricoeur's argument: reference as self-transcendence, reference as redescription and reference as an integrative process (see also Lategan 1994b: 128–134). I shall particularly draw from the last two aspects, which deal with the purpose of both discourse and reference, namely to effect and enable shifts in language and meaning, aimed at shifts in action and behavior: "The power of discourse is not undirected, nor is reference aimless. Discourse in its pragmatic form is aimed at persuasion and change. The rhetorical intent of discourse and the issue of reference are therefore intimately connected" (Lategan 1994b:131). According to the perspective of the Ephesians epistle, the freedom and constraints of imagination are ultimately governed by the love of God *in Jesus Christ* (cf. 4.3–4.5).

(1982:42) argues that all the biblical language used to refer to God, is metaphorical. This confirms the importance of metaphor for religious language: "(W)e have no language but *analogy* for speaking about God, inadequate as such language is" (McFague 1982:42; emphasis mine).

Because an understanding of the interactional and referential function of metaphors is basic to the understanding of human thinking and language in general, and of communicative processes of reinterpretation in particular, I briefly deal with a theory of metaphor here.

By means of comparison a metaphor creates a relation of meaning between two things, and in such a surprising way that something new comes to the fore about the unknown factor in the comparison (cf. Ricoeur 1976:45–69; McFague 1982).[44] It is especially this important observation that metaphors *redescribe* reality (Ricoeur 1976:67–69; 1977:239–246; 1980:25–27) which brings about a better understanding of our knowledge and experience of reality.[45] Chapters two and three of the book will concentrate on the remarkable way in which the author of Ephesians utilized and reinterpreted a network of metaphors and traditions as *lenses* or *shifting devices* in order to guide his readers toward a renewed self-understanding *in Christ* (cf. 2.1.3; 3.3.3).[46]

Drawing on ideas from John M. Murry, McFague (1982:32) describes the appearance of metaphor "as the instinctive and necessary act of the mind exploring reality and ordering experience." This essential aspect of language applies to all expressions or descriptions of human experience—the human, social and natural sciences, philosophy, the arts *and* religion. In the processes of learning and understanding reality, the most outstanding feature of the human mind, in

---

[44] Ricoeur (1976:67; cf. 1977:83–90) quotes well-known socio-linguist Max Black in this regard: "(A) memorable metaphor has the power to bring two separate domains into cognitive and emotional relation by using language directly appropriate for the one as a lens for seeing the other."

[45] There in an interesting resemblance between this description and function of *metaphors* (as interaction with one's environment in the light of new experiences) and Kelley's rather general definition of *communication* (i.e. to create meaning through one's interaction with reality; Kelley 1977:9, cf. 2–17; Rousseau 1986:279).

[46] The discussion on the role of metaphors and traditions in Ephesians will only serve as an illustration of the encompassing processes of reinterpretation typical of the document's discourse as a whole. "What is true of the metaphor, becomes even clearer on the level of discourse. In a more extended text, the scope for redescription is that much bigger. An alternative understanding of reality can be offered, an alternative position can be described in much more detail. In narrative texts, redescription can take the form of an alternative point of view or the offering of different roles with which the reader can identify. In argumentative texts, alternative positions or perspectives are developed with the help of logical and/or rhetorical devices" (Lategan 1994b:132). Although Ephesians is neither of these two *per se*, it contains elements of both, which eventually add up to new insights and which offer a comprehensive alternative view on the reality of God in relation to human existence.

fact the essence of human being, is its image- and story-making capacity, "its *mobility*, its constant, instantaneous power of *association*, its ability to be forever *connecting* this with that" (McFague 1982:33, cf. 34, 65; emphasis mine), its ability to move by indirection from the known to the unknown, which is the heart of metaphor.[47]

The importance of metaphor in philosophy and the sciences is illustrated by the recognition of any creative act (e.g. the solution of a moral problem) as the "selection, combination, and synthesis of the already familiar into new wholes.... The new way is not simply a reshuffling of the old, for metaphorical thinking recognizes the *unlike* as well as the *like*, but it uses the similar to move beyond it into the unknown.... The whole that one sees is not identical with anything with which we are familiar, but the similarity has enabled us to see a new thing" (McFague 1982:35–36; cf. Thiselton 1992:8–10, 31–54). The essence of discovery and creation is thus recognizing a similarity that has not been seen before in two previously unrelated matrices.[48] In this sense metaphor may be considered as "a competence, a talent.... a talent of thinking." If this is the case, "(r)hetoric is just the reflection and the translation of this talent into a distinct body of knowledge" (Ricoeur 1977:80; Lategan 1994b:131).

Although metaphor should not be absolutized as the *only* way of understanding reality and the nature of human language, McFague (1982:36) emphasizes that it is a highly suggestive and fruitful way "by which to understand

---

[47] This means that the search for "truth" is a continuous process by which language is stretched to bring new insight (see Van Huyssteen's quote, 1986:160, of Max Black: "*metaphorical thought is a distinctive mode of achieving insight*") and to understand what has previously not been understood, and analogies made with the familiar, but by which final answers are never reached (cf. Van Huyssteen 1986:161). Instead, approximations of truth are achieved to which people commit themselves—an ongoing process which search for better explanations of human experience, and which is therefore characterized by its tentativeness and open-endedness (McFague 1982:33–34). In this process metaphor obviously plays a central role (cf. Ricoeur 1977:247–256).

[48] For the necessary interaction between text and readers to be set into motion, for shifts (in language and meaning, aimed at shifts in understanding, perception and action) to be effected, a delicate balance between the known and the unknown, between the old and the new in metaphorical expressions has to be maintained. "If the difference is too big, a shift cannot take place and the metaphor will not work. If it is too small, it will likewise not succeed, because not enough new information is offered. On the one hand, the two elements must be close enough to ensure a spark of recognition or resemblance. On the other, there must be sufficient difference and distance to arouse curiosity and to achieve a shift. A theory of metaphor that is based merely on the idea of substitution or ornamentation is therefore bound to fail, because the metaphorical event entails much more than simply exchanging one element for another—a new entity is created in the process" (Lategan 1994b:132, cf. 131–133; 1987:115; 1992c:627). What a person would find to be significant in the process of understanding (i.e. the similarity or dissimilarity between events, people, structures, objects, etc.), will evidently depend on her/his own *perspective*.

particular aspects of human being, *especially those pertaining to expression and interpretation, creation and discovery, change and transformation"* (emphasis mine). Metaphor, therefore, has the potential power to orientate and reorientate readers in accordance with an author's perspective.

.2 Toward a Definition of Metaphor

Until the nineteenth century Aristotle's notion of metaphor prevailed as the basis for understanding metaphor (cf. Ricoeur 1976:46–49). He mainly considered the function of metaphor as *decorative*—a rhetorical device which does not represent any semantic innovation. As such, metaphor was *not* considered to furnish any new information about reality, or to be central to language. It was therefore seen as "substitutable." But increasingly, since the 1960s, that opinion was reversed and scholars started to recognize metaphor as the natural way in which human thought and language work, and therefore as "unsubstitutable" (McFague 1982: 37).[49]

It is especially the pioneering work of I. A. Richards which marked the overthrow of the classical notion of metaphor (Ricoeur 1976:49; 1977:76–83). Richards' definition of the 1930s, which was later refined by himself, Max Black and others, was indeed a good start: "In the simplest formulation, when we use a metaphor we have two thoughts of different things *active together* and supported by a single word, or phrase, whose meaning is a resultant of their *interaction*" (quoted by McFague 1982:37; emphasis mine).[50] The vitality of a metaphor would thus exist in the "two active thoughts which remain in permanent tension or interaction with each other", the tension which Ricoeur (1976:49–53) calls the "is and is not" quality of metaphor (cf. McFague 1982:37–38; Carmody 1992: 143–146).[51] While active metaphorical utterances are sufficiently unconventional and shocking, dead metaphors have lost their shock and tension and are viewed as literal in meaning. "Religious metaphors, because of their preservation in a tradition and repetition in ritual, are especially prone to becoming idols" (McFague 1982:38).

---

[49] As an essential aspect of human language, and like other aspects of written texts, metaphor could *inter alia* be approached from a philosophical, linguistic, or literary angle. In spite of different points of departure, these dimensions are implicitly dealt with here as complementing, and in interaction with each another (cf. Gräbe 1984:6).

[50] South African linguist Ina Gräbe has done important research in this regard (1984: 6–177). See also the section on metaphor in the authoritative work on the so-called "new rhetoric" by French-speaking linguists Chaïm Perelman and Lucie Olbrechts-Tyteca (1969:398–410).

[51] It is only the ensemble of two terms in tension which constitutes the metaphor. "So we should not really speak of the metaphorical use of a word, but rather of the metaphorical utterance. The metaphor is the result of the tension between two terms in a metaphorical utterance" (Ricoeur 1976:50).

Max Black's theory on metaphor gained wide recognition since the 1960s. He refers to a metaphorically used word (verb or noun) in a sentence as the *focus* of a sentence and the rest of the sentence as the *frame*. The identification of a metaphor would depend on the contrasting syntactical environment within which it is embedded. That environment is then redescribed by means of the metaphor.[52]

It is clear that metaphor is concerned with "meaning" (in the form of judg-

---

[52] In the sentence "War is a chess game," Black distinguishes between the two subjects by referring to "war" as the *principal subject* and "chess game" as the *focus* or *subsidiary subject* of the sentence. The effect of the identification between war and a chess game is determined by what the reader knows about the focus subject "chess game" in its literal function(s). Black (1962:40) speaks of a *"system of associated commonplaces"* (cf. McFague's "matrix of thought"—1982:36, 39) which comes to the mind of the reader, and which functions as a filter or screen through which the principal subject 'war' is understood in a new light. Black (1962:41; cf. Gräbe 1984:7–9) describes the dynamic interplay between metaphorical focus and literal frame as follows. (Brackets are used where Black's example in the particular quote, "man is a wolf," is replaced by another of his examples namely, "war is a chess game"):

"A suitable hearer will be led by the (chess) system of implications to construct a corresponding system of implications about the principal subject. But these implications will *not* be those comprised in the commonplaces *normally* implied by literal uses of '(war).' The new implications must be determined by the pattern of implications associated with literal uses of the word '(chess game).' Any (war) traits that can without undue strain be talked about in '(chess) language' will be rendered prominent, and any that cannot will be pushed into the background. The (chess) metaphor suppresses some details, emphasizes others—in short *organizes* our view of (war)." This organizing process of backgrounding and foregrounding in the understanding of metaphors will obviously differ from context to context.

Gräbe (1984:9–11) further draws on notions from Harald Weinrich, well-known German scholar of linguistics and literature studies, who elaborated on Black's theory by pointing out that the nature and meaning of a metaphor is determined by the tension between a metaphorical word and its contradetermining context. A surprise element is created by the tension between the original (literal) meaning of a word and the significance which is forced onto that word by its syntactical context. Weinrich calls this process "contradetermination" because the real determination of the context goes against the expectancy of the word in its literal meaning. Whereas Black would define the functioning of a metaphor as the interplay between focus and frame, Weinrich does this in terms of the tension between a word and its contradetermining context. For a further refining of Black and Weinrich's theories by Richards' concepts of *tenor* and *vehicle*, and David M. Miller's idea of *surface* and *submerged metaphors*, see Gräbe 1984:11–15. Yet, whatever the different fields or subjects are called ("tenor" and "vehicle" by Richards, or "principle" and "subsidiary" subject by Black), *the point is that both fields or subjects are influenced or changed by being brought into relationship with the other*. "This is a very important point for religious models because the human images that are chosen as metaphors for God gain in stature and take on divine qualities by being placed in an interactive relationship with the divine" (McFague 1982:38; cf., e.g., the history of interpretation of Eph. 5:23).

ments), and therefore belongs to the semantics of language (cf. Ricoeur 1976:1–23). McFague stresses the crucial importance of two points in the process of finding and creating meaning in people's interaction with the world: to remember that all judgments are indirect and tentative, and that metaphor has a structural or organizational power. Because of the "bifocal," "twinned" or "stereoscopic" vision of metaphors (the tension of actively entertaining the similarity and dissimilarity of two subjects—McFague 1982:136; cf. Van Huyssteen 1986:161), understanding will always contain the duality which is at the heart of human truth and judgment (McFague 1982:39). Moreover, the judgment of similarity and difference has structural and organizing possibilities because two systems of associated commonplaces are interacting with each other. "The most fruitful metaphors are the ones with sufficiently complex grids to allow for extension of thought, structural expansion, suggestions beyond immediate linkages" (McFague 1982:39).

Thus, metaphorical *meaning* depends upon a literal, conventional base as a point of contact (cf. God as *father* and *steward*; Jesus as *savior* and *lord*; the Spirit as *seal* and *deposit*), but through being applied to a new field, another matrix of thought, new meaning is created. We have seen that Ricoeur (1976:67–69, cf. 49–53) refers to metaphor as a *redescription* of reality (cf. McFague 1982:40; Lategan 1985b:75–85; Van Huyssteen 1986:162–163), that is a new or unconventional interpretation of reality. This assertion rests on metaphor's capacity to rely on a literal meaning, and at the same time to subvert and extend it through transformation. That means that the question of the "truth" of metaphor cannot be dealt with in a direct, literalistic or positivistic way (McFague 1982:40).

According to McFague (1982:41), the greatest danger of metaphor, therefore, is *assimilation*. That is when its surprising and shocking power is lost.[53] When a metaphor has become commonplace, and is literalized, the problem is that similarity has become identity, and that the tension which is so critical in metaphor, has been lost. This danger is ever present in religious metaphors, because religious images—through tradition and ritual—seldom change, and easily become accepted as ordinary language.

Hence, McFague (1982:42) summarizes the distinctive features of alive metaphors in the following way:

> (A) metaphor is an assertion or judgment of similarity and difference between two thoughts in permanent tension with one another, which redescribes reality in an open-ended way but has structural as well as affective power.

---

[53] McFague (1982:41) refers to Colin M. Turbayne who identified three stages of metaphor: Initially, when newly coined, it might seem inappropriate and unconventional, and responded to with rejection. During a second phase, when it functions as a living metaphor with dual meaning, it can be insightful. In a final stage, it might become commonplace, and consequently be liberalized and die.

The (re)orientating and persuading function of metaphor (and especially its ability to facilitate the communicative processes of association, disassociation and reassociation) will be explored further in chapter 3.3.3 as part of the Ephesians epistle's transformative potential or rhetorical power.

.3 Metaphor and Tradition as Windows through which the Moral World of a Text May Be Explored

Before subsequent readers can start asking questions such as: How could or should the language and ethos of the first century Christians influence the moral lives of Christians of later centuries? (cf. Smit 1991b), we first have to ask: What did their "moral world" look like, and how did it work? How were the lives of the first Christians (supposed to be) influenced? How were they persuaded toward a new ethos? What was their orienting life and world view, their basic values and commitments—before and after they were confronted with a specific text? And how were they supposed to respond to the moral challenges of their time? These are the questions which a socio-historical and rhetorical analysis of a text seeks to investigate.

As a refinement of several historical-critical and social-scientific methods, the valuable contribution of North American New Testament scholar Wayne A. Meeks is briefly investigated here, as one possible way of dealing with these ethical questions.

In his widely acclaimed book, *The Moral World of the First Christians*, Meeks (1986b:12–17; cf. 1986a:3–4; Botha 1994a:39) discusses the necessity for New Testament scholars to first try and explore, explain, or even better, *understand* something of the social processes that formed and shaped the symbolic universe ("moral world") which the early Christian communities shared with other people in their villages or cities. Meeks (1986a:4; 1986b:15) approaches the early Christian movement as a *cultural entity*, which he—in agreement with famous German sociologist and philosopher Max Weber and North American anthropologist Clifford Geertz[54]—sees as *a system of communication, a system of meaning*:[55]

> Understanding the ethics of the early Christians must therefore begin with a rigorous attempt to describe the ethos of the larger culture.... within which the Christian movement began and spread. What we would like to know, if it were possible, is what every morally

---

[54] Elsewhere, Meeks (1993:11) refers to Geertz as "the doyen of interpretive anthropologists."

[55] Some other anthropologists and philosophers also share this insight. Meeks describes *culture* (of which ethos, world view, and religious symbols all form a part) as "an elaborate set of signs, a system of communication. Understanding culture—and so, understanding any of these parts—is like learning a language" (Meeks 1986b:15; 1986a:4, 5).

competent person then knew simply by being part of that culture (Meeks 1986a:7; cf. Smit 1992:305).[56]

Meeks (1986b:11–12) further makes the very important observation that, in order to *understand* the ethos of the early Christians, later readers should not—in the first instance—be interested in the "moral argument or rules" of the New Testament. The essential aspect of the early Christians' moral life is their *identity awareness*, the *self-understanding* within which ethical requirements or directives were embedded. The crucial question is not What must we do?, but *Who are we?* Only following that, it may be asked: Which ethos would be worthy of such a moral person? (cf. Meeks 1993:109–110). This distinction will form a basic premise in the rest of this study (cf. Niebuhr 1941:1–66; Hauerwas 1981:129–152; Du Toit 1994:482; Hartin 1994:519–520). The unique character of the Ephesians

---

[56] It is necessary at this stage to clarify the concepts "ethos" (or morality) and "ethics," and the important difference between the two (cf. Smit 1991b:52; 1992:303–317; Meeks 1993:3–5; Botha 1994a:36–37). (Christian) ethos refers to the standards of character and conduct people use in the living of the practical moral life, while (Christian) ethics is the critical, intellectual discipline in the service of the moral life (cf. Birch & Rasmussen 1989:39). Both these words come from the Greek word *ethos* (character; cf. the Latin *mos*, from which "morality" is derived). Already found in the writings of Plato and Aristotle, *ethos* referred to "habit" or "custom" (practising certain virtues until they became second nature), which would eventually build "character" (Meeks 1986b:15). *Ethos* originally referred to "the shelter or dwelling place of animals. In order to provide for society what animals were raised to provide, they needed a place of protection and nutrition. The stall meant sustenance and security. It meant a daily routine that met their needs and a familiarity that gave them a sense of 'home.' The 'stable' offered 'stability'.... Customary behavior does for human society much of what the stall does for animals; it provides stability and security, and helps to sustain society. Morality is a kind of social glue.... It keeps society sufficiently intact to let people get on with the living of life.... Without compliance with some minimal moral stipulations, life together cannot happen" (Birch & Rasmussen 1989:38, cf. 52–58).

Within the context of Christian ethos and ethics, we are particularly interested in the development of "communities of moral discernment" or "communities of character" (cf. 4.3.5). In this respect the description of the term *ethos* as suggested by Geertz is extremely helpful. Meeks (1986b:15) draws upon some of his ideas (emphasis mine):

"A people's ethos.... is the tone, character, and quality of their life, its moral and aesthetic style and mood; it is the *underlying attitude toward themselves and their world* that life reflects. Their world view.... is their picture of the way things in sheer actuality are, their concept of nature, of self, of society.... Geertz further concludes that religious symbols are connected with both world view and ethos, and indeed serve in virtually all societies to synthesize the two. 'Such religious symbols, dramatized in rituals or related in myths, are felt somehow to sum up, for those for whom they are resonant, what is known about the way the world is, the quality of the emotional life it supports, and the way one ought to behave while in it'" (cf. Birch & Rasmussen 1989:71, 213–214 n.14; Smit 1991b: 56).

community's identity will be discussed in the next chapter.

One important way in which one can try to gain access to the moral world and identity awareness of the early Christians, according to Meeks (1986a:7–8; 1993:213–214), is to look at their treatment of *traditions* (which function in a way similar to metaphors). These would especially involve the traditions of Greece and Rome, and of Israel.[57] Like us, the early Christians did not live in a vacuum. They were consciously and unconsciously influenced by their historical-cultural contexts, their moral worlds, which inevitably determined the way in which they interpreted and redescribed existing traditions (cf. Van Huyssteen 1986:196–202). Their experience of the Christ event radically challenged their whole traditional-historical environment, and in particular their religious traditions (cf. Kaye 1984).[58]

In his historical investigation of early Christian ethics, Meeks (1986a; 1986b; 1993:1–17, 109–110) is not so much interested in the description of those ethics; or the abstraction of ideas, ideals, or principles; or even proposals about using early Christian writings normatively in the ethical discourse of later times—although he considers these to be valid and important. His main interest is—as I understand him—in the *dynamic, dialectic and metaphorical processes, the communicative networks underlying the moral formation of those communities* (cf. Ricoeur 1977:244; Lategan 1994b:133). For hermeneutics it is likewise of crucial importance how texts impinge on readers during moral formation, that is, "*what processes they set in motion, and whether these processes are valid*" (Thiselton 1992:5). These interests concern an ethical choice about what constitutes an adequate description of people's morals. "I believe," says Meeks (1986a:4), "that we cannot claim to understand the morality of a group until we can describe the world of meaning and of relationships, special to that group in its own time and place, within which behavior is evaluated."

The thrust of Meeks' inquiry therefore is to ask how the symbolic universe of the early Christians worked. "The culture of people does not only express who they are; it is *constitutive of* who they are. We become members of a community by the same process by which we become selves, and that is a cultural, com-

---

[57] "In the kind of account of the great traditions I am suggesting, a central question would be about the dialectic between social structure and the shape of the moral tradition" (Meeks 1986a:8).

[58] Therefore, this part of the multi-dimensional approach to texts is concerned with the *function* or *purpose* of the different tradition units and metaphors which an author incorporated into a writing. The communicative or transformative power of a document can be uniquely illustrated by the creative processes by which traditions have been re-interpreted and contextualized in new circumstances. To retell the narrative of the past in such a way that new elements are discovered in the old history, is to utilize those dormant traditions as a *shifting device* in helping the readers to think of themselves and their world in a new way. *To reinterpret the present situation as a redescription or reshaping of history can thus serve as a powerful communicative strategy* (cf. 2.2.1).

municative process" (Meeks 1986a:4–5; emphasis mine; cf. 1993:213–214). The processes of identity and moral formation, which form a crucial aspect of my argument, have to be understood against this background.[59]

Meeks himself devotes much time and energy to explain life in the first century villages and cities, which was the context of Greek ethics, and of which the Christians formed a part (1986b:12–13, cf. 19–39).[60] Only *after* doing that, he explains what kind of "resocialization" and changes of their symbolic world took place when people became Christians:

> (T)o join the Christian movement entailed 'conversion' or what some sociologists call 'resocialization.' That is, becoming a Christian was expected to affect some of the most fundamental relationships, values, perceptions of reality, and even structures of the self.... Thus the Christians could speak of their initiation variously as a dying and rising with Christ, as a second birth, as adoption into a new family of God's children. The radicality of the metaphors bespeaks a real experience of sharp displacement which many of the converts must have felt (Meeks 1986b:13; cf. 1993:18–36; Eph. 4:22–5:21).

Although one can never completely replace the primary early childhood socialization (and the Christians did not try to do so), some of the things they said may make us think they did. For example, Ephesians 4:22–24 reminds its readers:

> You were taught, with regard to your former way of life, to put off your old self, which is being corrupted by its deceitful desires; to be made new in the attitude of your minds; and to put on the new self, created to be like God in true righteousness and holiness.[61]

The typical admonitions which follow these words would be instantly recognizable in the moral rhetoric of that time. For, "(t)he Christians whose moral

---

[59] Within the parameters of the book, the construction of the moral world of the Ephesians author and addressees will largely depend on text-internal references. However, it is important to remain aware of the broader socio-historical context within which the text was probably embedded (cf. 2.2).

[60] "The first Christian groups did not exist on islands or in deserts. They lived in villages or cities. In the villages, daily behavior was controlled by the routines of necessity, the cycles of seasonal labor in the fields, customs as old as the oldest memory. Identity was a matter of family and clan, and family honor was a powerful sanction *affecting every choice*.... Within a few years, the majority of the Christian groups were to be found in the various cities around the eastern perimeter of the Mediterranean. There, to be sure, life was more diverse than in rural villages, and the ties of the clan and custom less firm. Nevertheless, city life was crowded and public.... It was not only that the Christians, wherever they lived, were under certain pressures from without to conform to the patterns of the larger society. Those patterns were part of themselves, *part of who they were, how they thought and how they felt*" (Meeks 1986b:12–13, cf. 19–39; 1983; emphasis mine).

[61] See Rm. 12:2, "Do not conform any longer to the pattern of this world, but be transformed by the renewing of your mind."

formation we are trying to understand lived in the world of the early Roman empire, and that world also lived in them: in their thinking, in their language, in their relationships" (Meeks 1986b:13).

It is important to note that the ethos of individuals and groups was not something added to this process of identity development. It indeed formed an integral part of it.[62] North American ethicist James Gustafson refers to the history of the early Christian movement as the development of "communities of moral discourse" (quoted by Meeks 1986b:12). Allen Verhey, another North American theologian, also employs this concept, but goes a step further by asking what kind of "community of moral discernment" is represented by each of the New Testament documents (Verhey 1984a:154–156, 72–152; cf. Meeks 1986a:5, 6). From a similar context Stanley Hauerwas (1981, 1985a) uses yet another descriptive term, "communities of character," arguing that "more than talk contributes to the shaping of behavior, and (that) 'character' suggests the essential dialectic between community and self" (Meeks 1986b:12; cf. Smit 1991b:52–53; Fowl & Jones 1991:56–109).

Because the early Christian movement can be described as *systems of communication, communities of moral discourse,* and *communities of character,* biblical scholars should be challenged to construct, in their imagination, the scattered (but not negligible) pieces of information that they do have of the social structure of each of the various forms of that movement—the moral world within which the words of the New Testament documents once worked, within which those fragments made sense.[63]

In the end, textual communication revolves around the dynamic interaction and reference between the perspective (life and world view) of an implied author and his/her addressees, and their socio-cultural and moral worlds. The ethos of the early Christian communities likewise emerged from the interplay between their distinctive beliefs and practices with their common cultural environment (cf. Hendrix 1988:15 n.43). According to their nature, the function of the biblical documents is to *orientate* and *reorientate* the perspective and concrete ethos of their readers. By disclosing an alternative moral world, these documents have the ability to enlarge and expand the finite and historically conditioned horizons of their readers, to re-order values, and to project new possibilities which can reach beyond prior boundaries of thought systems. This is where the *shifting, changing,* or *transformative* potential of the biblical texts lies:

---

[62] The New Testament writers repeatedly urged their readers to exhort, admonish, comfort and encourage one another, with the primary aim *"to live a life worthy of the calling (they) have received"* (Eph. 4:1; cf. 1 Ts. 2:12; Meeks 1993:150–173).

[63] From several recent studies we know that there is much to be learned about the early Christian ethos, for instance, by explaining the moral world of the Greco-Roman household (cf. Malherbe 1983; Meeks 1986a:10; 1993:37–41, 77–79, 103; Eph. 5:21–6:9).

Because of their capacity to bring about change, texts and especially biblical texts engage with readers in ways which can productively transform horizons, attitudes, criteria of relevance, or even communities and inter-personal situations. *In this sense we may speak of transforming biblical reading.* The very process of reading may lead to a re-ranking of expectations, assumptions, and goals which readers initially bring to. texts.... In actualizations of understanding or encounter between readers and texts, the boundaries of horizons may be extended and moved, and thus come to constitute *new* horizons (Thiselton 1992: 8, 6, cf. 1–54, 611–619).[64]

However, such a process does not occur inevitably or automatically. With reference to Gadamer, Thiselton (1992:8) warns: "*Only if we respect the distinctiveness of the horizons of the text* as against the distinctiveness of our own reader-horizon can a creative and productive interaction of horizons occur." In this sense, the distance between texts and readers may perform a positive hermeneutical function. By stimulating an ongoing critical interaction and engagement between the horizons of texts and readers, such a distance may prevent the hijacking of the reading process by pre-formed horizons of expectations (only to affirm the identity and ethos which people already enjoy). Or the distance may prevent premature assimilation between the horizons of texts and readers, which can result in an "*uneventful, bland, routine, and entirely unremarkable*" process of reading (Thiselton 1992:8). This challenge brings us to the rhetorical aspect of communication.

1.6.3   *THE PERSUADING STRATEGY OF THE RHETORICAL DIMENSION: APPROPRIATING THE TRANSFORMATIVE POTENTIAL OF A TEXT*

The third dimension in the analysis of textual communication is concerned with the dialectic interaction among the different elements of the communication process itself. It therefore focuses on the pragmatic *function* of different pericopes, but especially of a writing as a whole. The New Testament documents essentially reflect a communicative process of proclamation and appeal, by which their authors implicity and explicitly wished to *persuade* their addressees of a specific message.[65] The ongoing critical conversation between these writings and their

---

[64] Thiselton wrote two major works on the rapidly growing subject of hermeneutics and its significance for biblical studies: *The Two Horizons* (1980), and *New Horizons in Hermeneutics* (1992). The latter builds on the former, and focuses on the theory and practice of the transformative, surprising potential of biblical reading. It evaluates, and probably uniquely accounts for a comprehensive range of theoretical models of reading and interpretation, as well as the foundations on which they rest. These are skillfully combined with practical implications for Old and New Testament reading.

[65] Technically, this means that an author consciously or unconsciously arranged words and sentences on the linguistic-literary level, selected and reinterpreted traditional

subsequent readers therefore form part of this decisive phase in the communication process. Rousseau refers to the dialectic interaction between text and readers as a continual "battle between perspectives" (1986:372, 401, 412–414; cf. Mouton 1987:68–73, 159).

Because the reception and interpretation of a text actually rise beyond the static and dynamic dimensions to a level where the text develops a life of its own, Rousseau (1986:43, 64–69, 387–432) refers to it as the "metatextual dimension of textual communication." Since I am primarily concerned with the persuasive and transformative potential of text-immanent strategies in Ephesians, I refer to this phase as the *theological, faith,* or *rhetorical dimension* (cf. Lategan 1982:52).[66] The contributions of the structural and historical dimensions converge at this point to activate the pragmatic potential of the text. In this regard rhetorical analysis and speech act theory (cf. Combrink 1988; Patte 1988) have become important tools in understanding the original speech event, and in revealing persuasive strategies used by an author—as prerequisite for its appropriation in current situations:

> The concept of the implied reader sharpens the eye for directions given on all levels for the realization of the text. But not only is the reader as textual construct at stake, the interpreter has to take the real receptor and his or her existential situation into account. It is in this context that the world of the text plays a mediating role. What the text offers is an alternative way to look at reality.... Thus the self-understanding of the reader is challenged. Between the horizon of the text and that of the reader a creative tension develops which calls for the affirmation of the status quo or for the openness and courage to accept a new self-understanding (Lategan 1992b:154).

It is in this context that the literary category of "rhetorical situation" (Bitzer 1968) will be explored in 2.3, and elaborated on in chapter three. While rhetoric—in the classical and modern sense—has to do with power and persuasion (concepts which are radically redefined in Ephesians), I prefer to speak of the implied *communicative or transformative potential* of the document, as the culmination of all its underlying processes and functions.

Against this background, the book focuses on the ongoing dialectic pro-

---

material and metaphors on the historical level—with one goal in mind, namely to *persuade* the readers toward appropriating a new way of thinking and living (cf. Mouton 1987:176–210).

[66] It has already become evident that the re-discovery and re-invention of rhetoric in this century, together with the development of rhetorical criticism, hold tremendous promise also for the interpretation of biblical documents. Rhetoric refocuses traditional content- and structure-oriented analyses of texts "to a reading in which a text is allowed to interact, affect, strengthen and transform values and beliefs. Rhetoric concerns itself not simply with logical and rational dimensions of discourse, but emotive and imaginative" (Hester 1994:1; cf. Wuellner 1987:460–463; Combrink 1993).

cesses of *identification* (association), *estrangement* (alienation, disassociation) and *reorientation* (redescription, appropriation) involved in textual communication. These are typical processes involved in the functioning of metaphorical language (cf. Ricoeur 1975:122–128; McFague 1982:46–47; 3.3.3). According to Rousseau's model, this phase of ongoing interaction between texts and readers functions as pragmatic processes within *each dimension*, and essentially as the end result of the pragmatic modes within the syntactic, dynamic and dialectic dimensions respectively, with the latter as its focal point (cf. Rousseau 1986:64–69).

This phase is concerned with *how* an author uses linguistic devices to persuade her/his readers, and *how* the readers appropriate those strategies. That the Ephesians epistle was meant to communicate a powerful message, is *inter alia* implied by its recurring reference to God's purpose for the author and readers' lives, and by its numerous contrasting metaphors (cf. 2.1.3.1; Mouton 1987:155–223). Once the implied rhetorical processes within this ancient canonized text and its implied readers have been explored, the essential step has to be taken of bridging the historical gap between the document and its later readers.[67]

The three simplifying and integrating concepts of *thrust*, *perspective* and *strategy* have so far been utilized as useful keys to unlock the sometimes complicated interrelations of textual communication. It has been suggested that the potential of these concepts theoretically only comes to the fore within the dialectical phase, as the chronological result of the analyses of the previous two dimensions (cf. Mouton 1987:155–158). It is in this context that the communicative power, the persuading function, of the Ephesians epistle will be examined.

According to Rousseau's model (1986:430–432), it is obvious that the Ephesians author's rhetorical *strategies* would only make sense to its readers if they grasped the *thrust* of the text, shared its *perspective*, and complied with its requisites for frame of reference, experience of meaning, and relevance (cf. Vorster 1977:21). Reception in written communication is, therefore, decisively co-determined by the perspective of the receiver. It is in this sense that the "success" of the communication process is dependent on a mutual perspective and frame of reference between senders and receivers (Rousseau 1986:42–43). *Only if* the authors and readers of the New Testament documents shared a dynamic faith relationship with God in Jesus Christ, would these texts be able to communicate in a meaningful way—that is, in accordance with their *nature* and

---

[67] Accounting for the influence of readers' presuppositions will—as in the other phases—necessarily form part of this level of research. The application of a biblical text to a contemporary context includes an analysis of contemporary readers' socio-cultural world, and its influence on them. "The pursuit of scientific understanding does not necessarily cancel out such prejudices but should make the exegete sensitive to them. We all view reality through 'glasses' (presuppositions) of one sort or another; one of the things required of the scientist by sound scientific practice is an awareness of his (*sic*) own glasses—their nature and their effects" (Bosman 1986:10).

purpose. The Ephesians author's prayer for the readers in 1:18 implies that it would only be possible to recognize the wealth of his message by means of the *enlightened eyes of a believing heart*. This prerequisite would also apply to subsequent readers, and therefore necessarily forms part of an ethical reading of this document.

These observations have important consequences for the use of Ephesians and other New Testament documents in Christian ethics. A communicative approach—as reorientation of New Testament exegesis—*inter alia* implies that later readers be equipped to become "wise readers of Scripture" *and* their contexts, so that they might live faithfully before God (Fowl & Jones 1991:4–55; Botha 1994c). That means that they should be guided toward obtaining *a competence in ethical reading*—a competence which would enable them to experience and explain their role in a new world in a way as relevant as those reflected in the New Testament documents (cf. Deist 1989b; Fowl & Jones 1991:56–83).[68] It is in this sense that the Bible inspires subsequent readers not necessarily to act in the same way as those early believers, but "to do likewise" (Vorster 1977:18–23; cf. Rousseau 1985b:99).

The comprehensive processes underlying the different phases of textual communication represent what Meeks calls the "moral grammar" of a text. For him, an analysis of the moral grammar of the early Christian communities is of vital importance for the understanding of the formation of their moral world (cf. Meeks 1986a:10; 1986b:124–160; 1993:91–110). By moral grammar he does not mean a mere description of the linguistic structures of the New Testament texts—although that is always a natural starting point. Moral grammar at least includes a broader construction and understanding of the "rhetorical situation" of a document. Meeks is convinced however that such an analysis is only preliminary to the immensely more difficult task: to analyze the logic of the interactive world that the biblical authors and their readers shared, "*the meaningful structure of the process in which they were engaged before and after the writing of (those documents)*."

This approach ties up with the "cultural-linguistic" model of religion, as coined by George Lindbeck, renowned Yale theologian (cf. Meeks 1986a:5; Smit 1991b:55–61). Its aim is to find out what was particularly Christian about the ethos and ethics of those early communities—not by abstracting the "essence" of

---

[68] The inaugural address at the University of South Africa of Willem S. Vorster, authoritative South African New Testament scholar, was titled *'n Ou Boek in 'n nuwe wêreld—gedagtes rondom die interpretasie van die Nuwe Testament* (1977). Referring to the implications of a communicative-oriented approach to exegesis for New Testament science, and the use of the New Testament in the church, Vorster (1977:23) concludes: "Veral die Skrifgebruik staan hier onder 'n baie skerp fokus maar ook die vraag van hoe die gelowige gehelp sou kon word om in 'n nuwe wêreld 'n kompetensie aan te leer om teologiese uitsprake te maak wat net so relevant sal wees as wat die uitsprake 'was' wat ons in die Nuwe Testament vind."

Christianity from what they "borrowed" from the impure world around them, *"but by confronting their involvement in the culture of their time and place and seeking to trace the new patterns they made of old forms, to hear the new songs they composed from old melodies"* (Meeks 1986a:11; cf. 1986b:61–96; emphasis mine).

These were the processes, says Meeks, which shaped the moral life of the early Christians:

> Most, perhaps all, of the writings that now make up the New Testament, and a great many of the other earliest Christian writings as well, had as *their primary aim the shaping of the life of Christian communities.* Arguments and rules, of course, had their place in those writings, but we fail to understand the force of the arguments and rules if we take them out of the contexts in which they stand. A *much more comprehensive process* was going on, by which participants in the new movement we call Christianity were discovering a new identity— learning to think of themselves as 'the churches of God,' 'the holy ones,' 'children of God'.... 'brothers and sisters,' 'those for whom Christ died' (Meeks 1986b:12; emphasis mine).

When we compare the moral world of the first century to societies of the early twenty-first century, we realize that different people indeed have different symbolic and moral worlds. The world in which we live, is a world in which "our senses are organized and thus have meaning through a system of signs so much part of us that we are rarely aware of them as such" (Meeks 1986b:14). It is obvious that this symbolized, socially learned world in which we live affects the way we think, behave, and interpret history. And as the world changes, symbols change, and we are forced to relearn and resocialize. Thus we are engaged in a constant interaction with our world.

On the other hand, the world is also influenced and changed by people. According to the Christian paradigm, people are indeed *called* to be persuaded and transformed by the rhetorical power of the biblical texts. In Ricoeurian language, they are invited to adopt and inhabit the "proposed world," the "new way of looking at things" suggested, opened up and mediated by these writings (Ricoeur 1975; 1980:26; cf. 1976:89–95; Lategan 1992b:154; 1994b:131–133), and thus to proactively create meaning from their interaction with the world (cf. Eph. 4–6; Kelley 1977:9). In short: Christians are called to follow the example of Jesus Christ, and to decode his message and lifestyle in their specific moral worlds—as his body of disciples, representatives, and image bearers (cf. Hays 1990:47–48, 53). It will be argued in the next two chapters that the Ephesians vision, the basic ethos, responsibility and challenge of being *in Christ*, is to live— verbally and non-verbally—from the paradoxical power of his exalted position as lord. The implications of this perspective for the formation of moral people, for taking responsible actions, and for influencing a moral society, will be the focus of the last chapter.

READING EPHESIANS ETHICALLY:
TOWARD CONSTRUCTING ITS RHETORICAL SITUATION

(God) raised (Christ) from the dead and seated him at his right hand....
far above all rule and authority, power and dominion.... And God
raised us up with Christ and seated us with him in the heavenly realms
in Christ Jesus.... I urge you (then) to live a life worthy of the calling
you have received....

(Eph. 1:20, 21; 2:6; 4:1)

I have argued in the previous chapter that the New Testament documents form part of a dynamic communication process, which occurred within specific socio-cultural circumstances, and with specific rhetorical aims in mind. This realization has led to the conviction that these documents—like any communication event—function on different levels, at least with regard to a static linguistic-literary or structural level, a dynamic socio-cultural or historical level, and a dialectic theological or rhetorical level (cf. Lategan 1982:50–52). Subsequent readers are challenged to read and understand these writings in accordance with their own *nature* and *intention*—a conviction which necessarily calls for an integrated, multi-dimensional and interdisciplinary approach (cf. Rousseau 1986; 1988a; J. N. Vorster 1990; 1991; Jonker 1993).

The first aim of this chapter is to identify major linguistic and literary elements in the Ephesians document, and to determine its broad thrust and coherence—*particularly in relation to the need(s) it implicitly wished to address.*[1] While a detailed structural and discourse analysis would take us beyond the scope of this study, I hope to be sensitive to the risks attached to such a selective endeavor.

Secondly, this chapter explores the "moral world" of the document by briefly constructing relevant traditio-historical and socio-cultural aspects of the Asia Minor (Christian) communities around the first centuries C.E. The primary

---

[1] If later readers wish to infer normative guidance for their own moral behavior from an ancient canonized text, they have to be guided by its linguistic-literary pointers or textual instructions. Such elements represent the encoded author's usage of every possible technique "to communicate with his reader, *to entice him (sic) to get involved in the possibilities opened by the text.* Textual communication therefore is a cooperative enterprise. Author and reader stand in a 'chiastic' relationship to one another: the implied reader is a construct of the real author. The first is necessary to prepare the expected response to the text, the latter is a textguided image in order to get a grip on this intended response" (Lategan 1985b:73; cf. 1989a). The main purpose for studying readers' instructions in the Ephesians text, would thus be to construct the rhetorical strategies by which the author provided his readers with a new perspective on their extratextual reality (cf. Lategan 1985b:74). Such strategies were meant to stimulate a dialectic interaction between the document and its readers (cf. 1.6.1 n.33; 2.3).

aim of this section is to identify the dynamic processes of resocialization underlying the formation of the Christian communities, and in particular, the probable
pragmatic function of Ephesians during those processes.

Thirdly, and as a result of the foregoing, the chapter investigates the "rhetorical situation" of the epistle in terms of its text, author and the status and behavior
of its implied readers. The relation between the historical and rhetorical situations
will also be dealt with briefly.

2.1 READING EPHESIANS FROM A LINGUISTIC-LITERARY PERSPECTIVE: IDENTIFYING IDENTITY- AND BEHAVIOR-ORIENTED ELEMENTS

Reading any text—particularly an ancient text—presumes that the most original
or reliable copy of that text be considered as the gateway toward understanding
the different syntactic, semantic and pragmatic relations within that text (i.e. its
structure, socio-cultural or moral world, and rhetorical function).[2] For the purpose
of an ethical reading of Ephesians, I shall use the third edition of *The Greek New
Testament* text of the United Bible Societies (1983).

It has to be noted further that masculine terms are used exclusively in
reference to God and the Ephesians author throughout this chapter. It is done in
concurrence with the male-dominated God and human language of the original
text. For this reason the New International Version of the *The New Testament and
Psalms* (1989) is used alongside the Greek text instead of—for instance—the
New Revised Standard Version (1989) which uses human inclusive language. All
references to the English Bible are to this version, except where indicated
differently. This is a deliberate choice in order to illustrate the dangers of a one-
sided literal approach toward biblical understanding. It should be noted, however,
that the very thrust of the Ephesians epistle requires that gender-sensitive
language be used by later interpreters.

For the identification of major structural elements, the demarcation of pericopes, and the underlying macro-structures of Ephesians, I mainly depend on the
detailed discourse analyses done by two South African New Testament scholars,
Johnnie Roberts (1991, first edition 1983 in Afrikaans) and his former student,
Richard Lemmer (1988). This section of the project has simultaneously been en-
riched by the different perspectives, approaches, and emphases of extensive and
thorough research on Ephesians by, among others, Heinrich Schlier (1957), Nils
A. Dahl (1965), Markus Barth (1974a; 1974b), Andrew T. Lincoln (1990), and
Rudolf Schnackenburg (1991).

Most scholars who have devoted time and energy to the form and structure
of Ephesians, agree that the document can be divided into four major sections,

---

[2] It has been argued in the previous chapter (1.6.1) that, "even when we read the
'original' texts, both these texts and we as readers are the products of centuries of tradition, and our readings are social activities, fundamentally determined by our communities
and societies" (Smit 1994d:2).

namely the *opening* (1:1–2), the *body* consisting of a *first* and *second main section* (1:3–3:21 and 4:1–6:20 respectively), and the *ending* (6:21–24; Roberts 1991:14–19; Lemmer 1988:appendix). The first main section contains various elements such as utterances of praise, thanksgivings, intercessory prayers, and confessions of faith. This section is sometimes broadly referred to as the theological, christological, pneumatological and ecclesiological *indicative* of the Ephesians message (cf. Schnackenburg 1991:293–310; Lategan 1984b:323–324; Roberts 1978:167, 169; 1991:15). The second main section primarily consists of paraenetic elements, which are interwoven with theological and christological motivations, and intrinsically linked to and informed by the first main section. It is often described as the ethical *imperative* of the Ephesians message (cf. Roberts 1984a:139–141; Furnish 1968:224–227, 262–264; Jordaan 1990; Gräbe 1990).

2.1.1   *PERICOPE DEMARCATION*

Identifying a document's major building blocks is by no means an objective endeavor. Right from the outset, the reading process is necessarily determined by the presuppositions and choices of later readers—which often reveal the distance between them and the oral culture of the first century Mediterranean world. This is *inter alia* illustrated by the divergence of opinion concerning the demarcation of pericopes in Ephesians (cf. Schlier 1957; Barth 1974a; 1974b; Lemmer 1988; Lincoln 1990; Roberts 1991; Schnackenburg 1991). As indicated, I limit myself to the analyses of Roberts and Lemmer.

Roberts (1991:18–19) divides the Ephesians text into thirteen pericopes, while Lemmer (1988:appendix) demarcates fifteen units. Roberts considers the pivotal confessional pronouncement in 1:22–23, as well as the conclusions based on it (1:22–2:22), as one long pericope (his pericope IV). Lemmer in turn sees the confession as part of his pericope III (1:15–23), followed by three separate pericopes in chapter 2 (2:1–10, 11–18, 19–21). While Roberts treats chapter 3 as two pericopes (3:1–19, 20–21), Lemmer prefers three units (3:1–13, 14–19, 20–21).

Concerning the second main section, Roberts divides the exhortations directed to the *church* into two pericopes (4:1–6, 7–16), as opposed to Lemmer who considers it a single unit. Roberts further divides the section containing exhortations on a *personal* level into three pericopes (4:17–24; 4:25–5:14; 5:15–6:9), whereas Lemmer demarcates three slightly different sections: 4:17–32; 5:1–14; 5:15–6:9. This means that Roberts interprets 4:25–32 as belonging to the conclusion on the *practice* of the new life in 5:1–14, while Lemmer deals with it as part of the conclusion on the *principle* of the new life in 4:17–24.

What really matters for the purpose of this study, is the *function* of each pericope in terms of the implied rhetorical effect of the document as a whole. For that matter I chose one particular outline—that of Roberts (1991)—to serve as basis for further reference to the macro-context of the document. My pericope demarcation follows the linguistic and literary considerations of his sub-divisions (cf. Roberts 1991:18–19):

PERICOPE DEMARCATION OF EPHESIANS

PERICOPE I:

(Eph. 1:1–2)   Letter opening: Implied author and addressees, greetings

First main section: Praise to God for God's grace and salvation in Christ, as markers of the new community's identity (1:3–3:21)

PERICOPE II:

(Eph. 1:3–14)   Doxological exclamation (1:3a) and reasons for praise-giving, namely the blessings of God's Spirit in fellowship with Christ (1:3b–14):

- Election and sonship (1:4–6)
- Salvation and destination as God's people (1:7–12)
- Assurance of incorporation with God's people as God's possession (1:13–14)

PERICOPE III:

(Eph. 1:15–21)   Intercession for the Spirit's enablement toward an understanding of their inheritance:

- Thanksgiving and report on intercession (1:15–16)
- Prayer for deeper knowledge among new Christians (1:17–21)

PERICOPE IV:

(Eph. 1:22–2:22)   Explication of intercession: Confessional pronouncement (1:22–23) and its consequences

- No longer dead under the power of sin, but alive in union with Christ (2:1–10)
- No longer lost and far off, but near and reconciled with God (2:11–18)
- No longer estranged, but the family and dwelling-place of God (2:19–22)

PERICOPE V:

(Eph. 3:1–19)   Intercession (3:1, 14–19) with digression (3:2–13):

- Intercession: A prayer for experiencing the fullness of God's salvation (3:1, 14–19)
- Digression: The author's commission—his *bona fides* as herald of the divine mystery (3:2–13)

PERICOPE VI:

(Eph. 3:20–21)   Doxological conclusion to the intercession

Second main section: Exhortations based on the new identity awareness developed in the first main section (4:1–6:20)

PERICOPE VII:

(Eph. 4:1–6)   Exhortations directed to the church to live a life worthy of God's calling (4:1–16):

- Maintaining the unity of the church (4:1–6)

PERICOPE VIII:

(Eph. 4:7–16)   A χάρισμα for each believer to serve the unity of the church

- The triumphant lord gives a special gift to individuals (4:7–10)
- The lord gives gifts to the church (4:11–15a)
- Résumé: The whole body brings about its own growth and upbuilding (4:15b–16)

PERICOPE IX:

(Eph. 4:17–24)   Exhortations on the personal level (4:17–6:9):

- Conclusion on the *principle* of the new life: to be like God in true righteousness and holiness (4:17–24)

PERICOPE X:

(Eph. 4:25–5:14)   Exhortations on the *practice* of the new life in Christ:

- Concerning lies, anger, and an opportunity for the devil (4:25–27)
- Concerning theft, vain talk and grieving the Spirit (4:28–30)
- Concerning noisy brawling, mutual forgiveness and the imitation of God (4:31–5:2)
- Concerning immorality, lewd talk and thanksgiving (5:3–5)
- Concerning deception through foolish talk, and abiding in the truth by living in the light (5:6–10)
- Concerning the secrets of darkness, the revelation of light, and the new life where the light of Christ shines forth (5:11–14)

PERICOPE XI:

(Eph. 5:15–6:9)   Conclusion on the *practice* of the new life with reference to various relationships (5:15–21): living wisely under the influence of the Spirit

- The relationship between husband and wife in marriage, based on the relationship between Christ and the church (5:22–33)
- The relationship between children and parents (6:1–4)
- The relationship between slaves and masters (6:5–9)

PERICOPE XII:

(Eph. 6:10–20)   Exhortation: Call to arms and victory

PERICOPE XIII:

(Eph. 6:21–24)   Conclusion: Bearer of letter, Tychicus, encouragement and blessing

2.1.2 *STRATEGIC PERICOPES AND STRUCTURAL COHERENCE*

The purpose of this section is to indicate the thrust of the Ephesians discourse by highlighting strategically important pericopes. According to the arrangement of units of thought in Ephesians (2.1.1), and the concentration of metaphors and traditional material (cf. 2.1.3), these pericopes determine the tight structural coherence of the document.

.1 The Opening and Ending (Eph. 1:1–2; 6:21–24)

In the formal Hellenistic letter form, the letter opening and ending were naturally considered as strategically important (cf. Johnson 1999:268–269; Du Toit 1984a: 9–12; Stowers 1986:27–31). This also applies to the opening and ending (pericopes I and XIII) of Ephesians, which frame the document as a whole. Both the greetings at the beginning (1:1–2), and the farewell wishes at the end (6:21–23), contain the powerful blessing of χάρις and εἰρήνη (1:2; 6:23, 24). These orienting symbols announce, and to a large extent summarize, the main thrust of the document (cf. 1:6–7; 2:5–8, 14–17; 3:1–2, 7–8, 14; 4:3; 6:15). Its literary function is also confirmed in the final greetings, where the author explicitly says that he is sending Tychicus "for this very purpose.... that he may *encourage* you" (6:22).

.2 The First Main Section (Eph. 1:3–3:21)

A discourse analysis of the *first main section* of Ephesians (Roberts 1991:18–19, 15; Lemmer 1988:appendix) brought the following primary elements to light: an exclamation of praise (1:3a); reasons for praise-giving to God (1:3b–14); intercession (1:15–21); confession of faith with explanations (1:22–2:22); intercession with excursion (3:1–19); and a doxology (3:20–21).

   The *direction* of the discourse, the arrangement of units of thought, and the concentration of metaphors and traditional material, thrust in my view pericopes IV (1:22–2:22)—the confessional pronouncement and conclusions—and VII (4:1–16)—exhortations based on the first main section and as a heading for the second main section—to the fore as the pivotal points of the two main sections. I briefly substantiate this by dealing with the immediate contexts of these pericopes.

Pericope II (Eph. 1:3–14)

Pericope II introduces the first main section of the document. A structural and discourse analysis of this pericope (Schnackenburg 1977; O'Brien 1979; Kourie 1980:25–60; Mouton 1987:75–101; Lemmer 1988:appendix; Barkhuizen 1990) shows that the expressions ἐν Χριστῷ, with its equal variant forms ἐν αὐτῷ, διά, Ἰησοῦ Χριστοῦ, ἐν τῷ ἠγαπημένῳ, ἐν τῷ Χριστῷ, and the pronominal form ἐν ᾧ and ἐν αὐτῷ (referring to Christ) form the most important grammatical connections between the different units of thought. The main verbs which are linked in this way are εὐλογήσας, ἐξελέξατο, προορίσας ἡμᾶς εἰς υἱοθεσίαν, ἔχομεν τὴν ἀπολύτρωσιν, ἐκληρώθημεν, and ἐσφραγίσθητε, which together form the main reasons why God should be praised (1:3a; Barkhuizen 1990:402–408; cf. Denton 1982). Because of what God has done for them in Christ, they are encouraged to respond in a practical lifestyle of praise and thanksgiving (1:6, 12, 14; cf. 4:1ff). Purpose and consequence clauses (with prepositions or conjunctions such as εἰς and ἵνα) abound in this pericope (1:4, 6, 10, 12, 14, 17; cf. chapter 2 n.17). A similar pattern is continued elsewhere in the document (2:7, 9, 10, 16; 3:16, 18, 19; 4:14, 29), highlighting its probable intended pragmatic effect.[3]

The recurrence of εὐλογητὸς indicates that 1:3–14, and possibly the whole of chapters 1–3, represents a eulogy—a song of thanksgiving and praise.[4] The reasons for praising God are divided into three cola (cf. Roberts 1978:169; Mouton 1987:78–81).[5] From the implied author's point of view, the first two cola (1:7–10 and 11–12 respectively) deal with "our" (ἡμῶν) redemption, and the third (1:13–14) with "you" (ὑμεῖς) and "your" salvation and inclusion in Christ. With the linguistic movement from "we" to "you" the particular structure focuses on verses 13–14. God is especially praised because Gentiles (cf. 2:11)—as part of God's elected people in Christ—now also participate in God's redemption (Roberts 1978:169, 172; cf. 1993b:100; Schnackenburg 1991:35–36, 63–64; Jayne 1974).

Several scholars (cf. Kourie 1980:61–67; 1987; Barkhuizen 1990:391, 407; Corley 1979; Mouton 1987:83–84, 92–94, 164) have shown that ἐν Χριστῷ forms a basic theme right through Ephesians, and that the majority of motives associated with Christ are already announced in the introductory pericope of 1:3–14. Pericope II thus functions as a "basic plan" for the structure of the document. Its mere occurrence directly after the opening, points toward its strategic function

---

[3] To mention two examples: (1) Eph. 1:4 (cf. 5:27) describes the overarching purpose of the readers' election in Christ as being "*holy and blameless in (God's) sight*" (cf. 2:10, 21; 4:1–6, 13, 22–32; 5:1–33; 6:1–20), thereby introducing the close relation between identity and ethos as a major characteristic of the document. (2) In 1:10 (cf. 1:21–22) the author describes God's encompassing goal at the fulfillment of the times as to sum up, to unite, to bring all things in heaven and on earth together in Christ as head. For an informative discussion on the function of 1:10 within the wider context of Ephesians, and its implications for the ethos of the church, see Hartin 1986.

[4] Deist (1990:88, 76) distinguishes as follows between eulogy and doxology: Eulogy is "(w)ritten or spoken praise of a person's life and qualities." Doxology is "(a) hymn of praise or formula of praise to God." For the structural differences between eulogy and doxology, and its application to Eph. 1:3–12 and 3:20–21, see Havemann 1976:4–12, 75–109, 177–197. According to these distinctions, Eph. 1:3–14 may be considered a eulogy, and Eph. 3:20–21 a doxology.

[5] In discourse analysis, a *colon* (plural *cola*) is defined as "a grammatical unit consisting of at least a nominal and a verb phrase" (Deist 1990:48).

with regard to the document as a whole (cf. Roberts 1986c:187–192). This would create a specific expectancy with the audience. The christological references implicitly serve to remind them to consistently reconsider and revision their position *in Christ*, and to live accordingly. By the strategic use of ἡμῶν (*our* Father, and *our* Lord Jesus Christ) in 1:2–3, they are encouraged to identify—right from the beginning—with what was to be said about Christ. As such 1:3–14 also functions as basis for the ethical-social guidelines in chapters 4–6 (cf. Mouton 1987:98–99, 164–175).

Pericope III (Eph. 1:15–21)

Pericope III, which directly leads to the climax of the confessional pronouncement in 1:22–23, consists of two intercessory prayers. The formal introduction to each prayer (1:17a, 18a) clarifies the purpose of the intercession: that the readers may *know* God (cf. Roberts 1991:49).[6] Of particular importance is the second prayer (1:18–21) which comprises three petitions linked to the request for inner enlightenment. These clauses (beginning with τίς and τί) summarize the content of the understanding the author wishes them to obtain: the hope God's calling brings, the wealth of glory contained in God's inheritance in the saints, and *the immensity of God's power*. Verses 19b–21 elaborate on this last petition (cf. the four almost synonymous uses of power in v. 19: δύναμις, ἐνέργεια, κράτος, ἰσχύς). Structurally the focus of the author's prayer is on Christ's power, and especially the power of his exaltation (Lincoln 1990:61):

> καὶ τί τὸ ὑπερβάλλον μέγεθος τῆς δυνάμεως αὐτοῦ εἰς ἡμᾶς τοὺς πιστεύοντας κατὰ τὴν ἐνέργειαν τοῦ κράτους τῆς ἰσχύος αὐτοῦ ἣν ἐνήργησεν ἐν τῷ Χριστῷ ἐγείρας αὐτὸν ἐκ νεκρῶν, καὶ καθίσας ἐν δεξιᾷ αὐτοῦ ἐν τοῖς ἐπουρανίοις ὑπεράνω πάσης ἀρχῆς καὶ ἐξουσίας καὶ δυνάμεως καὶ κυριότητος καὶ παντὸς ὀνόματος ὀνομαζομένου οὐ μόνον ἐν τῷ αἰῶνι τούτῳ ἀλλὰ καὶ ἐν τῷ μέλλοντι (1:19–21).[7]

> (That power is like the working of his mighty strength, which he exerted in Christ when he raised him from the dead and seated him at his right hand in heavenly realms, far above all rule and authority, power and dominion, and every title that can be given, not only in the present age, but also in the one to come—1:19b–21).

---

[6] The concepts of knowledge and wisdom are themes reflected upon at some length in the entire epistle. The emphasis is consistently on that kind of knowledge and wisdom *which leads to proper behavior* (cf. Porter 1990:274).

[7] In Greek the end of a sentence frequently contains the apex of the whole, although this can by no means considered to be a rule. In this particular instance, the structure of the sentence reveals a climactic effect towards the end, which foregrounds the concept of God's power (cf. Du Toit 1984a:16).

The composition of 1:15–23 (one long sentence in Greek) is of such a nature that the recipients' attention is drawn to the active deeds of the glorious Father (1:17). In both prayers God's initiative is emphasized (cf. the two aorist participia ἐγείρας and καθίσας: He raised him, He made him sit, followed by two aorist indicatives ὑπέταξεν and ἔδωκεν: God placed all things under his feet, and gave him as head to the church; Cloete & Smit 1988:59–60; Hays 1996:62–66). All this was done *in their interest* (εἰς ἡμᾶς τοὺς πιστεύοντας—v. 19), which indicates the rhetorical function of the particular prayer. By focusing the readers' attention on the ultimate authority, power and glory of Christ, pericopes II and III fulfil an important strategic function in guiding them toward recognizing their new identity in Christ (cf. Arnold 1989:41–69; Mouton 1993; Keathley 1979).[8]

Pericope IV (Eph. 1:22–2:22)

The credal or confessional statement of 1:22–23 (as summary of pericope III, and strategic transition or introduction to pericope IV) consists of two closely related elements: (1) God subjected all things to Jesus and made him head over all; and (2) God gave him to the church. The first has to do with the nature of Christ's rule, and is linked to the intercession of 1:20, 21 as a kind of conclusion. The second element concerns God's gift of Christ as supreme ruler to the church, which at the same time indicates the theme of that which is to follow in chapter two. In this sense the credal statement of 1:22–23 serves as an important transitional technique between the prayer of 1:15–21 and the discourse on the church's identity and ethos in the rest of the document (Roberts 1991:56–60; 1986c:192–199; cf. Howard 1974; Mickelsen 1981).[9]

The structure of 1:22 reveals a remarkable contrast: "God placed all things

---

[8]   References to enthronement psalms (110:1 in v. 20 and 8:6 in 22a) strengthen the notion of Christ's ultimate authority and power (cf. Roberts 1991:53–55). In the Ancient Near Eastern world occupying a place on a god's right hand was associated with a position of supreme honor. In the Old Testament itself Yahweh's right hand is represented as the position of favor, victory and power (cf. Lincoln 1990:61–65; 1982:40–42). In the New Testament this metaphor is often used (e.g. in the Gospels and Acts) to refer to Christ's position of sovereign power and authority (cf. Meeks 1993:166–169). Although the intra- and extra-textual reference of these elements would normally be the interest of a traditio-historical analysis (cf. 2.2.1), it is mentioned here as part of the rhetorical function of a linguistic reading of Ephesians. By reinterpreting such traditions and metaphors in terms of Christ, the author uses it as *shifting devices* to guide his readers toward a new vision of God and themselves. He prays that they may learn to think of themselves in terms of their primary identity as people belonging to Christ seated at God's right hand! The rhetorical power of the extreme contrast between Christ's shameful—yet honorable—death, resurrection and exaltation within an "honor and shame" value system will be discussed in chapter three (cf. 3.2.3).
[9]   For an in-depth study of the structure and rhetorical function of this and other transitional techniques in the Pauline letters, see Roberts 1986a; 1986c; 1988.

under his feet" (ὑπέταξεν ὑπὸ—22a), and He "appointed him to be head *over* everything" (ὑπὲρ πάντα—22b; cf. "far *above* all rule," ὑπεράνω—21a). This language underlines the author's concern to emphasize the supremacy of Christ's heavenly status. The image of Jesus as *head* confirms his sovereign rule over all things, all rule and authority (cf. 1:10; Hartin 1986). It is noteworthy—and rhetorically important—that the strategic verb ὑποτάσσω in 1:22 (to subject to, or to bring under someone's control—Louw & Nida 1989:476) recurs in its passive form ὑποτάσσομαι in the second main section of the document (5:21, 24).[10] This verb seems to embody not only the essence of the church's relationship to Christ (in terms of honor, reverence, respect, service and dependence), but also emphasizes that same relationship between the members of the body (cf. other semantically related terms such as φοβέομαι—5:33, ὑπακούω—6:1, 5, and τιμάω—6:2).

Syntactically the weight of 1:22 falls on the ἐκκλησία (Lincoln 1990:67, 73, 77)—an emphasis which continues in the two descriptive clauses of verse 23.[11] Although the triumphant theology and christology of 1:19–22 appear to be the focal point of the prayer, it is important to follow the direction of the author's thought (cf. Barth 1974a:145–210). He stresses that what God has done in Christ was *toward those who believe*. The rhetorical function of the whole prayer is in-

---

[10] Cynthia B. Kittredge, North American theologian whose doctoral dissertation at Harvard Divinity School was published under the title *Community and Authority: The Rhetoric of Obedience in the Pauline Tradition*, made a useful analysis of the semantic field of "obedience" in contemporary Hellenistic and Jewish writings, as background to her exposition of the rhetoric of obedience in the Pauline tradition (Kittredge 1998:37–51). The verb ὑποτάσσω was used as a military term in the first century Mediterranean context (e.g. with regard to a king), referring to the acknowledgement of a person's status, dignity and authority—embodied in obedience, loyalty and submission to that person's directives and wishes (cf. Louw & Nida 1989:468). The Ephesians author uses another metaphor from this sphere of life, namely the *armor of God* in 6:10–20. Both concepts are radically reinterpreted from a christological perspective (cf. Meeks 1993:38–39, 166–169).

[11] Verse 23 presents extremely difficult questions concerning grammatical construction, which has to do with the nature of Christ's reign over the cosmos. Although Christ is described as *head over everything* in v. 22 (καὶ αὐτὸν ἔδωκεν κεφαλὴν ὑπέρ πάντα τῇ ἐκκλησίᾳ), the body metaphor for the church specifically expresses the notion of Christ as head of *his church*. It is clear that Christ's headship over the church is confessed here, but it is not obvious whether this is the *only* way in which his authority is manifested. "(I)s his ecclesiastic rule in and over the church paralleled, perhaps undergirded, by his cosmic headship" (Barth 1974a:156)? Many exegetes discover some traces here of the cosmic lordship of Christ, in addition to his more direct lordship over the church—an exegetical problem which has to be solved within the wider contours of the New Testament. In the context of Ephesians, the church appears to be the focus and medium of Christ's presence and supreme rule in the world. This means that the power of God has been given to Christ in order that it be used primarily by the church (Lincoln 1990:66–78). For the public responsibility of the church in its fullness or catholicity, see Müller & Smit 1994:402–403.

deed that the readers may *know and experience* God in the power and glory of the resurrected and exalted Christ, and redefine themselves in the light of their relation to him. This would be the substance of their *hope* (cf. 1:12, 18; 2:12).

The images of *body* (cf. 4:12–16; 5:29–30) and *fullness* (cf. 3:19; 4:13) in 1:23 both stress the close and inseparable relationship between God's people and Christ (cf. Perriman 1990). He included (incorporated) all who belong to him into *one body* when he accomplished their salvation. What has happened to him, has happened to them: When He was raised from the dead, they were raised *with him.* When He was seated at God's right hand, they were seated *with him* (2:4–6; cf. Hoch 1982). The structure of 2:6 is syntactically parallel to that of 1:20, which would be of particular rhetorical significance (cf. the two aorist indicatives συνήγειρεν and συνεκάθισεν in 2:6, and the two aorist participia ἐγείρας and καθίσας in 1:20).

The meaning for πλήρωμα that probably best fits the context, is to consider the church as the community which is *filled* and *completed* (in the sense of *making complete provision for*—Roberts 1991:59) by Christ's dynamic presence and rule (cf. 2:21, 22; 3:17, 19; Hermans & Geysels 1967; Foulkes 1956:66–67). "The Church is nothing in itself. It is a special community only because Christ is its head and his presence fills it" (Lincoln 1990:80). These two metaphors can thus be described as revealing the essence of the church (Barth 1974a:183–210).

In sum, the confession of 1:22–23 deals with two matters: The exalted position of Jesus as resurrected and sovereign lord, and the significance of Jesus as gift of salvation to the believers. The second aspect defines the first in a surprising way. In the broad context of Ephesians, Christ's power (as *lord* and *head*) is decisively, but paradoxically defined in terms of his sacrificial love and care (as *servant*—cf. references to his death, blood and cross: 1:7, 20; 2:13, 16; 4:32; 5:2, 25, 29).[12] The metaphors of *head, body* and *fullness* in 1:22–23 (cf. 3:19; 4:12–16; 5:29–30) therefore seem to function as major *shifting devices* in thrusting the readers' thoughts toward a full understanding of their new identity and ethos *in Christ.* According to the Ephesians perspective, the Christ event—and especially his exaltation in power and glory—is the vantage point from which humanity is to be viewed.

The potential rhetorical and pastoral power of the statements in pericope IV (1:22–2:22) should not be underestimated. For the recipients who were previous-

---

[12] In this way the core values of honor and power—typical of a patriarchal culture—are decisively reversed and reinterpreted in terms of Christ's example. The paradoxical nature of Christ's power also determines the implied readers' *ethos*, which is primarily dealt with in the second main section of the document. Their lifestyle should be characterized by the style of his reign, i.e. by works of *service* (cf. 4:12). They should be "kind and compassionate to one another, forgiving each other, just as in Christ God forgave (them)" (4:32; cf. 5:2). They should "live a life of love, just as Christ loves (them) and gave himself up for (them)" (5:2). They should be "completely humble and gentle.... patient, bearing with one another in love" (4:2).

ly considered to be "without hope and without God in the world" (2:12), to hear that their head is head over everything, that their lord is LORD over all powers, and that their God is leading the world to a final end where he will fulfil all things (cf. 1:10), would certainly encourage and empower them to understand and experience their unique position in the world (cf. Smit 1983a:141–143; Cloete & Smit 1988:60–61; Lincoln 1990:78–82, all with reference to J. Gnilka).

The confession of 1:22–23 leads to three conclusions regarding the identity of the readers in chapter two (2:1–10, 11–18, 19–22), in each instance described by means of different metaphors. Because of what God has done *in Christ* (1:3–14), those who were formerly dead in their transgressions and sins have been made alive with Christ because of God's love and grace, and seated with him in the heavenly realms (2:1–9; cf. Lincoln 1973; 1981:135–150; 1983; Best 1981).[13] Because of what God has done *in Christ*, the previously powerless and statusless believers—excluded from citizenship in Israel, and foreigners to the covenants of the promise (2:12; cf. ξένοι καὶ πάροικοι, 2:19)—have been brought near and became fellow-citizens of God's holy people, yes, even members of his household (οἰκεῖοι τοῦ θεοῦ, 2:19), a "dwelling in which God lives by his Spirit" (2:11–22; cf. Lincoln 1981:150–154).

With reference to a detailed linguistic-semantic analysis of the discourse relations in Ephesians by V. Krüger, Combrink (1986:227) emphasizes the concentric structure of 2:11–22. According to this view, 2:13–18 forms the centre of 2:11–22, which focuses on Christ's reconciling death on the cross. This centre is framed by 2:11–12 and 2:19–22, which form an antithetical parallelism. By means of powerful metaphors (depicting people's legal status in society), the parallelism dramatically contrasts the Gentiles' former position outside Christ to their new status in Christ. In this way a new body, a new corporate entity, "one new humanity" consisting of reconciled Jews and Gentiles is created *in Christ* (2:15; cf. 1:23; 4:4, 12), which would have radical cultural and socio-ethical implications (cf. Schnackenburg 1991:105–127; Combrink 1986:227–234).

The important rhetorical shift in terms of ownership and loyalty which occurs in chapter 2, may also be phrased as a shift in emphasis from traditional activity-related Jewish symbols (circumcision, law, temple, dividing wall) to relationally oriented metaphors (God's people, household, spiritual temple, dwelling place). It is clear that the Ephesians author profoundly shifts the Jewish concep-

---

[13]   From a different perspective, and within the prophetic-apocalyptic *genre* of the book of Revelation, John describes his vision of the throne of God in the most vivid language (Rev. 4–5). In this vision God's throne is surrounded by twenty-four other thrones, on which twenty-four elders—representative of the entire Christian church—are seated, and also by four living creatures, representative of creation as a whole. Characteristic of this picture, is that the elders and living creatures praise God day and night—which reminds of the eulogical and doxological nature of the prayers in Eph. 1:3–21 and 3:14–21 in which the announcement of Christ's and the church's exaltation is embedded, and which implicitly includes "all things in heaven and on earth" (Eph. 1:10).

tual system of the Torah, recentering the divine drama in Jesus Christ. The recipients' relation to God is consequently redescribed by means of a new set of metaphors (cf. Ricoeur 1980:26; Combrink 1986:226–229). The relational nature of these metaphors essentially constitutes the unique identity and ethos of those who are *in Christ*. The *in Christ* reality would henceforth determine who they were and how they would live—a relationship in which prayer would play a decisive role (Eph. 1:15–23; 3:14–21; 6:18–20). As opposed to previous categories of ethnicity, social stratification and gender (cf. Eph. 5:21–6:9), this relationship would be characterized by a new set of *christologically oriented* values and criteria (cf. Roberts 1984b:294–319; Lincoln 1973; 1987).

Pericopes V and VI (Eph. 3:1–19; 20–21)

In pericope V, of which the second intercessory prayer (3:1, 14–19) forms a part, the element of Christ's power is underlined once more (cf. 1:19; 3:16, 18, 20). The substance of this power is defined in terms of Christ's multi-dimensional *love*. The author asks that God may strengthen his audience with *the power to grasp how wide and long and high and deep the love of Christ is* (3:18).

The pattern of thought represented by the intercession of 3:14–19, together with the doxology of 3:20–21, forms an interesting chiastic structure.[14] An analysis of recurring elements in 3:14–21 reveals the following pattern:

---

[14] Chiastic structures represent a famous Greek stylistic device "for expressing a contrast through a parallelism in reverse order of grammatical or semantic categories or even of whole sentences or groups of sentences" (Deist 1990:43; cf. Du Toit 1984a:14–15). An example of a more complex and extended kind of chiasmus is where a non-repeating element occurs in the middle, and where a pattern like a-b-c-b-a can be discerned, also known as a *palindrome*—"a word or sentence that reads the same backwards and forwards" (Deist 1990:182). *In the case of an a-b-c-b-a chiasm, not only the recurring elements are emphasized by the specific structure, but in particular the non-repeating middle section.* Chiastic structures in the Ephesians text are the following: 2:19; 4:9–10; 5:3–5; 5:19–21 (Roberts 1991:13–14; Porter 1990). See also Argentinian theologian Beatriz M. Couch's very interesting analysis (1988) of a chiastic structure in 1:3–14, emphasizing the abundance of God's grace, love and wisdom in bringing about a new humanity in Christ. This would mean that Eph. 1–3 (itself representing a chiastic structure) is framed by two similar structures in 3:1–14 and 3:14–21.

In a discussion of the chiastic structure in Eph. 5:3–5, Stanley E. Porter, authoritative North American scholar on New Testament Greek, draws on David Clark's criteria for distinguishing between different forms of chiasmus, namely "parallelism of content; form or structure; language, including catchwords; and setting and theology" (Porter 1990:273). According to these criteria, the pattern of thought in Eph. 3:14–21 resembles a parallelism of *content and theology.*

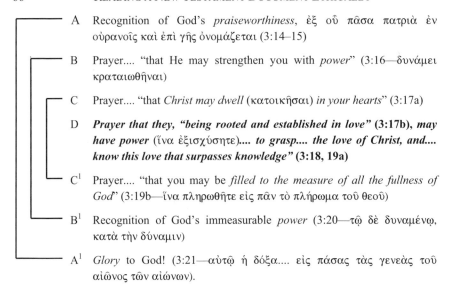

A　Recognition of God's *praiseworthiness,* ἐξ οὗ πᾶσα πατριὰ ἐν οὐρανοῖς καὶ ἐπὶ γῆς ὀνομάζεται (3:14–15)

B　Prayer.... "that He may strengthen you with *power*" (3:16—δυνάμει κραταιωθῆναι)

C　Prayer.... "that *Christ may dwell* (κατοικῆσαι) *in your hearts*" (3:17a)

D　***Prayer that they, "being rooted and established in love" (3:17b), may have power* (ἵνα ἐξισχύσητε).*... to grasp.... the love of Christ, and.... know this love that surpasses knowledge" (3:18, 19a)***

C¹　Prayer.... "that you may be *filled to the measure of all the fullness of God*" (3:19b—ἵνα πληρωθῆτε εἰς πᾶν τὸ πλήρωμα τοῦ θεοῦ)

B¹　Recognition of God's immeasurable *power* (3:20—τῷ δὲ δυναμένῳ, κατὰ τὴν δύναμιν)

A¹　*Glory* to God! (3:21—αὐτῷ ἡ δόξα.... εἰς πάσας τὰς γενεὰς τοῦ αἰῶνος τῶν αἰώνων).

The non-repeating D section of the chiasm focuses on the experience of God's love and power—particularly in terms of the presence and involvement of the ascended lord (the two C sections; cf. 2:22). The two B sections underline the petition for power, while God is acknowledged and glorified in the two A sections.

The structure of Ephesians 3:14–21 thus forms a remarkable *palindrome,* with special emphasis on the *love* and *power* of God.[15] Such an observation would be of particular rhetorical significance at the end of the first main section. Bonnie Thurston, a North American theologian, considers this prayer as the bridge between the two main sections of the document, summarizing its primary intention (1993:78–89). This is indeed the persuading function of the great doxology in pericope VI, namely to emphasize the glory of Christ's presence in the church throughout all generations, for ever and ever! At the same time, the doxology directly leads to the second main section on the readers' ethos as practical *response* to the gospel of Christ in the first main section.[16]

---

[15]　The linguistic features of Eph. 3:14–21 serve as motivation for considering pericopes V and VI as a tight structural unit. However, because it contains two distinguishable elements of the author's prayer (intercession and doxology), it is demarcated as two separate pericopes, both serving a strategic function in the broad chiastic structure of Ephesians 1–3 (cf. "Structural coherence of Ephesians" at the end of section 2.1.2).

[16]　The power and love of Christ indeed form the primary motivation for the ethical imperatives in the second main section of the document (4:2, 15, 16; 5:2, 3, 25, 28, 33; 6: 21, 23, 24). It is also noteworthy that *love* is added to the final greetings of grace and peace in 6:23. The promise of grace in 6:24 is in the final instance "to all who love our Lord Jesus Christ with an undying love."

It is also rhetorically significant that the prayer of 3:1, 14–21 is interrupted by an explanation of the encoded author's commission in 3:2–13. The interruption consists of two sections, both connected to the commission referred to in 3:2. In verses 3–6 the accent is on the *content* of that which the author proclaimed at God's command. It once again summarizes an essential consequence of the gospel of Jesus Christ, namely the unity of his body—here referred to as the *mystery* of Christ (3:3, 4, 6, cf. 9). This had been made known to Paul by revelation from the Spirit (3:3, 5). Verses 7–12 treat the *execution* and *fulfillment* of the commission—through the empowerment of Paul—as the disclosure of God's good news (cf. Lincoln 1981:154–155; Blevins 1979).[17] The whole is concluded in verse 13 with a request to the audience to continue courageously in order that they may execute this commission, which is the task of the whole church (3:10). This in turn calls to mind the interrupted intercession which began in verse 1, and which continues in verses 14–21 (cf. Roberts 1991:86; 1993b:101–102; H. H. Culpepper 1979).

Such an interruption by a new construction in a discourse, as a peculiar stylistic feature, is referred to as an *anacoluthon*.[18] The function of this particular digression seems to emphasize the author's integrity and authority as a servant of the gospel (3:7), especially in terms of the revelation which he received from God (3:3). A prerequisite for the readers' acceptance of the epistle and its message would be the acceptance of the author's authority (cf. J. N. Vorster 1991:32).

---

[17] Syntactically and semantically 3:10–11 links up with other purpose and consequence clauses in the preceding and following contexts of the document, emphasizing the practical ethos associated with the implied readers' new status (cf. Hartin 1986:230–236; Mouton 1987:82):

- εἶναι ἡμᾶς ἁγίους καὶ ἀμώμους κατενώπιον αὐτοῦ ἐν ἀγάπῃ (1:4)
- εἰς οἰκονομίαν τοῦ πληρώματος τῶν καιρῶν, ἀνακεφαλαιώσασθαι τὰ πάντα ἐν τῷ Χριστῷ (1:10)
- εἰς τὸ εἶναι ἡμᾶς εἰς ἔπαινον δόξης αὐτοῦ (1:12)
- εἰς ἔπαινον τῆς δόξης αὐτοῦ (1:14)
- ἵνα ὁ θεὸς.... δώῃ ὑμῖν πνεῦμα σοφίας καὶ ἀποκαλύψεως ἐν ἐπιγνώσει αὐτοῦ (1:17)
- εἰς τὸ εἰδέναι ὑμᾶς τίς ἐστιν ἡ ἐλπὶς τῆς κλήσεως αὐτοῦ (1:18)
- αὐτοῦ γάρ ἐσμεν ποίημα, κτισθέντες ἐν Χριστῷ Ἰησοῦ ἐπὶ ἔργοις ἀγαθοῖς οἷς προητοίμασεν ὁ θεὸς ἵνα ἐν αὐτοῖς περιπατήσωμεν (2:10)
- ἵνα τοὺς δύο κτίσῃ ἐν αὐτῷ εἰς ἕνα καινὸν ἄνθρωπον ποιῶν εἰρήνην (2:15)
- εἰς ναὸν ἅγιον ἐν κυρίῳ (2:21)
- εἰς κατοικητήριον τοῦ θεοῦ ἐν πνεύματι (2:22)
- Παρακαλῶ οὖν ὑμᾶς.... ἀξίως περιπατῆσαι τῆς κλήσεως ἧς ἐκλήθητε (4:1ff).

[18] According to Deist (1990:10), an *anacoluthon* can be defined as "the violation of syntactic sequence (word order) as a result of strong emotion" (cf. Blass & Debrunner 1961:243–245; Du Toit 1984a:16).

Conclusions on the Structure of Ephesians 1–3

According to Roberts (1978:167–169; 1984a:139–141; 1991:15–17), the different elements in Ephesians 1–3 also reveal an extended and rather complicated chiastic structure—that of a *palindrome* (with pericopes II and VI as the A sections, III and V as B sections, and pericope IV as non-repeating C section—cf. "Structural coherence of Ephesians" on page 75). This structure emphasizes the recurring elements—and in particular the non-repeating centre, pericope IV.

The rhetorical function of an extended chiastic structure in Ephesians 1–3 would be of particular interest for the purpose of this study. That the faith confession about God's radical saving event *in Christ* (1:22–23, with its three illustrative explanations in 2:1–22) forms the centre of the chiasm in 1:3–3:21, would be of vital importance for the understanding of the rhetorical function of the "theological indicative" of Ephesians 1–3, as well as the essentially "paraenetic imperative" of 4–6 (cf. Barth 1974a:275–276; Combrink 1986:227–229). This confession reads as follows:

> καὶ πάντα ὑπέταξεν ὑπὸ τοὺς πόδας αὐτοῦ, καὶ αὐτὸν ἔδωκεν κεφαλὴν ὑπὲρ πάντα τῇ ἐκκλησίᾳ, ἥτις ἐστὶν τὸ σῶμα αὐτοῦ, τὸ πλήρωμα τοῦ τὰ πάντα ἐν πᾶσιν πληρουμένου.

> (And God placed all things under his feet and appointed—'gave'—him to be head over everything for the church, which is his body, the fullness of him who fills everything in every way.)

The intended pragmatic effect of this confession is strengthened by its immediate linguistic context, namely the two prayers of intercession in pericopes III and V (B sections of the chiasm), and the recurring exclamation of praise in pericopes II and VI respectively (the C sections). The tight structure of the first main section is further underlined by the introductory conjunctions διὰ τοῦτο (1:15) and τούτου χάριν (3:1, 14), which indicate the prayers of pericopes III and V as a logical consequence of the foregoing sections. *Since* the recipients have been elected, adopted, redeemed and sealed as God's people in Christ (pericope II), and *since* they were made alive and brought near as members of God's family (pericope IV), the author sincerely prays for a deeper understanding of their new status and its consequences (pericopes III and V). He prays that they may live according to a growing vision of God's presence (1:15–23; 3:1, 14–21; cf. 2:19, 22; 3:17, 19; 4:6, 10). In effect this seems to mean that, because of the practical experience of the confession in 1:22–23, they should respond in spontaneous and continuous praise-giving to ὁ θεὸς καὶ πατὴρ τοῦ κυρίου ἡμῶν Ἰησοῦ Χριστοῦ (1:3; cf. 1:6, 12, 14; 3:20–21).

It is generally accepted that the structural elements of Ephesians 1–3 are somehow related to the elements encountered in a typical Jewish prayer form called the *berakah*, a specific form of laudation or praise-giving. The *berakah* was fundamentally an act of remembrance, where God was to be praised for the way God had worked in the past. By remembering God's deeds, his people were moved again to praise him (Johnson 1999:59–60). The *berakah* always comprised two elements, namely a doxological exclamation or appeal for praise-giving to God, followed by the reasons why God was to be praised (cf. 2.2.1.1). In addition still other elements could occur, for example intercession, confession of sin and confession of faith. The whole could also be concluded with a doxology (Roberts 1978:167–169; 1991:15; cf. Schnackenburg 1991:45–47; O'Brien 1977:233–258). In the light of these remarks, it is evident that Ephesians 1–3 is related in one way or another to the Jewish *berakah* (O'Brien 1979). Indeed, considering the elements mentioned, it is only a confession of sin that is absent (Roberts 1991:15). The author certainly must have had a specific rhetorical aim in mind by making such extensive use of a Jewish tradition in a mainly non-Jewish environment (cf. 2.2.1, 2.3; Wessels 1990a:53–55).[19]

From this point of view, Roberts (1978:169; 1991:17) argues that the actual focus or rhetorical aim of Ephesians 1–3 lies in the eulogy at the beginning, and the doxology at the end of these chapters. Although Ephesians 1–3 essentially explain God's redemptive work *in Christ* (the confession of faith), Roberts emphasizes that everything in the end revolves around the redeemed community praising and adoring God's glory (verbally and non-verbally by means of a God-pleasing ethos—cf. 4–6).

To identify a communicative focal point in the first three chapters, as well as the Ephesians text as a whole, once again depends on the perspective and exegetic-hermeneutical choices of the interpreter. It seems that the movement within the text focuses the implied recipients' attention on two aspects in turn: the reality of God's actions *in Christ* and, at the same time (on the same linguistic level), the faith community's response to those actions. To my mind, the text considers these symbiotic and reciprocal aspects of divine initiative and human response (*responsibility*) to be equally important within a mutual relationship. Ultimately, this matter can only be dealt with satisfactorily by exploring the pragmatic *function* of the text as a whole (cf. 2.3.4).

---

[19] If the *genre* of an extended eulogy and doxology (probably as part of a sermon) forms the background to the first three chapters of Ephesians, it speaks for itself that it necessarily would have influenced the language structure, idioms and metaphors used in this section. The long and densely structured sentences, the solemn expressions, would all be due to the probable "liturgical" nature of these chapters (cf. Roberts 1991:16; Jeal 1990: 16–90). For further discussions on the *genre* of Ephesians (and its corresponding form/ structure and function), see 2.1.4.2 and 3.3.1.

.3 The Second Main Section (Eph. 4:1–6:20)

The *second main section* of Ephesians consists of three major parts, namely

- exhortations related to the new life in Christ directed to the *church* (4:1–16);

- exhortations and conclusions about the principle of the new life on a more *personal* level (4:17–6:9); and

- a call for armor and victory as *conclusions* from the previous two sections (6: 10–20; cf. Roberts 1991:18).

The structural and semantic coherence between the first and second main sections of the document is *inter alia* indicated by conjunctions such as οὖν, τοῦτο οὖν, and διὸ in 4:1, 17, 25; 5:15 (introducing pericopes VII, IX, X and XI respectively). In the case of διὰ τοῦτο and τούτου χάριν at the beginning of pericopes III and V, these conjunctions indicate the particular pericopes as a direct and logical consequence of what had been said before (see also 6:14). The conjunctions thus function retro- *and* prospectively: While referring to what had gone before, they lead to new encouragement. The admonitions which are to foll-ow in chapters 4–6 are indeed motivated by the *indicatives of God's redemptive work in Christ*, which He had already given to the church (Jordaan 1990). The essence of Ephesians 1–3 (a new identity awareness in relationship with Christ) is thus explicated in terms of a life worthy of their calling (4:1). Within the main argument, such a way of living decisively *replaces* any possible "outward" iden-tity marker which could serve as a "dividing wall" (2:14) among the members of the one body of Christ. In this sense Ephesians 1–3 *inform* chapters 4–6.

Pericopes VII and VIII (Eph. 4:1–6; 7–16)

Pericope VII directly links the two main sections of the document by introducing the central theme of the second main section, namely a life worthy of the calling (identity, or character) the audience has received from God:

> Παρακαλῶ οὖν ὑμᾶς ἐγὼ ὁ δέσμιος ἐν κυρίῳ ἀξίως περιπατῆσαι
> τῆς κλήσεως ἧς ἐκλήθητε.... (4:1)
>
> (As a prisoner for the Lord, then, I urge you to live a life worthy of the calling you have received.)

The very first practical admonitions in this respect are the following: "Be completely *humble* and *gentle*; be *patient*, bearing with one another in *love*. Make every effort to keep the unity of the Spirit through the bond of peace" (4:2–3). These lead to a rhetorical accumulation of the words "one" or "unity" (εἷς, μία, ἓν) in 4:4–6, whereby the unity of Christians is stressed as a dominant theme in Ephesians (Meeks 1977:214–217). Other elements which reflect, or are closely related to the readers' implied ethos and unity frequently occur in chapters 4–6:

περιπατέω (6 times), ὁ Χριστός (19), ὁ κύριος (15), τό πνεῦμα (7), ἡ ἀγάπη (14), ἡ ἀλήθεια (6), πληρόω or τό πλήρωμα (3), ἡ εἰρήνη (3). All of these (except Χριστός, πληρόω and ἀλήθεια) occur in the introductory pericope (VII), although Χριστός and πληρόω (4:10, 13; 5:18) should be viewed as semantically related to κύριος (4:1, 5) and εἷς θεὸς καὶ πατὴρ πάντων, ὁ ἐπὶ πάντων καὶ διὰ πάντων καὶ ἐν πᾶσιν (4:6).

In Ephesians 4:6, 10 the theme of Christ's presence, which has been the focus of 3:14–19, is taken up again. The new life is characterized by a real sense of the triumphant Lord's creative presence, which is represented by the wise, enlightening influence of the Holy Spirit (1:17; 4:3, 4, 30; 5:17, 18; 6:17, 18), and the unity of the body of Christ (pericopes VII and VIII). In pericope VIII (4:7–16) Christ's ascension is explicitly associated with the purpose to fill all things with his presence (ἵνα πληρώσῃ τὰ πάντα—4:10; cf. 1:22–23; 2:19, 22 with reference to the church as his πλήρωμα; Lincoln 1981:155–163; Hermans & Geysels 1967; Yates 1972; Theron 1973). In order to prepare and guide the church toward the full experience of God's presence in Christ, He provided the gifts of apostles, prophets, evangelists, pastors and teachers (4:11–16). Almost all the themes of 1:15–23 recur in this pericope: the calling of the readers, the role of the Spirit, Christ's ascension, and his gifts to every member of the body (the church), for the sake of its unity.

Pericopes IX to XI (Eph. 4:17–24; 4:25–5:14; 5:15–6:9)

A discourse analysis of pericopes IX to XI—as a conclusion on the principle and practice of the new life—reveals the following main line of thought (cf. Roberts 1991:18, 134–178; Lemmer 1988:appendix; Johnson 1999:417–419; Smit 1983b: 172):

- 4:17–19 is an introductory warning against a possible continuation of the readers' previous way of living;

- 4:20–24, being one sentence in Greek, forms the actual paraenesis in the form of (1) a reminder of the new teaching which they had received (20–21b), and (2) a brief summary of the contents of this teaching, namely to put off their former way of life, the old self, and to put on the new self, "created to be *like God* in true righteousness and holiness" (21c–24);

- 4:25–5:2 gives a number of concrete examples, mainly consisting of a *description* of their former lifestyle, an *admonition* to a new way of living, and the strong theological *motivation* and *encouragement* in 4:30, 32 (cf. 5:18) and 5:1–2 (cf. 5:23, 25, 29) not to grieve the Spirit, but to be imitators of God and Christ in their behavior towards one another;[20]

---

[20] In this regard a close syntactic and semantic relation exists in the second main section of Ephesians between the concepts *unity, love and truth* (as opposed to *deceit and*

- 5:3–14 exhorts the readers to avoid pagan vices like sexual immorality, and to act as children of the light;

- 5:15–6:9 illustrates the principle of the new life under the influence of the Spirit in terms of three different relationships: husband and wife, children and parents, slaves and masters. The general introduction of 5:15–20 is followed by a reinterpreted version of the well-known Jewish and Greco-Roman *Haustafel* in 5:21–6:9 (cf. 2.2.1). The radical example of the indwelling Christ (cf. 4:32; 5:2), and the consoling Spirit (4:30; 5:18; 6:18) serve to *empower* and *transform* these relationships (cf. O'Hagan 1976; Lincoln 1981: 163–164; Barnard 1983; Smit 1983b; Wall 1988; Wessels 1990d; Hays 1996: 64–65). In this sense, 5:21 and 6:9c frame the Ephesians *Haustafel* by emphasizing its underlying perspective: "Submit to one another *out of reverence for Christ.... and there is no favouritism with him.*"[21]

---

falsehood in 4:14, 25; 5:6). These concretize the author's prayer in 3:14–21 that the readers' may be filled with God's presence.... so that they may know and experience his love. No wonder that Barth (1974b:547–550; cf. Smit 1983b:177; Sampley 1972; Bruce 1967:308–311) considers Ephesians 4:30 (*"Do not grieve the Holy Spirit of God"*) as taking a central structural position within the paraenetic section of chapters 4–6. It is the dynamic Spirit of God who implicitly fills the readers (5:17–18), and who seals and protects them in their commitment to Christ (1:13–14), in their reconciliation with God and one another (2:15b–18; 4:3–4), and in their moral growth (4:12–13; 6:17–18). This leads Barth (1974b:525; cf. H. H. Culpepper 1979) to consider the whole of Eph. 4 "a manifesto declaring the inseparability of ecclesiology and ethics."

[21] As a general injunction and motivation, respectively, Eph. 5:21 and 6:9b frame the household code by reinterpreting its patriarchal structure from a christological perspective. Ephesians 5:21 is a transitional verse "completing the series of participles which are dependent on the verb πληροῦσθε, 'be filled,' from v. 18, while itself providing the verbal form on which the first injunction in the.... household code is dependent" (Lincoln 1990: 365). The idiomatic expression in 6:9b, "There is no favouritism with God" (NIV) or "With God there is no partiality" (NRSV), literally means 'God does not lay hold of someone's face,' that is, 'God does not esteem anyone according to face value' (καὶ προσωπο-λημψία οὐκ ἔστιν παρ' αὐτῷ, from λαμβάνω προσωπον—cf. Dt. 10:17; 16:19; Lv. 19: 15; Mt. 22:16; Mk. 12:14; Lk. 20:21; Ac. 10:34; Rm. 2:11; Gl. 2:6; Col. 3:25; Louw & Nida 1989:768). It probably originated from within the context of slavery, where slaves were chained to one another while waiting to be sold on the market. As inferiors they were not allowed to lift up their heads until a potential buyer would do so, sometimes brutally, in order to examine their teeth and general health. In Eph. 6:9, as well as parallel expressions in Dt. 10:17; 16:19 and Lv. 19:15, this phrase occurs in a context which emphasizes God's sovereignty and almighty power. In contrast to the often abusive power of contemporary authorities, the essence of God's power is defined in terms of loving care and concern for people, and particularly by God's restoring what was lost to them, namely their dignity and humanity. The Ephesians author thus seems radically to reverse the patriarchal connotation of ὑποτάσσω (as imposed loyalty and obedience) to reflect not only the essence of the relationship between Christ and the church (in terms of willing

The thrust of the Ephesians text has been identified as a renewed awareness of the implied recipients' identity in Christ. Recurring elements in the first six pericopes of the first main section focus on the glory of Christ's *grace* (referred to 11 times), *love* (6 times) and *power* (6 times). The admonitions of the second main section reflect the ethos worthy of their new status, and have to be interpreted within that context. The intended rhetorical function of admonitions such as μετὰ πάσης ταπεινοφροσύνης (4:2), ὑποτασσόμενοι ἀλλήλοις (5:21, 24), φοβῆται (5:33), ὑπακούετε (6:1, 5) and τίμα (6:2) indicate the essence of these relationships. All these seem to implicitly reflect a mutual, reciprocal attitude of honor and respect, acknowledging the other's new authority (new humanity— 2:15; 4:24) *in Christ*. In this sense the paradoxical example of Christ as *servant-lord* serves to empower and radically redefine these relations. In their *redescribed* form these relations reflect the ethos worthy of the readers' new status, and have to be interpreted within that context.

Throughout this section, Christ's *transformative power*, qualified by his humility as *sacrificial love*, serves as ultimate motivation for their new behavior (4:32–5:2; etc.; cf. Pfitzner 1978; R. A. Culpepper 1979). The second main section is characterized by a remarkable repetition of expressions such as καθὼς καὶ ὁ θεὸς ἐν Χριστῷ, and ὡς or καθὼς καὶ ὁ Χριστὸς or ὁ θεὸς (cf. Eph. 4:32; 5:2, 23, 25, 29; 6:5, 6, 7). This linguistic device represents a peculiar Greek stylistic figure called *tertium comparationis*, "'a third of (a) comparison,' the shared feature on which a comparison is based" (Deist 1990:255). In Ephesians 4:32 and 5:2 the quality of the mutual relationship among members of the body of Christ is compared to and substantiated by Christ's sacrificial love toward them. Sacrificial love—in terms of Christ's concrete example of kindness, compassion and forgiveness—thus serves as a *tertium comparationis*.[22]

In 5:23, 25, 29 the Christian husband's role in the marriage relationship is compared to God. Once again, the feature which God and the husband have in common, is their sacrificial love and care toward the ἐκκλησία/wife. Sacrificial and caring love, accordingly, may be said to serve here as the *tertium comparationis*. In accordance with the communication model discussed in chapter one, the

---

honor and reverence), but also among the members of the body itself. On this point, it is important also to note the semantically related terms φοβέομαι in 5:33, ὑπακούω in 6:1, 5, and τιμάω in 6:2, which all relate to the guiding principle for wise living in the Old Testament covenant, namely the "fear of YHWH," which is reinterpreted here as the overriding motivation for wise Christian living (1:8, 17; 5:15) and for liberating, healing relationships within the new community. It is an attitude that looks to Christ in awe at his overwhelming love and power (Lincoln 1990:365–68). These expressions implicitly resemble the thrust of the document as a radical reinterpretation of human relations in the light of the Christ event.

[22] See Furnish 1993 for an informative discussion of the expression "He gave himself up for us" as christological assertion in Pauline literature.

rhetorical impact of these expressions has to be explored against the background of the ethical context of the Jewish and Greco-Roman *Haustafeln* (cf. Stagg 1979; 2.2.1.4).

Pericope XII (Eph. 6:10–20)

In the final part of the second main section, pericope XII (literally introduced by τοῦ λοιποῦ), the author exhorts his audience to be "strong in the Lord and in his mighty power" (6:10), and to "put on the full armor of God" (6:11, 13), so that they may take their stand "against the rulers, against the authorities, against the powers of this dark world and against the spiritual forces of evil in the heavenly realms" (6:12; cf. Lincoln 1981:164–168; O'Brien 1984; Wild 1984). Since their previous position of shame had been changed radically to a position of honor, they are once more encouraged to adhere to the positive example of their Lord Jesus Christ. The exhorting verb στῆναι recurs three times in 6:11, 13, 14, while ἀντιστῆναι occurs once in verse 13.

The metaphorical use of the different parts of the armor summarizes both the theological motivations and the ethical paraenesis of the second main section. References are made to the strength of the *Lord* (6:10; cf. 1:19–21; 3:16–9), the armor of *God* (6:11, 13), the sword of the *Spirit*, which is the word of God (6:17), and praying in the *Spirit* (6:18; cf. 4:30; 5:18) as the context of the recipients' protection in the battle against other forces and perspectives. The essential parts of the Christian believers' armor are *truth* (6:14; cf. 1:13; 4:25), *righteousness* (6: 14; cf. 4:24), the gospel of *peace* (6:15; cf. 1:2; 2:14, 15, 17; 6:23), *faith* (6:16; cf. 2:8; 3:12; 6:23) and *salvation* (6:17; cf. 1:13; 2:5, 8; also 1:7; 4:30—redemption).

˙   Pericope XII thus serves not only as a conclusion of the previous two parts of the second main section, but in a very dramatic sense of the document as a whole. It also places the final greetings of peace, love and grace (pericope XIII) in the perspective of a paradoxical experience of God's presence amid the reality of conflict and struggle.

Conclusions on the Structure of Ephesians 1–6

The direction of the Ephesians discourse thrusts pericopes IV and VII to the fore as the pivotal points of the two main sections (IV being the centre of the chiasm in chapters 1–3, and VII as heading for chapters 4–6). Schematically, the broad structural coherence and direction of the document can be presented as follows:

STRUCTURAL COHERENCE OF EPHESIANS

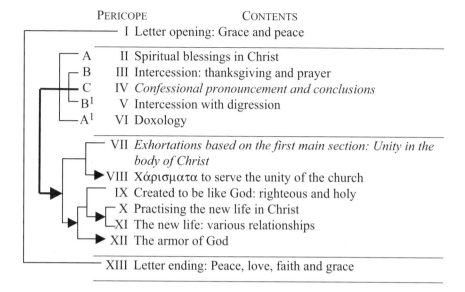

PERICOPE   CONTENTS

           I Letter opening: Grace and peace

A   II Spiritual blessings in Christ
B   III Intercession: thanksgiving and prayer
C   IV *Confessional pronouncement and conclusions*
B¹   V Intercession with digression
A¹   VI Doxology

VII *Exhortations based on the first main section: Unity in the body of Christ*
VIII Χάρισματα to serve the unity of the church
IX Created to be like God: righteous and holy
X Practising the new life in Christ
XI The new life: various relationships
XII The armor of God

           XIII Letter ending: Peace, love, faith and grace

2.1.3 *MAJOR IDENTITY- AND BEHAVIOR-ORIENTED ELEMENTS*

An ethical reading of the Ephesians document is concerned with its thrust, perspective, and strategy as major functions of its underlying communication processes. As a starting point, the study of its structural coherence (2.1.2) brought aspects to the fore which focus on the implied recipients' or readers' identity and behavior. This needs some further elaboration.

The recurrence of structural markers (strategic words, expressions, themes, metaphors, traditional material, actantial roles[23]) in Ephesians can be considered

---

[23] "Actantial roles" is a French linguistic category referring to the "spheres of action" (Patte 1976:42), interpersonal roles, or basic functions fulfilled by different actors in a narrative text. Although the Ephesians *genre* is not primarily narrative in nature, particular roles are implied in its "story" (cf. 4.2). It is the *interaction* among these roles which actually produce the narrative of the document. I have analyzed the metaphorical actantial structure of Eph. 1:3–14 elsewhere (Mouton 1987:61, 90–91, 140–143), and found that these roles reflect a radical shift from a previously shameful position to a new honorable position in Christ. The Triune God (as *protagonist*) takes the initiative in the Ephesians story, whereas the roles of the author and recipients are determined by their relation to God, Christ, and the Spirit, as well as to one another. If they would adhere to the divine purpose for their lives, according to Ephesians, they are portrayed as God's *adjuvants* (helpers). If they however do not accept the honorable position *in Christ*, they are viewed as *antagonists* or *opponents* of God. See Mouton 1987:164–175 for the implied consequences of these relations.

as important signals toward understanding the communicative focal point of the document. The encoded author's choice of language was—by implication—meant to thrust the audience's attention in a specific direction. A multitude of significant personal designations, purpose clauses, and other phrases pertaining to the new status and behavior of the author and readers can be indicated (cf. Mouton 1987:82, 89). In this regard I found the discourse configuration of Ephesians by Lemmer (1988:appendix) interesting and helpful. Within the parameters of the study, I focus on appropriate *metaphors and traditions* in the document—particularly as *literary devices* aimed at *shifting* the recipients' minds toward a new identity awareness and corresponding ethos.[24]

Metaphors and traditions as metaphorical expressions are important elements of rhetorical persuasion in communication as a whole.[25] By identifying a document's metaphors and traditional material, one can to a large extent construct the implied author's view of the recipients' moral world, as well as the alternative s/he wished to communicate (cf. 1.6.1; Rousseau 1986:246; Meeks 1986a:7–8).[26]

.1 Metaphors

The Ephesians author uses a large number of potentially influential metaphors and traditions from his Old Testament, Judaistic and Hellenistic environment, in order to explain his experience and understanding of the crucified, resurrected and exalted Christ (cf. Du Toit 1984a:17). To my mind, the rich metaphorical language of the Ephesians document—together with the processes of reinterpretation and redescription underlying it—represents the essence of its *perspective*.

The following nominal and verb metaphors and metaphorical expressions occur in Ephesians, which basically constitute the narrative, the *story* of the document's discourse (cf. 4.2). At the same time the contrasting nature of these metaphors illustrates the unique identity and ethos of the Ephesians faith community (cf. Meeks 1993:21–23).[27]

---

[24] It has been argued in 1.6.1 that the *recurrence* of specific themes, metaphors, traditional material, and interpersonal roles, as well as their underlying coherence and reference, forms part of the researcher's task in determining the thrust of a document. The recurrence of specific words and themes may serve as a "foregrounding device," meant to focus the readers' attention on major aspects of the message.

[25] See 1.6.2.1–3 for a brief theory on metaphor.

[26] It has to be noted that the mere identification of metaphors and traditions in Ephesians already presumes a certain competence on *text-external* matters on the researcher's side, which brings such an endeavor into the sphere of a socio-historical reading of the text. It is almost impossible to tear the different dimensions fully apart, even for the sake of theoretical investigation.

[27] In this section metaphors or metaphorical utterances are written in italics.

Metaphors referring to God, Jesus Christ, and the Spirit

The title most frequently used for Jesus, is *Christ*. Apart from references to *Christ*, the expression *in Christ* occurs in 1:3, 4, 7, 9, 11, 12, 20; 2:6, 7, 10, 13; 3:6, 11, 21. Jesus is also confessed as the *peace* of both the author and audience (2:14). He is *Lord* (1:2, 3, 15, 17; 2:21; and 15 times in chapters 4–6), ruling with mighty *power* over all *rule and authority, power and dominion*, and *every title* (1:21; 3:10; 6:10, 12)—as *head* of his body, the church, and the cosmos (1:10, 22; 4:15; 5:23); as *savior* of the church (5:23); as the *Son of God* (4:13); as *king* (5:5).

The following metaphors seem to be intrinsically related to God's work in Jesus as *the Christ*: God is (re)described as *father* (1:2, 3, 17, 18; 4:6), *creator* and *manager/steward* (2:10, 15; cf. 1:10—εἰς οἰκονομίαν τοῦ πληρώματος τῶν καιρῶν), as *king* (5:5), and in terms of his *fullness* (1:23; 3:19) and ultimately great *power* (1:19, 21, 22; 3:7, 16, 18, 20). Christ is the foundation and motivation for the *election* of author and recipients (1:4), for their *adoption* as God's *children* (1:5), their *redemption* and *salvation* through his *blood, flesh,* the *cross* (1:7, 13, 14; 2:13, 15, 16), the *revelation* (1:9, 17, 18) of a *mystery* (1:9; 3:3, 4, 6, 9), and their receiving of an *inheritance* (1:14, 18; 3:6). In Christ they received the *Holy Spirit* (1:13, 17; 2:18, 22) as *a seal/stamp of ownership* (1:13), or *deposit* (1:14), as the *spirit of wisdom and revelation* (1:17, 18). The believers' victorious position is also described in relation to Christ, *under whose feet God placed all things* (1:22, 10): God *made them alive, and raised them up* with Christ (2:5, 6), and *seated them with Christ at God's right hand* (1:20; 2:6). In sum: The grace by which they have been saved, is a *gift* of God *in Christ Jesus* (2:8–10; 3: 7, 8).

Metaphors for the Church

Ephesians describes the community of believers as the *body of Christ* (1:23; 3:6; 4:12, 16, 25; 5:23, 30), his *fullness* (1:23), *one new man* (2:15; *sic*), a *family* of believers (3:15), *God's (holy) people, members of God's household* (2:19; 5:3), *heirs* of God's final redemption (1:14), and the *bride of Christ* (5:25–30). Built on the *foundation* of the apostles and prophets, with Christ as *chief cornerstone* (2:20), the whole *building rises* in him to become a *holy temple* (2:21). They are built together to become a *dwelling* in which God lives (2:22; 3:17). Likewise, the body is *built up/grows up* (4:12, 16, 20) toward the whole measure of the *fullness of Christ/God* (4:13, 10; 5:18). They are God's *workmanship* (God's creation: τό ποίημα αὐτοῦ—2:10), God's church (ἡ ἐκκλησία—1:22; 3:10, 21; 5:23, 24, 25, 27, 29, 32).

These metaphors reveal the positive and unique identity awareness of the Ephesians faith community. The qualifying genitive combinations "of God" and "of Christ" reveal the uniqueness of their self-understanding: They belonged to, and were determined by God, Christ and the Spirit (cf. Du Toit 1994:482–485).

Metaphors referring to their Former Status and Lifestyle

In sharp contrast to metaphors used for the church, the implied recipients' previous position is described in terms of the following metaphors: They were *dead* in their transgressions and sins (2:1, 5), under control of the *ruler of the kingdom of the air* (2:2), as *objects of wrath* (2:3). They were called *uncircumcized* by those who call themselves *the circumcision* (2:11), they were *excluded from citizenship in Israel and foreigners to the covenants of the promise* (2:12, 19). According to their former position, they were *darkened* in understanding, *separated* from the life of God, their hearts were *hardened* (4:18), and they were given over to every kind of *impurity* (4:19; 5:3).

However, they who were once *far away*, have been brought *near* (2:13), they have been made *heirs* together with Israel, *members* together of one body, and *sharers* together in the promise in Christ Jesus (3:6). This was made possible because Christ destroyed the *barrier, the dividing wall of hostility* (2:14, cf. 2:16), by abolishing the *law* with its commandments and regulations (2:15).

Metaphors referring to the New Ethos of the Church

In contrast to the implied recipients' previous ethos, they now have to *put off the old self and put on the new self* (4:22, 24), they who were once *darkness*, are now *light* (5:8, 11, 13, 14). They should not *grieve* the Holy Spirit of God (4:30). As *dearly loved children* they should be *imitators of God* (5:1), they should be *wise* instead of *unwise* (5:15), understand *the Lord's will* instead of being *foolish* (5:17), be *filled with the Spirit* instead of getting drunk on wine (5:18), they are to be *holy and blameless* in God's sight (1:4), *cleansed by the washing with water through the word* (5:26). In brief, they have to *live a life worthy of the calling they have received* (4:1), that is, they have to *live a life of love, just as Christ loved them and gave himself up for them as a fragrant offering and sacrifice to God* (5:2, 25). Their new behavior should be characterized by the image of God and Christ, that is, by *humility, gentleness, patience, peace, truth, righteousness, goodness, holiness, obedience, submission* (4:2, 3, 12, 21, 23, 24; 5:6, 9, 12, 21, 22, 26, 27). They have therefore to put on (Christ as) the *full armor of God* (6:10, 11; cf. 4:24), consisting of the *belt of truth* (6:14), the *breastplate of righteousness* (6:14), the *shield of faith* (6:16), and the *helmet of salvation* (6:17).

It is hardly possible *not* to be overwhelmed by the exuberant and powerful metaphorical language of Ephesians. It also strikes the reader that metaphorical references to *Christ* occur in every single pericope of the document.[28] The contrasting nature of these metaphors—referring to different positions of human

---

[28] The occurrence of the *in Christ* expression is relatively higher in the Ephesians epistle than in any of the other New Testament and specifically "Pauline" writings (Rienecker 1961:35; cf. Barth 1974a:69–71). For its use in the undisputed Pauline documents, see Wedderburn 1985.

identity and ethos *in and outside Christ*—gives a strong indication of the document's implied function. On a syntactic level the emphasis on Christ is implicitly meant to thrust the readers' attention toward the writing's orientation or point of view—their unique identity and ethos in relation to God in Jesus Christ (cf. Mouton 1987:164–175).

In the first main section, references to Christ focus on different aspects of *God's redemptive work in him.* All this had been accomplished *for the readers* (cf. 1:19, 22–23; 5:2). Their identification with Christ was thus meant to bring about a radical shift in their self-understanding. The implications of such a shift are explicated in the second main section, which is dominated by practical ethical imperatives with christological motivations. The faith community's new life is consistently measured by the quality of God's sacrificial love for them *in Christ.* They had to respond with "a life of love, *just as Christ loved them*" (5:2; cf. 1:7; 2:16; 5:25). The functioning of the body would thus depend on its members' vision of the identity and ethos of their head—the resurrected and exalted Lord Jesus Christ. This observation confirms the strong interdependence between the two main sections of the document.

The purpose of this section has been to *identify* or *catalogue* metaphorical expressions in Ephesians on the syntactic level. Together with other structural markers, these constitute the *thrust* or *direction* of the document. The difficult yet extremely important issue regarding the dynamic *reference* of these metaphors within the first century Mediterranean moral world of Ephesians (the semantic level), will briefly be discussed as part of a socio-historical reading of the text (2.2.1.1). The rhetorical strategies underlying the reinterpretation and appropriation of these metaphors—which represent the communicative power or transformative potential of the document (the dialectic level)—will be dealt with in 3.3.

.2 Traditional Material

When one compares the Ephesians text to contemporary inter- and extra-biblical texts, its high degree of intertextuality becomes obvious. Together with the numerous metaphors mentioned above, the author integrated several traditional motives (as extended metaphors) into the document to support his understanding of the Christian narrative. The purpose of this section is once again to *identify* probable traditional material in Ephesians. The dynamic *reference* and *orientation* of some of these traditions will be discussed in 2.2.1. The persuading strategy underlying the appropriation of these traditions will be dealt with in the next chapter (3.3).

Scholarship on Ephesians over the past three decades—especially Schlier 1957; Roberts 1963; 1991; Dahl 1965; Käsemann 1966; Sampley 1971; 1972; Barth 1974a; 1974b; 1984; Roetzel 1983; Lincoln 1982; 1990—has been dominated by a growing awareness that Ephesians probably has to be understood against the background of a mosaic of traditional materials.[29] Although quotations with introductory formulae are used only twice in Ephesians (4:8; 5:14), unmarked quotations—which probably stem from oral and written, hymnic and prose, liturgical and ethical, and perhaps mystical and proverbial traditions—abound in this document (cf. Barth 1984:3; Hendrix 1988).[30]

Since the influence of the *Religionsgeschichtliche Schule*[31]—which became notorious for its employment of sometimes remote parallels as direct influence between the New Testament and different traditional materials—the contribution of scholars such as Elisabeth Schüssler Fiorenza (1976; cf. Smith 1989:207–208) is to be welcomed. She—for instance—finds it methodologically inadequate and misleading to define the relationship between the Qumran and New Testament writings *only* by means of parallels and similarities pertaining to the history of religions. "What is necessary is to search for the concrete situation and theological motives that in each community led to the transference of cultic language" (Fiorenza 1976:161; cf. 2.2.1.3).

It is to the exploration of such a "concrete situation and theological motives" that the present *identification* of traditional material hopes to lead (cf. 2.2; 2.3). In the end, it would be of vital importance to find a responsible way by which the ongoing processes of identification, estrangement and reorientation underlying the documents of the New Testament, can be fully acknowledged and appreciated—that creative practice by which one group or individual can take over a concept from another and (sometimes considerably) reinterpret that concept for its own theological purposes (cf. Smith 1989:208; Meeks 1986a; 1986b; 1993).

---

[29] Barth (1984:3) introduces his article, *Traditions in Ephesians*, by saying that "Ephesians is a most rewarding, perhaps inexhaustible hunting ground for everyone eager to detect traditions whose forms and contents were used in the composition of a New Testament book." At the same time he concludes with a warning "that Ephesians should not be called an exponent of a coarse or subtle *Traditions-Prinzip*.... The guarantee of its truth and effectiveness lies neither in its antiquity, nor in its continuity.... but in the Holy Spirit (1:13–14; 4:30 etc.)" (Barth 1984:15). The author's use of these traditions can nevertheless shed important light on how he understood and substantiated the guidance of the Spirit in his situation.

[30] This viewpoint began to replace the well-known hypothesis of the American Baptist scholar Edgar J. Goodspeed which to a large extent dominated the interpretation of Ephesians since the early 1930s. Goodspeed maintained that the document was best understood as an introduction to or a covering letter for a newly formed collection of Paul's letters, which had been provoked by a reading of Acts. As such it was not considered as having much creativity and individuality of its own (Sampley 1972:101; Mitton 1981:7–11, 25–32; Rowston 1979:121–122; Lincoln 1990:lxxix; cf. Barth 1984:3).

[31] At the beginning of the twentieth century the *Religionsgeschichtliche Schule* studied the development of individual religions and religious systems, and the influence between them. With regard to the study of the New Testament, this approach endeavored to set the religious presuppositions of early Christianity in their contemporary Near Eastern and Greco-Roman contexts (cf. Marshall 1977:48–50; Deist 1990:116).

These processes revolve around the dynamic perspectives and intentions of the New Testament writings, and will be the focus of a socio-historical reading of Ephesians (2.2).

Probable Old Testament and Jewish traditions

The Ephesians author's probable usage of material from the Hebrew Bible or "Old Testament" has briefly been illustrated in 2.1.2.2.[32] When the Ephesians text is compared to its intertextual canonical context, it is significant that *enthronement psalms* were probably used in 1:20–22 (Ps. 110:1 in Eph. 1:20; and Ps. 8:6 in Eph. 1:22a) to strengthen the notion of Christ's ultimate authority and power (cf. n.8 of this chapter; Roberts 1991:53–55; Lincoln 1990:61–65; 1982:40–42). It has also been argued that the classic structure of the Jewish *berakah* prayers (the great benediction as a form of traditional Jewish worship), can almost inevitably be discerned as the basic form represented in chapters 1–3 (Roberts 1984a: 139; 1991:15, 31–34; Barth 1984:6–8; Johnson 1999:58–62, 414–416; Kirby 1968:83–138; Mouton 1987:118–121; Barkhuizen 1990:392; cf. 2 Cor. 1:3–4; 1 Pet. 1:3–5).[33]

The unique doxological formula εὐλογητὸς (Eph. 1:3) is another illustration of the Ephesians author's usage of Jewish traditional material. In the Hebrew Bible this expression consistently refers to "the God of Israel" (cf. Gen. 24:27; 1 Kings 8:15, 56; Pss. 111:1–10; 145:1, 2–21), but is profoundly reinterpreted in Ephesians as referring to "the God and Father of our Lord Jesus Christ" (cf. Roberts 1983:96–98; 1984a:139–140; Mouton 1987:126, 180).

Apart from individual instances of Old Testament motives in Ephesians, overall study of the particular use of Old Testament material and later Jewish traditions in this epistle—in contrast to Christian traditions, particularly from the Pauline writings—has remained a relatively neglected aspect.[34] Among possible

---

[32] It has to be borne in mind that the documents which would collectively become known as the canon of the *Old Testament*, were not yet known in that form during the time of writing of what is today known as the *New Testament*. Traditional material from the period of the Hebrew Bible was available to authors of the first century C.E. mainly in the form of oral traditions, but also in the loose form of written documents (cf. Du Toit 1989: 100–102).

[33] The Jewish *berakah* is a popular prayer form in the Old Testament (cf. Gn. 24:27; Pss. 103–106; 111; 117–118; 135–136; 138; 144; 145; 149; 150; Roberts 1991:32–33). It is adopted in Eph. and reinterpreted—with significant changes suitable for liturgical use—in terms of a christological content.

[34] Among the few scholars who have recently devoted some focused or extended discussion to this topic were Schlier (1957), Dahl (1965), Käsemann (1966), Sampley (1971; 1972), Barth (1974a:27–31; 1984), Lindemann (1975) and Lincoln (1982; 1990). The findings of these scholars on the use of Old Testament sources in Ephesians sometimes vary considerably. Sampley—for instance—makes fairly extensive claims about the Old Testament's role in Ephesians, while Lindemann considers its significance as fairly minimal.

reasons why the Old Testament has not attracted much scholarly attention with regard to the religious background of Ephesians, is the relatively small number of direct Old Testament citations in the document, as well as the focus that has often been directed toward either an early form of *Gnosticism* (cf. Schlier 1957:19 n.1; Dahl 1965; Käsemann 1966; Moore 1982), or cultic language from *Qumran* (cf. Sampley 1972:101–102). The widespread assumption that the author's audience was predominantly Greek or Hellenistic, has also frequently contributed to the notion that Jewish traditions are of no consequence in the interpretation of the document (Sampley 1972:102).

Lincoln (1982) deals in a comprehensive way with the difficult questions pertaining to the use of Old Testament material in Ephesians. He focuses on what he sees as the most significant "actual" quotations from the Old Testament in Ephesians, namely the use of Psalm 68:19 (LXX; Ps. 68:18 NIV) in Ephesians 4:7–13; Isaiah 57:19 (NIV) in Ephesians 2:17; Genesis 2:14 in Ephesians 5:31, 32; Exodus 20:12 in Ephesians 6:2, 3; Psalms 110:1 and 8:6 in Ephesians 1:20, 22; Zechariah 8:16 in Ephesians 4:25; Psalm 4:4 in Ephesians 4:26; Proverbs 23:31 in Ephesians 5:18; and Isaiah 11:4, 5; 52:7; 59:17 in Ephesians 6:14–17. In the first four instances mentioned above, Old Testament passages are not only cited, but also discussed and unfolded by hermeneutic comments (Barth 1984:3–4). Earlier, Lincoln (1973; 1981:135–168) also did useful research on the Hebrew Bible and Jewish concept of "the heavenlies" which often recurs in Ephesians. In several publications, Roberts has further explored the Old Testament background of "temple" and "building" imagery in the document (cf. Roberts 1963:18–19, 22–30; 1991:76–83; Marshall 1989).

To this can probably be added the artistic combination of elements from Ezekiel 16:1–8 and the Song of Songs in Ephesians 5:25–27, as well as allusions to Old Testament imagery like the "cornerstone" in 2:20 (cf. Is. 28:16), sacrificial imagery in 5:2 (cf. Ps. 40:6; Gn. 8:21; Ex. 29:18, 25, 41), and the general theological influence of essential Old Testament themes such as *election*, *salvation*, and *the people of God* (cf. Mouton 1987:102–154).

When shorter allusions are included, Barth (1984:4) indicates that "about 17 references to the Pentateuch (especially to Exodus and Deuteronomy), 30 to prophetic books (almost half of these to Deutero-Isaiah), 11 to the Psalms and 10 to the (partly apocryphal) Wisdom books can be counted." To these he adds references to "the Christ" (the Messiah), his sacrificial death, the temple, circumcision, and the use of terms such as peace, grace, fear, secret (or mystery), which—according to him—all presuppose a pre-given significance.

The large number of possible allusions to Old Testament motives in Ephesians would be significant structural markers pointing toward the document's thrust, perspective and strategy. This will be illustrated in 2.2.1.2 through analyzing the dynamic reference of material from Psalm 68:19 as adopted in Ephesians 4:8–13.

Possible Qumranic, Hellenistic, and early Christian Traditional Material

Apart from a large variety of Old Testament traditions, it is possible that the Ephesians author also employed motives from the cultic language of Qumran, the Hellenistic moral world, and early Christian material. The incidence of these traditions will be discussed together with their possible reference, as part of a socio-historical reading of the Ephesians document (2.2.1).

2.1.4 *CONCLUSIONS: THE PRAGMATIC FUNCTION OF A LINGUISTIC-LITERARY READING OF EPHESIANS*

The present section has mainly been concerned with the *identification* of linguistic-literary elements in the Ephesians text—those devices which would be conducive to a positive response from its audience. It revealed a coherent and symbiotic interrelatedness among the different main sections, pericopes, themes, metaphors and traditions found in the document. The *function* of these devices is briefly discussed here—under the rubrics of *literary effect* and *genre*—as part of a linguistic-literary reading of a text. Chapter three of the book will however be devoted to a more detailed discussion on the transformative potential of these devices as rhetorical strategies.

.1 Literary Effect

A linguistic reading of a text is ultimately concerned with the *intended literary effect* of the encoded author's choice of words, metaphors, traditions, expressions, and text type. Reading a text from a literary perspective has become a fine scientific art, and forms an important part of the ethics of interpretation (cf. Botha 1994b:63–120). A literary reading of Ephesians would be interested in questions such as: What kind of a shift or *moral effect* did the author wish to bring about through those words, metaphors, *et cetera*? What was the text supposed to *do* in the lives of its readers? And what strategy did the author employ to persuade the readers of the radical impact of his message?[35]

The thrust of Ephesians has been established as the author and readers' focus on *Christ* (especially the *power* of his resurrection and exaltation), and a corresponding attitude and behavior of praise-giving, which is closely related to virtues such as reverence, obedience, humility and submission. In the wider context of the epistle the power of Christ is paradoxically defined in terms of his sacrificial love and service *for them* (ὑπὲρ ἡμῶν; cf. 4:32; 5:2, 25, 29). The paradoxical nature of his power would also determine the nature of their communal identity and ethos (cf. 4:1–6).

The implied author and recipients' focus on Christ represents a continual re-

---

[35] These questions will be of significance in the construction of the document's rhetorical situation (2.3).

orientation in their self-understanding and ethos, and can be referred to as the *intended literary effect* of the document. This effect was implicitly intended to be brought about by the document's particular linguistic elements. I limit myself to the function of metaphors and traditional material as shifting devices in this process.

It has become clear that the nature of metaphorical expressions in Ephesians reflects a sharp contrast between the old and new status of the audience, as well as the corresponding behavior of those positions. These reinterpreted metaphors and traditions seem to highlight one major aspect: *The result of God's active presence in the community of believers.* Those who once were far away, have been brought near, and now live in God's presence. They are described as God's *household*—"a dwelling in which God lives by his Spirit" (2:19, 22). In 3:17 the author prays that God "may strengthen you with power through his Spirit in your inner being, so that Christ may dwell in your hearts through faith." In 5:18 (cf. 4:30) the series of socio-ethical admonitions is motivated by a *theological* motive concerning God's presence: "Do not get drunk on wine, which leads to debauchery. *Instead be filled with the Spirit*" (i.e. with God's presence—cf. 3:19b). The author's primary appeal to his audience is to recognize in their midst the mighty presence of God *in Christ* and *in the Spirit.* By implication this vision was meant to empower and encourage them to respond in accordance with Christ's example (4:1, 23, 24, 32; 5:1, 2, 23, 25, 29).

The nature of the *metaphors* further reveals the essentially *social* or *communal* character of the implied recipients' new life.[36] The emphasis on their life in God's presence is substantiated in terms of their relationship to one another as the *community* of faith: They are God's body, fullness, household, temple.... Evidently this is why the unity of the church is such an important issue for the author (4:1–16). The audience had to translate the reality and authenticity of God's presence into their practical way of living. It therefore makes sense that all the admonitions deal with the *communal* sphere of life: They had to speak truthfully, "for we are all members of one body" (4:25). They were not to be angry, not to steal, not to talk in an unwholesome way, but only in a manner that would be "helpful for building others up according to their needs" (4:29), forgiving (liberating) each other (4:32).[37]

---

[36]   In Eph. 1–3 there is a very close relation between the purpose to be holy and the believers' collective destiny to "praise God for his glorious grace" (1:6, 12, 14; cf. 3:21; 2:10). We have seen how chapters 4–6 describe this praise-giving in terms of the believers' ethos—always within the social context of the functioning of the church, marital and family relations, and the *social-ethical* relation between masters and slaves. The *social* implications of Christ's redemptive death and resurrection are so radical, that they are described in terms of the metaphorical contrast between life and death (Eph. 2:5, 6; cf. 1:19–21; 3:16, 20; 4:9, 10; 5:14–20; 6:10).

[37]   The implied ethos of the Ephesians document as *community* ethos has crucially important implications for its use in Christian ethics. This will be discussed further in

Likewise, the *traditions* adopted and reinterpreted by the Ephesians author were meant to refocus and reorientate the receivers in accordance with their new identity *in Christ*. Remembering their past history in the light of the Christ event, would redefine and redescribe their present reality in a radical way (cf. Ricoeur 1976:67; McFague 1982:46–48).

How the first historical readers physically responded to the intended pragmatic effect of the document, is not known from the text itself. All that we do know, is how the author envisaged them to respond. The essence of his challenge to them was to acknowledge Christ, and to live in accordance with his example. This necessarily implied a radically alternative way of thinking and behaving.

.2 Literary *Genre*

Apart from the shifting device of metaphor and reinterpreted traditions, the aspect of *genre* is briefly dealt with here. The nature and structure of a document, and how it is read, how its words and sentences are interpreted, will decisively be determined by what its literary *genre* or text type, and the specific rhetorical function of that *genre* is considered to be (cf. Smit 1987:22–24; Classen 1993:280). The function of the *genre* of a text is concerned with what an author intends to communicate (i.e. what *effect* s/he wants to facilitate), and *how* s/he implicitly brings that about by her/his specific choice and employment of that genre.

The broad *literary form* of the Ephesians document is that of an ordinary letter, that is, part of the Greco-Roman epistolary genre (cf. Du Toit 1984a:5–12; Stowers 1986; Johnson 1999:267–268; Schnackenburg 1991:21–24; Roberts 1991:14–15), however other forms like prayers and songs are also embedded within this primary *genre*.[38] Both the opening and ending of the document reflect the typical characteristics of the undisputed Pauline letters in the New Testament (Roberts 1984a:139; cf. Reed 1993:305–308). Charles Robbins (1986) has demonstrated that the opening blessing of Ephesians 1:3–14, for instance, is not so peculiar when analyzed in terms of classical composition and rhetoric, although not without its exceptions according to those conventions. Following Adolf Deissmann's earlier classification of Paul's letters (cf. Reed 1993:292; Furnish 1968:10), some scholars distinguish between the structure and function of occasional, everyday, non-literary *letters*—i.e. personal discourse not intended for the public—and formal, literary, artistic *epistles* intended for public reading. Although Ephesians may be considered to contain elements of both these genres, it seems to primarily characterize the features of an *epistle*—a formal writing of a

---

4.3.5.

[38] Another possible view on the Ephesians *genre* (namely Holland Hendrix's interpretation of the form and ethos of Ephesians as reinterpretation of Greek and Roman honorific schemes—1988) will be dealt with in 3.3.1, where it forms part of a discussion on the document's persuasive strategies or communicative power.

religious nature written by a person or persons in authority, either by the apostle Paul, one of his disciples or a group of disciples as authoritative person(s) (cf. Du Toit 1984a:20–21), and probably intended to be read aloud to the congregation(s) to which it was addressed (Johnson 1999:267–269; Du Toit 1984a:1–5, 18; cf. Deist 1990:84–85; Hendrix 1988).

The art of letter writing was a highly valued and developed form of communication in the cultural setting of the first century Mediterranean world. "Letters were composed for a variety of purposes. Perhaps the only universal function was that of making one who was absent, present: in a real sense, the letter was viewed as bearing the presence of the sender" (Johnson 1999:268; cf. 2.3; Stowers 1986: 15–47; Vorster 1992b:10–12). In the case of the Ephesians epistle, the sender advocated the presence of the one who authorized him (1:1; 3:1; 4:1). Among the great variety which marks the Pauline (and deutero-Pauline) correspondence, Ephesians is usually grouped with the so-called *captivity letters*, those written from prison (Philippians, Philemon, Colossians and 2 Timothy). Among these— and in contrast to Philemon and 1 and 2 Timothy which are personal letters, and Philippians and Colossians which are addressed to specific churches—Ephesians is the most public letter. It can perhaps best be understood as an encyclical, a kind of circular sent to different congregations in Asia Minor, the Roman province of Asia (Johnson 1999:268; Roberts 1991:13–14, 27–28). It will become clear that the literary style by which the document deals with the exigency of its implied readers, points toward its essentially *pastoral* character (cf. Du Toit 1984a:4), a description which would perhaps do more justice to the basic perspective of the document. As a general circular letter it would also be capable of addressing the needs of a wide variety of audiences.

On a personal level Ephesians contains various linguistic references to the author (who is identified as "Paul"—cf. 1:1; 3:1), and the circumstances of the recipients (cf. Roberts 1991:14). For the sake of the mainly rhetorical concern of the study, it is sufficient at this point to say that the Ephesians author identified his readers as believers in Christ (1:1, 15), and presumed that they would accept his authority as "an apostle of Christ Jesus" (1:1; 3:2–23) and therefore respond to his proclamation and appeal (4:1). This focused on the strengthening of their new identity in relation to Christ. In order to persuade them toward such a perspective, the author had to make use of a powerful *genre*, and emotionally the most appealing language at his disposal. For this purpose he utilized the communicative potential of a circular letter. The letter genre leaves room for a combination of different techniques such as narrative and argumentation—which could appeal to the emotional and cognitive senses of its readers.

To summarize, one can say that the ultimate purpose of a structural analysis of Ephesians is the exploration of its pragmatic function. This function was obviously communicated from within a specific *perspective*, which—in accordance with the communication theory outlined in chapter one—leads to a next dimension in textual communication, namely the construction of the moral world of the text, and the concrete socio-historical world within which the implied readers needed comfort and strength, and within which the language of the document made sense.

2.2 READING EPHESIANS FROM A SOCIO-HISTORICAL PERSPECTIVE: TOWARD UNDERSTANDING ITS MORAL WORLD

Various procedures involved in the socio-historical reading of an ancient canonized document have been discussed in 1.6.2. We have seen that a historical analysis focuses on the dynamic relation among the different elements within a text, its relation to other texts, as well as the socio-cultural and moral world to which it refers. It has also been argued that the historical nature of the New Testament writings presents itself in terms of at least three facets—a traditio-historical, socio-cultural, and historical-literary facet.

It is especially with regard to the historical dimension that the dynamic faith *perspective* of the New Testament authors has to be explored as the orientation from which they integrated, reinterpreted, and appropriated the language of their moral environment. This has in fact often been implicated during the linguistic-literary reading of the Ephesians epistle. The aim of the present section is to identify the complex processes of resocialization underlying the formation of the early Christian communities, and in particular the probable pragmatic function which the document could have played during those processes.

Research on the *purpose* of Ephesians has in the past mainly been situated in the historical situation of either the Asia Minor communities, or that of Paul, his disciple(s), or both. Because of the complexities and uncertainties surrounding introductory issues on the document (cf. 2.2.2), it will be argued that investigation into its purpose needs to be refocused and relocated in its so-called *rhetorical situation* (2.3). I shall therefore concentrate on text-internal information and the reader competence presumed by the Ephesians author.

This, however, does not mean that historical considerations are totally disregarded, but that the emphasis shifts toward a different approach to the text. "To address the problems of 'what the text says' and 'what the text meant' satisfactorily, the historical situation of the text needs to be bracketed and a more specific focus, allowing for the peculiarities of the textuality (for example its literariness and rhetoricity) of the material under investigation, deserves priority" (Botha 1994b:143; cf. Lincoln 1990:lxxiii–lxxxvii). A rhetorical reading of Ephesians therefore hopes to nuance and qualify the historical situation which is briefly discussed below.

As a document probably dating from the first century C.E., the epistle to the Ephesians is the product of a certain "historical situation" (cf. Botha 1994b:141; J. N. Vorster 1991:30–31) and "moral world" (Meeks 1986a, 1986b). The historical situation and moral world within which the origins of a text are embedded, are mainly constituted by the traditio-historical and socio-cultural facets of that document (cf. 1.6.2). The term "moral world" has been described as the collective moral network of a group or society—in terms of customs, rules, taboos, and traditions (cf. Meeks 1986b:11–17). The category "historical situation" needs some further explanation.[39]

Botha (1994b:141) gives the following working definition for "historical situation." It includes

> a very broad field of reference, encompassing the events, objects, persons, abstractions and relations (social, political, personal, cultural, ideological, ecological, or whatever) which constituted a situation which existed in the past in time and space and which could have been or was in actual fact experienced by human beings.

Two remarks will at least have to be made with regard to a possible construction of both the historical situation and moral world of Ephesians. Firstly, narration of history is never simply a reconstruction of so-called historical facts, but always a *construction* or *redescription* of reality by the particular narrator (Botha 1994b:141; Lategan 1985b:75–85).

Secondly, it is indeed very difficult even to construct a *probable* historical setting for the Ephesians epistle, simply because of the limited external information available from contemporary writings and other sources. One can therefore understand why scholars differ to such an extent with respect to its historical setting. The history of interpretation of Ephesians has, for example, been characterized by an ongoing debate on issues of authorship and address. Yet, despite the ambiguity of historical data, and the creation of more ambiguity in the process of describing these data, everything is not so vague that the text can be totally cut loose from the ideal of providing and clarifying historical information (cf. Botha 1994b:142). In so far as historical information can inform the rhetorical situation of Ephesians, such an endeavor will certainly be worth our while.

2.2.1 *THE TRADITIO-HISTORICAL FACET OF EPHESIANS*

The historical distinctness of the New Testament documents is first and foremost to be seen in the way in which their authors used written symbols—i.e. language as a cultural convention—to transmit and preserve the radically new message of

---

[39] As explained earlier, I shall only briefly deal with the "historical situation" of the Ephesians document, and rather concentrate on the "moral world," which is embedded in, determined by, closely related to, and dependent on its socio-historical situation. The "moral world" or "ethos" of a group is their collective morality, the moral or ethical side of their culture (Smit 1992:303; 1991b:52–55; Meeks 1986b:15; Birch & Rasmussen 1989:38), and is concerned with those—sometimes abstract, "invisible," yet very influential—virtues, values, and conscious or (more often) unconscious moral choices of a concrete society. Understanding the moral world of a New Testament document is therefore of crucial importance for the construction of its "rhetorical situation" (2.3) and, consequently, for its use in Christian ethos and ethics by later readers (cf. Smit 1991b:55–65).

Jesus Christ. This was done by means of a metaphorical process (in terms of what was known to the recipients), namely through a variety of metaphors and traditional material (e.g. Old Testament quotations, creeds about God, Jesus and the church, hymns, references to the Greco-Roman environment, etc.—cf. Meeks 1993:66–90, 211–213). In this way it may be said that the text of the New Testament itself has a history of development behind it—a traditio-historical facet (cf. Rousseau 1989a:16–22, 44–48; Furnish 1968:25–92). West (1991a:107–117; 1991b) and Lategan (1994b:127), among others, refer to this aspect as "the world behind the text" (cf. 1.6.2 n.36).

.1 The Dynamic Reference of Metaphors and Traditional Material

It has been argued in the previous chapter (1.6.2) that an author's use of metaphors and traditions provides valuable, though sometimes hazy "windows" through which the socio-cultural and moral world of a document can be explored (cf. Breytenbach 1990:257; Meeks 1986a:7–8).[40]

Although a detailed study of the referential and potentially life-changing power of Ephesians' metaphorical language would be more than interesting, it would exceed the limits of this book. The (standard) commentaries on the document (cf. 2.1.1) supply fascinating and rewarding material in this regard. I have explored elsewhere some aspects of the referential wealth of metaphors occurring in Ephesians 1:3–14 (Mouton 1987:123–140). This shows that the author utilized powerful and well-known images—everyday language from the Judaistic, Hellenistic, and Christian moral worlds—to explain his experience and understanding of the Christ event, as well as its (perhaps less known) implications.[41]

Of major concern for the purpose of this study is the creative process by which the author used those metaphors to redefine and redescribe his and the audience's experience and interpretation of their present reality. The characteristics of this process will be discussed in more detail in the following chapter. By way of example, *Christ*—as metaphor or parable for understanding God, and as model for the readers' new ethos—will be singled out as expression *par excellence* reflecting the potential persuasive or transformative power of the document.

Like the metaphors mentioned in 2.1.3, written and oral *traditions* formed an intrinsic part of the socio-cultural, and specifically the religious-historical

---

[40] In reality traditions function *as extended religious metaphors and symbols* (cf. 1.6.2.1–3). The study of metaphors and traditional material is thus very closely related, and meant to complement each other.

[41] For informative discussions on the content and experience of the self-disclosure of God according to metaphorical descriptions of the early Christians, especially with reference to God as Father/Parent, God as Steward/Householder, God as Monarch, and God and the cross, see Smit 1994e:47–53; Meeks 1993:45–47, 48–51, 61–65, 77–79, 84–88, 103–106, 150–173; McFague 1982:145–192.

environment of the historical author and first readers of Ephesians. I subsequently attend to the use of several traditional motives in the document, as illustration of the metaphorical processes of identification, estrangement, and reorientation underlying their interpretation. Although fragmentary, these traditions collectively contribute toward a tentative construction of the document's moral world. Their appropriation by the Ephesians author significantly illustrates how reinterpretation in actual fact takes place, and how the "proposed world" of the text is mediated to its readers.

.2 The Probable Use of Old Testament Traditions

According to Gary V. Smith (1975:181), the use of Old Testament sources by the New Testament writers "continues to be one of the most difficult areas in the field of hermeneutics." He argues that many of the problems of interpretation are due to an inability to understand the (mainly typological and allegorical) methods of exegesis used by the New Testament and other first century authors (cf. Van der Watt 1989:70–71). The wrestling to understand this and other aspects of the New Testament is, among other factors, connected with the dynamic and multi-dimensional nature of the New Testament documents themselves, and with the continuously changing interpretive contexts of researchers (cf. Lategan 1982).[42]

To explore the possible allusions to Old Testament and other motives in Ephesians (2.1.3.2) in detail, would once again take us beyond the scope and intention of this book. What would be of primary interest, however, is the (re)appropriation of these traditions as a persuading strategy in the fortification of the implied readers' identity awareness and character. This process will be the focus of the next chapter. Yet, in order to illustrate the difficulties involved in a traditio-historical reading of Ephesians, as well as the communication processes underlying it, a brief excursion on the creative reinterpretation of Psalm 68:19 (LXX) in Ephesians 4:7–13 is undertaken here.[43]

---

[42] *Inter alia* due to the rise of rationalism and the wide use of critical methods, a twenty-first century approach to the Scriptures would—for example—necessarily differ from that of the first century (cf. Smith 1975:187).

[43] For a detailed discussion on the possible influence of other Old Testament motives referred to above—particularly that of *kingship*, peace, the *Spirit of God*, and major elements from Jewish domestic codes—see Lincoln 1982:25–43; Barth 1984:3–8; and Sampley 1972:101–109.

[Excursion: The Functioning of Psalm 68:19 in Ephesians 4:7–13]

Being the only direct citation from the Old Testament, Eph. 4:8 has probably been the focus of attention as far as the role of Old Testament traditions in Ephesians is concerned. Of all possible usage of the Old Testament in Eph., 4:8–13 is the only citation which is accompanied by an introductory formula (διὸ λέγει), designating the authority of the quoted words (cf. Lincoln 1982:18).

After the author has stressed the maintaining of the unity of the Spirit in 4:1–6, he introduces the diversity of gifts to individuals by Christ in 4:7 (cf. Eph. 1:3). Both Lincoln (1982) and G. V. Smith (1975) discuss in detail—albeit with different emphases—how the author (probably) used and modified the Septuagint (LXX) and Masoretic text of Ps. 68: 19. The major change in Eph. 4:8 is ἔδωκεν δόματα τοῖς ἀνθρώποις ("he gave gifts to men") instead of ἔλαβες δόματα ἐν ἀνθρώπῳ ("you received gifts from men") in the LXX and Masoretic text. The New Testament writers sometimes quoted the Old Testament in a way that is described as a kind of *midrash-pesher*: The Old Testament text is interpreted (*pesher*) and supplied with commentary (*midrash*) in the citation itself. This procedure was not unusual in contemporary Jewish exegetical techniques (cf. Roberts 1991:117–119). It is also significant that in the *targum* on the Psalms (Aramaic translation) the concept of *receiving* has been changed to that of *giving* in the same way as in Eph. 4:8 (Smith 1975:182–183).

Lincoln (1982:18) considers the key concept in the argument of Eph. 4:7–13 to be that of *giving*, which probably sparked off the citation from Ps. 68:18 in v. 8, and which enabled the *midrash* of 4:9–10 to follow naturally. He argues that the "original force of Psalm 68:18 was in praise of Yahweh's deliverance of his people," while being pictured as triumphantly ascending Mount Zion (Lincoln 1982:19; cf. Ps. 68:8, 16, 17 NIV; Schmidt 1983:207–220). Barth (1984:5) remarks that the psalm "may have played a role in a Holy war and/or in an Enthronement Festival. Or it may have expressed the expectation of a glorious king" (cf. Old 1985). References to gifts being presented to and by Yahweh recur in the psalm (68:18, 29, 31, 35 NIV). It was probably these parallel (military) notions of "Yahweh's triumphant ascent" and the "gifts" which interested the Ephesians author. And although he does not explicitly develop the concept of "leading captive a host of prisoners," it certainly fits his earlier depiction of Christ's exaltation over the powers in 1:21–22.

Lincoln (1982:19) further describes the use of Ps. 68:19 in Eph. 4:7–13 as contrasting its use in rabbinical tradition where it could refer to an ascension to heaven by Moses: "Ps. 68:18 was linked with Moses going up Sinai and interpreted as an ascent to heaven to receive not only the Torah but also other heavenly secrets" (cf. Schmidt 1983:38–52). The "Moses mysticism" with which this interpretation is to be associated occurred quite frequently in the rabbinic writings. The Ephesians document however pictures Christ in a "new Moses typology" as a link with the heavenly world which exceeds all previous parallels (cf. Smith 1975:184). Lincoln (1982:20; cf. 1990:61–65; 1981) confirms this: "Christ has ascended far above all heavens in order to fill all things (cf. v.10). His gift is not the Torah but his grace (v.7) nor are his various special gifts heavenly secrets for the enlightenment of a few but people whose ministries will build up the whole body (vv.11 ff)." According to this view, the *function* of the reinterpreted citation is to underline the reality that it is the exalted Christ who is the *giver* of *gifts* and blessings to members of his body (cf. Lincoln 1982:18).

Apart from the connection between Psalm 68:19 and Ephesians, Psalm 68 has often been associated with *Pentecost* (cf. Smith 1975:184; Yates 1977:518). Besides celebrating the harvest, Pentecost was more and more coming to be regarded as "the feast which commemorated the law-giving at Sinai" (Lincoln 1982:20). Lincoln finds substantial reason to believe that this association existed from the middle of the second century B.C.E. "The Book of Jubilees, which is usually dated between 135 and 105 B.C., makes Pentecost or the Feast of the weeks the most important of the annual festivals in the Jewish liturgical year, associating it with the institution of the various covenants in Israel's history but above all with the covenant at Sinai" (Lincoln 1982:20; cf. Yates 1977:519). Together with other factors, the two central themes of the christological interpretation of the citation in Eph. 4—the exaltation of Christ and his distribution of gifts—might suggest *Pentecost* as the probable background to the psalm's use there (cf. various references to the Spirit in Eph.).

To understand the *midrash* following the Old Testament citation in Eph. 4:8–10, the interpretation of the "descent" mentioned in these verses is of vital importance. Textual criticism has shown that a variant reading exists in several manuscripts with reference to the temporal relation between the ascent and descent, which suggests that the sequence of the ascent and descent in the original could be taken either way (cf. Aland *et al.* 1983:671 n.9). Lincoln (1982:21–25) discusses three major possibilities, namely a descent into Hades with a possible reference to Christ's death, the descent of the pre-existent Christ in his incarnation, and the descent of the exalted Christ in the Spirit at Pentecost.

For several reasons the third possibility seems to be more attractive (cf. Yates 1977: 519). This interpretation maintains the central function of Christ's ascent and the giving of gifts in the passage. It seems natural that the author, having dealt with the Spirit's unifying work in the body (4:3–4), should include the vital connecting link between Christ's gift via his ascent, and the coming of the Spirit (cf. Lincoln 1982:23; 1 Cor. 12:4, 7, 8, 11, 13). Ps. 68 would thus no longer be viewed as a Jewish Pentecostal psalm concerning Moses, but as "a Christian Pentecostal psalm, celebrating the ascension of Christ and his subsequent descent at Pentecost to bestow spiritual gifts upon the church" (G. B. Caird, quoted by Lincoln 1982:23). See also the close association and interchange between Christ and the Spirit in Eph. 1:13 and 4:30; 3:16 and 17; 1:23 and 5:18.

For Lincoln (1982:24, 25) this interpretation of Eph. 4:8–10 fits the context, as well as the probable background and associations of the psalm citation, best. In sum, it may be said that—by means of a *pesher* quotation of Ps. 68:18/19 and a rabbinical type of *midrash* on the psalm citation—the Old Testament has been *reinterpreted christologically* in Eph. 4:8–10, as the author found scriptural support for his statement about Christ's various gifts of grace to his people.

Smith (1975:184–189), with reference to the contradictory and complex history of the interpretation of Ps. 68, also discusses different situations within which exegetes found the historical context and purpose of the psalm. Somewhat different from the views of Lincoln and Barth, he finds the scope of Ps. 68 much broader than that of a hymn of praise concerning a military victory (Smith 1975:185–186). For him, the psalm as a whole is a revelation of a *theophany* (vv. 1–2) which is attended by singing and praise to God who is in his holy habitation (v. 6). The praises of God are naturally associated with his presence and his acts. God went before his people (v. 7), appeared to them at Sinai (v. 8), and accompanied by heavenly hosts, ascended to the heights, led captive captives, received gifts among people, even from the rebellious, so that the He might dwell among them (v.

18). This is followed by a hymn of praise (v. 19).

According to Smith (1975:186), the specific occasion (*Sitz im Leben*) for the psalm is by far not obvious. He suggests its focal point being seen as *a song of praise* which was used after the Levites placed the ark in the inner sanctuary of Solomon's temple (II Chron. 5–6). The Levitical singers and musicians praised God (5:12), and suddenly "the glory of the Lord filled the house of God" (5:14).

Smith sees the captives whom God captured for Godself as the often rebellious *Israelites* (cf. Ps. 68:5–6, 18b). More specifically, says Smith, these refer to the Levites who were taken "as captives" from among the sons of Israel, and separated from them (Nm. 8:6, 14, 16, 18; 3:45; cf. Is. 66:20–21). The purpose for which the Levites were taken captive was "that they might be able to perform the service of the Lord" (8:11) and "to make atonement on behalf of the sons of Israel" (8:19), so that the Lord might dwell among them (cf. 2 Chr. 7:19–20). Smith finds further support for this notion in Numbers 8:19a, where the Levites are referred to as *gifts given* to Aaron (cf. 18:6—"to you they are *given* as a *gift* for the Lord"). He concludes by saying that the captives are the gifts, and both (captives and gifts) refer to the Levites (Smith 1975:187; cf. Kirby 1968:146).

In this way Smith illustrates the Ephesians author's imaginative use of *analogy* as an effective principle of teaching. "The principle of analogy is the heart of poetry and many prophetic utterances.... An analogy is used to express the new on the basis of the known. The power of poetry is often due to its use of illusive analogies which presuppose a psychological appreciation of the author's connotations" (Smith 1975:187–188).

Smith's exposition has indicated that the Ephesians author's quotation of Ps. 68:19 in Eph. 4:8–10 goes *beyond* the mere fact that the verbs "ascended" and "gave" occur in both verses. The psalm's use in this context is characterized by a process of dynamic and radical reinterpretation. Like the Levites were given privileges and responsibilities in order that God might dwell among the *Israelites*, God now equipped people with special gifts *in the body of Christ* (consisting of Jews and Gentiles *in Christ*), so that the body may be built up, and be prepared for works of service. Smith is convinced that the Ephesians author wanted his audience to understand that God had—throughout history—chosen special people as leaders of God's community of believers. Those leaders are responsible for teaching, preaching, etc.—for the one purpose of bringing humankind into a living relationship with God (Eph. 4:12, 13).

Smith rejects the idea that the Ephesians author availed himself of a *midrashic* exegesis or a *pesher* treatment of a textual deviation, or that he made use of the *targum* to Psalm 68:18/19. He rather sees it as

> a remoulding of the thought of Psalm 68:18 on the basis of the Scriptural commentary in Numbers 8:6–19; 18:6 which the Psalmist used.... Paul takes his quote from the Psalm which he interprets histor-ically, and applies analogously the thought of Numbers 8:19; 18:8 in the words of Psalm 68:18. Paul explains the gifts given to the church by using the example of the Levites who were given to Israel.... The understanding of this text and the hermeneutical methods used are securely linked to the controlling factor of a grammatical-historical understanding of the text quoted (Smith 1975:189).

Although Smith's suggestions with respect to the Levites sound interesting and attractive, a word of caution—regarding the presuppositions of a grammatical-historical approach[44]—may be appropriate here. While the idea of the Levites as "gifts" to the Lord is indeed present in Numbers 8, none of the Hebrew texts of that chapter indicates that the Levites are "taken captive." To conclude that the gifts of Ps. 68:19 refer to the Levites, seems to be risky. With reference to W. F. Albright and others, Smith (1975:184–187) connects the text of Ps. 68 with the time of David, and the dedication of the temple during the time of Solomon. In that case it is problematic to accept literary dependence on Numbers 8 or 18, since Numbers is considered nowadays to be mainly the result of the Priestly redaction, which would make it almost impossible to date these texts to the Solomonic period (cf. Deist 1990:201).

To conclude, it is clear that the christological interpretation of Ps. 68 in Eph. 4 leaves room for multiple hermeneutic choices, each with its own presuppositions. The Ephesians author probably used the psalm in his own creative way—and with his own rhetorical strategy in mind—without necessarily thinking of the concrete reference of the psalm, or a clear historical analogy. The immediate and broader context of Eph. 4:7–16 (pericope VIII) focuses on the ascended Christ's presence as a basic characteristic of the new life pictured in chapters 4–6. His ascension is explicitly associated with the purpose to fill *all things*, and specifically *his body*, with his presence (4:10–16; cf. 1:22–23). In order to prepare and guide the church toward the full experience of Christ's presence, God provided the gifts of apostles, prophets, evangelists, pastors and teachers (4:11). Almost all the themes of the prayer of Eph. 1:15–23 recur in this pericope: the calling of the readers, the role of the Spirit, Christ's ascension and gifts to every member of the body—for the sake of its unity.

The Ephesians author's reinterpretation of Ps. 68:19 thus serves as an important rhetorical strategy to emphasize Christ's exalted position, together with the gracious gifts to members of his body associated with that position. Their identification with him was meant to bring about a radical shift in their self-understanding and behavior.

Some Conclusions on the Role of the Old Testament in Ephesians

Motives from the Hebrew Bible undoubtedly played an important part in the Ephesians author's understanding of the Christian gospel. Generally, one may say that the remembrance of Jewish traditions in some or other way served to strengthen the Christian community's identity. By referring to the roots of their

---

[44] *Historical-grammatical exegesis* is an offshoot of the sixteenth century Reformation, and the precursor of historical criticism. Despite the rise of historical criticism, it still has its adherents today. The greatest contribution of historical-grammatical exegesis was its emphasis on the *original languages* and the *philological* and *stylistic* detail of a text. Some of its salient features are that it seeks to interpret the biblical texts *historically*, accepting them at face value as referring to actual events in history. In the process *literary genre* receives little attention. This approach further ignores the long history of origin which historical criticism attributed to these texts, and consider a text as a *unit*, written at a particular time by a particular author. The text is also expounded as if it had a *universal meaning* which, being God's word, is true for all times and all situations (Scheffler 1991:52–53, 64). These are some of the dangerous presuppositions which may underlie Smith's hermeneutics.

faith, the Ephesians author situates the story of the recipients within the larger narrative of Israel's history. However, in terms of actual use, the Old Testament is hardly ever quoted in Ephesians as a "proof text" (Barth 1984:6). To use Hays' terminology (1989): The "echoes of Scripture" in Ephesians are typical of the dynamic hermeneutical process represented by the document. As such it marks a dialectic "intertextual fusion that generates new meaning" (Hays 1989:26). Although Old Testament motives play more of a supportive than a formative role in the document, they seem every time to have been creatively selected and reinterpreted to serve the author's particular christological, ecclesiological and ethical purposes (Lincoln 1982:49–50; cf. Van der Watt 1989:71; Furnish 1968:42–44, 65–67). "In all cases.... exegetical techniques are subservient to a christological perspective whereby the OT texts are read in the light of the new situation which the writer believes God has brought about in Christ" (Lincoln 1982:45). The purpose of the Ephesians document is summarized by Lincoln (1982:49–50) as a reminder to Gentile Christians of their privileges and responsibilities as members of the body of Christ.[45] It is this distinctive setting which ultimately determines the cohesive and unifying function of the Old Testament and other traditions in Ephesians (cf. Lategan 1985b:92).

Whatever the historical situation of Ephesians' first readers, it is important to bear in mind that Christian believers of the first centuries C.E. worshipped God in manifold ways. The production of Christian literature was always

> related to the cultic and ethical service of God.... In oral and written form, narrative, legal, and moral traditions were kept alive, continued and adapted to meet contemporary needs.... The hermeneutics of Ephesians.... was traditional and suggests a Jewish-born author who knew of learned intra-mural Jewish discussions and cared for them. Only the results of the expositions proposed in Ephesians are different.... Sometimes the exegesis offered in Ephesians seems far removed from the intention of the author or final editor of the OT text in question. Still it is not certain whether modern scholarship is better

---

[45]   On the other hand, the occurrence of Old Testament references might also have been meant to strengthen the Jewish Christians' identity as being a continuation with their past. In his persuasively argued book, *Echoes of Scripture in the letters of Paul*, Hays (1989:ix) argues, with reference to the letter to the Romans, that Paul never allowed the new world of Christian interpretation completely to supersede the symbolic world of earlier Jewish texts, because he remained "passionately driven, to the end of his life, by the desire to demonstrate that God had not abandoned Israel." However the setting of Ephesians may differ from that of Romans, this seems to be a possibility to be kept in mind. Paul's readings of the Old Testament are generally carried out in the context of pastoral situations, and they are done in the service of forming communities of faithful disciples (Fowl & Jones 1991:24 n.14, with reference to Hays).

> equipped than ancient Jewish interpreters and the author of Ephesians
> to penetrate into the psyche of the OT writers and to reconstruct their
> real intention (Barth 1984:4–5).

To this Barth (1984:5) adds that Ephesians was rather part of, or the result of, an ongoing dialogue with contemporary Jewish exegesis than a matter of private interpretation.

A hasty and unnuanced solution concerning the relationship between the Old and New Testaments would be untenable. Except for the development of different motives within the Old Testament, late Jewish writings and the New Testament itself, the unique situation within the Asia Minor congregations—to which Eph. was addressed—might have called for such a radical reinterpretation of traditional material, that a "logical" explanation of the Ephesians author's exegetical and hermeneutic methods (without proper background information) would be forced and almost impossible. To interpret an ancient text which interprets in turn still more ancient texts, is indeed a daunting task. However, defining the dynamic *Christological perspective* or orientation of Ephesians, would to my mind relativize the frantic and often futile search for sources behind the text in order to understand the author's intention (cf. Mouton 1987:164–175).

While respecting the internal constraints of the Ephesians text, as well as the implied situation within which it was meant to function, later readers should at all times be open to be surprised by the dynamics within the text itself.

The excursion on the functioning of Psalm 68:19 in Ephesians 4:7–13 illustrated some of the complexities involved in the construction of a document's historical situation and moral world via reinterpreted traditional material. These complexities also characterize the interpretation of the use of other traditional material in Ephesians (cf. 2.2.1.3–.6 below). Understanding something of the nature and intention of an ancient text, therefore, necessarily involves a multi-dimensional approach (cf. 1.6).

.3 The Possible Use of Cultic Language from the Qumran Writings

The discovery of the Qumran scrolls in 1947 has led many exegetes to postulate that the New Testament authors, in using cultic language, were dependent on Qumran theology (cf. Mitton 1981:18–20). In this regard, the divergent contributions of two North American scholars, Elisabeth Schüssler Fiorenza (1976) and Derwood C. Smith (1989), are briefly discussed here.[46]

---

[46] Barth (1984:6–8) also indicates the probability of Ephesians allusions to Qumranite and apocalyptic literature (cf. Lohse 1976:55–73; 89–115), since the document has much to say about "angels, powers, the devil, the heritage of the saints, a mystery, the decisive role of knowledge, the priestly contrast between light and darkness." One significant difference between the two would, for example, be the Qumranite militance and the spiritual war described in Ephesians 6:10–18 (Barth 1984:6).

Ephesians 2:19–22 combines different terms, such as building, temple, cornerstone, and plantation of a people, which are found in similar combinations in the Qumran texts (Fiorenza 1976:173; cf. Smith 1989:211–216; Roberts 1963: 19–21). Smith (1989:211–212, 217) and Fiorenza (1976:164–168) identify 1 QS 5:5ff, 8:4ff, 9:3ff, and 4 Q Flor as the most important Qumran texts for the purpose of this investigation. These texts do not only contain the idea of the spiritual temple, but also a striking number of other concepts which occur in Ephesians 2 in connection with this metaphor. "The Qumran community is here referred to as the sanctuary in Aaron, the house of truth in Israel, the eternal plantation, the holy house for Israel, an assembly of supreme holiness for Aaron, the tested wall, the precious cornerstone, a most holy dwelling place for Aaron, a house of perfection and truth in Israel, the holy house for Aaron, the holy of holies, the house of the community, the house, the sanctuary, and a sanctuary of men" (Smith 1989:212).

Fiorenza (1976:162–164) discusses G. K. Klinzing's careful analysis of the usage of cultic terminology in different texts from Qumran and various writings of the New Testament. Klinzing defines the relationship between Qumran and the New Testament in terms of "*religionsgeschichtlich* parallel phenomena that share a common apocalyptic view of salvation history." He discerns two reasons for such a shared view. The cultic notions of temple, priest, and sacrifice were transferred to the community of Qumran and its activities because the temple and cultic institutions of Jerusalem had been desecrated and polluted by the Hasmonean priests in the second century B.C.E. (cf. Smith 1989:208). The loss of the Jerusalem temple cult forced the Qumran community to create a new possibility of worshipping God in cultic purity and of experiencing God's presence. Since the Torah did not allow them to build a new temple outside of Jerusalem, the *community* now became the place where God was worshipped in cultic purity and holiness. The sacrifices offered in the community in terms of "the new temple," consisted of a life lived in perfect obedience to the law. Ritually unclean persons were, therefore, not allowed to join the community (Fiorenza 1976:165; cf. Eph. 1:4; 5:27).[47]

Klinzing finds a second reason for the transference of cultic notions to the Qumran community, namely the belief that they *already* lived in the end-time, and that God was, therefore, already in their midst. The application of the "temple" notion to the community would thus be rooted in their apocalyptic understanding of salvation history. According to this view, the Qumran community's self-understanding as God's new eschatological temple formed the centre of its theological thinking (cf. Fiorenza 1976:163).

---

[47] "In all those texts of the Qumran writings which transfer the concept of temple to the community, the community has replaced the temple of Jerusalem and its cult. The social contexts of this theological understanding is the actual separation of the Qumran community from the Jerusalem cultic institutions. The function and goal of the community is to be a community of cultic purity" (Fiorenza 1976:166).

This is exactly where Klinzing finds a parallel with New Testament writings.[48] According to him, the comparison between the cultic language in the literature of the Qumran and Christian communities shows that the theological reinterpretation of cultic institutions in both types of literature was rooted in the mutual self-understanding of these communities as belonging to the endtime, and who thus already experienced eschatological salvation (cf. Fiorenza 1976:163).

Fiorenza finds this common theological denominator proposed by Klinzing insufficient to understand the theological differences between the two communities. "It is necessary in my opinion to search for the *social context* and the *theological interest and function* which the transference of cultic language upon the community had in Qumran and in the NT" (Fiorenza 1976:164; emphasis mine). By suggesting this shift in emphasis, she takes a meaningful step towards a rhetorical approach to these texts.

Unlike the Qumran texts, Fiorenza argues, the New Testament writings do not employ cultic language for the sake of *reform*, but to *redefine* cultic and religious reality. "Whereas the transference and re-interpretation of cultic language in Qumran underlined the basic validity of the Jerusalem cult and expressed the hope for its renewal, the transference and usage of cultic language in the NT presupposes the conviction that the eschatological salvation in Jesus Christ meant the end of the temple of Jerusalem and of all cultic institutions" (Fiorenza 1976: 168, cf. 170). Therefore Fiorenza considers the theological centre and interest of the transference of the notion of *temple* to the community of Ephesians 2:22 to be the affirmation of the indwelling of the Spirit in the community, that is, of the community's status as the temple of God.

Despite the similarities between Ephesians and the Qumran writings, Fiorenza views the concrete situation for the transference of cultic language to the Ephesians community as "not a sectarian separation but the early Christian missionary endeavor" (Fiorenza 1976:171). She considers the missionary context and interest of Ephesians 2:18–22 to be evident:

> The theological argument stresses that Jews and Gentiles are made in one new being in place of two. Through Jesus Christ the Jews and Gentiles have cultic access in one Spirit to the Father. The Gentiles are no longer strangers and foreigners who are excluded from the holy temple of the endtime. Instead they have become full members of the temple community. The theological motifs that Eph. 2:18–22 shares with Qumran theology are made to serve the opposite purpose to that in Qumran. The cultically unclean strangers and foreigners can now enter the temple community and become members of the household of God. They grow into a holy temple and are fellow citizens with the heavenly angels (Fiorenza 1976:173).

---

[48] Klinzing's contribution has to be seen against the background of the prior "history of religions" search for parallels and similarities among those early documents (cf. 2.1.3.2 n.31).

Fiorenza (1976:177) concludes by saying that the theological interest guiding the transference of cultic and specifically temple imagery to Ephesians 2:19–22, is "the affirmation of the self-identity of the Christian community as a special, religious, and holy group of people in a cultic-religious environment." By pointing out these differences in theological interest and purpose, she however *excludes* the possibility of any dependence of the Ephesians text on the Qumran writings (cf. Smith 1989:211, 215).

In his response to Fiorenza, Smith (1989:207) makes a strong claim in favor of the effect of the Qumran documents on the New Testament authors. He considers these writings as the "most significant source" for the understanding of the metaphorical concept of the spiritual temple in Ephesians. His conclusion is that dependency between two or more documents does not imply identity in the use of the language and concepts. The latter is obviously determined by the perspective, needs and purpose of the author. "Certainly the New Testament writers reinterpreted the Qumran temple language (as they did the language of the Old Testament) in the light of their understanding of the meaning and significance of Jesus Christ. To notice these differences, however, does not prove there is no dependence; *rather it sharpens what is new and distinctive in Christianity*" (Smith 1989:217; emphasis mine). Contrary to Fiorenza's one uniform "apologetic-missionary" motif of interpretation, Smith allows for creative and surprising possibilities of diverse interpretations in the adaptation of such rich language. "The use of the temple language in Ephesians is an excellent example of this creative process" (Smith 1989:217).

Referring to the *purpose* of the use of cultic language in Ephesians 2:11–22, Smith (1989:216) argues that the passage deals with "the problem of Gentiles who were first converted to an esoteric type of Judaism and then to Christianity. These 'Gentile-Jewish-Christians' are now claiming superiority over native Jews who have become Christians. The purpose of the text is to counter such claims. In either case, the problem concerns a situation within the congregation and is not directly related to a missionary-apologetic function. The purpose of the passage is not to convert Gentiles" (Smith 1989:216).

Smith (1989:211–216) is further convinced that the cluster of terms and ideas which Ephesians and Qumran have in common, demonstrates a developed tradition of temple symbolism behind the specific use of cultic language in Ephesians. He indicates that the combination of the terms *temple* and *house* does not occur anywhere in Jewish sources *except in the Qumran texts*, and believes that this cannot be incidental. The same would apply to the controlling image of the *temple* in Ephesians 2:19–22 in combination with the *building* concept. "The use of the image of building to refer to the Jerusalem temple or the heavenly temple occurs in Jewish sources in general, but again it is only at Qumran that this combination of language is used in a spiritual sense to refer to the people of God" (Smith 1989:214).

In conclusion, this section has emphasized the need that each document in the New Testament be looked at separately within its context, and against the background of its specific theological or rhetorical purpose. The reinterpretation of possible cultic language employed by the Qumran and early Christian communities saliently illustrates the processes of identity and ethical formation in these communities. These processes also broaden contemporary readers' view of the moral world in which those communities functioned, and which simultaneously lived in them. Accounting for such processes forms a vital part of the ethics of New Testament interpretation.

.4 The Use of Hellenistic Traditional Material in Ephesians

It is almost unthinkable that the Ephesians author would so strongly proclaim the unification of Jews and Gentiles mainly *to people of Gentile origin* without also considering Hellenistic traditions (cf. Furnish 1968:44–51).

Probably the most striking example of a christological reinterpretation of a Hellenistic symbol is the use of the title κύριος for Christ (cf. Du Plessis 1981: 120–125; Van Huyssteen 1987:26). This title was *inter alia* used for the head of a household, but also for the emperor as head of the Roman Empire. Paul (like the LXX) normally uses this title for Yahweh, especially when he quotes from the Old Testament (cf. Schmidt 1983:53–92). This could perhaps be a reason why Paul ended up in prison.

Late twentieth century readers can only but vaguely imagine the impact of the early Christians' witness—as interaction with their moral world—when they called their leader by the same name as the emperor. By dynamically reinterpreting this title from their christological perspective, those believers openly declared their ultimate loyalty and dedication to their *Lord* Jesus Christ (Eph. 1:2, 3 etc.; cf. Mouton 1987:34–46). This title would thus be one of the most important identity markers in the Ephesians text, indicating the implied readers' new self-understanding.

Although no tangible trace is found in Ephesians of the classical Greek and Roman gods (cf. Lohse 1976:222–226), the reference to God as "the Father, from whom the whole family in heaven and on earth derives its name" and the "kneeling" before him in 3:14–15, may be an allusion to the title Zeus πατήρ. The Stoic conception of the universe was that of one huge body ruled by its one head, Zeus (cf. Eph. 1:10, 22). In the Old Testament and in Judaism contemporary to Ephesians, kneeling is more often the attitude of prayer found among pagans (Barth 1984:15, 17).

The description of the new lifestyle in Ephesians 4–6 does not only essentially coincide with that of Old Testament and Jewish ideals for life, but also reminds of Persian, Greek and Roman paraenetical traditions (cf. Stagg 1979; Hendrix 1988; Meeks 1993:66–90, 211–213). These also have parallels in other New Testament writings, which may have been influenced by Jewish and Gentile moral teaching *before* Ephesians began to take them up and reshape them (cf. Barth 1984:12–13).

While earlier scholars from the *Religionsgeschichtliche Schule* such as Martin Dibelius (cf. Marshall 1977:50–51; Furnish 1968:81–92, 259–262) saw little more in the *Haustafel* ethics of Ephesians than a compromise with the culture of the Roman Empire (Barth 1984:18)[49], the ongoing exploration of the vocabulary and structure of the document has gradually lead to another conclusion (cf. Stagg 1979; Sampley 1971:17–30, 109–163)[50]. The primary difference between Ephesians and its extra-textual sources may be identified in terms of its perspective or intended literary effect, namely the recurring motivation offered for the new ethos of its readers, which is exclusively christological (4:25, 30, 32; 5:2, 23, 25, 29; 6:5, 6, 7). Barth aptly phrases this difference: "(W)hile in Stoicism Socrates is the radiant example of ethical conduct, in Ephesians Jesus Christ, through his sacrificial death, is the *sacrament* of ethics" (Barth 1984:19).[51]

---

[49] Other exponents of the History of Religions School, such as Bultmann, recognized the creative role of the early communities in the shaping of the Jesus tradition from the outset (Lategan 1989a:4; Furnish 1968:262–264).

[50] See Barth 1984:17–19 for possible references in Ephesians to Stoic *Haustafeln*, as well as Stoic legendary examples of virtues such as knowledge, love, and suffering.

[51] The Ephesians perspective on relations would *inter alia* challenge first and later readers' understanding of the role of wives, which is described in 5:21–33 in deceptively familiar *Haustafel* terminology, yet with a new qualification: "Wives, *submit* to your husbands *as to the Lord*" (cf. Sampley 1971:17–30). The intended rhetorical function of pericope XI, and of this particular command, would obviously have to be explored within the multi-dimensional macro-context of the document. According to the linguistic-literary analysis, the transformative potential of "submission" is located in its reference to the radical and paradoxical power of the cross, resurrection and exaltation of Christ (cf. pericope IV). This notion is developed with great care by Sally Purvis, a North American Christian ethicist, in her recent book, *The Power of the Cross* (1993). Contrary to many contemporary Christian feminists, she asserts that the cross does not glorify or justify suffering, death, or power as control, but represents a free and playful passion which is the healing, life-giving power of God (cf. also Johnson 1990:97–127). In terms of Ephesians, this means that the redefined virtue of submission belongs to the paradoxical status and ethos of *beloved, empowered servants in Christ* (5:21; 6:1, 5). It therefore embodies the wives' acknowledgment not only of *their own, and their husbands' new identity in Christ, but also of their mutual submission to him*. In fact, such an ethos would equally apply to *all* members of Christ's new community, whether they were Gentiles or Jews, wives or husbands, children or parents, slaves or masters (4:16; 5:21, 25, 29; 6:4, 9).

Although Fiorenza (1983:140–154) would probably agree in principle, she however finds the Ephesians author's use of patriarchal language restrictive, and even in conflict with the document's probable intention. Under the rubric "Ephesians and the Household Code" in her well-known *In Memory of Her* (1983:266–270), Fiorenza discusses interesting similarities between Eph. 2:11–22 (the unification of Gentile and Jewish Christians) and 5:21–33 (the marriage relationship between husband and wife). Her conclusion is that the relationship between Christ and the church—as paradigm for Christian marriage—

The term μυστήριον also plays a significant role in Ephesians (cf. Schlier 1957:60–66, 148–151; Ryrie 1966). Although this is a well-known term in contemporary *mystery-religions* and *-cults* (cf. Lohse 1976:232–243), terms like fullness, mystery, body, and spirit receive an entirely different sense in Ephesians. "In this letter, '*mysterion*' is neither a fixed divine plan, nor a blind fate, nor a secret communication.... nor a magical performance or ritual.... The substance of the revealed secret is the eternal election, carried out in the historical co-option and insertion of Gentiles into full membership in the one people of God.... Once, in Col. 1.26–27, the term *mysterion* is defined most briefly and precisely: the mystery.... that is Christ among you (Gentiles)" (Barth 1984:19; cf. Mouton 1987: 136–137).

Assuming that Ephesians was addressed to the Asia Minor Christian congregations, the absence of any hint to the cult of the great Artemis of Ephesus, the goddess of blessing and fertility, and widely honored in the Roman provinces, would come as a surprise (Barth 1984:15, 16). Like other unmentioned cultural matters influencing the New Testament writings, also this aspect might have formed a tacit background to the Ephesians epistle, though not specifically mentioned—"*because they were so commonplace and well known that they did not need elaboration*" (Rogers 1979:250). It was simply the moral world in which

---

"reinforces the cultural-patriarchal pattern of subordination, insofar as the relationship between Christ and the church clearly is not a relationship between equals, since the church-bride is totally dependent and subject to her head or bridegroom.... The instruction to the wives thus clearly reinforces the patriarchal marriage pattern and justifies it christologically." Although patriarchal domination is radically questioned in the exhortation to the husband, with reference to the love relationship of Christ to the church, Fiorenza doubts whether "this christological modification of the husband's patriarchal position and duties does.... have the power, theologically, to transform the patriarchal pattern of the household code, even though this might have been the intention of the author. Instead, Ephesians christologically cements the inferior position of the wife in the marriage relationship.... *(T)he cultural-social structures of domination are theologized and thereby reinforced.*"

This interpretation emphasizes the very fine line between the Christian perspective on power as sacrificial love, service and humility, and the naive approval of power as androcentric control, and particularly the language used to express these attitudes. On the one hand, I am convinced that the transformative potential of the Ephesians document—including the ethos of the redescribed household code—lies in its reference to a new unified humanity *in Christ*. To what extent, on the other hand, such a vision indeed impacted on the socio-political status of women, and the "honorable" virtue of submission within a predominantly patriarchal society, becomes a next question, which has to be investigated against the socio-cultural history during and since the document's writing (cf. Domeris 1993; Kittredge 1998:151–174). To use the Ephesians household code in constructing or evaluating a Christian feminist or womanist ethics, consequently asks for a double ethics of interpretation (Fiorenza 1988). It will be argued in chapter four that this primarily means to respond to the revelation of God in new situations, and not to a creed or code for behaviour (cf. Carmody 1992:147–168; Ackermann 1992a; 1993).

they lived consciously or unconsciously, and which lived in them.

Likewise Rogers (1979), inspired by Markus Barth's extensive two-volume commentary on Ephesians (1974a; 1974b), argues that "the wild, drunken practices connected with the worship of Dionysus or Bacchus, the god of wine, form the general cultural background for Paul's two commands in Ephesians 5:18," as well as for the general commands against sexual sins. He investigates the widespread character of the cult of Dionysus which was well established throughout Asia Minor during the New Testament period (Rogers 1979:250–253). Common features of the festivals celebrated in honor of Dionysus were the emphasis on fertility and sex, as well as

> the wild, frenzied dancing and uncontrolled ravings, in connection with wine drinking and the music of flutes, cymbals, drums, or tambourines.... The purpose of the intoxication by wine and also the chewing of ivy, as well as the eating of raw animal flesh, was to have Dionysus enter the body of the worshiper and fill him (*sic*) with 'enthusiasm' or the spirit of the god. Dionysus was to possess and control such ones so that they were united with him and partook of his strength, wisdom, and abilities. This resulted in the person doing the will of the deity.... and having the ability to speak inspired prophecy (Rogers 1979:254–255).

Rogers further explicates the consequences of viewing the Dionysian cult as background to Ephesians 5:18. "The grammatical parallels and contrasts reveal a close connection between the two commands. 'Do not be drunk' is a present negative imperative prohibiting a manner of life, while the command 'be filled' is a positive present imperative calling for a continued consistent manner of life.... The wisdom and power, the intellectual and artistic ability, the freedom from the drudgery of life, as well as a prophetic message from the true God, are not to be found in the Dionysian drunkenness, but in the control of the Spirit of the true God" (Rogers 1979:256–257).

Rogers also finds it significant that in the section following Ephesians 5:18 the author deals with matters which played a vital part in the Dionysian worship, namely singing (v. 19), giving of thanks (v. 20), as well as marriage and the responsibilities of each partner (vv. 21–33). All these are strong indications for him that the Dionysian worship could well have formed the background against which the author gave his general instructions, and against which he wanted to stress his message that "spiritual strength, wisdom, and divine help to live a godly life are obtained by being controlled by the Spirit of God, not by any other means" (Rogers 1979:257; cf. Arnold 1989).

This argument, I believe, may serve as motivation to explore the possibility of the Dionysian background to other sections in Ephesians as well—particularly the concepts of salvation and holiness, and the paraenetical section in 4:17–5:20. The language of passages such as 3:16, 20; 6:10 (power of God); 4:22–24; 6:11, 13 (putting off/on the old/new self in accordance with the will of God); 5:3–5,

10–12 (immorality contrasted with thanks to God); and possibly 1:21; 2:2; 3:10; 6:11–12 (principalities and powers), also reminds of the practices of the Dionysian cult, albeit from a radically different perspective.

In a challenging article, Calvin J. Roetzel (1983) investigates the background of the—what may sound like a—very anti-Jewish statement in Ephesians 2:15a. He argues in favor of a strong influence of Hellenistic Judaism on the Ephesians author (particularly via the writings of Philo):

> His adoption of the hymn of cosmic reconciliation seen in 2 14–16(17) suggests an openness to the Hellenistic worldview that is significant. A sampling of the vocabulary of Eph. offers further evidence of Hellenistic influence on the author of Eph. The Hellenistic background of such expressions as 'strangers and exiles' (ξένοι καὶ πάροικοι, 2 19), 'fellow citizens' (συμπολῖται, 2 19), 'fullness of God' (πλήρωμα τοῦ θεοῦ, 3 19), and 'unto a perfect man' (εἰς ἄνδρα τέλειον, 4 13) is unmistakable (Roetzel 1983:86).

In the context of pericope IV (Eph. 1:22–2:22), the author is probably suggesting in 2:15a that—with the coming of Jesus Christ—the old division between heavenly and earthly human beings has been overcome, and that the commandments which belong to the "former way of life" or the "old self" have become obsolete (cf. 4:22, 24, 13, 14, 16). "And if that be the case, this new existence, since it transcends the commandments, would serve as the basis for the unity of Jewish and gentile Christians" (Roetzel 1983:88). Roetzel concludes that the understanding of this verse might provide the key toward understanding the purpose of Ephesians as a whole.

In this context, the early Christians' adaptation and reinterpretation of the Greek *household*, as the microcosm and basic moral unit of the πόλις, needs to be mentioned briefly. Within the household relationships of power, protection, dependence, submission, honor, duty, and friendship were formed and governed. The household became an extremely important shelter and the fundamental unit for early Christian groups in the Greco-Roman cities, which explains why the subject of "household management" figures so frequently in their hortatory literature (cf. Eph. 5:21–6:9; Col. 3:18–4:1; Meeks 1993:37–51, 77–79, 101–110). The Mediterranean household was especially well-known for its *hospitality* (protection and care for legal foreigners, strangers and aliens)—a virtue which also became highly prized and cultivated by the early Christian communities. In Ephesians 2:19 the "household of God" (with its reinterpreted structure—cf. chapters 4–6) functions as a hallmark for the implied recipients' new identity.

It has further been suggested (*inter alia* by Bultmann, the early Käsemann and Schlier, who all belonged to the *Religionsgeschichtliche Schule*) that Ephesians was thoroughly influenced by *Gnosticism*, and particularly "the Myth of the Redeemed Redeemer," which is considered to be the heart of the Iranian "Mystery of Redemption" (Barth 1984:20; cf. Schlier 1957:60–74; Lohse 1976: 253–277; Marshall 1977:48–51; Mitton 1981:20–24; Moore 1982; Hartin 1986:

233). Barth however is convinced that the interpretation of Pauline literature—especially that of Rm., I Cor., and Eph. with its emphasis on the knowledge of God—has influenced the development and substance of second century and later Gnosticism (Barth 1984:20–21).

This cursory discussion on the possible use of Hellenistic material in the Ephesians document confirms the multi-faceted picture of the moral world, and the fascinating processes of reorientation which it represents.

.5 The Use of Christian Traditional Material in Ephesians

Among the many elements of early Jewish-Christian and Christian worship which are found in Ephesians—such as prayer, Scripture reading, biblical exposition or preaching, hymns or the public praise of God, confessions, with different possible *Sitze im Leben*—the elements of hymnic and paraenetic character stand out (cf. Barth 1984:8–12; Merklein 1973a; 1973b; Sanders 1965). Although constructions of the moral worlds of New Testament documents (centuries after their writing) are extremely difficult, Barth (1984:12) is convinced that the epistle to the Ephesians, with its wealth of recreated hymns and confessions, can be fully appreciated "without blind confidence in certain methods of reconstructing their origins."

In his article, *Hymnic elements in Ephesians 1–3*, Jack T. Sanders (1965: 214–232) identifies three passages (1:20–23; 2:4–10; 14–18) which probably refer to early Christian hymns or fragments thereof.[52] Sanders further argues that it is likely that the entire section of 1:20–2:7 gives evidence of a hymnic alteration and expansion of Colossians 2:10–13. He shows that the Ephesians author used hymnic and liturgical material from Colossians to create his own hymn-*like* passages, thereby supporting his understanding of Christianity.

It is striking that the Ephesians author often used the traditional material of a *song* to illustrate his point (cf. 1:3–14).[53] Through the ages songs communicated

---

[52] See Helmut Merklein's criticism (1973:86–88) on Sanders' exposition of Eph. 2:14–18.

[53] This strategy is emphasized when the tradition of a song (possibly of Hellenistic origin) is applied to awaken those who sleep as dead people *outside Christ* (5:14). In 5:19, 20 the author inspires his audience to "(s)peak to one another with psalms, hymns and spiritual songs. Sing and make music in your heart to the Lord, always giving thanks to God the Father for everything, in the name of our Lord Jesus Christ" (see also Paul's experience in Acts 16:25; Phlp. 1:12). "In the light of the liturgical character of the opening chapters, the instruction of the author in 5:19 gains in significance" (Barkhuizen 1990: 392).

The content of the song in 5:14, and particularly the occurrence of the verbs ἐγείρω and ἀνίστημι (cf. ἵστημι and ἀνίστημι in 6:11, 13, 14), is—in the broad semantic context of Eph—most probably to be understood in the light of the pivotal occurrence of ἐγείρω and συνεγείρω in 1:20 and 2:6 respectively. Expressions similar to ἐκ τῶν νεκρῶν in 5:14 occur 1:20 and 2:1, 5.

humankind's most intimate hopes, dreams, desires, needs and fears. The praise-giving to which the author encouraged his recipients, was not only meant to be to God's glory (1:6, 12, 14), but also to strengthen and substantiate their identity awareness and new lifestyle in Christ (4:1–6:20).

Within the New Testament, Colossians is quite widely accepted to be the most likely immediate literary background for the Ephesians epistle (Sanders 1965:227; Polhill 1973:449; Mitton 1981:11–13; Roetzel 1983:85–86). Without going into any detail on this difficult relationship, I agree with Polhill (1973:449–450) and Fiorenza (1976) that mere literary resemblance will not fully settle the question. Decisive factors like liturgical background, the purpose and occasion of the epistle, and its theological *Umwelt* need to be taken into account.[54] This confirms that considering the use of traditional material in any New Testament document necessarily forms part of its ethical reading (cf. 1.6.2, 1.6.3).

Many scholars consider the reference to the strategic verse 4:30—"the Holy Spirit of God, with whom you were sealed for the day of redemption"—as a reference to baptismal terminology (Schlier 1957:227–228; Kirby 1968:150–161; Smit 1983b:173), although there is not much agreement on what the metaphor of sealing exactly means (cf. Smit 1983b:173–176). Despite this strong trend, Barth (1974a:135–144; 1974b:547–550) is convinced that Ephesians 4:30 ought not to be understood as a reference to baptism.

Of importance however is that the thrust of chapters 4–6 as a whole points toward the kind of teaching or instructions that would naturally form an essential part of a baptismal service—baptism being the initiation ceremony representing the rebirth, resocialization or transformation of an individual or group into a new status and ethos (cf. Dahl 1976:11–29; Meeks 1993:34, 67, 92–96). The possible strategic reference to Christ as *sacrament*, symbol, metaphor or parable for the revelation of God (cf. Barth 1984:19; McFague 1982:48–54), will be dealt with in 3.3.3. Within the context of identity formation, reference to baptism as a collective experience within a family or congregation would necessarily be of profound significance.

.6 Conclusions: The Use of Moral Traditions in Ephesians

The discussion on possibilities surrounding the dynamic reinterpretation of metaphors and traditional material in Ephesians has hopefully created some appreciation for the unique "moral world" of the Ephesians document.[55] An endless, kaleidoscopic picture of Old Testament, Judaistic, Hellenistic and

---

[54] In a previous study I investigated possible resemblances or parallel motives between Ephesians and other New Testament writings (Mouton 1987:108–122; cf. Mitton 1981:13–18). This, for me, confirmed the strong intertextual character of the document, as well as the broad moral world it shared with contemporary communities of the Christian faith.

[55] Cf. De Villiers 1980 for a discussion of the uniqueness of Christian morality.

Christian motives unfolds the deeper one delves.

However, the base on which this investigation has proceeded is not broad enough to permit any final conclusion about the author's ideological and moral roots. With respect to this larger issue, the present narrower inquiry allows only for a modest conclusion with respect to the Ephesians author's pluralistic and complex background. All the examples mentioned above nevertheless consolidate the creative *processes* of identification, alienation, and reorientation which are typical of the integration of familiar sources in the light of new experiences. For the implied author and recipients of the ancient epistle to the Ephesians, these essentially revolve around the document's christological and communal orientation.

2.2.2   *THE SOCIO-CULTURAL FACET OF EPHESIANS*

The historical distinctness of the New Testament is also clear from the fact that it was written against the background of a world and reality of almost two thousand years ago—a world that differs in so many ways from contemporary contexts. The individual and collective characteristics and needs of specific historical persons and groups would form an integral part of this aspect, which reflects the socio-cultural facet of a text. This necessarily leads to an inquiry into introductory issues of the document concerned.

According to Barth (1974a:10–12), Black (1981), Roberts (1984a:125–137; 1991:13; 1993b), Smith (1975), Rogers (1979) and Rienecker (1961:20), the Ephesians epistle was written by *the apostle Paul*, probably while he was in captivity—either in *Caesarea* (round about 58/59 AD—Reicke 1970:277–2282) or *Rome* (59–61 AD—Lategan 1983:216; cf. Guthrie 1977:515). Johnson (1999: 407–412) argues that Ephesians could have been written by *Paul and his fellow workers*.[56] Many scholars—such as Furnish 1968:11; Sampley 1972:102; Howard 1979; Mitton 1981:2–11; Schnackenburg 1991:24–29; Lincoln 1990:xxxv–lxxiii; Meeks 1993:34—however, consider Ephesians to be *deutero-Pauline*, written by a (Jewish) student/follower (e.g. the author of Luke-Acts—Rowston 1979) or a

---

[56] Bo Reicke (1970:277–282) bases his position on an interesting discussion of the political situation in Caesarea at the time of Paul's imprisonment there, which he dates from 58–60 C.E.: "Politically oriented concepts in Ephesians suggest that Caesarea fits best as the background for his letter (whether it was written by Paul or by a disciple). While in Jerusalem in A.D. 58, Paul himself experienced the animosity which the majority of the people there had for Greeks. The occasion was the claim that he had brought Greeks into the sanctuary (Acts 21:28f). On the wall between the court of the Gentiles and the court of the women, where the so-called Holy Place started, there were inscriptions containing restrictions which encouraged the division of mankind (*sic*) into Gentiles and Jews. A transgression of this line of demarcation by the uncircumcized meant the death penalty for the transgressor" (Reicke 1970:281). For an in-depth discussion of the "broken wall" imagery in Eph., see Barth 1959a and 1959b.

school of students who/which was well familiar with the Pauline documents and Paul's thinking. These scholars date the epistle between 80–100 C.E., which could change the historical situation of the text, and the specific reinterpretation of metaphors and traditions rather dramatically.[57] Among other introductory issues regarding Ephesians, the aspect of its historical situation and setting seems to remain enigmatic to a large extent. This complicates matters for later readers, because the choices which we make on the document's authorship and historical setting will have direct bearing on our understanding of its theological purpose and communicative spearhead (cf. Roberts 1993b, with reference to the positions of Arnold and Schnackenburg).[58]

As far as the addressees are concerned, very little is known from the text itself, except that they were "saints.... the faithful in Christ Jesus" (1:1; cf. 1:15). Lincoln (1990:lxxvi) describes the Ephesians picture of its readers and their assumed competence as follows:

> The implied readers are assumed to know of Paul (1:1; 3:1; 6:21, 22), of his special proclamation of the gospel and ministry to the Gentiles (3:2, 3, 7, 8; 6:19), and of his suffering and imprisonment (3:13; 4:1; 6: 20). The readers envisaged by the author, although they are Gentiles, are also assumed to know the Jewish Scriptures, to accept their autho-rity, to be conversant with the author's method of interpreting them and persuaded by the results of that interpretation (cf. 2:17; 4:8–10; 5:31, 32; 6:2, 3). In addition they accept the authority of Christian liturgical traditions (e.g., 5:14) and have received Christian instruction which included paraenetical material (cf. 4:20–24).

---

[57] A significant question with regard to the date of Ephesians is whether it was written before or after the Jewish War of 60–66 C.E. (cf. references to the broken wall and the building of a "spiritual" house of God, consisting of former Jews and Gentiles—Eph. 2:14, 20–22; Barth 1974a:12; 1984:7). If the underlying tension between Jewish and Gentile Christians in Ephesians is more or less the same as the tension underlying the book of Acts (cf. Acts 8–28; Reicke 1970; Du Plessis 1983; Ogletree 1983:152–159; Meeks 1993:43–45; Thurston 1993), we could infer that the epistle refers to a situation where it was not obvious to Jewish Christians that non-Jews could become Christians without ac-complishing the traditional Jewish religious laws and regulations. During that time it was indeed a struggle for the Jews to break through to the Gentiles (cf. previous note), and to accept that God could save them by faith in Christ alone. The thrust of the document would make more sense against the background of struggle for identity among Jewish and Gentile Christians, especially during the period after the War (70–85) when the tension between Jews and (mainly Gentile) Christians gradually led to a total break between the synagogue and Christian communities. In the light of such a possibility, and the crumbling of the *pax Romana*, Verhey (1984a:123–126) argues that the Ephesians author announces the good news and the requirements of the *pax Dei*.

[58] In this respect Johnson (1999:410) rightfully remarks: "The real challenge to Ephesian authenticity comes—or ought to come—from its distinctive theological perspect-ive."

Because of the impersonal style of the letter, as well as the absence of the destination "in Ephesus" (1:1) in the oldest Greek manuscripts (Chester Beatty papyrus P46, *Codex Sinaiticus*, and *Codex Vaticanus*), it seems probable—however argued against by Black 1981—that the epistle functioned as a circular letter to different congregations in the Judaistic-Hellenistic environment of first century Asia Minor (cf. Santer 1969; Roberts 1984a:138–139, 119; 1991:13–14; Johnson 1999:410–412; Lincoln 1990:lxxiii–lxxxvii).[59] Passages such as 2:11–22; 3:1–13; 4:17–24; 5:6–20 give the impression that these congregations predominantly consisted of Hellenistic converts (cf. Wessels 1990a:50–56; Thurston 1993:73).[60]

The probability that Ephesians functioned as a circular letter does not mean that the author did not have a specific audience with concrete needs in mind. It is difficult and frustrating, however, to gain access to historical information of such a group or groups.[61] Virtually all that we do have, is the document's picture of the implied readers, whether that picture corresponds with a physical audience or not

---

[59] The particular Chester Beatty papyrus dates from about 200 C.E., while the two codices are both from the fourth century (Aland *et al.* 1983:xiv–xv).

[60] Because this study is mainly concerned with rhetorical devices in the Ephesians text, I do not further elaborate on introductory issues concerning its historical author and addressees. For the debate on these issues, and especially the issue of Pauline or deutero-Pauline authorship, see Schlier 1957:22–28; Barth 1974a:10–12; Roberts 1984a:17–124; 1993b; Lincoln 1990:lix–lxxiii; Schnackenburg 1991:24–29.

[61] In order to construct the best possible picture of the historical situation and moral world of Ephesians, one would at least have to explore the socio-cultural circumstances in Asia Minor during the (second half of the) first century C.E., and in particular the *sociological role and status* of Greeks, Romans, Jews, Jewish and Gentile Christians, women, children and slaves, and the relations among the different groups (cf. Malherbe 1986; Meeks 1975; 1982; 1986a; 1986b; 1990; 1993; Stowers 1984; Stambaugh & Balch 1986; Theissen 1987; Roetzel 1987; Kee 1989; Moxnes 1989; Balch, Ferguson & Meeks 1990; Perdue 1990; Kraemer 1992; Keener 1992; Van der Horst 1992; Gottwald 1993; Kittredge 1998). Although the position and roles of these groups may have differed in time and place, one can to a large extent assume that all, after joining the Christian movement, had to redefine their identity during the time of transition—a time in which old certainties and structures were being questioned. Ephesians seems to have functioned within this transitional, liminal context, and with the intention of supplying people with new direction. Regarding the socio-cultural embeddedness of the biblical documents, it has to be borne in mind that these writings were composed and transmitted in a patriarchal society. Its language is androcentric, and does not always reflect the radical shift in human relations as advocated in this analysis (cf. Meeks 1983:23–25; 1993:138–147).

To further obtain a picture of the *religious, political, economical and geographical* background of Ephesians, one would have to investigate the Roman Empire under the rule of the Caesars, and the circumstances of Greeks, Romans, Jews, and Christians in Palestine (cf. Reicke 1970), and the cities and countryside of Asia Minor (cf. Perkins 1988; Meeks 1983; 1993:37–51; 1986c; Freyne 1980; Du Plessis & Lategan 1983; Lohse 1976; Foerster 1968; Reicke 1968; Neyrey 1990). I have elsewhere attended briefly to some of these diverse aspects (Mouton 1987:144–151).

(which need not be an issue). This is why it seems to be more viable—in terms of understanding the document's persuasive power—to locate research on its purpose in a *rhetorical* reading of the document.

However, if a suggestion *has* to be made with reference to a probable historical situation for Ephesians (as a prerequisite for further choices regarding its rhetorical function), I would follow Roberts (1993b:97; cf. 1986c:76–77; 1991: 60–83; Schnackenburg 1991:33) in locating a possible general relation of tension among the Jewish and Gentile (Christian) communities in western Asia Minor during the first century C.E. His argument is motivated by the ecclesiological thrust of the document:

> When one views.... the theme of the church as the overarching, even single, issue about which the letter revolves, one might postulate a context for this letter where the sociological and political enmity of Jews and Greeks in the Hellenistic world, and especially in the Roman province of Asia (western Asia Minor) spilled over into the church once its membership became mixed and even predominantly Greek (Roberts 1993b:97).

This situation thus seems to be similar to that which underlies the book of Acts. Jewish Christians namely wrestled with the idea that Gentiles (people who did not know the God of *Israel*, the God of the *covenant*) could become Christians by faith in Christ alone—without accomplishing the traditional Jewish laws and regulations (cf. Eph. 2:14–15). The Jews used to contemptuously refer to them as "the uncircumcized" (Eph. 2:11). I therefore agree with Roberts (1963: 42–188; 1984b:294–300; 1986b:76–77; 1993b:97, 103) that linguistic pointers such as the Ephesians document's emphasis on the readers' *collective identity* as the one body of Christ (4:4), and their behavior toward one another as fellow-members of God's household (2:19), confirm the notion that such a situation may supply the key toward its understanding.

Several other scholars investigated the major *purpose* of the Ephesians epistle against the *background* of (their views of) the probable historical context and the primary need(s) it wished to address. Schlier (1957:21–22), typical of previous studies in the setting and aim of Ephesians, sees the document as a theological treatise or meditation on the mystery of Christ and the church, meant for a general occasion. Kirby (1968) probably marks a shift in Ephesians introductory studies—from a general to a more specific situation and purpose. He proposed that its liturgical structure (with special reference to Jewish liturgical traditions) pertains to a baptismal service, meant to affirm the converts' new status.[62] This designation is endorsed by Dahl (1965), who also treats the docu-

---

[62] Hendrix (1988:5) finds Kirby's analysis extremely optimistic with regard to "what can be known of first century C.E. Jewish and Christian prayer, liturgy, and sermons.... (T)he rather slim evidence for early Christian adaptation of Jewish prayers and forms of worship does not compare positively with Ephesians. The prayers and liturgical

ment as a homily for a baptismal occasion. For him the structure of Ephesians indicates that it is *"Taufanamnese und Taufparaklese"* (cf. Meeks 1977:209–210).
Meeks concurs by emphasizing that Ephesians "reproduces elements from the
baptismal liturgy and catechism of the Pauline churches of Asia" (1977:214, cf.
214–217; Fiorenza 1983:267–268). Käsemann (1966) argues that it was written
for a Gentile audience who was in danger of forgetting the Jewish origins and history of the gospel. According to him, Ephesians was meant to remind the church
of its continuity with the Jewish faith (cf. Meeks 1977:215; 1993:214–215).
Ralph P. Martin (1967–68:299–300), in a similar fashion, believes that the document reflects a situation in which the early Christian communities experienced
antinomian tendencies. According to this view, the Gentile Christians were apparently boasting of their independence of Israel, while showing a lack of tolerance
for Jewish Christians. These positions do not necessarily exclude one another.

One of the most impressing efforts to link the Ephesians epistle and its
socio-religious environment, is probably Clinton E. Arnold's book, *Ephesians:
Power and Magic—The concept of power in Ephesians in light of its historical
setting* (1989). Arnold notes that the highest concentration of power terminology
in the New Testament occurs in this document, and investigates probable reasons
for that (Arnold 1989:1–4, 167–172; cf. Thurston 1993:75). It is well-known that
the female deity Artemis was worshipped more widely than any other goddess in
the ancient Greek world (Arnold 1989:5–40; cf. Thurston 1993:68–71). Hellenistic magic, astrology and spiritual powers formed an integral part of this cult. The
city of Ephesus—one of the probable addresses for which the epistle, today
bearing its name, was intended—was a great religious centre, and therefore also a
centre for magical practices. In a refreshing way, Arnold (1989:41–69, 123–166)
indicates how knowledge of Hellenistic magic and astrology provides important
background for understanding the "powers" in Ephesians.

Lincoln (1990:lxxxi, 62–65, 94–97), on the contrary, is much more hesitant
to link the frequent references to principalities and powers in Ephesians to the
pervasive interest in astrology during that period. Lincoln's analysis (1990:lxxiv–
lxxxvii) leaves room for a larger variety with regard to the readers' needs than
that of Arnold.[63] Arnold argues that at least some, if not a majority, of the con-

---

elements of Ephesians stand in stunning contrast to, for example, the liturgical portions of
Didache and the prayers presumed to be Jewish in the Apostolic Constitutions.... A
nagging fact about Ephesians is that there is little evidence from antiquity or even since
then that anyone ever preached or verbally directed a service in the manner of the author of
Ephesians" (cf. 3.3.1). Apart from Kirby's useful literary analysis of the Jewish *berakah*
and its probable function as background to Eph. 1–3, Kirby's speculations on the origins of
Eph. were not met with widespread approval.

[63] The extraordinarily fine commentary on Ephesians by Andrew T. Lincoln, New
Testament scholar from Sheffield, represents a major shift in the approach to the
document. It namely locates the setting and purpose of the document in its "rhetorical
situation" instead of the "historical situation." Lincoln (1990:lxxv), followed by his former

verts entering the Ephesians church were formerly associated with the worship of Artemis and the practice of magic. For them, the powers were demonic and threatening (cf. Meeks 1993:112–117). The Ephesians author has as his task to convince them that no "power" is outside the realm of God's sovereignty or Christ's supremacy. Through Christ, in fact, they have a means of access to "the power of God" (Arnold 1989:70–122).

Arnold's contribution significantly adds to a better understanding of the probable mind-set and historical situation of the first readers of Ephesians, and of some of the document's terms and concepts. Without diminishing the over-whelming importance of the church in Ephesians, Arnold has drawn attention to the fact that spiritual powers—and over against them the idea of God's power and the readers' empowerment—play an important role in the document, and most probably form the backdrop to its setting and theology (cf. Roberts 1993b:96–105). His research in actual fact *accentuated* the close relation between the triumphant *power* of God and Christ which transcends all else, and the *unity* of the church as a manifestation of that power. This relation gains in significance against the background of an implied situation of disunity among Jewish and Gentile Christians which could *inter alia* have been caused by the persisting be-lief in foreign powers.

However fragmentary (and sometimes vague and confusing), these aspects do help to construct the historical situation and moral world within which the Ephesians epistle originated. To my mind, all these bits of information contribute toward a better understanding of what seems to be the main "exigency" (Bitzer 1968:6) behind the document: *The empowerment of the readers' identity and ethos in relation to Christ*. It is toward this vision that the document was clearly supposed to function as a shifting device.

2.2.3   THE HISTORICAL-LITERARY FACET OF EPHESIANS

Language and handwriting are human products, products of cultural-historical creativity. The New Testament documents have therefore to be considered as part of the literary creation of the early Christians, and—historically speaking—as the primary documents of Christianity. After they had been written down, they were gradually accepted by Christian believers as canon for their lives, and were since then treasured by the church. As was the case with the other New Testament documents, it was the Ephesians epistle's *christological perspective* which would function as criterion for its canonization as authoritative, inspired writing (cf. Guthrie 1977:480–482; Rousseau 1986:420–422). This is referred to as the his-torical-literary facet of the New Testament (Rousseau 1989a:16, 25–27, 49–53).

In the history of the development and closure of the New Testament canon

---

student Roy R. Jeal (1990:16–90), also considers the document as a *written homily* or *sermon in epistolary form*, but comes to that conclusion from a different angle, which does not negate historical questions (cf. 2.3).

(cf. Du Toit 1989:171–272), the epistle to the Ephesians was probably one of the first documents to be accepted as authoritative by the early Christian church. The earliest writing from the sub-apostolic era, the *First Letter of Clement* (round about 96 C.E.), probably already alludes to Ephesians. Allusions to Ephesians by *Polycarp's Letter to the Philippians* (round about 135 C.E.) also illustrates the recognition of its authority at an early stage (Du Toit 1989:192–198). The canon history of the New Testament thus testifies to the fact that Ephesians played a significant role in the identity formation and self-understanding of Christians during the early centuries C.E.

An empirical investigation into the *Wirkungsgeschichte* of the epistle, its influence and functioning in the lives and writings of people since its enscripturization and canonization, and especially its functioning in contemporary church documents, creeds, and sermons, would be a fascinating enterprise. Within the limitations of the present study this facet cannot be explored.[64]

West (1991a:124–131), among others, refers to this continuing process as "reading in front of the text" (cf. Lategan 1994b:127). Guidelines toward an accountable use of Scripture in contemporary Christian ethics will, however, be suggested in chapter four.

2.2.4 CONCLUSIONS: THE PRAGMATIC FUNCTION OF A SOCIO-HISTORICAL READING OF EPHESIANS

We have seen that an important function of a socio-historical interpretation of a text is to determine the crucial *perspective* from which an author selects and edits transmitted oral and/or written material, and from which s/he interprets, redescribes and reshapes her/his environment (cf. Rousseau 1986:374–380). It is therefore vital to the reinterpretation of the text by later readers. For us, the purpose of identifying the perspective of an ancient canonized document such as Ephesians, would be to (re)orientate our own perspective in accordance with that of the text (cf. Fiorenza 1988:13–17; 1999:26–30).

With regard to the communicative power of a document, this aspect is also of particular interest for understanding its "rhetorical situation" (cf. 2.3; J. N. Vorster 1991:31). An author's perspective indeed forms the *cornerstone* and *orientation* of the dynamic processes involved in the communication of ancient canonized texts (Rousseau 1986:374–380).[65]

---

[64] An appropriate example of such an analysis is William Rader's *The Church and Racial Hostility: A History of Interpretation of Ephesians 2:11–22* (1978), originally presented as a doctoral dissertation under Oscar Cullmann. It investigates the interpretation by different church traditions and commentators of Eph. 2:11–22—from the Apostolic Fathers to the twentieth century.

[65] Jesus Christ, who is the orientation point from where the Ephesians author (re)interpreted his environment, is metaphorically described as the "chief cornerstone" of God's household. "In him the whole building is joined together...." (2:20–21).

Another function of a historical analysis is to bring about a necessary though not absolutized alienation between a text—especially an ancient text—and its readers, and would enable the interpreter to ask critical questions about the communicability and relevance of that text (Vorster 1984:104; Fiorenza 1988:14; Hays 1990:43).

A socio-historical reading of Ephesians is also meant to enable later readers to tentatively construct elements from its moral world and historical situation. The present study is particularly interested in the way in which Jesus Christ—amid other possible influences—was supposed to affect the moral world of the first century Asia Minor Christian communities. In that sense we are not only interested in *what* Jesus and the early Christians taught, and what the symbolic and social universe was within which that teaching made sense, but particularly in *how* these communication processes took place, or were supposed to take place. The brief socio-historical reading of Ephesians has indeed started to shed valuable light on the question: What was the moral effect the author expected from his readers? And eventually: What is the moral effect later readers presume when appealing to the same text as normative for their personal lives and society?

It has become clear that the Ephesians perspective is in the first place christologically oriented, and aimed at the reorientation of the readers' identity awareness and ethos. The most important rhetorical question arising from the brief investigation of the document's historical situation and moral world, is what the document was supposed to *do* to this particular environment. This brings us to the persuading function of the document and the exploration of its "rhetorical situation."

2.3 READING EPHESIANS FROM A RHETORICAL PERSPECTIVE: TOWARD CONSTRUCTING ITS RHETORICAL SITUATION

The third dimension of textual communication is concerned with the dialectic interaction among the different elements of the communication process itself, and specifically as strategy to *persuade*. It therefore focuses on the pragmatic *function* of a text. With regard to the New Testament documents, this means that an author arranged words and sentences on a linguistic-literary level, selected and reinterpreted traditional material and metaphors on a historical level—with one goal in mind, namely to *persuade* the readers toward an alternative way of thinking and living (cf. Mouton 1987:176–210). The ongoing critical conversation between—the perspective of—these writings and—the perspective of—their subsequent readers forms part of this phase in textual communication.

As a manifestation of a goal-specific social interaction, the epistle to the Ephesians presupposes a certain communicative or "rhetorical situation" (Bitzer 1968:4–6; J. N. Vorster 1991). A linguistic-literary and socio-historical reading of the document naturally brought questions to the fore concerning the situation or circumstances which inspired its writing. By bringing its rhetorical situation into focus, a provisional attempt can now be made to establish the relation between linguistic-literary aspects of the document, and the socio-cultural context of which the author and recipients probably formed part.[66]

---

[66] South African New Testament scholar Johannes N. Vorster (1992b:2–5) draws on notions from Robert Fowler, and distinguishes three different communicative contexts which do not only *contribute* toward the birth of a document's rhetorical situation and meaning, but which actually *constitute* or *create* it. These are respectively a context of *utterance*, a context of *culture*, and a context of *reference*. To these Vorster adds a fourth category, namely the context of *the reader*. There is a continuous and dynamic interaction amongst these various contexts, and it can sometimes be extremely difficult to distinguish between them. (Most of these aspects have been implicated or referred to during the course of the discussion—sometimes by means of different categories—but are briefly integrated here in order to highlight the dynamics involved in textual *persuasion*.)

The context of *utterance* is that context in which discourse is produced, or uttered. It refers to the participants (senders and recipients) in their localization and immediacy toward each other in terms of time and space, as well as the channel of communication. The participants in textual communication have been identified as the encoded author and implied readers, which should not be equated with the real author and real readers. The context of utterance should therefore not be viewed in physical and historical terms only. The Ephesians epistle implies a context of utterance within which the author and readers are separated in terms of time and place.

The context of *culture* influences the context of utterance decisively. It can be described as a "network of social conventions and institutions as they bear upon the context of utterance. That means that the context of culture comprises the world of knowledge shared by participants in communication, their mutual value-systems, their adherence to mutual codes of behaviour, symbols and rituals, their recognition of various roles and their accompanying statuses within their midst" (Vorster 1992b:3). In the case of Ephesians, this means that the issue is not whether there were Jews and Gentiles in the Asia Minor communities, or how many they were, but *what their social significance within the context of utterance was*, and what the specific terms were by which status was designated to, or taken away from them (cf. 2.2 n.39 on the relation between "historical situation" and "moral world").

The context of *reference* is concerned with the subject matter of a text. We have seen that a text can refer to the world *behind* it, *in* it, and *in front of* it (Lategan 1994b:126–128; cf. 1.6.2 n.36). As such it can refer beyond the here and now, to the future and the past, and will therefore not necessarily be a reflection of reality. "(A)lthough human imagination and creativity can here be extended to its full potential, it is always part of the contexts of *utterance and culture*" (Vorster 1992b:4). Without these, communication would be impossible. In order to communicate a radical alternative to his implied readers' self-understanding, the Ephesians author creates a "presence" between him and his audience, and a "world" with which they can identify. These are typical literary-social conventions in letters of antiquity (cf. Stowers 1986:27–31).

The context of *the reader* also adds to the creation of a document's rhetorical situation. Reception criticism has since the late seventies emphasized the role of readers in the interpretation of texts (cf. Lategan 1984a; 1991a; 1992a; 1992c). It is important to account for the role of readers, because they are co-responsible for the creation of meaning (cf.

2.3.1 *THE EXIGENCY OF A RHETORICAL SITUATION*

What is a rhetorical situation, and how does it come into existence? Lloyd F. Bitzer, who introduced this concept in 1968, defined the rhetorical situation as

> a complex of persons, events, objects and relations presenting an actual or potential exigence which can be completely or partially removed if discourse, introduced into the situation, can so constrain human decision or action as to bring about the significant modification of the exigence (Bitzer 1968:4–6; cf. Kennedy 1984:34–35; Botha 1994b:144–149).

According to this definition, the origin of the rhetorical situation—that which generates, creates, actualizes the rhetorical situation—is the notion of "*exigency*" or "*exigence.*" Bitzer (1968:6; cf. Vatz 1973:156) states: "Any exigence is an imperfection marked by urgency; it is a defect, an obstacle, something waiting to be done, a thing that is other than it should be." Within a given set of circumstances one or other kind of need or problem (cf. the Latin *dubium*, i.e. doubt), giving rise to the rhetorical situation, must thus be recognizable (cf. Vorster 1992b:6).

Bitzer's definition needs some further explanation. Defining the exigency that constitutes a specific rhetorical situation, is not a matter of merely recognizing specific living persons, "objective" events, objects and relations within a concrete historical situation, and appropriating a specific strategy in solving that situation (an impression which one gets from Bitzer's definition—cf. J. N. Vorster 1991:53–54; Vatz 1973:156). Epistemologically the rhetorical situation is only possible through the perspectivistic perception and choices of a rhetor. "The very choice of what facts or events are relevant is a matter of pure arbitration. Once the choice is communicated, the event is imbued with *salience*" (Vatz 1973: 157). Vatz further refers to this process as "the myth of the rhetorical situation"— a "translation" or "linguistic depiction" of a situation (1973:156–157). A rhetorical situation is thus constituted or recognized the moment when the interest of a rhetor is imposed on what s/he regards as the exigency of a specific situation (Vorster 1992b:8). As such, the *purpose* of a document can be described as the author's interest in and response to the exigency of a situation.

Quite often the exigency behind a document is not mentioned explicitly, simply because it would have been well-known to the original readers. For later readers to *reconstruct* this exigency would be impossible. The best that can be done—as in the case of the "historical situation"—is to *construct* the most prob-

---

1.3). "Meaning does not reside *in* the text, but is given *to* the text. That implies a self-awareness as to our points of departure, our presuppositions, the difference between our world view and that of the text. If we as interpreters concretize the meaning of the text, a context of *utterance, or culture or reference* cannot be *re*constructed, but is always a construction, a figment of our imagination" (Vorster 1992b:5).

able situation from the available sources, realizing that such an attempt would always be determined by the reader's perspective, and therefore always be provisional and tentative, and open to further discussion.

For this reason contemporary readers of the Ephesians epistle may find it rather difficult to construct the exigency of its implied readers. It is nowhere stated explicitly. We simply have to read between the lines. Several linguistic-literary pointers toward such a direction have been identified in 2.1. It appears that the type of problem which prompted the writing of the document, has to do with the quality of the implied recipients' identity and behavior. This is decisively measured by what God has done for them *in Christ*.

2.3.2 *ROLES OF PERSONS WITHIN THE RHETORICAL SITUATION*

Various persons may participate in the rhetorical situation, but a basic distinction can be made between those people who have an *interest* in the situation, and those who do not only have an interest, but who *control* the situation and wish to modify it. The latter is responsible for the rhetorical process (J. N. Vorster 1991: 56).

The category *rhetorical audience*, as active participant in the rhetorical situation, consists only of those persons who are capable—according to the implied author's perception—of being influenced by discourse and of being *mediators of change* (Bitzer 1968:7–8; cf. Botha 1994b:145). This corresponds with Perelman and Olbrechts-Tyteca's definition of *audience* (1969:19) as "the ensemble of those whom the speaker wishes to influence by his argumentation" (cf. Vorster 1992b:11).[67]

The audience "does not only function as cause for communication, but it also determines the selection of linguistic entities, the selection of arguments, the selection of τόποι" (Vorster 1992b:11). Τόποι are defined as those techniques of argumentation by which an author wishes to control and modify a situation, and specifically with the purpose of persuading an audience toward a new way of thinking and acting (cf. Perelman & Olbrechts-Tyteca 1969:185–410; Corbett 1990:32–143). These will be dealt with in chapter three.

According to these views, the Ephesians author would consider his readers as potential controllers of its rhetorical situation. They were in a position to modify or transform the exigency of that situation. Therefore he would have to know his audience well, but also to adapt himself to them in order to establish a mutual frame of reference between them. This underlines the important aspect of the interaction between author and readers. How the author would create and shape

---

[67] Perelman and Olbrechts-Tyteca (1969:19) confirm that the audience who decisively create and shape the discourse, is not to be equated with a real flesh-and-blood audience, but is a construct of the rhetor's imagination. Reception criticism has supplied us with the useful category of *implied readers* as a means to designate the visualized audience (cf. 1.6.1 n.33).

the discourse, would decisively be determined by his construct of the audience. He had to select those characteristics, expressions, metaphors and traditions which would not only be appropriate to the exigency of the situation, but which would also be acceptable to the audience.

2.3.3   *THE RELATION BETWEEN THE HISTORICAL AND RHETORICAL SITUATIONS OF A TEXT*

With regard to the relation between the "historical" and "rhetorical situations,"[68] J. N. Vorster (1991:30–33) asks: If the purpose of a document is concerned with the *rhetorical* situation, to what extent is the rhetorical situation *historical*? This question is concerned with whether, or to what extent, the constituents of a rhetorical situation—situated within the first century C.E.—can be seen as matters of "fact." In other words, when speaking of an exigency, are we referring to a "real" exigency, or a deficiency created by the perspectivistic interest of an author? And further, what are the differences and similarities, the points of contact, between the concepts historical situation and rhetorical situation?

This is indeed an extremely complex issue. It has been indicated that the rhetorical situation only comes into existence when the exigency of the situation enters into relationship with the interest of the rhetor. The exigency of a rhetorical situation is, therefore, always relational and determined by an external term. While there is a basic set of facts, whether and how these facts are exigent, is fully determined by the "interest" component (J. N. Vorster 1991:30). If the interest of the rhetor acts upon a basic set of facts to constitute an exigency, the creative role of the rhetor in regard to the rhetorical situation has to be acknowledged and accounted for as an essential element of the ethics of interpretation.

The thrust of this discussion again leads to the acknowledgement that, if the interest of the rhetor plays the role of catalyst in the constitution of the exigency of the rhetorical situation, then we can no longer talk of a so-called "objective set of facts." It is epistemologically impossible to know anything independent of its relations and metaphorical language (cf. J. N. Vorster 1991:30, 38 n.34; Van Huyssteen 1986:151–168).

This means that the rhetorical situation of a document cannot be equated with its historical situation. The rhetorical situation is concerned with what the author (or rhetor) deems defect, and only comes into existence as a creation of that person. As such, the purpose or meaning of a letter is concerned with the *perspective* of its author (cf. J. N. Vorster 1991:310). The *purpose* of a letter can therefore be described as a reflection of the interest of an author. This recognition consequently asks that research on the purpose of a letter should be relocated in its *rhetorical* rather than in its *historical* situation (cf. Lincoln 1990:lxxiv). Such

---

[68]   That is, if such a relation can be identified at all (Botha 1994b:140–145; cf. Vatz 1973).

an approach would take the focus away from a so-called "set of facts," which "does not mean that a construction of the rhetorical situation is an a-historical endeavor, it is more likely the point of departure for further historical studies; however, in a different manner" (J. N. Vorster 1991:31; cf. Botha 1994b:143).[69]

The ethical implications of such a view on the purpose or meaning of a New Testament document would be crucial. If—*contra* Bitzer—the communication of persons, events, *et cetera* is considered as a choice, a decision, an interpretation or translation, the *implied rhetor's responsibility* becomes of supreme concern. "To view rhetoric as a creation of reality or salience rather than a reflector of reality clearly increases the rhetor's moral responsibility" (Vatz 1973:158). In other words, the rhetor is responsible for what s/he chooses to make salient. With respect to Ephesians, this introduces the question of the implied author's responsibility and interest in what he considered as the major need of those communities.

Because the rhetorical situation cannot be equated with the historical situation, the audience of the rhetorical situation can also not be equated with a real audience. An author's interest in the audience is determined by her/his view of the audience. Because discourse is decisively shaped by the rhetor's image of her/his audience, the reception-critical category of implied reader has been used consistently in the analysis of Ephesians. The function of the implied reader is to illustrate and stimulate reader-engagement (cf. Vorster 1992a:11). It is a device "to engage the real reader by offering a role to be played or an attitude to be assumed" (Lategan 1989a:10), and is therefore particularly helpful in the ongoing conversation between an ancient canonized text and its later readers.

2.3.4 *CONCLUSIONS: THE PRAGMATIC FUNCTION OF A RHETORICAL READING OF EPHESIANS*

It has been indicated that the possibility that Ephesians functioned as a circular letter (Roberts 1991:27–28), does not mean that it did not have a specific audience with concrete needs in mind. The author evidently wished to strengthen his addressees' vision of what God had done for them *in Christ*, and to encourage them toward a collective lifestyle of praise-giving which would be worthy of the calling they received from God. Yet, is there any substantial evidence in the text which could illuminate the situation and needs which called for such a message? Are we able to identify "the issue that mattered" for the author (Mack 1990:20)?

The picture which the text presents of its audience is that of a group of people known as τὰ ἔθνη or *Gentiles by birth* (2:11–22). They were called "uncircumcised" by those who call themselves "the circumcision" (2:11), which indicates that the Jews treated them with some degree of contempt (cf. Wessels

---

[69] Kittredge (1998:111–174) provides a good example of such a procedure. She wisely starts by analyzing Ephesians rhetorically and by subsequently defining its *rhetorical* situation. From there she moves toward constructing its *historical* situation.

1990a:52–55; Roberts 1991:66). The Gentiles' former religious and sociological position is described as that of "foreigners and aliens" who used to be "far away"—people separated from Christ, "excluded from citizenship in Israel and foreigners to the covenants of the promise, without hope and without God in the world" (2:12, 13, 17, 19; cf. Lincoln 1990:120–165; Roberts 1991:67–76).

These and other linguistic and literary aspects of the Ephesians text give the impression that the implied recipients primarily consisted of Gentile Christian believers. Although the Christian communities of first century Asia Minor consisted of Jewish and Gentile Christians, Ephesians mainly addresses the Gentiles. While Gentile citizens would presumably enjoy a sociologically superior position in the Roman Empire (of which there is no indication in the text), the author's perspective on the Jewish Christians' ideological perception of the Gentile Christians is that they belonged to an inferior class of people (cf. 2:11). The thrust of the document reveals an emphasis on the implied Gentile readers' new status *in Christ* (2.1)—specifically against the backdrop of a (previously) tense situation between these two groups. By means of various identity markers the author stresses that—because of the Christ event—the Gentile Christians are *"no longer foreigners and aliens, but fellow-citizens with God's people and members of God's household"* (2:19).

Such a situation may, for instance, help to explain the large number of re-interpreted *Old Testament* motives and traditions which occur in the document, while the majority of its audience probably consisted of non-Jewish Christians. Could it be that these religious symbols still functioned verbally or non-verbally as part of the "dividing wall of hostility" (2:14) which previously separated them—in spite of their common Christian belief? Or, could this be the reason why the author so emphatically reinterpreted these traditions in terms of Christ's act of reconciliation on the cross (cf. 2:14–16), the unity of the church (4:1–16), and the different relations expressing that unity (5:21–6:9)? Such a notion seems quite probable.

The tension among Jewish and Gentile Christians implied in Ephesians does not necessarily seem to pertain to a specific historical conflict between these groups. It most probably refers to the author's perspective of a *general situation* in which the Jewish nation consistently refused to grant status to the new movement of Jesus-followers within its fold. This probably meant that the tension regarding religious and sociological status between Jewish and Gentile communities in the villages and cities of Asia Minor, still influenced their relationship after they had become members of the one body of Christ (cf. Meeks 1983:32–139, 164–170; Roberts 1986b:76–77; 1993b:97). These complexities were caused by the fact that conversion to the Christian faith implied a complete reorientation of the value systems and lifestyle of *both Jews and Gentiles*:

> For Jews this transition was difficult enough, but it did not entail the abandonment of their own tradition—it was rather understood as its continuation and completion. For Gentiles, the break was much more incisive. They found themselves at a double disadvantage—new to the Christian faith, but also unfamiliar with its Jewish roots (Lategan 1993: 400, with reference to the argumentative situation of Galatians).

A probable rhetorical situation reflecting the Jews' continuous maintenance of exclusivity, and the Gentiles' resultant disposition of rejection and inferiority, compels the Ephesians author to revalue their roles. Several of the numerous rhetorical strategies which he employed to shift their attitudes and behavior—or, in terms of Bitzer's definition, that particular language which was supposed to constrain human decision or action in such a way as to bring about the significant modification of the exigency involved—have been identified in the previous two sections of this chapter, and will be discussed further in chapter three.[70]

As a tentative point of departure toward exploring rhetorical strategies in the Ephesians text (3.3), I suggest that its exigency be investigated as a—rhetorical and not necessarily historical—situation of tension among Jewish and Gentile Christians, and in particular the implied author's view of some kind of an imperfection or obstacle (Bitzer 1968:6) regarding their (especially the Gentile Christians') identity awareness and ethos (cf. Wessels 1990a:52–55; Roberts 1991:66–70, 75–76; Lincoln 1990:79–80, 134–136). Other social imbalances are implied by the redescription of relations between husbands and wives, parents and children, masters and slaves. The metaphors by which their new status is described (2:19, 21, 22) strengthen the notion that the document's exigency was of a predominantly religious and sociological nature.

The communicative, transformative power of the Ephesians epistle lies in its

---

[70] The analysis of rhetorical strategies in Ephesians holds the potential to help us understand something of the "moral grammar," *the logic of the interactive world* which its author and readers shared—that process in which they were engaged before and after the writing of the document (Meeks 1986a:10; 1986b:124–160). In terms of the communication model discussed in 1.6, this refers to the *functions* of the structural, historical and theological *dimensions* of a written text—as the end result of an analysis of their dynamic and dialectic *modes*.

potential ability to persuade its readers toward appropriating their honorable position in Christ, toward inhabiting its alternative moral world. How the author could have envisaged this, is the focus of the next chapter.

READING EPHESIANS ETHICALLY: TOWARD EXPLORING ITS TRANSFORMATIVE POTENTIAL

> What is indeed to be understood—and consequently appropriated—in a text? Not the intention of the author, which is supposed to be hidden behind the text; not the historical situation common to the author and his (*sic*) original readers; not the expectations or feelings of these original readers; not even their understanding of themselves as historical and cultural phenomena. *What has to be appropriated is the meaning of the text itself, conceived in a dynamic way as the direction of thought opened up by the text. In other words, what has to be appropriated is nothing other than the power of disclosing a world that constitutes the reference of the text.... (I)t is.... the disclosure of a possible way of looking at things, which is the genuine referential power of the text.*
>
> (Ricoeur 1976:92; emphasis mine)

In the previous chapter attention has been given to the linguistic-literary and referential *contexts* of biblical texts through analyzing the Ephesians epistle. It has gradually become clear how the different communicative contexts of *utterance*, *culture*, *reference*, and *the readers* (the rhetorical context) function interactionally in the constitution and creation of a text and its meaning (Vorster 1992b:2–5; cf. 2.3 n.66). Eventually, all these aspects (un)consciously contribute toward the process by which readers concretize or actualize what they understand as the meaning or intended effect of a text. This observation confirms that all texts—including biblical texts—represent a dynamic and multi-dimensional process of communication.

3.1 THE INTERACTION BETWEEN TEXT AND CONTEXT

We have seen that it is especially the notion of *the readers' context* in the process of textual communication that has lately become the focus of attention among biblical scholars (Lategan 1984a; 1987; 1989a; 1991c; 1992a; 1992b; 1992c; 1994a). The process of reading involves much more than just the recognition of meaning which is seemingly inscribed into a text. It is indeed more than the sum total of the meaning of words and syntactical structures within a text (cf. J. N. Vorster 1991:40).

It has become clear that reading is an *interactive* process between a text and its readers, which evokes different responses from different readers. Readers assign meaning to a text and actualize that meaning in potentially different ways (cf. W. S. Vorster 1991:1099). It is therefore obvious that language cannot be studied in isolation, but that it has to be done in relation to its context. It is in this respect that a *pragmatic* approach toward texts, which acknowledges that meaning is constituted by the interaction between text and context, can be of help. According to this approach, language has to be studied within the speech situation, or situation of utterance. Meaning is thus believed to reside in the interaction of a speech situation and its linguistic elements. "The question is no longer simply *what* does this sentence *mean* or *say*," but rather "*why* is this utterance appropriate to the context and not any other?," or "*what* does this utterance *do* within this context?" (J. N. Vorster 1991:41, cf. 42; emphasis mine).

It is in this sense that J. N. Vorster (1990; 1991) suggests an *inter-actional* model for analyzing the communicative (functional) aspects of biblical texts, and in particular for the *letter genre*. The *genre*-typical element of the New Testament letters is their persuasive nature—that is their communicative function. Even where these letters convey information, it is done in terms of their communicative objective (cf. J. N. Vorster 1991:44). Vorster suggests that aspects within the sphere of general pragmatics, and specifically conversational analysis, can be of help in analyzing the communicativeness of New Testament letters (cf. Lategan 1992c).[1] This kind of approach integrates *deixis* (linguistic-literary pointers or constraints within a text) and the reception critical categories of implied author and readers. The interaction between text and readers will also have to take notice of *rhetoric* as the art of persuasion, and specifically as it was employed by speakers and authors of the first century Greco-Roman world—that world within which the New Testament authors produced their writings (cf. Kennedy 1984:3–38; Mack 1990; Perelman & Olbrechts-Tyteca 1969).

The distinctive feature of the New Testament letters lies in their being a response to a specific situation in which one or other form of need existed (cf. Stowers 1986). The previous chapter identified characteristic communicative devices in the Ephesians epistle, which served to create a frame of reference within which its rhetorical context can now be discussed further. The aim of this chapter is to identify the author's response to the context of his audience, and to determine the pragmatic function or potential persuasive force of the document within that context. It is an effort to construct—by means of ancient *and* twentieth century categories—some of the everyday communicative instruments utilized by Greek and Roman rhetoricians of the first century.

3.2 READING EPHESIANS RHETORICALLY

Up to now, the *persuading dimension* of the Ephesians epistle has been considered a major characteristic of its nature as ancient canonized text. At the same time, a so-called "rhetorical reading" of the document has almost been taken for granted. Yet, is such a premise valid? Can we assume that Ephesians allows for

---

[1] "Because of the persuasive nature of biblical literature, which presupposes a response from its readers, reader response theory is of special significance for this type of material.... With the growing interest in reader response theory and its application on biblical material, the challenge remains to clarify the referential potential of these texts and their relationship to extratextual reality" (Lategan 1992c:627–628; cf. 1987:116–117).

TOWARD EXPLORING ITS TRANSFORMATIVE POTENTIAL   125

an investigation in accordance with the methods and presuppositions of classical and modern rhetoric? And if so, *how* can these contribute toward a better understanding of the persuading function of the document, and the metaphorical, communicative processes facilitating that purpose? In what sense, then, may Ephesians be read *rhetorically*? By investigating these questions, this chapter aims to analyze the dynamic and dialectic operation of some of the major rhetorical strategies or persuading devices within the document's overall genre, composition, and function. As such, the chapter amplifies the procedures and results of sections 2.2 and 2.3 of the previous chapter—the *how* and *why* questions according to the communication theory discussed in 1.6.

Although it has become popular to deal with biblical material from a rhetorical perspective, this approach is not without its risks. In the published essays from the 1992 Heidelberg Conference on *Rhetoric and the New Testament* (Porter & Olbricht 1993), at least three scholars (Stanley Porter, Joachim Classen, and Jeffrey Reed) explicitly warn against the unnuanced application of formal ancient rhetorical categories to New Testament epistles.[2] Although both similarities and differences existed between epistolary traditions and rhetorical practices, the ancient writers clearly *differentiated* between rhetoric as *oratory* and epistles as *writings*, and contrasted the formal theories and techniques associated with the two *genres* (cf. Porter 1993:112; Classen 1993:288–291).[3] I take a brief look at the characteristics of both *genres*.

3.2.1 *MAJOR CHARACTERISTICS OF ANCIENT RHETORIC*

The rhetorical handbooks generally discuss five aspects of rhetorical practice, which recapitulate five stages in the act of composing a speech: invention (Latin *inventio*), which deals with the planning of a discourse, including the selection of arguments[4] and familiar material, themes or τόποι[5] to make the point; arrange-

---

[2] After having done a survey of Greco-Roman epistolary theorists and the extant work of well-known ancient letter writers—such as the Greek writer Demetrius and premier Roman letter writer Cicero, both of the first century B.C.E.; the Roman Stoic Seneca, court philosopher and advisor of Nero, and Quintilian, both of the first century C.E.—Porter (1993:111–116) and Reed (1993:294–314) conclude that, although these writings might have been rhetorical in nature, or evidenced rhetorical features in their composition, little if any theoretical or practical justification was given by these writers for the *analysis* of letters or epistles according to the categories found in ancient Greek and Roman rhetorical handbooks. (For an overview of such ancient letter writers, cf. Malherbe 1986:23–29; Du Toit 1984a:4; Johnson 1999:32–35; Porter 1993:111–114; Meeks 1993: 26, 76.)

[3] See Akinnaso (1982; 1985) for a very interesting contemporary yet general discussion on the differences and similarities between spoken and written language.

[4] Aristotle (referred to by Reed 1993:301 n.28) mentions two kinds of arguments available to a speaker: non-artistic, and artistic discourses (i.e. creating λόγος—rational appeal, πάθος—emotional appeal, and ἔθος—ethical appeal). The method which the

ment (*dispositio*)[6], the composition of the various parts into an effective whole; style of words into sentences, including the use of figures; memory (*memoria*), and delivery (*pronunciatio*; cf. Kennedy 1984:13–33; Mack 1990:31–34; Corbett 1990:22–28; Cunningham 1990:20, 27; Vorster 1992a; Reed 1993:296, 301–308).

In addition, ancient oratory was—as a *genre* of argumentation—typically divided into three *sub-genres* or types of persuasive discourse: judicial (forensic), deliberative (hortative, advisory), and epideictic (ceremonial).[7] Because *genres* are function-specific, they develop a customary form and pattern appropriate to the basic function they serve. (*elocutio*), which involves both choice of words and the composition.

3.2.2 *CHARACTERISTICS OF ANCIENT LETTER WRITING*

We have also noted that letter writing was a highly developed form of communication in the cultural setting of the first century Mediterranean world (Stowers 1986; Meeks 1993:79–84). Different letter types were composed for a variety of purposes.[8] Perhaps the most universal function was that of making one who was

---

classical rhetoricians devised to aid the speaker in discovering matter for the three artistic modes of appeal was the topics (Greek τόποι, Latin *loci*; cf. Corbett 1990:23–24; Kennedy 1984:15–16; Mack 1990:35–41).

[5] Different letter types would obviously have different τόποι, e.g. topics of friendly correspondence included the health wish, prayer formula and closing greeting (Meeks 1993:77–79; Reed 1993:303). "In summary, the epistolary theorists stressed the importance of carefully selecting the topic of one's letter based on the type of letter to be written.... That is, they show concern for how one 'invents' or composes a letter. This concern at least functionally parallels *inventio* in the rhetorical handbooks—viz. the speaker's sensitivity to what he or she should say and how it should be said" (Reed 1993: 304).

[6] After *selecting* the type of speech to be delivered, and *inventing* the subject matter, a rhetor would often proceed to *arrange* the material into the best possible order. According to Reed (1993:304), "the epistolary theorists apparently say nothing about arranging letters after the fashion of the rhetoricians. What they do say instead, conforms to the standard pattern of letter writing. In part, the reason epistolary theorists do not prescribe rhetorical arrangements to epistolary structures is due to the formulaic traditions long established in letter writing."

[7] Generally, *judicial* speech functioned in the courtroom before a jury or judge, *deliberative* speech in the political assembly, and *epideictic* speech in the public arenas, frequently at ceremonial occasions. "Did he do it or not?" was an essential question scrutinized by judicial speech. "Is it more beneficial (expedient) to do this or that?" was the question explored by deliberative speech. "Should something or someone be praised or blamed?" was the question discussed by epideictic speech (Reed 1993:297; cf. Kennedy 1984:36–37; Corbett 1990:28–29; Mack 1990:34–35; Hester 1994:2–6; Perelman & Olbrechts-Tyteca 1969:47–51).

[8] According to Stanley K. Stowers' well-known work, *Letter Writing in Greco-*

absent, present. The letter was in actual fact viewed as bearing the presence (παρουσία) of the sender (Johnson 1999:268; Du Toit 1984a:4; cf. Reed 1993: 303, 311; Kelber 1987). The ancient Greek letter essentially contained a *conversation* (ὁμιλία), and was meant to communicate the author's *positive attitude* (φιλόφρονεσις) toward the reader or readers (cf. Du Toit 1984a:4).

Standard conventions found in the large majority of ancient letters were the opening (sender, recipient, greetings), health wishes and thanksgiving, body, and ending (Du Toit 1984a:5–12; cf. Reed 1993:305–308).[9] The special τόποι for letter writing would serve the function of each section.

3.2.3   *THUS, MAY EPHESIANS BE READ RHETORICALLY?*

The question therefore is whether rhetorical aspects of discourse are found in ancient epistles—particularly in the New Testament epistles—and whether a rhetorical analysis of Ephesians would be justifiable, and if so, to what extent it could contribute to and complement the results of other analyses.

Lategan (1993:397) deals with this general issue in the following way:

> To my mind, there is no need to impose a rhetorical framework, which was originally designed for speech, on letters by categorizing them as 'speech at a distance' or 'deferred speech.' The specific nature of epistolography should rather be respected for what it is. Written communication with its accompanying feature of the presence/absence of the writer and reader has its own mysteries and fascination and should be studied in its own right. *But, in as far as letters have a pragmatic intent, their illocutionary and perlocutionary force have to be taken into account.*[10] *This provides all the scope for rhetorical analysis of letters in the broader sense of the word* (emphasis mine).

Roman Antiquity (1986), these situations could pertain to friendship, family, and client-patron relationships, occasions for praise and blame, exhortation and advice, mediation, etc. (Stowers 1986:49–179; cf. Malherbe 1986:79–85). One can imagine that such communicative situations would have their own essential *purpose*, and their intention would be to bring about a particular response by means of persuasion.

[9] The combined functions of opening, body and closing correspond broadly to the three chief operative factors in rhetorical speech: speaker, speech and audience, which confirms the basic nature and structure of any communicative event.

[10] Illocutionary force is the particular *function* in which one uses an utterance produced on a particular occasion (Deist 1990:120–121; Ricoeur 1976:14; Thiselton 1992: 291–298), while perlocution refers to the *effect* on hearers/readers caused by utterances (Deist 1990:190). The perlocutionary act—what we do by speaking—has less an intentional function (i.e. calling for an intention of recognition on the part of the hearer), "than a kind of 'stimulus' generating a 'response' in a behavioral sense. The perlocutionary function helps us rather to identify the boundary between the act character and the reflex character of language" (Ricoeur 1976:18).

Since I am particularly interested in the implied or potential pragmatic intent and persuasive force of the Ephesians epistle (i.e. how the author wished to effect a change in the thinking, attitude and behavior of his readers), it becomes an interesting and important question as to whether, and to what extent, the historical author could have been influenced by rhetorical aspects from his environment. Pertaining to ancient letters in general, Reed (1993:296) surmises that the first three parts of ancient rhetorical practice (invention, arrangement, style) could have played a significant role in epistolary theory and practice, inasmuch as they would be conducive to the function and persuasive power of a particular document.[11]

In addition, Classen (1991; 1993:289) and Reed (1993:296) argue that the various species or sub-genres of rhetoric may have influenced the epistolary traditions (3.2.1 n.7). Because the ancient epistolary genre allowed individuals to handle different situations with a variety of letter types, "it is no surprise to find types of letters which parallel the three sub-genres of rhetoric" (Reed 1993:299). In this regard it is noteworthy that,

> (o)f the three rhetorical sub-genres, the epideictic type is most at home among the epistolary theorists.... (T)his is perhaps because of the widespread importance of honor and shame in Graeco-Roman culture,

---

[11] *Style (elocutio)* seems to be an important exception here: "So far as the ancient rhetorical handbooks are concerned with respect to letters, the only significant discussion of epistolary material concerns stylistic matters" (Porter 1993:122; cf. Classen 1993:269). Put differently, the rhetoricians' concern for style was also a concern for the epistolary theorists (Reed 1993:308). Indeed, "the effectiveness of one's persuasiveness hinged on one's style" (Reed 1993:311; cf. Corbett 1990:380–538).

Style, according to the ancients, did not pertain to mere ornamentation, but formed part of the way in which substance was conveyed (Porter 1993:116). The ancient classical definition for rhetoric was indeed "*the art of persuasion*" (Mack 1990:15), which was revived by Perelman and Olbrechts-Tyteca (1969) in their extensive work on (modern) rhetoric as "argumentation." "Indeed, for the ancients, rhetoric was generally concerned with speech designed to persuade—*and specifically, to induce others to action*" (Cunningham 1990:12, cf. 28–48; emphasis mine). In ancient rhetoric, different styles would be appropriate to different circumstances and needs. Style may be characteristic of a particular work of art, a particular author or a specific literary *genre*. In the case of an author, it is an expression of her/his artistic choice and arrangement of elements such as words, sentences, themes, figures of speech, metaphors and citations, and would therefore involve questions of grammar, syntax (structure described with reference to constituents like comparison, contrast, chiasmus), and features such as clarity and appropriateness for the situation (cf. Reed 1993:308–311). This also concerns the application of the formal categories of rhetoric, and particularly that of *style*, to analysis of the New Testament epistles (cf. Du Toit 1984a:13–18). Significant stylistic features in Eph. are repetition, antitheses, chiasmus, anacoluthon, climax, hyperbole, metaphor, the use of traditional material, etc. The study focuses on the function of metaphors and traditions in Eph., as important features of its style, and therefore of its rhetorical persuasion as a whole.

in which the 'praise' and 'blame' style characteristic of epideictic rhetoric would have been important to other literary modes as well (Reed
1993:300–301).[12]

These possibilities allow Reed (1993:301, 322–324) to concede that Paul
could conceptualize a letter in terms of, for instance, "praise or blame" and "ex-
pediency or non-expediency," although his use of epideictic-like and deliberative-
like argumentation did not necessarily indicate a direct parallel to formal Greco-
Roman rhetorical systems.[13] *If* such a parallel does occur between say, paraenetic

---

[12]   The epideictic genre formed a central part of the art of persuasion in antiquity. It
was meant to strengthen a disposition toward action by increasing adherence to specific
values. "The speaker tries to establish a sense of communion centered around particular
values recognized by the audience, and to this end he uses the whole range of means
available to the rhetorician for purposes of amplification and enhancement" (Perelman &
Olbrechts-Tyteca 1969:51, cf. 47–51).

Among others, *honor and shame* were the most significant values in the Mediterranean moral world before and during the New Testament era. In order to understand something of the possible role which these values may have played in the mind of the Ephesians
author, it is important to explore these concepts in both the Jewish and Hellenistic worlds
(cf. Domeris 1993:285–288; Meeks 1986b:40–96; 1993:39–41, 61–90, especially 86;
Solomon 1990:280). Domeris (1993:291) refers to J. Pitt-Rivers' definition of the
Mediterranean honor concept: "Honour is the value of a person in his (*sic*) own eyes, but
also in the eyes of his society. It is his estimation of his own worth, his *claim* to pride, but
it is also the acknowledgment of that claim, his excellence recognized by society, his *right*
to pride." In these contexts honor was acclaimed to the worth of one's possessions, social
status, reputation, and recognized role in society. It was a grant of recognition accorded to
a person by her/his community. One could for instance lose honor through one's actions
and so be shamed, or gain honor and so be exalted.

Significant in this regard was the human response to the Jewish law. Honor was
considered as the reward given to a person for obedience to the Torah. (Hence the question
to Jesus from one of the Pharisees, an expert in the law, in Mt. 22, Mk. 12 and Lk. 10:
"Teacher, which is the greatest commandment in the Law?" In his response, Jesus does not
single out a particular commandment, but summarizes the essence of the law: "Love the
Lord your God with all your heart.... and your neighbour as yourself.") If an attitude of
strict obedience to the Jewish law was prevalent in the Ephesians communities, one can
only imagine the dramatic impact, on the Jewish Christians, of the shift brought about by
Christ's *abolishing* of the law (Eph. 2:14–15).

Further, "(t)he keynote for both the biblical and rabbinical view of humankind is that
people are created in the image of God.... The honor of any person derives ultimately from
his or her possession of the image of God" (Domeris 1993:286; cf. Eph. 4:24; 5:1). In the
Greek world honor was shown toward the various deities, by means of sacrifice or praise.
It is important to bear in mind though, that honor and shame did not operate as fixed
values, but varied from one community to another, with significant changes in nuance
(Domeris 1993:288). It is evident that nuances in rhetorical strategies would change
according to variations in value systems (cf. Vorster 1990:123–126).

[13]   Yet, the methodological issue is not whether Ephesians exhibits features of praise

letters and deliberative rhetoric, Reed (1993:300, 307–308) is convinced that it would in the first instance be *functional*.[14] The most important aim of both letters and speeches was indeed to persuade, *to communicate effectively*.

Although it is extremely difficult to establish whether the Ephesians author consciously utilized formal categories of ancient rhetoric, I grant with Reed, Porter and others that there are universal communicative and persuasive practices and trends at play in the everyday use of *all* human interaction, irrespective of time and place (cf. Kennedy 1984:10, 19; Du Toit 1992:279–282).[15] This is particularly true about theological language—human language about God (cf. Cunningham 1990:1–9). It is therefore "possible—though difficult to defend—that some rhetorical practices of the orators may have influenced ancient letter

---

and blame, advice, and dissuasion (which it certainly does—cf. the vivid picture of Christ's triumphant resurrection and exaltation in chapters 1–3, and the exhortations in 3–6), but whether such features should be categorized as evidence of the author's use of ancient rhetorical formulas. Why not describe the document's discourse according to epistolary categories, without appealing to the terms of ancient rhetorical handbooks (cf. Reed 1993:314–322 with regard to his criticism of D. Watson's rhetorical analysis of Philippians)? The Ephesians author's emphasis on identity, and his usage of praise as persuasive device would in any case be characteristic of a *culture* based on honor and shame. Apart from the ancient Greek letter *genre*, the Ephesians author could also have been influenced by the Hebrew letter style, as well as Jewish and/or Christian liturgical traditions (cf. Du Toit 1984a:7).

[14] However, even *functional* similarities between Paul's argumentative style and the rhetorical handbooks do not prove a *formal* and conscious relationship between them (Reed 1993:322, 324). On the other hand, it would be "shortsighted to assert that there is no trace of ancient rhetoric in Paul's letters. No literary genre, including that of the epistle, exists in isolation. Genres exist in an intertextual system, each genre containing features common to other genres. However, the larger evidence from the letter writers and epistolary theorists suggests that Paul probably did not incorporate a *system* of ancient rhetoric into the epistolary genre.... Perhaps Paul was familiar with some of the rhetorical conventions of his day. Perhaps he did implement some of these in his use of the epistolary genre. But to claim that all or most of his writings are undeniable examples of the classical rhetorical genre is.... methodologically dubious" (Reed 1993:323).

[15] In this sense every language and culture has its own rhetoric. The *koine* language itself contained linguistic elements that allowed for several persuasive features in discourse, without the aid of formal rhetoric. However, "the classical rhetorical schemes, no matter how rudimentary and scientifically deficient they may have been, can provide us with valuable clues, especially since they reflected in many respects the cultural context within which the Pauline documents emerged. It should also be accepted.... that Paul at least possessed a basic knowledge of Greco-Latin rhetoric. It should also be kept in mind that the latter had, to a considerable extent, only identified and formalized certain strategies basic to all human interaction" (Du Toit 1992:280). Drawing on various models, Du Toit applies these insights to a pragmatic analysis of Galatians, by using what he calls "a common sense approach to the dynamics of interpersonal reciprocity" (Du Toit 1992:280–295).

writers" (Porter 1993:115).[16]

With this possibility in mind, as well as the limitations involved in utilizing a theory developed for *another genre*, I shall—by way of experiment—read Ephesians from a universal and formal, ancient and new rhetorical perspective, with the hope of becoming a more considerate reader of this text, while being open to be continuously surprised by it.[17] Or to phrase it in the words of South African pianist, Daniël-Ben Pienaar, with reference to his interpretation of a nineteenth century text, Brahms' astounding Handel Variations, Opus 24: "To me the challenge in playing this piece is to achieve a meticulous attention to detail of colour and meaning without sacrificing the overall architectural coherence."[18]

3.3 THE TRANSFORMATIVE POTENTIAL OF EPHESIANS: THE IMPLIED FUNCTION OF ITS RHETORICAL STRATEGIES

The rhetorical or communicative situation presented by the Ephesians document—the position *from which* the author wished to shift his readers' thoughts and behavior through discourse—has been dealt with in 2.3.4. It has been suggested that its exigency be investigated as an imperfection concerning the implied readers' identity and ethos. To persuade the mainly Gentile Christian

---

[16] This possibility is to my mind strengthened by the Ephesians author's creative use and reinterpretation of various other oral and literary elements from his environment—be it formal or informal, conscious or unconscious—such as the ancient letter genre, the form of an honorific decree (Hendrix 1988), different aspects of traditional material, etc. (cf. 2.2). He adapts these and fills them with new content to serve his particular purpose (cf. Du Toit 1984a:9–12). The *form* of the document, for instance, is therefore not merely aesthetic, but significantly contributes toward its persuasive function. This illustrates once again that the strategic metaphorical processes of *identification* (with familiar material, traditions, people), *estrangement* (from old positions and ways of behavior), and *reorientation* (toward a new perspective, in this case the alternative, "proposed world" of the text—Ricoeur 1980:15–32), indeed form the essence of human understanding and experience (cf. Lategan 1993:406; Rousseau 1986:246–252, 317, 381–385, 415–416, 432; Johnson 1999:14–16, 612–613).

[17] Two remarks seem appropriate here. When reading Eph. from a rhetorical perspective, it needs to be taken into account that this document is *not* in the first instance an argumentative discourse like Galatians or Romans. Secondly, aspects like praise and thanksgiving which abound in the document, have first and foremost to be considered as part of the *epistolary* form—not necessarily as a distinctly epideictic form (cf. Mitchell 1991:10 n.33). Yet, although it cannot be established beyond a doubt that these features should be categorized as evidence of the Ephesians author's use of ancient rhetorical formulas (n.13 above), it is just possible that the *functions* of epideictic and deliberative rhetoric could have been at the back of his mind, namely to create a vision of who and what is honorable, and to persuade the readers to act in accordance with that vision.

[18] Program for a recital presented under the auspices of UPE Cultura, Port Elizabeth, 7 Aug. 1994.

readers of their equal status with Jewish Christians, would certainly call for a fine strategy. We have already seen how the author imaginatively utilized a large number of metaphors and traditional material as persuading or shifting devices. One such tradition which he adapted for his purpose, was the *genre* of the Hellenistic epistle.

Against the background of an honor and shame value system (typical of the Mediterranean moral world of the early centuries C.E.—cf. 3.2.3 n.12), and the tentative observation that Ephesians might contain elements of the ancient rhetorical *genres* of epideictic and deliberative speech, the issue concerning the literary *genre* of Ephesians is taken up again.[19] This has briefly been investigated in 2.1.4.2, where it formed part of a discussion on the pragmatic function of a linguistic-literary reading of the document. It is however done here from a different perspective, and particularly in the context of its reinterpretation as strategic rhetorical device.

---

[19] Lincoln (1990:lxxv) is convinced that "the mixture of rhetorical genres—epideictic in the first half of the letter and deliberative in the second half—reflects the writer's twofold strategy. He wishes both to intensify the readers' adherence to the Christian convictions, values, and concepts that he and they have in common and to persuade them to take action that will bring their lives in greater conformity to what he deems to be appropriate to their shared perspective. The first part reinforces their sense of Christian identity, the privileges and status they enjoy as believers who are part of the Church. The second part appeals to them to demonstrate that identity as they live in the Church and in the world. The first part has a congratulatory tone and attempts to secure the goodwill of the recipients through its language of blessing, thanksgiving, intercessory prayer, and doxology. It does not, however, simply repeat what they already know adequately but, particularly through.... the sharp contrasts between the readers' past and present.... indicates that the readers are not as aware as they should be of some of the dimensions of their Christian identity.... In addition, through its intercessory prayer-reports, it suggests knowledge, love, and the experience of God's power as areas for the readers' growth. The ethical exhortations of the second part build on the rapport established with the readers in the first part and set out the sort of conduct to which the writer wishes them to attain. The final rhetorical strategy, the *peroratio* of 6:10–20, combines the emphases of both parts of the letter by stressing the identity of believers.... and by spelling out again the virtues they are to demonstrate—truthfulness, righteousness, peace, and faith. The main concluding exhortation—to stand in the cosmic battle—also sums up the two emphases, appealing to the readers to maintain and appropriate their identity and position of strength as they practice distinctively Christian living. This exhortation is not so much a call to changed behavior as a call to firm resolve in preserving the values the writer hopes will by now have been instilled in his readers."

3.3.1   *A Closer Look at the Ephesians Genre as Reinterpreted Tradition*

Classen (1993:280; cf. Smit 1987:22–24) underlines the importance of a document's *nature* or *genre,* and the specific function of that *genre,* for its proper understanding:

> Anyone attempting to understand and appreciate a speech or a written composition will first determine in a very general way the nature of the piece: literary, non-literary.... casual or serious, personal or general, with emphasis on content or form.... and, finally, the intention of the writer.

The broad *literary form* of the Ephesians document has been established as that of an *epistle* (with significant parallels to the typical Greco-Roman epistolary *genre*), although other forms like prayers and songs are also embedded within this primary form. As an epistle, Ephesians was probably intended to be *read aloud* in the congregation(s) to which it was addressed. However, even if this was the case, it is still important to respect its *genre* as that of an epistle, *not* a public speech (cf. Du Toit 1984a:5; 1992:280–281).[20] Thus, when the document is read from a rhetorical perspective, such an approach applies to the discourse *as embedded in the epistle.* It does not replace the epistle as *genre* of the text. For example, to describe Ephesians as an *epideictic-deliberative-like* epistle, means to acknowledge it as an epistle which probably employs epideictic and deliberative rhetoric in its body—a combination which was not uncommon in ancient literature (cf. Mitchell 1991:22 n.5).

North American theologian Holland L. Hendrix looks at the subject of the Ephesians *genre* from a somewhat different point of view, which might broaden and enrich what has been said thus far—especially with regard to the interpretive processes underlying the document. In a thought-provoking article, *On the form and ethos of Ephesians* (1988:3), Hendrix describes the text's peculiar form as:

---

[20]   If a text such as Ephesians has to be approached in terms of its communicativeness rather than the information it conveys, it will however be important to look at aspects of the interaction or *conversation* between the encoded author and its intended recipients. Conversational analysis is built on speech act theory, according to which a speech act is defined as "an utterance produced by a speaker within a context and addressed to a hearer with an intended effect" (Traugott & Pratt as referred to by J. N. Vorster 1991:45). This would imply that aspects such as speaker and hearers' perceptions, speaker's point of view, and the social values and relations of speaker and hearer determine meaning (cf. J. N. Vorster 1991:45–52). Contemporary readers of ancient letters thus have to be sensitive to the various elements involved in the original utterance of a text as "speech act," although they are only able to trace some of those elements between the lines and within the boundaries of a *written* document (cf. Thiselton 1992:16–19, 283–312, 361–368).

the Gordian knot of epistolary criticism. The opening blessing.... is extended remarkably; the single sentence runs from Ephesians 1:3 through to 1:14. The author then launches into thanksgiving which runs off and on to the end of chapter 3. At 4:1 we are beseeched suddenly with a *parakalo* leading into an exhortation which comprises the rest of the letter. The form-critical problem is rather acute in Ephesians. There is no body[21] or body middle. We have a letter opening, a thanksgiving heaped onto a blessing, a concluding exhortation and the letter closing.

What else then could Ephesians be, and how are its different components related to each other *formally* and *rhetorically*? How does one account for its sometimes cumbersome and overwhelmingly dense structure?[22] And to what extent does its particular formal variant—compared to other New Testament epistles—reflect something about its exigency?[23]

Hendrix looks for an answer to these questions by linking the style of Ephesians to its paradoxical nature:

There is a central paradox of Ephesians which scholars have recognized implicitly for some time. The document appears to be emphatically public, but its loquacious style renders it *publically in-comprehensible*—especially if one supposes it were a sermon or public speech framed as an epistle (1988:5; emphasis mine).

The one other public documentary phenomenon manifesting this kind of paradox, Hendrix discovered, is that of the typical *honorific decree* found on monuments and inscriptions of antiquity. Honors for benefactors were a well-known phenomenon in Greco-Roman antiquity—a culture which particularly treasured the values of honor and shame:

A Greek benefactor in the Classical and Hellenistic periods was someone who was honored for an important public or private service.... Individuals benefiting from the service might honor their benefactor with a crown to be presented on a formal occasion, perhaps a statue to

---

[21] Contra Roberts 1991:16.

[22] Some scholars tried to solve this problem by considering Ephesians as something other than an epistle. Kirby, for instance, has proposed that the document be regarded as a *baptismal liturgy* of the Ephesians church, framed as a general epistle addressed to Jewish and Gentile Christians (1968:170; cf. 2.2.2). Lincoln (1990:lxxv), followed by Jeal (1990: 42–51), also designates the document as a written *homily* or *sermon* in epistolary form, combining epideictic and deliberative rhetorical genres. In his doctoral thesis, Jeal (1990) presents a detailed rhetorical critical examination of Ephesians, providing a possible way through the difficulties of explaining how the theological and ethical sections of the document may be related to each other—an explanation which, according to him, is not rendered by epistolary analysis.

[23] For example, "(o)f the letters attributed to Paul, only Ephesians contains both an introductory blessing and thanksgiving" (Hendrix 1988:4).

be displayed conspicuously and crowned periodically, an inscribed testimonial to the benefactor's generosity and excellence together with a record of the honors accorded him or her.... In the Hellenistic kingdoms, the functions and honors of the Classical Greek benefactor were appropriated by leaders claiming royal authority. This was accompanied by an escalating emphasis on Alexander's divine status. The title 'benefactor' and '*soter*' (savior) became personalized epithets of an increasingly divinized Hellenistic royalty (Hendrix 1988:6).

Among the outstanding examples which Hendrix quotes (1988:5–8), is that of an ancient honorific decree which describes the deeds of one Menas towards his home city Sestos. After his honorable attitude and deeds are described in eighty more lines (containing ponderously cumbersome sentences, often starting with "*whereas*"), a pivotal "*therefore*" (οὖν) appears, followed by the honor, glory and gratitude which the people of Sestos owe him. "Normally in civic honorifics, *the resolution declares the types of honors granted in response to the benefactions received.* First, it is important to remember that the social, if not moral obligation to honor benefactors was expressed explicitly in many honorifics" (Hendrix 1988:8; emphasis mine; cf. Perelman & Olbrechts-Tyteca 1969: 49).

Subsequently, Hendrix (1988:7) deals with the question as to whether ancient honorifics provide us with a possible analogy for understanding Ephesians:

> Formally, Ephesians reads like an honorific preamble which cites an honorand's benefactions (in this case, those of God and Christ) followed by a resolution introduced by 'therefore I beseech you' (*parakalo oun hymas*). The resolution then spells out the implications of receiving the benefactions cited.

It has been argued that conjunctions such as οὖν, τοῦτο οὖν, and διὸ in Ephesians 4:1, 17, 25; 5:15 stress the structural and semantic coherence between the two main sections of the document. What follows these conjunctions has been indicated as a *direct consequence* of what was said before. Hendrix (1988:8–9) finds these moral obligations both formally and socially comprehensible in view of the benefactor/honorific phenomena:

> What is 'resolved' in Ephesians, what follows the preamble is precisely those honors appropriate to the benefactors God and Christ. How does one honor this God? How does one reciprocate for the enormous benefactions received? The question becomes all the more pressing since access to a benefaction network previously exclusive to the Jews has been thrown open to the Gentiles. The 'dividing wall' which defined who was within and who was without the covenant and the blessings.... had been abolished in Christ according to the author of Ephesians. How does one, especially Gentiles, honor this benefactor?.... Being thankful here involves more than simply reciting blessings and thanksgiving. It requires living a life worthy of God's benefaction....

> *The exhortation of Eph. 4–6 is cogent formally as a resolution which sets forth the honors one is obliged to offer the benefactors God and Christ* (emphasis mine).

For Hendrix (1988:9) these analogies are too striking to be coincidental, so that he concludes:

> I propose as a working hypothesis that Ephesians is an epistolary decree in which the author recites the universal benefactions of God and Christ and proceeds to stipulate the appropriate honors, understood as the moral obligations of the beneficiaries. This hypothesis might account for other peculiar features of the document.... The density of its diction is appropriate to its public task: proclamation of benefaction and the fulfillment of the beneficiaries' obligations. While the author has framed the document in an epistolary genre, its form follows the general conventions of honorific decrees.

Hendrix's research does not only throw valuable light on the dynamic process by which the Ephesians author creatively reinterpreted forms and concepts from his moral environment, but also illuminates more fully a *significant leitmotiv* of the document, namely the strengthening of the implied readers' identity and ethos worthy of their new status in Christ. "In the rehearsal of benefactions, the ancient reader would not have missed a singular honor bestowed by the benefactor—namely, the grant of citizen status in the divine commonwealth to aliens and sojourners" (Hendrix 1988:9). From this Hendrix infers the rhetorical function of the Ephesians language and style:

> As with many decrees, Ephesians is a prescription of reality. The author adapts a pervasive social reality, the benefactor-beneficiary phenomenon, and through his adaptation prescribes a new network of benefaction. *What is achieved is a powerful reinforcement of Christian identity and cohesion. Christians are those who honor their divine benefactor through moral behavior, animated by love as expressed in mutual benefit* (Hendrix 1988:10; emphasis mine).

Hendrix emphasizes the ethos associated with a specific social identity, and again finds a striking parallel in Ephesians:

> An ethos of reciprocal benefactions and honor *for the common good of the People and the glory of her patrons* was the social premise of the benefactor-beneficiary phenomenon. It is precisely this ethos which is articulated in a 'Christianized' form in Ephesians. As the ultimate benefactors, God and Christ are honored through moral behavior that mutually *benefits God's people* (Hendrix 1988:10; emphasis mine; cf. Eph. 4:1–32).

Understanding the Ephesians document as an honorific decree embedded in the epistolary *genre* in my opinion further illuminates its overwhelming emphasis on different rather unique aspects: Christ's lordship, and his and the implied recipients' exalted position of power (1:10, 19–23; 2:5, 6); the heavenly dimension of the recipients' new status (1:3, 20; 2:6; 3:10; 6:12; cf. Lincoln 1973; 1981:135–168); the document's alternative ethos of praise-giving (1:6, 12, 14; 3:20–21; 5:20), unity (4:1–16) and mutual respect/submission (5:21) associated with those who believed that what He did, was for their benefit (1:19; 5:25).[24] The author acts as mediator of the universal gifts of God's grace and love *in Christ* (1:3–14), and calls the readers to appropriate honor of God and mutual caring for one another (cf. 4:25–32; 5:1–21) as possible expressions of this "common good of the people and the glory of her patrons."[25] All these aspects function within the author's main rhetorical strategy of reassuring his audience of their new status. This emphasis, as well as his use of praise as persuasive device, are typical rhetorical characteristics of an honor and shame culture.[26]

From the structure of ancient honorific decrees it has become clear that these writings were not meant to be merely aesthetic, but to *persuade* the beneficiaries toward specific action (cf. Cunningham 1990:12, 301–374). *This is the essence of rhetoric.* Although it cannot be indicated beyond a doubt that the Ephesians author consciously applied categories of formal rhetorical traditions, Hendrix's work strongly suggests that *epideictic-like* and *deliberative-like* features could be intertwined in the discourse of the document—even though he does not use these categories (cf. Reed 1993:301; Lincoln 1990:lxxiv–lxxv).

3.3.2 *TEMPORAL AND SPATIAL INDICATORS*

Various persuasive techniques are embedded within the encompassing rhetorical device of the Ephesians *genre*, by means of which the author wished to persuade his audience from one position to another. The ancient rhetoricians referred to such tactical shifting devices as τόποι, also known as indicators or *deictics* (from the Greek verb δείκνυμι, i.e. to point out, explain, reveal, inform, prove). Τόποι are defined as "techniques of argumentation" which an author employs in

---

[24]   The rhetorical function of the two intercessory prayers (1:17–21; 3:14–19) has been indicated in 2.1.2.2—that the readers may know and experience God's love in the power of the resurrected and exalted Christ, and redefine themselves in the light of God's relation to them.

[25]   Of particular interest is the purpose clause in 4:29 (ἵνα δῷ χάριν τοῖς ἀκούουσιν—"that it may benefit those who listen"), as well as the recurrence of the reciprocal pronoun ἀλλήλων (4:25, 32; 5:21).

[26]   The main terms used in Ephesians for honor are εὐλογέω (1:3), δόξα (1:6, 12, 14, 17, 18; 3:13, 16, 21), ὑποτάσσω (1:22; 5:21, 24), φοβέομαι (5:33), ὑπακούω (6:5) and τιμάω (6:2). Within the moral context of an honor and shame value system, and the rhetorical argument of the document as a whole, these terms seem to radically redescribe the relationship between Christ and the church, and the members of the body among themselves. All these reflect an attitude of honor, reverence, respect for the other's new authority and status *in Christ*. It is in this sense that the paradoxical example of Christ is supposed to redefine all those relationships.

discourse, in order to control and modify a situation, and specifically with the purpose of persuading the audience toward a new way of thinking and acting (cf. Perelman & Olbrechts-Tyteca 1969:185–410). It refers *inter alia* to aspects of people, time and place, which decisively anchor a discourse in a specific situation (cf. Perelman & Olbrechts-Tyteca 1969:185–514; Corbett 1990:94–143; Vorster 1990:123; 1991:65–68; 1992c; 1992d).

Τόποι necessarily reflect the value system of a group or society, and can therefore not be separated from the socio-historical situation and moral world within which they function. In the context of classical rhetoric, Aristotle identified three means by which people are persuaded, namely the *speaker*, the *audience* and the *speech* itself—which coincides with the three major categories of *sender*, *receiver* and *message* used in twentieth century communication theories (cf. 1.6). These three modes of persuasion can respectively be phrased as the appeal of the speaker's character (ἔθος), the appeal to the emotions and context of the audience (πάθος), and the appeal to reason (λόγος—cf. Malherbe 1986:30–47). Various τόποι appropriate for different occasions would then be selected and used in each mode.[27] Which τόποι would be considered as suitable, how they were used, and with what emphasis, would depend on factors such as the subject matter involved, the perspective of the speaker, and the kind of audience addressed (cf. Cunningham 1990:67–300; 1991:414–418; Corbett 1990: 37–94; Malherbe 1986:48–67).[28]

Deeply concerned about his audience's perception of their primary status, the Ephesians author uses every possible means to contrast their previously *shameful and powerless* position and behavior with that of their present *honor-*

---

[27] The implied audience of a writing "does not only function as cause for communication, but it also determines the selection of linguistic entities, the selection of arguments, the selection of τόποι" (Vorster 1992b:11).

[28] North American systematic theologian David S. Cunningham's doctoral thesis, "Faithful persuasion: Prolegomena to a rhetoric of Christian theology" (1990), is a comprehensive—and in itself a persuasive—argument for appropriating rhetoric within theology. (It was published in 1991, entitled *Faithful Persuasion: In Aid of a Rhetoric of Christian Theology*. Notre Dame, I.N.: University of Notre Dame Press. My references are to the unpublished work though.) Cunningham explores the three modes of persuasion identified by Aristotle—which were developed and extended by modern commentators such as Wayne Booth, Kenneth Burke, and Chaïm Perelman—and skillfully adapts their potential to the sphere of theology. The thesis contains useful information on the three modes of persuasion and their sub-sections, as well as the *praxis* (ethics, politics) of theology as rhetoric. It illustrates how the hermeneutical, transformative potential of the ancient canonized texts is set into motion and unfolds within the creative context of a dynamic, reciprocal, interactive process between the ἔθος of the sender, the λόγος of the medium, and the πάθος of contemporary receivers. In general, Cunningham advocates a paradigm shift for theological method toward a *rhetorical hermeneutic* similar to that proposed by Fiorenza (1988), which is a promising suggestion with regard to the use of the Bible in contemporary Christian ethics (see also Cunningham 1991:422–430).

able and powerful situation and corresponding ethos. To clearly differentiate between these alternative modes of existence (Best 1993), he—in terms of ancient rhetorical categories, probably—employs different τόποι.[29] These constitute significant features of the document's style, and pertain *inter alia* to τόποι of *person-construction* (with regard to the author's ἔθος) and *time* and *space* (with regard to the readers' πάθος). Temporal and spatial deictics are briefly dealt with here, whereas personal indicators will form part of a discussion on the deliberative use and function of *examples* in ancient rhetoric (3.3.5.3).

In different ways temporal and spatial indicators mark the decisive "before" and "after" of the Ephesians readers' coming to faith (cf. 2:1–6, 11–13, 19–22; 4:17–24; 5:8). The period of their present status is seen as *fundamentally* different from their previous status. Their position of dishonor has been replaced by a position of honor. In contrast to a shameful and powerless position where they had been looked down upon by the Jews (2:11–13), excluded from citizenship in Israel and aliens to the covenant (2:12, 19), they are now depicted as fellow-citizens of God's people and members of God's household—a dwelling in which God lives by the Spirit (2:22).

1. The *time* division in Ephesians confirms other indications of their former and present status, in particular what Perelman and Olbrechts-Tyteca (1969:345–349) would call a difference in *order*. This is also expressed by the "old-new" antithesis in the document (4:23–24). Vorster (1992d:5) explains as follows the use of temporal indicators in the Ephesians epistle:

> In.... Ephesians.... temporalisation is effectively used to promote a difference between the status and corresponding behaviour of the implied audience in the past, and their status and behaviour in the present. Their past is seen as a period in which their status was decisively different from their status in the present. Consequently, a certain

---

[29] We have seen how the author strategically assigned a specific identity or status to himself and his audience (2.1). Right through the document, but especially in chapters 4–6, the logical consequence of this status is described in terms of an appropriate ethos. This argument forms the crux of the Ephesians message. As such, the thrust of the document seems to pertain to what Perelman and Olbrechts-Tyteca (1969:293–296; cf. Vorster 1992d:3) describe as the relationship between the *essence* of a phenomenon and its *manifestation*. According to this thesis, the status assigned to the Ephesians author and readers would belong to the *essence* of their being. However, because appropriate behavior would be considered as the *manifestation* of that status, the need for a certain kind of behavior is consistently prompted from their position of honorable status.

In Eph. 2:2 their previous behavior is described in correspondence with their previous status. But, because of God's great love (2:4), they were given a new status: They were made alive, were resurrected, and were seated in a position of power *with Christ* (2:5–6). Therefore (οὖν, τοῦτο οὖν, διό) they were compelled to live accordingly (cf. 4:1, 17, 25). This seems to be the major τόπος within which other τόποι in Ephesians are embedded.

appropriate behaviour could also have been expected from them in the past. Their past is seen as a period without honour and status, but associated with shame and powerlessness. Their earlier conduct portrayed their earlier status as 'natural children of the flesh' (2:2–4; cf. also 4:22–24). That earlier status is on a par with the current status of those that are disobedient, that is in a position of shame (2:3). As children of the flesh they occupied the most shameful state, that of death (2:1, 5). Their earlier status is further described as a period in which they were excluded from being part of Israel, since they were strangers and estranged from the covenant; they were without God and without Christ (2:12).

Thus the new dispensation in Christ (2:13) brought them a totally different and superior—yet at the same time a paradoxical—position of honor (cf. 4:2; 5:2). Their new status and conduct are brought into the closest possible relation to each other (2:10; 4:1, 17; 5:2, 8, 15): Because they were given a new status in the present, their conduct should correspond to that position.

2. Parallel to temporal and other contrasts in Ephesians are *spatial* indicators which emphasize positions inside and outside faith. The most famous of these is the ἐν Χριστῷ formula which appears prominently in chapters 1–3 (cf. Mouton 1987; 1993; 1994). The counterpart to the *in Christ*-position are several negative allusions to indicate a non-preferred shameful position and conduct (cf. 2:1–3, 11–12, 19; 4:17–19, 15–31; 5:3–7, 12). The most important term used in the New Testament to render the idea of shame is αἰσχρός (cf. Domeris 1993:285), which occurs in Ephesians 5:12.[30]

---

[30] Another important τόπος which is often found in Pauline literature, and which is closely related to temporal and spatial indicators, is that of *dissociation* (not to be confused with "disassociation"—Lategan 1993:402). Dissociation refers to that part of the rhetorical process in which a profound change or modification is suggested "that is always prompted by the desire to remove an incompatibility arising out of the confrontation of one proposition with others, whether one is dealing with norms, facts, or truths" (Perelman & Olbrechts-Tyteca 1969:413; cf. Vorster 1992c:6). The objective of dissociation is to compromise, to reconcile. By using shared knowledge, an author would present a modified (metaphorically redescribed) structure of reality, and thus establish a new hierarchy of values. Owing to the strong "in-group" values of religious communities, dissociation becomes a key for the understanding of related religious movements (Vorster 1992c:6).

Dissociation can be used in interaction with various other τόποι. It can for instance be embedded within a pragmatic argument, the concern of which is the link between an event and its consequences. "The consequences function as criterion for the favourable or unfavourable appraisal of the event" (Vorster 1992c:9). In Ephesians the implied audience is challenged with a decision to elevate one of two possible pragmatic effects to the position of a normative criterion, either a lifestyle worthy of their calling which would be positively associated with their new status in Christ (4:1), or humanly made signs such as circumcision and the regulations of the law (2:11, 15), which would communicate the negative value attached to an inferior status. Their choice would designate them as either

The temporal and spatial indicators in Ephesians function on two important levels. Firstly, they are used to *identify* different dispensations, and preferred or non-preferred positions. Secondly, they are used as a rhetorical strategy "*to effect the shifting of position*" (Lategan 1993:402). *Indicating* preferred and non-preferred positions is one thing. However, to achieve a shift in the right direction is another matter. But that is precisely what rhetoric is about, and that is clearly the purpose of the Ephesians author. How does he go about ensuring the desired result?[31] How does he influence his readers to accept their new, advantageous position—even after they have come to faith (cf. 1:1, 15)? How is their change of attitude and behavior supposed to take place?

---

wise or foolish (cf. 5:15–17).

As we have seen thus far, the author of Ephesians is concerned with the confirmation of the status of Gentile Christians. By emphasizing their equal position to that of Jewish Christians, he does not wish to induce conflict between the two groups, but to bring about compromise and harmony between them. His objective is not to sever the ties with Jewish Christians, but to justify the reconciliation of Jewish and non-Jewish Christians and their integration and unity within one body (1:23; 4:15, 16), a holy temple with Christ as the chief cornerstone, in whom they are "joined together" (συναρμολογουμένη—2:20, 21) and "are being built together (συνοικοδομεῖσθε) to become a dwelling in which God lives by his Spirit" (2:22). The redescription of other roles referred to in the document should also be viewed within this context.

The norm or criterion for this justification is *Christ* (cf. 4.3.4), who is their peace (2:14). He has destroyed the dividing wall of hostility (2:14, 16), that element which defined the position of those who were within and those who were without the covenant and its blessings (cf. Hendrix 1988:9). "His purpose was to create in himself *one new man* (*sic*) out of the two, thus making peace, and in this one body to reconcile both of them to God through the cross, by which he put to death their hostility" (2:15, 16). In this way Christ destroyed every "boundary marker" (e.g. circumcision—2:11, the law with its commandments and regulations—2:15) which were observed by the Jews, and which created a very strong "in-group" consciousness with exclusivist tendencies. Within the new (functional) hierarchy of values proposed by the Ephesians author, Christ functions as criterion for a practical ethos that would be in accordance with God's will (5:17) and that would fit their new status. This ethos is described in terms of different relationships within the church, society, marriage and family, and has a consistent christological orientation (1:7; 2:16; 5:2, 25). Their new status and conduct is thus brought into the closest possible relation (2:10; 4:1, 17; 5:2, 8, 15).

We have seen that the symbol of reconciliation by which the ethos of the new faith community is orientated—the cross—is a symbol of shame, powerlessness and social rejection. It now becomes "a symbol to strengthen group-identity and -consciousness. *Dissociation* functions.... in the sense that the 'actual' meaning of the cross is to be seen in the way it provides access to a position of honor within the circle of the Jews" (Vorster 1992c:14, referring to the rhetorical function of the cross in the letter to the Galatians). In this sense dissociation corresponds closely with the communicative processes of identification and estrangement.

[31] Cf. Lategan 1993:404, with reference to Paul's letter to the Galatians.

For the Ephesians author the key to change is provided by the interrelated communication processes of *orientation,* *disorientation,* and *reorientation* (Ricoeur 1975:122–128; 1976:46–53, 89–95; 1977:65–100; 1980:21–27; McFague 1982:46–48), *identification* and *estrangement* (Rousseau 1986:317), *alienation* and *re-identification* (Du Toit 1992), *association* and *disassociation* (Lategan 1993:402), or *distancing* and *appropriation* (Hartin 1994:514–516). We have seen in the theoretical section (1.6.2) that these processes reveal the essence and (re)orientating potential of metaphorical language, which forms the heart of (biblical) hermeneutics. As illustration of the Ephesians epistle's essentially interpretive nature, its wealth of metaphorical language and traditional material was subsequently explored through a multi-dimensional analysis of the document (2.1.3; 2.2.1). Those results are developed further now within the context of metaphor as rhetorical strategy.

3.3.3   *THE PERSUADING POTENTIAL OF METAPHORICAL LANGUAGE*

It has been indicated that the Ephesians author adapted potentially influential metaphors and traditions from his moral world to explain his experience and understanding of the Christ event (cf. Du Toit 1984a:17).[32] These serve as windows through which the implied processes of *identification and estrangement* can be viewed—those processes typical of the image-making capacity of the human mind, of its ability to move by indirection from the known to the unknown (McFague 1982:33). Any creative act of interpretation, discovery, decision-making, change or transformation can thus be recognized as the imaginative combination and synthesis of the familiar into new wholes (McFague 1982:35–36)—which is a *redescription of reality* (Ricoeur 1975:122–128; 1976:45–69; 1980:26).

This process can also be applied to the metaphorical language of the Ephesians epistle, and particularly to the descriptions of Jesus Christ as "metaphor or parable for God," and as "model for Christian behavior"—to use McFague's terms (1982:31–66, 90–194; cf. 1.6.2.1–2). To follow her argument from metaphor to Jesus as parable, and Christ as model or example for Christian behavior, McFague's description of the relation between metaphor and parable is briefly discussed here. The purpose of this section within the ambit of the study, is to investigate the implied significance of the Christ event *as story* for an imaginative functioning of the New Testament in Christian ethics.

---

[32]   For example, we have seen how a creative reinterpretation of the only direct citation from an Old Testament tradition in Eph. (Ps. 68:19 in Eph. 4:8–10) serves as rhetorical strategy to emphasize Christ's exalted position, as well as the gracious gifts to members of his body associated with that position (2.2.1.2).

.1 The Relation between Metaphor and Parable

McFague argues that the basic characteristics of metaphorical language (indirection, extravagance, mundanity) also apply to Jesus' parables, and to Jesus as parable (McFague 1982:31–54).[33] "A parable.... is a metaphorical process in narrative form. A parabolic metaphor, in the strangeness of its plot, institutes a shock which redescribes reality, and opens for us a new way of seeing and being. The Kingdom of God is like 'what happens' in the story. What happens, despite its everyday setting and circumstances, is 'odd.' More, it is 'extravagant.' This form of metaphorical process opens an otherwise matter-of-fact situation to an open range of interpretations and to the possibility of new commitments" (Ricoeur 1980:26).

In the Synoptic tradition the parables of Jesus are concerned with relations among people. The kingdom of God is always explained *indirectly* through telling a story.[34] Confirming Ricoeur's reference (1975:94–112; 1980:21–27) to the interactive patterns in permanent tension in a parable as two ways of being in the world (the conventional way and the way of the kingdom), McFague (1982: 45) defines parable as "a judgment or assertion of similarity and difference between two thoughts in permanent tension with one another: one is the ordinary way of being in the world and the other, the extraordinary way." Reality is re-described and reshaped through the tension generated by these two perspectives, and the listener is implicitly or explicitly asked to make a decision (cf. McFague 1982:45–46, 50–51). It is in this sense that the potential power of metaphors and parables as strategic "shifting devices" becomes important—not only for understanding the moral world and underlying communication processes of an ancient text, but also for its appropriation by later readers.

Apart from its indirectness, the language of the parables is characterized by its *extravagance*, by the element of the extraordinary, of radicalism, of surprise and reversal. They are metaphors with considerable shock value, because their intention is to upset conventional interpretations of reality. Events occur and decisions are made in the parables which are absurd, radical, alien, extreme. The extreme quality of the parables appears in *the passion for the rule of God* and its

---

[33] Ricoeur's discussion (1976:53–70) on the movement from metaphor to symbol, and metaphor to model (1977:239–256) develops along similar lines (cf. Van Huyssteen 1986:159–168; 1987:24–31). In this sense Jesus Christ may also be considered as a *symbol* or *sacrament* of God and God's mighty presence.

[34] The stories of the parables are indeed extended metaphors providing exemplars or models for the kingdom: "(T)he structure of human relationships which it suggests; its inversion of expectations; its intimation of a set of priorities; its existential, ordinary and secular quality—all of this is the grid or screen which allows us to see what life in the rule of God is like" (McFague 1982:46). The parables do not define that life, but provide models for it.

overriding importance in relation to everything else (McFague 1982:43, 44, 46).[35]
At the same time, most of the New Testament parables (like the Old Testament imagery for God) are personal and relational, concerned with different ways of dealing with other people. This implies that, in the continuing (re)description of people's understanding of God, "many as well as novel images are appropriate and necessary to both avoid idolatry and remain relevant to a people's experience of God" (McFague 1982:43).

In general, we can say that parables function in the play of two different basic perspectives or orientations to reality (cf. Birch & Rasmussen 1989:61–62). McFague (1982:46–47), drawing on Ricoeur' notions (1975:122–128), suggests in this respect that parables work on a pattern of *orientation, disorientation, and reorientation*: "A parable begins in the ordinary world with its conventional standards and expectations, but in the course of the story a radically different perspective is introduced that disorients the listener, and finally, through the interaction of the two competing viewpoints, tension is created that results in a redescription of life in the world." She concludes by saying that a parable is "an assault on the accepted, conventional way of viewing reality. It is an assault on the social, economic, and mythic structures people build for their own comfort and security. A parable is a story meant to invert and subvert these structures and to suggest that the way of the kingdom is not the way of the world" (McFague 1982:47). Parables were thus meant to shock and reverse the expectations of their listeners and readers, and to shift their moral vision and behavior in radical ways (cf. Lategan 1992b:154; Birch & Rasmussen 1989:61–62).[36]

A third characteristic of New Testament parables is their notably *mundane* or *secular* nature: They are introduced as ordinary stories about ordinary people

---

[35] In this sense the scope and intention of Jesus' parables are closely related to that of the Ephesians epistle.

[36] Throughout the parables, then, two standards or perspectives are in constant tension with each other, and the effect of their interaction is profound *disorientation* (cf. Ricoeur 1975:122–128). Not "liking" the parables (because they upset conventional security) is the appropriate initial reaction to them. Like the first phase of understanding, the next one (that of *reorientation*) should be considered as open-ended and provisional. "What the parables stand for is opposition to all forms of idolatry and absolutism, *even* the new orientation to reality brought about through the parables' redescription of reality. The permanent function of parables is to enhance consciousness of the radical relativity of human models of reality, even when these models are 'divinely inspired,' that is, based on the new way of the kingdom" (McFague 1982:47).

From this view on the parables, McFague comes to two important conclusions regarding the basis for a metaphorical theology. Indications for *method* can be summed up in the following way: "A theology influenced by the parables would be open-ended, tensive, secular, indirect, iconoclastic, and revolutionary" (McFague 1982:48). As far as the *content* of metaphorical theology and ethics is concerned, the focus is on relational life. These observations provide valuable criteria for the construction and criticism of the use of Scripture—and particularly its language—in Christian ethics (see chapter 4).

engaged in ordinary, every day matters and decisions (cf. McFague 1982:42–44). This is also a distinctive feature of the metaphorical language of the Ephesians document (cf. 2.2.1).

.2 Jesus Christ as Metaphor and Parable

All the abovementioned characteristics of metaphor and parable come into clearer focus and are epitomized when Jesus himself is considered as an extended metaphor, a parable of God (cf. McFague 1982:48–54). The story of Jesus of Nazareth indeed functions as the parable *par excellence* of the New Testament. His life and work form the central "critical interpretive framework for under-standing the divine-human relationship" during and after the formation of the identity and ethos of the early Christian communities (McFague 1982:44; cf. Johnson 1999:93–153). For McFague, the categories of metaphor and parable function as a key to Christian ethics and the formation of moral people, in a way similar to the functioning of "story" in the narrative ethics of Stanley Hauerwas and others (cf. 4.4.4.3; Spohn 1984:89–102). According to them, both these notions have the potential to impact on biblical readers by continuously reorient-ing and transforming their self-understanding and ethos as disciples of Jesus Christ:

If we say.... as I would want to, that Jesus of Nazareth is par excellence the metaphor of God, we mean that his familiar, mundane story is the way, the in-direct but necessary way, from here to there.... Metaphoric meaning is a *process*, not a momentary, static insight: it operates like a story, moving from here to there, from 'what is' to 'what might be' (McFague, as quoted by Spohn 1984: 100).

Like metaphors and stories, the essence of parable is that it works through the ordinary, mundane, and secular—by indirection—to bring about new insight. This means that we start with the (more familiar) work of Jesus from "below," and move *indirectly* to his person, and to the invisible (unfamiliar) God whom He represents.[37] The whole network of Jesus' life, his words and deeds, and par-

---

[37] We can accept that this was the way by which the early church arrived at its con-fession of Jesus as the Christ: "(F)rom experiences of healing, forgiveness, and renewal in relation to this man came the attempt to say who he was. The work of Jesus forces the question of his person.... The many titles ascribed to him—Messiah, Son of God, Son of man, and so on—are metaphors from the Hebraic tradition which provide familiar screens through which to interpret the strange and marvelous work of this man" (McFague 1982: 49). With reference to Richard Schaeffler, the Catholic philosopher of language, Müller and Smit (1994:393–394) further illustrate this metaphorical process by showing how believers spontaneously address and name God (which is the fundamental act in prayer): "These names have a narrative structure, they summarise, recall, and appeal to specific events, acts, histories, memories. The identity of the God addressed in prayer is given in the narratives that underlie the divine name or names. In prayer, this naming of God

ticularly his death, resurrection and exaltation, provides a grid or screen through which the understanding of God can be realigned (cf. McFague 1982:49–54; Hays 1990:45–46; 2.1.2). In this way McFague (1982:49) regards the metaphor of "parable" as ideally suited to express the work and person of Jesus Christ. At the same time however she considers it as *one* provisional way to confront the question of God, while taking seriously both the central concerns of the New Testament and the sensibilities of contemporary readers.

How then does Jesus' designation as parable of God *realign, redefine* or *re-orientate* later readers' understanding of God? (Ricoeur 1975:122–128; 1976:89–95; 1977:216–256). As a true and novel metaphor, Jesus as parable reorders and upsets familiar, conventional preconceptions and understandings of God. "The interactive partners in permanent tension in the parable that is Jesus' life are the prior understandings we have of proper life under God in the world, and the way of the kingdom, which was the focus of his entire existence. Just as the parables center on the kingdom, so does the life and death of Jesus" (McFague 1982:50). She believes that the heart of the drama of Jesus' life and death is the tension that it manifests between *accepted ways of relating to God and to others*, and *a new way of living in the world*. As such Jesus' life and especially his death has to be viewed as "extravagant, radical, and shocking"—a scandal which calls into question the comfortable and secure homes that our interpretations of God have built for us (cf. McFague 1982:51).[38]

---

develops into further narrations, narrations of the history of God, reminding the One addressed of his own identity and previous acts, as well as narrations of the history of the person or people who pray, their experiences, needs, suffering, hopes."

[38] To be consistent, McFague (1982:51) suggests that the characteristic "is" and "is not" tension of metaphor be maintained—and idolatry be avoided—by not *identifying* metaphors for Jesus with God. "(T)o see Jesus as a parable and thus to deny his identity with God is important for peoples whose experience has been excluded due to the particularity of Jesus' person and history, for instance, for women who feel excluded by Jesus' maleness" (McFague 1982:51–52).

I am hesitant, though, about some of the conclusions McFague draws from Jesus as a parable for God. The same applies to her explanation of the ethos of his disciples (cf. McFague 1982:48–54). Even in a religiously pluralistic society, Jesus Christ remains, *according to the Christian paradigm, the* ultimate parable (or "ground metaphor" to use Geertz's term) for explaining God. North American Christian feminist Denise L. Carmody (1992:143–136) raises similar criticism against McFague: "(T)here is a contradiction between presenting a theology as Christian and not making Jesus its crux—not finding in Jesus the unique revelation of what God is like, what humanity might become through God's grace, and where salvation (utterly radical healing) has taken place" (1992:145; cf. Müller & Smit 1994:404–406). Yet, an ethically responsible use of the Bible has also to account for other expressions of the divine—especially in the light of its exclusively monotheistic claims about God (cf. Dt. 6:4; Is. 40:12–31; Mt. 11:27; Jh. 14:6). Various questions arise from this: Are Christians then supposed to opt for a *henotheistic* view on reality—acknowledging the existence of more than one god, but worshipping only one—or

Another essential characteristic of Jesus' ministry related to parable, is the *personal* and *relational* focus of his work. This is illustrated by his calling God "Father," which does not provide the foundation for a patriarchal model for God, but which reveals the great intimacy and affection which describes his own sense of utter trust in God. Likewise, the thrust of his teaching and healing was toward people, their way of relating to others, and their physical and spiritual wholeness and health (cf. Smit 1994e:49–51). "Thus, a theology dependent on Jesus as parable will focus on the quality of relationships among differing kinds of persons; *in such theology ethics can never be an appendage to systematic theology, but at its heart*" (McFague 1982:52; emphasis mine).

This further implies that Jesus' mode of relating to people and God, can be characterized as *radical, shocking and unconventional* (McFague 1982:52). Jesus constantly created tension with established ways, and reversed expectations wherever He went.[39] Jesus' life, as an embodiment of the kingdom, is one partner in the drama; the other is the economic, political, religious, national and social mores of his time. The cross becomes the focal point of the scandal and thrust of Jesus' life, "for the cross is both the supreme offence to the ways of the world and the greatest test of trust against conventional evidence. The cross.... is also a parable of God's way of dealing with evil, a way different from that of conventional ways" (McFague 1982:53, cf. 52; Meeks 1993:61–65, 86–88, 129, 131–135). The shocking part of the cross is that a conception of good is found *not* by separation from evil, but by suffering identification with it (McFague 1982:53, drawing on notions from a British theologian, Maurice Wiles; cf. Eph. 1:7; 2:15, 16; 5:2).

To summarize, it can be said that the consideration of Jesus as parable of God reveals the same characteristics as that of metaphor: mundane, indirect, unconventional, and radical. His early and later followers were/are therefore challenged to reflect the same parabolic qualities. "Like Jesus, 'who' we are depends to a great extent on what we do; the intimate relationship between being

---

should they maintain a *monotheistic* view on God and reality? (cf. Ephesians' reference to Christ's power and dominion over all rule and authority). And what are the implications of considering Jesus as one legitimate expression of the divine among others for Christian missionary work? (cf. Eph. 3:10). What is the relevance and ultimate reference of Christian theology as human thinking about God? One way of dealing with these and other related issues, would be to encourage interreligious dialogue, where the unique claims (ultimate commitments) of different religions can be discussed and respected according to minimum criteria such as problem-solving and reality-depicted potential—accounting for both the nature and intention of their different canonical writings, and the context of successive readers (cf. Van Huyssteen 1986:169–214). These questions are important, but do not form part of the immediate scope of the book.

[39] In the Gospel of Mark, for instance, the most frequent responses to Jesus are surprise, awe, wonder, and fear at the disturbing, unsettling quality of his words and deeds (cf. Mk. 1:22, 27; 2:12; 4:41; 5:42; 6:2, 51; 7:37; 9:6, 32; 16:8).

and doing in the Judeo-Christian tradition militates against both empty spirituality and over-intellectualism.... Moreover, like Jesus we are called to life *in* but not *of* the world, to lives that always stand in criticism of the status quo and that press toward fulfillment in the kingdom" (McFague 1982:54).

.3 Identification with Christ as Model

The ultimate purpose of the Ephesians author's use of metaphorical language is to provide a basis for the readers' new self-understanding and perspective on reality (cf. Lategan 1993:404–406). In the linguistic-literary and socio-historical readings of Ephesians (2.1; 2.2) it has become clear that he employs two major strategies in order to accomplish this goal. Firstly, he emphasizes his own, as well as the readers' identification with Christ, and, secondly, his own identification with them (cf. 3.3.4).

The Ephesians author reminds his readers that their own dramatic change was not self-initiated, but was effected by the closest possible association with Christ—in his death and resurrection, and especially his exaltation to the right hand of God (1:18–21; cf. Lincoln 1990:61). "Change cannot be achieved on one's own or in isolation—only in solidarity with Christ and with fellow-believers" (Lategan 1993:405). Being "raised up *with Christ* and seated.... *with him* in the heavenly realms" (2:6) is therefore pictured by the author in the most practical terms (Eph. 4–6). "Change becomes a reality through this association with the greater power of a living God" (Lategan 1993:405).

Christ functions decisively in terms of time and status. It is He who brought about the new era by destroying the "dividing wall of hostility" through the cross (cf. 2:14–22). However, as the decisive element in creating the distinction between old and new, Christ actually symbolizes *the power of God* (1:5–7, 9). In the confessional pronouncement of 1:20–23 (which has structurally been identified as the chiastic centre of Eph. 1–3) it is explicitly stated that it was *God's* power which ensured Christ's absolute position. As symbol of God's power, Christ is also symbol of the faith community's unity (2:20–22; 4:15, 16).

"Identification with this symbol means sharing in and interacting with that which the symbol symbolizes, that is God's power and the unity of the community" (Vorster 1992d:7; cf. Meeks 1993:92–96, 131–135). In this sense the many prepositional phrases identifying the implied audience's position ἐν Χριστῷ are indeed remarkable (1:3, 10, 12, 15, 20; 2:6, 7, 10, 13; 3:6, 11, 21; 4:32), and particularly the designations in 2:5, 6: συνεζωοποίησεν τῷ Χριστῷ.... καὶ συνήγειρεν καὶ συνεκάθισεν ἐν τοῖς ἐπουρανίοις ἐν Χριστῷ Ἰησοῦ. All these strategies serve to create a healthy consciousness of their new status (cf. Hoch 1982).

However, Christ does not only function as a parable and symbol, but also as a *model* inducing specific behavior. That means that specific values which are associated with Christ are generated towards those who identify with him (cf.

2.1.2.3). In the macro-context of the document these refer to love, grace, peace, forgiveness, holiness, humility, honesty, unity.... In Ephesians the implied audience is urged to imitate not only Christ (5:2), but also God (5:1; cf. 4:24).[40] Husbands are told to model their behavior toward their wives on Christ's relationship with the community of believers (5:23–25).

Yet, while their association with Christ seems to induce a stronger in-group awareness, and confirms their new status as a counteract of any thoughts of inferiority they might have had, their new position of power and glory should *not* be absolutized at the cost of the full nature of Christ's example. Ephesians pictures Christ as model particularly in terms of his *servanthood*. Part and parcel of the process of associating with him, is therefore an experience of surprise, shock and estrangement. This is implied when the Ephesians readers' exalted position *with Christ* (2:5, 6) is simultaneously described in terms of *the paradox of his status and ethos* as an "offering and sacrifice to God" (5:2), and the giving up of himself for them (cf. 1:7; 2:13, 16; 4:2; 5:2, 25). God's grace and peace are concretized in the *blood* of Christ, a symbol for his *death*. His position is further characterized by the sociologically shameful symbol of a cross (Rome's most shaming form of execution), which is reinterpreted and turns out to be an honorable deed for the benefit of those who adhere to him by faith (1:7; 2:16; cf. Seeley 1989; Meeks 1993:14–15, 48–50, 61–65, 86–88, 129, 131–135).[41] After having been *alienated* from the initial perception of the cross as a symbol of shame, the audience is *re-oriented* according to a new perspective on the cross as a symbol of honor, confirmed by Christ's resurrection and exaltation. It is by the glory of these strange events that the "theology" and "ethics" of the Ephesians epistle are shaped.

It seems as if the author deliberately stressed the paradoxical aspect of Christ's position of power to emphasize the implied readers' identification with him as *servant*. Right through the document their status and conduct are seen in the closest possible relation to that of Christ (2:10; 4:1, 2, 17; 5:2, 8, 15).[42] Like

---

[40] Cf. the ideal of the Platonists and Stoics "to be like God," i.e. to live *in accord with nature* (Meeks 1986a:43, 47). To use Christ and even God as model for human behavior, might thus be another example of the Ephesians author's strategy to reinterpret well-known moral traditions from a new perspective.

[41] Faith, in terms of obedience to God and Christ, is in such a context likewise linked with honor.

[42] During a discussion of her paper *The contributions of feminist theory to Biblical studies as rhetorical studies* at an international conference on *Rhetoric and Religion* at UNISA, 15–18 Aug. 1994, Elisabeth Schüssler Fiorenza phrased the orientation point of the New Testament documents in terms of God's "energizing" (not "dominating") power in and through Christ.

Bearing the abovementioned rhetorical strategies in mind, it is doubtful whether the abundant references to Christ in Ephesians (2.1.3.1) were meant (only) to introduce him as a theological theme. In nearly every instance of reference to him, the confirmation of the implied audience's status is in focus. Christ's vital role in the document thus seems to *put*

him, they were also called to serve—not only by (verbally) making known "the manifold wisdom of God.... to the rulers and authorities in the heavenly realms" (3:10), but also to live (non-verbally) as "the 'theatre of God's works".... for the benefit of the world" (Barth 1974b:364; cf. Eph. 2:7; 5:8; Wessels 1990b:66). If they were to "prove" the quality of their status in their everyday moral world, they had to make themselves known in terms of concrete signs of peace, that is, by being *peacemakers* (cf. Mt. 5:9). As the body of the resurrected Christ, they were meant to *represent* him as their model (literally *to make him present*—cf. Roberts 1978:171), by living as God's dwelling, and as symbols of his grace and love (cf. Eph. 2:14, 22).

Roberts (1978:169–177) explains how the ecclesiological viewpoint of the document—which underlies the first main section—is strategically perpetuated in the second main section. The paraenetical section starts with an exhortation (4:1–6) to maintain the unity of the church which has been described in chapters 1–3. We have seen how the author develops a picture of the ascended Christ, reigning over God's people from a position of power and authority, and empowering them with certain gifts (4:7–11). This is followed by an exposition of the church's equipment and practical functioning under the guidance of Christ as head of his body (4:11–16).

The thrust of these passages is the intended pragmatic effect of the church's equipment, namely to *serve*. While their new status challenged them to identify with Christ as lord in his exalted position, they were at the same time challenged to be reoriented in accordance with the essential nature of that status, namely as servants. The reason why the body has to build itself up in love, is "to prepare God's people for works of service" (4:12, 16; cf. 2:10).[43]

Their new position of power was thus defined (after the paradoxical model

---

into motion and strengthen the main rhetorical argument, namely that a position of such honorable status as to be *in Christ*, to live under his lordship, power and authority, should accordingly correspond with a distinctive kind of behavior (cf. Hendrix 1988).

[43]   Roberts (1978:172–177) further explains how different metaphors for the church (especially the church as God's *inheritance/ possession*—1:11, 14; as *the building of God*—2:19–22; 4:11–16; and as *the body of Christ*—1:22–23, 5:22–30) function to strengthen the vision of the church *as servant* in the macro-context of the document. He discerns two levels in the church's role of servanthood:

   • *service directed to God* (liturgical service in terms of praise-giving and prayer—1:20, 21; 5:18–20, and a personal commitment to God in terms of knowledge of God's will, obedience to him by renewing the attitude of their minds and a practical ethos that pleases God—1:9; 5:17; 4:21–24; 4:17–6:10);

   • *service directed to others* (as members of the body "inwardly" serving and teaching each other, effectively building one another up towards the fullness of Christ—4:11–16, and 'outwardly' proclaiming the Lordship of Christ over all creatures, even against the powers and principalities—1:20–22; 3:1b, 9, 10; 5:14, 15; 6:15, 18–20). This would implicitly include the church's enlightening, empowering, pastoral role directed toward society as a whole (2:13–18; 5:18–20).

of Christ) in terms of self-sacrificing love (5:2, 25). On the one hand their love and service was geared toward the strengthening of their in-group identity, yet on the other hand, to be a dynamic proclamation to Jewish and Gentile outsiders.

3.3.4 *IDENTIFICATION OF IMPLIED AUTHOR AND AUDIENCE*

It is this association with Christ, this radical reorientation, *this decisive change*, which the Ephesians author so intensely desires for his addressees. In order to facilitate such a shift, it is of crucial importance that he develops and establishes another form of close association—alongside his identification with Christ—namely *with his audience*. In the process, his use of personal pronouns and the terms in which he addresses them play an important role. He does not approach them from a distance. In order to persuade them of "the issue that mattered" (Mack 1990:20), he uses at least four further strategies: in-group identity markers, person deictics, exaggeration and the relativization of defects.

.1 In-group Identity Markers

There can be little doubt that identification between implied author and readers is of paramount importance in the Ephesians epistle. The strategies which the author uses to identify with his audience, suggest that he wants to persuade them toward specific action. With a particular exigency in mind, he apparently wants to move them toward a renewed vision of their status in Christ, and a particular behavior in accordance with that status.

In order to establish a common ground between him and his audience, the Ephesians author firstly uses various in-group identity markers, which show that he acknowledges their new status (cf. Vorster 1992d:2). They are addressed as "saints.... the faithful in Christ Jesus" (1:1), as those who are the object of God's blessings (1:3), those who are chosen and "predestined.... to be adopted as his sons through Jesus Christ" (1:5, 11), those to whom God has revealed "the mystery of his will" (1:9), those who were marked by the seal of the Holy Spirit (1:13). Every action performed by God or Christ is described in terms of the mutual relationship between implied author and readers, signifying the common ground between them.

.2 Person Deictics

Secondly, it is noteworthy to see how the author anchors his audience to himself by means of the inclusive first person plural deictic ἡμᾶς. In comparison to ὑμεῖς which occurs only three times in 1:2, 13 for instance, the accusative, genitive and dative cases of the pronoun ἡμᾶς, ἡμῶν and ἡμῖν occur eleven times in 1:2–14. By affirming that they belong to the same in-group, he stresses the common ground between them, and assures them of his positive attitude toward them and his appreciation of, and concern for them (cf. 1:15–16). As a summary of everything they have in common, he greets them with χάρις ὑμῖν καὶ εἰρήνη ἀπὸ θεοῦ πατρὸς ἡμῶν καὶ κυρίου Ἰησοῦ Χριστοῦ. (1:2; cf. 6:23–24). The first main section starts with an introduction of ὁ θεὸς καὶ πατὴρ τοῦ κουρίου ἡμῶν Ἰησοῦ Χριστοῦ (1:3). Both author and readers have been blessed "with every spiritual blessing in Christ" (1:3). Both were chosen in Christ "before the creation of the world to be holy and blameless in his sight" (1:4). Both were—in accordance with God's pleasure and will—predestined to sonship (*sic*; 1:5). Both received redemption through the blood of Christ—in accordance with the riches of God's grace (1:6, 7). Both were in possession of God's secret knowledge and wisdom—according to God's good pleasure (1:9). They both put their hope in Christ (1:12). In the final analysis they were all meant to be to the praise of God's glory (1:6, 12, 14).

On the negative side the author identifies with his readers by reminding them that at one time they *both* lived among the disobedient, "gratifying the cravings of our sinful nature and following its desires and thoughts" (2:2, 3). Author and audience thus shared decisive past and even pre-past experiences.

It becomes clear that in a number of cases these in-group markers identify both author and readers as recipients of God's gifts and grace. All these gifts relate to a position of status. Although the primary function of the *berakah* (Eph. 1–3) would formally be to thank and praise God, it seems that—from a rhetorical perspective—the author utilizes it mainly to signify the common ground between him and his readers.

In 1:15–23 and 3:14–21 he further illustrates his goodwill towards them by mentioning his prayers for them. The contents of these prayers serve as a strategic reminder of their position of honor and power (cf. Mouton 1993). Of vital importance is the analogy drawn between that which has happened to Christ and to them. He prays that they may know God's "incomparably great power for us who believe. That power is like the working of his mighty strength, which he exerted in Christ when he raised him from the dead and seated him at his right hand in the heavenly realms...." (1:17, 19, 20). Parallel to this, he continues in 2:6 with a similar structural pattern: "And God raised us up with Christ and seated us with him in the heavenly realm in Christ Jesus...." This is an empowerment strategy *par excellence*.

Reference has been made in 2.1.2.2 to Ephesians 3:2–13 as an *anacoluthon* within the larger context of the prayer of intercession in 3:1, 14–21. The rhetorical function of an *anacoluthon* is to emphasize the *content* of the interruption, as well as the *context* within which it "interrupts" the basic line of thought. This concerns the status of the readers as members of God's new family (cf. 3:6 as a summary of what has been said before), but also the status of the author as an authoritative servant of the gospel. The introduction of the "person" of the author therefore does not constitute a new argument, but serves the underlying argument concerning a difference in order. "(I)t is exactly this mystery knowledge which proves yet again that a totally different order has dawned (3:5) and this different order signifies a new status for the Gentiles (3:6)" (Vorster 1992d:8). It has been indicated (3.2) that the "person"—character, ethos, appellative power—of the sender is of ultimate importance in the communication event (cf. Cunningham 1990:153–221; 1991; Perelman & Olbrechts-Tyteca 1969:293–327; Vorster 1992c:1–4).

The Ephesians author's claim to authority primarily lies in his possession of mystery knowledge (μυστήριον) which he obtained by means of revelation (3:3, 4, 9; 6:19). He derives his apostleship from the almighty God who showed his power by raising Jesus from the dead (3:2, 7–9). Although he is less than the least of all God's people (3:8), he received the commission to administer the grace and mystery of God, namely to preach to the Gentiles the unsearchable riches of God (3:2, 8–9). The following syntactically and semantically related symbols recur in 3:1–20, which—in concurrence with the broad coherence of the document—further depict the author's perspective on his paradoxical authority as "an apostle of Christ Jesus by the will of God" (1:1): καταλαμβάνω (3:18), γνῶσις (3:19), χάρις (3:2, 7, 8), δύναμις (3:7, 16, 20), ἀγάπη (3:17, 19).

The audience might have wondered why the author waited until "chapter 3" before disclosing his authority. One possibility is that he wished to ensure thier goodwill directly before he paid attention to their behavior in chapters 4–6. In fact, the ultimate reason why God had revealed the mystery of the Gentiles' new identity is already stated in 3:10–11: "His intent was that now, through the church, the manifold wisdom of God should be made known to the rulers and authorities in the heavenly realms, according to his eternal purpose which he accomplished in Christ Jesus our Lord."

Another striking feature of the author's reference to himself, is the designation "Paul, the prisoner of Christ Jesus for the sake of you Gentiles...." (3:1; cf. 4:1; 6:19). In 6:20 he refers to himself as "an ambassador in chains." Analogous to Christ's paradoxical position of honor as servant, "Paul" finds himself in a paradoxical position of shameful and powerless imprisonment—yet, redeemed and raised up with Christ to a position of power and honor (cf. 1:7; 2:6). In speaking from a shameful and powerless position, "Paul" would probably identify much better with his audience who apparently found themselves in an inferior situation of little or no power and honor. From this position the person deictics "we" serves as a powerful tool to anchor them to himself, and to encourage and empower them toward a new perspective on reality.

The encoded author's awareness of his own, as well as his audience's identity, is further emphasized by the way in which he involves them in his ministry (6:18–20). In spite of his self-description in 3:8, he does not reckon himself unimportant (in a kind of false humility). He does not pretend as if he could afford to be forgotten by the congregations just because he was a powerless prisoner. On the contrary, he recommends himself to his readers with confidence and urgency, so that they would intercede on his behalf. Once again his plea is paradoxical, because everything does not in the final analysis revolve around himself and his personal interests, but around his calling and position in Christ. "Pray also for me, that whenever I open my mouth, words may be given me so that I will fearlessly make known the mystery of the gospel...." (6:19). The real point is not Paul's apostleship, nor his person, but the truth and legitimacy of the gospel of Jesus Christ. Ultimately the loyalty he wants to gain is not a loyalty to himself, but a loyalty to God and Christ (cf. Du Toit 1992:279–280).

Thus everything the author emphasizes about himself seems to be geared toward a pastoral motive—that is to strengthen the *in Christ* status and in-group awareness of his recipients—which is directly linked to a certain behavior.

.3 Exaggeration

Thirdly, the τόπος of exaggeration is employed by which admiration for the other is expressed in order to establish common ground. This technique, *inter alia*, occurs in the following sections:

- 1:3—ἐν πάσῃ εὐλογίᾳ ("with every spiritual blessing");

- 1:4—πρὸ καταβολῆς κόσμου ("before the creation of the world");

- 1:8—ἐν πάσῃ σοφίᾳ καὶ φρονήσει ("with all wisdom and understanding");

- 1:16—οὐ παύομαι εὐχαριστῶν ὑπὲρ ὑμῶν ("I have not stopped giving thanks for you");

- 1:19—τὸ ὑπερβάλλον μέγεθος τῆς δυνάμεως αὐτοῦ.... κατὰ τὴν ἐνέργειαν τοῦ κράτους τῆς ἰσχύος αὐτοῦ ("his incomparably great power.... the working of his mighty strength"; cf 3:20);

- 2:7—τὸ ὑπερβάλλον πλοῦτος τῆς χάριτος αὐτοῦ ("the incomparable riches of his grace");

- 3:8—ἐμοὶ τῷ ἐλαχιστοτέρῳ πάντων ἁγίων.... τὸ ἀνεξιχνίαστον πλοῦτος τοῦ Χριστοῦ ("I am less than the least of all God's people").

.4 Relativization of Defects

Fourthly, the Ephesians author relativizes any defect which might have occurred on the side of his audience. In 1:15 he mentions their love for all the saints (εἰς πάντας τοὺς ἁγίους), while ἅγιοι normally referred to Israel as the people of God.

This process of identification between author and readers unfolds right through the document, and serves a twofold purpose (cf. Vorster 1992d:3). *Firstly*, because the author does not seem to be well-known to the Ephesians communities, it serves to establish common ground between them. He does not want to claim any special merit, and is indeed very careful to absolutize his own power and authority (cf. 3:2). The revelation which he has received—the ultimate sign of apostolic authority in this context—is not unique, although it "was not made known to men in other generations" (3:3–5). In this way he shows that his status is on a par with that which had been assigned to other apostles and prophets.

Secondly, the process of identification serves to create a mutual frame of reference in the interaction between author and readers, which would be conducive to further argumentation and exhortation on the basic theme of a mutual position of honorable status and appropriate conduct.

3.3.5 *ANALOGIES BETWEEN EPHESIANS AND ANCIENT DELIBERATIVE RHETORIC*

To summarize the persuasive force of these and many other rhetorical strategies in Ephesians, and to highlight the processes of *identification* and *estrangement* once more, I now briefly compare the document to ancient—mainly deliberative—compositions.

Contra the hesitancy of Porter, Classen and Reed in applying formal rhetorical categories to New Testament letters, North American theologian Margaret Mitchell finds deliberative rhetoric—albeit in a nuanced sense—an appropriate *genre* for appreciating the language and argumentation of 1 Corinthians. Her book, *Paul and the Rhetoric of Reconciliation: An Exegetical Investigation of the Language and Composition of 1 Corinthians* (1991), is an important contribution to the reading of New Testament texts against the background of Greco-Roman rhetorical traditions pervasive at the time of the letter's composition.[44] To construct these traditions, she uses numerous ancient handbooks, speeches and letters.[45] She deliberately stays away from the modern "new rhetoric" which she considers to be "an essentially synchronic investigation of human communication," though it draws upon classical sources at times (Mitchell 1991:7).[46]

---

[44] This work stands in the tradition of rhetorical criticism as practised by her mentor, Hans Dieter Betz. His pioneering work on Galatians in 1979 rests on the premise that Paul's letters undeniably contain argumentation, and could therefore "be elucidated by comparison with the conventions for the invention and arrangement of arguments in rhetorical compositions in Greco-Roman antiquity" (Mitchell 1991:6).

[45] In Mitchell's meticulous investigation of these resources, the dialectic relation between form, function and content is taken very seriously. After exploring the basic features of deliberative rhetoric as a *genre* in antiquity, she finds 1 Cor. to share its essential characteristics, and therefore appropriate to an analysis of the text. Her conclusion is that 1 Cor. consists of a series of arguments which all turn on the appeal for the cessation of community division, a feature which is commonly found in ancient deliberative discourse (cf. Mitchell 1991:65–183). When dealing with the composition of 1 Cor. in the light of ancient rhetorical features (1991:184–295), she considers the rhetorical *genre and function* of each part or pericope of the document as determined by the compositional whole, which I find methodologically responsible and convincing.

[46] According to Mitchell (1991:7 n.19), the impressive philosophical work by Perelman and Olbrechts-Tyteca, *The New Rhetoric: A Treatise on Argumentation*, "does not claim to be a handbook of ancient rhetoric, but rather a revision and reappropriation of

On the basis of these sources, Mitchell constructs four common features of deliberative rhetoric (1991:20–64):

- a focus on *future time* as the subject or realm of deliberation;

- employment of a determined or fixed set of *appeals* or ends, most distinctive and commonly the appeal to group advantage;

- uses of *examples* for imitation—as proofs; and

- appropriate *subjects* (*topics*) for deliberation, of which factionalism and concord are especially common (cf. Mitchell 1991:23; Kennedy 1984:36–37).[47]

Although an analysis of the *genre* and style of 1 Corinthians would not necessarily be applicable to the Ephesians epistle, I briefly indicate that possible traces of each of these elements of deliberative rhetoric occur in the discourse of Ephesians, and are strategically employed as shifting devices toward reorienting the recipients' perspective and behavior.

.1 Future-Directed Statements

Mitchell (1991:24) defines deliberative rhetoric as

> argumentation which urges an audience, either public or private, to pursue a particular course of action in the future (emphasis mine; cf. Stowers 1986:108).[48]

Possible future-directed statements occur in Ephesians 1:14, 17, 18; 2:7, 15, 22; 3:10, 17, 21; 4:10–16, 23–24; 6:13, 18. These are all described as a result of the *present* position of honorable status which has been brought about by God's work in Christ in the *past* (cf. the discussion on spatial deictics in 3.3.2). Numerous purpose clauses (starting with εἰς or ἵνα) which deal with the document's alternative moral world, and metaphors referring to the *ongoing processes of growth* (4:12–16) and *building* (2:21–22), strengthen the underlying notion that God will eventually bring "all things in heaven and on earth together under one

---

it to modern philosophical problems, particularly that of epistemology. Its intention is at basic points contrary to that of (those) New Testament scholars [who depended upon Perelman-Olbrechts-Tyteca for their rhetorical analyses of Paul's letters]—it aims at *expanding* the realm of argumentation rather than classifying particular texts according to genre or arrangement." Classen (1993:291 n.78) criticizes Mitchell for restricting herself to the categories of ancient literary criticism. (See conclusions to the discussion in 3.2.)

[47] I accept the integrity of Mitchell's procedure, as I am not capable of evaluating the content of (all) her sources.

[48] Although Aristotle distinguished deliberative rhetoric according to time frame (a speaker's advice about things to come), he admitted that deliberative argumentation also deals in some way with the present, because that is the situation which calls forth some future response (Mitchell 1991:24). In contrast, forensic or judicial rhetoric deals with the past and epideictic with the present.

head, even Christ" (1:10; cf. 3:19; 4:10, 13 and the strategic use of πληρόω). This perspective on the readers' future position is obviously aimed at affirming and broadening their present vision on life in the presence of the triumphant Lord (cf. Meeks 1993:174–188).

.2 The Deliberative Appeal to Advantage

What is the appeal or purpose of deliberative rhetoric?

> According to the handbooks, deliberative speeches either exhort an audience to or dissuade them from a specific course or action in the future. Deliberative rhetoric may be distinguished from the other two species, according to Aristotle, by its τέλος: 'the end of the deliberative speaker is the expedient or harmful'.... If one wants to convince people to pursue a particular course of action in the future, one must demonstrate that it is to that audience's advantage. Likewise if one wants to dissuade an audience from a course of action one must demonstrate that it is not advantageous (Mitchell 1991:25, cf. 26–32).

In a number of ancient languages the idea of "advantage" (οὐ συμφέρον) implies some comparison, either a benefit which is greater than what someone else has, or a benefit which makes one's later state better off than the previous state (Louw & Nida 1989:626). The benefactor-beneficiary scheme of proclamation and ethos in Ephesians vividly illustrates this point (cf. 3.3.1). As a whole it abounds with rhetorical descriptions, appeals and dissuasions in the form of contrasting positions of status and corresponding ways of behavior (cf. 1:3–14; 2:1–5, 12, 19; 5:1–20). The purpose clauses also point toward the benefits of the implied readers (cf. Hendrix 1988:10 with regard to "the common good of the people").

.3 The Use and Function of Examples

According to Mitchell (1991:39–42; cf. Malherbe 1986:135–138) there is general agreement among ancient handbooks that examples are most suitable for deliberative speakers and writers. In this case

> the author brings to mind a past person or situation and either says that the course of action proposed, like the example, will be advantageous, or in the negative, that the proposed action will, like the example, bring ruin and despair. Often the orator puts forward a person (or persons) from the past or present whom the audience respects, and then tells the audience to act as they had (Mitchell 1991:40–41).

Whereas the use of examples *per se* does not make Ephesians a deliberative document—since examples were used throughout a wide variety of literary genres in antiquity—it is significant that, "of the three *rhetorical species*, the deliberative most appropriately employs proof by example. Even more telling than the mere presence of examples, however, for determining the rhetorical species, is the *function* which those examples play in the argument" (Mitchell 1991:42). The first implicit premise of the Ephesians author's overall strategy is his faithful acceptance that people can change for the better. By providing the concrete example of Christ—as metaphor and parable for God, and as model for Christian behavior—he wishes to make the possibility for change more feasible. Two aspects are involved here:

The Call to Imitation in the Deliberative Use of Example

"The deliberate proof by example functions with an implicit or even explicit appeal to imitate the illustrious example (or avoid the negative example)" (Mitchell 1991:42, cf. 43–46). Mitchell found that in addition to illustrious figures and ancestors, also deities and specific historical persons are used as heroes or examples in deliberative rhetoric, including deliberative letters.[49] At the same time, the exhortative term παρακαλῶ and the exact formula παρακαλῶ οὖν ὑμᾶς is commonly employed in deliberative speeches and letters (cf. Mitchell 1991:44 n.114).

When these features are taken into account in a rhetorical analysis of Ephesians, it is all the more striking that the recipients are not only urged to imitate *Christ* in their attitude and behavior toward one another (4:32; 5:2, 23, 25, 29), but also to imitate *God* (4:24; 5:1). Indeed, the transformative potential of Ephesians is embodied in the radical example of Christ, who consistently reflects the will and love of God. Another important parallel is the pivotal Παρακαλῶ οὖν ὑμᾶς in Ephesians 4:1 (cf. Hendrix 1988:10).

We have seen in 3.3.4.2 that the Ephesians author emphasizes his authority as apostle of Christ on several occasions (1:1; 3:1–13; 4:1; 6:20). Although his rhetorical method of self-exemplification may not be as deliberate and explicit as that of Paul in 1 Corinthians (cf. Mitchell 1991:49–60), or Galatians (Du Toit 1992:282–294), it is still very significant in creating a positive relation with his audience, and in assuring them of his concern.

---

[49] An orator could even present *himself* (*sic*) as the example which his audience should imitate, in which case his moral character (ἔθος) and authority would be absolutely essential to constitute an effective means of proof (cf. 3.3.4.2 on the Ephesians author's claim to authority). "(W)hat really carries greatest weight in deliberative speeches is the authority of the speaker" (Quintilian, quoted by Mitchell 1991:46). Mitchell (1991:50) further remarks that New Testament scholarship has to a large extent in the past restricted "appeal to example" and the "call to imitation" as only belonging to paraenesis. For the possible appropriation of these devices by later readers, see the important section on 'The character with which theology speaks' in Cunningham 1990:153–221.

Proof by Example

It has been indicated at different stages of the analysis that the Ephesians author's major rhetorical strategy is the readers' reorientation and motivation in accordance with the example of Christ (4:32; 5:2, 23, 25, 29).[50] Put negatively, they are explicitly advised "no longer to live as the Gentiles do, in the futility of their thinking" (4:17, cf. 18–32; 5:3–20)—an ethos which belonged to their previous status (2:1–19).

Especially in the second main section Christ plays a vital role as a *model* inducing specific behavior. I have argued elsewhere (Mouton 1993:78–83) that the picture of Christ in Ephesians particularly pertains to his triumphant position of power and honor. A discourse analysis of the document has shown that the pivotal confession of Ephesians 1:22–23 (which forms the centre of the extended chiasm in Eph. 1–3) deals with two matters: the exalted position of Jesus as resurrected and sovereign Lord, and his significance as gift of salvation to the believers (cf. 2.1.2.2). It has further been indicated how decisively the second aspect defines the first: Ephesians paradoxically describes Christ's power in terms of his sacrificial love and care.[51] The values of honor (power) and shame are thus reversed and radically reinterpreted in terms of Christ's example.[52] His death on a cross serves as ultimate expression of this process (Meeks 1993:61–65, 86–88, 129).

The paradoxical nature of Christ's power also determines *the readers' ethos*, which is primarily dealt with in the second main section of the document. Their

---

[50] A central notion in Birch and Rasmussen's *Bible and Ethics in the Christian life* (1989) is that the essential characteristic of Christian ethics is its *communal* thrust and awareness. In this process "Jesus and the Spirit were the community's experience of God's presence, and the social form of their faith took its clues from that. So when the question was the moral one, 'What ought we now to be and do?' the answer of early Christians appealed to Jesus as *Pattern, Teacher, or Example*; or it looked to other clues from 'the Jesus story'" (Birch & Rasmussen 1989:30; emphasis mine).

[51] Because the notion of power is so radically reinterpreted in Ephesians, I prefer to speak of the document's *communicative or transformative power* (i.e. its potential to appeal to, to invite or "lure" its readers to willingly adhere to God), instead of *rhetorical strategies*, which might have the connotation of subtle or forceful persuasion with self-centered, ulterior aims and interests. Indeed, the transforming power of the cross, resurrection and exaltation of Christ reevaluates self-affirming, self-assertive, manipulative, dominating power as self-destructive (see Thiselton 1992:611–619; Purvis 1993).

[52] "There is a deep paradox here, one which surfaces often in biblical materials: Human wholeness arrives as a gift which happens in the unguarded openness of our lives to the lives of others and theirs to ours, and in meeting their needs as they meet ours. Paradoxically, an intense and deliberate focus upon our own self-fulfillment reduces the possibilities of reciprocal relationships, and thus of fulfillment itself" (Birch & Rasmussen 1989:70).

lives should also be characterized by works of *service* (cf. 4:12).[53] Like Christ, their power would lie in humility[54], patience, kindness, compassion, forgiveness.... (4:2, 32; cf. 5:2). This shows how their value system would be fundamentally reoriented by their faith in Christ.[55]

When applying the "proof by example" principle to 1 Corinthians, Mitchell (1991:48) observes another striking parallel:

> In 1 Cor. 12 (and 6:12–20) Paul makes use of the body of Christ imagery for the church community, which is a clear modification and employment of one of the most common παραδείγματα for concord and cessation of factionalism in Greek political thought and rhetoric— the body.

This particular metaphor—combined with the call for unity—plays a central role in Ephesians (1:22; 4:4, 15–16; 5:29–30). The metaphors of *head, body* and *fullness* in 1:22–23 (cf. 3:19; 4:12–16; 5:29–30) thus seem to function as major shifting device toward a new understanding of the community's ethos in Christ.

.4 Peace and Unity as Subjects for Deliberation

Mitchell (1991:21–23) explores a great variety of ancient speeches and letters, *inter alia* the famous *Panegyricus*—a deliberative speech by Isocrates, one of the most influential Greek rhetoricians of the fourth century B.C.E. This speech urges

---

[53] For the church, the *in Christ* relation is not meant to separate them from society or "the world" in an exclusivist way. Their new ethos is—after the example of Christ— specifically geared at *serving* one another and society at large (cf. Mouton 1987:188–190). The *only* standard of living that would reveal their new status as children of God, would be that of love, holiness and righteousness in their entire daily reality (cf. Roberts 1983:32; Guthrie 1981:917–925). This is qualified by means of various practical admonitions: "They are to give up falsehood (4:25), hostility (4:26), stealing (4:28), evil talk (4:29), bitterness, wrath, anger, and malice (4:31), all fundamentally antisocial behaviors. In exchange, they are to speak the truth because they are—according to the body analogy of 4:15–16—members of each other (4:25). Moreover, they are to do honest work so that they can share their possessions with each other (4:28); they are to speak so as to build one another up in their identity (4:29); and they are to be kind and forgiving to everyone (4:32). The desired result of this is manifest in 5:1–2: Therefore be imitators of God as beloved children, and walk in love, as Christ loved us and gave himself up for us, a fragrant offering and sacrifice to God" (Johnson 1999:418).

[54] In the context of Ephesians humility is reinterpreted to become a virtue—a notion which would be quite strange to most Greeks and Romans (Meeks 1993:86).

[55] The Afrikaans word for example—"voor-*beeld*"—literally links up with the Christian believer's mandate to be God's "*beeld*-draer" (image bearer, representative, shadow—Gen. 1:26, 27; cf. Eph. 4:24). Christ, as life-giving metaphor and parable, delegates his authority to his followers. Like him, they also have to be life-giving, healing stories and image bearers of God, referring to God's alternative reality in what they are, think, say, decide and do (cf. Rousseau 1988a:13–19).

the Greek states to unify against the common enemy (cf. Mitchell 1991:62, especially n.198).[56] She further observes that ὁμονοια was one of the universally recognized political values (some poets and philosophers referred to it as "the greatest of human blessings for the cities") to be discussed in a wide variety of literary genres, including the epistolary form (Mitchell 1991:62–63; cf. Malherbe 1986:144–148).[57]

The *leitmotiv* of the epistle to the Ephesians is often phrased in terms of the unity of the ἐκκλησία or the *body* of Christ (cf. Roberts 1986c; 1993b). In urging the readers to "make every effort to keep the unity of the Spirit through the bond of peace" (4:3), the author is likely to employ typical features of the appropriate rhetorical species for treating the subject, namely deliberative rhetoric—as in the ancient literary works where the family or household was a common image of concord and unity. Ephesians makes ample use of these and other related metaphors for the church, revealing its most essential characteristic (cf. 2.1.3.1; Meeks 1983:74–110; 1993:38–41, 45–51). As in the case of other—to the audience familiar—images, these are radically reinterpreted from the perspective of the *in Christ* orientation. In this way the processes of association and disassociation reflect the dynamic interaction among author, readers and their moral worlds.

These are but various strategic techniques which can be identified in the Ephesians epistle. Although the author did not necessarily use these τόποι consciously, rhetoric at least provides us with an apparatus by means of which any communicative situation—even that of an era far removed in time—can be investigated. Therefore these τόποι provide us with a potential hermeneutical key, or at least a starting point from which to approach the writing in a meaningful way (cf. 1.6.3). "This is due to the interrelationship between language and rhetoric and the insight that language is functional to human communication" (Vorster 1992c: 16).

Returning to the rhetorical situation of Ephesians, one may say in conclusion that the preceding rhetorical strategies do not necessarily leave the im-

---

[56] Mitchell (1991:62) refers to many (other) examples of deliberative arguments urging unity on divided factions, or urging one group to be reconciled to another, right "into the second century C.E., most notably the speeches of Dio Chrysostom and Aelius Aristides to cities throughout Asia Minor, which are thus quite close, both chronologically and geographically, to the cultural milieu inhabited by Paul" (cf. Malherbe 1986:24–28).

[57] "There is uniformity among the handbooks that deliberative rhetoric, the rhetoric of the assembly, treats such topics as: 'religious ritual,' or legislation, or the form of the constitution.... or war, or peace.... Alongside deliberations on war and peace emerges the important and related political topic of ὁμονοια, 'concord,' or unity within the political body. This is not surprising, as ὁμονοια, the opposite of factionalism, is also discussed as a common subject of deliberative rhetoric in the rhetorical handbooks. Deliberative rhetoric.... is often primarily concerned with such matters as political stability and unity" (Mitchell 1991:60). For other conventional subjects regarding moral instruction in Greco-Roman antiquity, see Malherbe 1986:144–161.

pression that any direct conflict or controversy was lurking behind the document. The author presented the recipients with neither an abstract theological treatise, nor a response to specific local problems, but with a more generalized epistle aimed both at strengthening the core identity of their Christian faith and at encouraging to act more in accord with that faith (Lincoln 1990:lxxiv–lxxxvii). To that end the document stresses the unity and harmony that should exist among believers:

> There seems to be a need to strengthen in-group consciousness. This is done by locating the implied audience within an entirely different order, decisively established by Christ, who is simultaneously responsible for their status and power. Since they have acquired a position of honor, shameful conduct should be shunned, while honorable behavior is an inevitable consequence (Vorster 1992d:9).

This honorable behavior was meant to be concretized with regard to the fellow members of their faith community.

3.4 CONCLUSIONS: THE TRANSFORMATIVE POTENTIAL OF EPHESIANS

The essential starting point of all rhetorical strategies—and prerequisite for effective communication—can be described as the delicate tension between *identification, alienation* and *reorientation* as ongoing processes during the reading and rereading of a text (Rousseau 1986:415–416, 432). These processes—characteristic of the referential and relational nature of metaphorical language, and representative of all human experience and explanation—I believe, hold the key to unlock the *transformative potential* of the ancient canonized biblical documents in contemporary situations (cf. Lategan 1985b; 1992b; 1994b; Ricoeur 1975; 1976; 1980). "In a co-operative shared work, the Spirit, the text, and the reader engage in *a transforming process*, which enlarges horizons and creates *new horizons*" (Thiselton 1992:619).

Through these processes the Ephesians author encourages his audience to think of themselves in terms of the new position they ought to assume—as fellow-citizens with God's people and members of God's household, as one in Christ, as a new humanity…. "As soon as this happens, a range of new possibilities opens up. Believers from the Gentiles no longer have to feel inferior and in a disadvantaged position in comparison to believers from a Jewish background…. Being one in Christ suddenly has all kinds of social and political consequences— cultural, social and sexual differences have somehow lost their divisive and destructive force" (Lategan 1993:406; cf. Volf 1996:167–190; Combrink 1986:

223–226; Eph. 5:21–6:9).[58] Ephesians 4:23–24 therefore summarizes the epistle's pragmatic intent (cf. Johnson 1999:417–419:

> .... ἀνανεοῦσθαι δὲ τῷ πνεύματι τοῦ νοὸς ὑμῶν, καὶ ἐνδύσασθαι τὸν καινὸν ἄνθρωπον τὸν κατὰ θεὸν κτισθέντα ἐν δικαιοσύνῃ καὶ ὁσιότητι τῆς ἀληθείας.

> (You were taught, with regard to your former way of life.... to be made new in the attitude of your minds; and to put on the new self, created to be like God in true righteousness and holiness.)

The preferred position indicated by persuasive strategies in the document is *the continuous renewal of the readers' spirit and ethos in accordance with God's righteousness and holiness.* By inviting them to assume their honorable status in Christ—a gift of God's grace (2:5, 8–10)—Ephesians offers its readers a radically new self-understanding, a new identity awareness, leading to a new ethos, new attitudes and actions. Appropriating the document's thrust and perspective, in-habiting its alternative moral world, would result in a different perspective on reality, opening up a series of pragmatic, ethical consequences. The next chapter investigates this potential with respect to contemporary challenges in Christian ethics.

---

[58] Typical of its patriarchal embeddedness, the language of Ephesians is (still) over-whelmingly androcentric, and does not—necessarily—openly reflect a radical shift in human relations. Although it is even doubtful whether its intended effect made a dramatic difference in the subordinate role of women in the first centuries C.E. (cf. P. J. J. Botha 1992; Fiorenza 1983:266–270; Meeks 1983:23–25; 1993:49–50, 138–147), I believe that the implied *direction* or *tendency* (cf. Combrink 1986:218) of the document—the identification with Christ's paradoxical status and ethos—was meant to reorientate both men and women according to their previous social status of either power or powerlessness. See Sampley 1971:109–163 for a detailed analysis of Eph. 5:21–33, and an interesting discussion on the influence of the document's perspective on the relationships in the *Haustafel*.

CHAPTER FOUR

READING EPHESIANS ETHICALLY: TOWARD HERMENEUTIC APPROPRIATION AS "AN INTEGRATIVE ACT OF IMAGINATION"

> The task of hermeneutical appropriation requires *an integrative act of imagination....* (W)henever we appeal to the authority of the New Testament, we are.... placing our community's life imaginatively within the world articulated by the texts.
>
> (Hays 1990:45–46)

4.1 WHERE DO WE FIND HOPE? (A CASE STUDY)

While reading for this chapter, the mass media continuously reminded me of the earth's numerous bleeding wounds: lingering wars and labor unrest; ghastly measures of famine and other faces of socio-economic misery on the one hand, and greed, materialism and corruption on the other; tragic forms of people, power, and substance abuse; an increasing incidence of serious crime, violence, and potential ecological disasters.... These—together with other ethical issues—constantly appeal to the *moral responsibility* of this generation, and will continue to do so in future.

However, circumstances always appear to be worse when getting nearer to oneself. In the spring of 1994, a tragic thing happened in the otherwise fairly quiet neighborhood where I live. A talented thirteen year old girl was brutally and senselessly murdered in her parents' house, shortly after she returned home from school in the early afternoon. Like the entire neighborhood, I was overwhelmed with horror and grief, and forced anew to account for, and accept as moral concern, the *society* which produces such occurrences—even though this particular instance turned out to be a family tragedy.

A couple of weeks later, on 5 November 1994, the world was shocked by the assassination of well-known South African theologian and ethicist, Johan Heyns, in his Pretoria home. This incident sadly reminded of the assassination of Chris Hani, secretary general of the South African Communist Party, in the driveway of his Boksburg home, at midday on 10 April of the previous year.[1] However diverse the circumstances surrounding these three occasions, they are presumably symptomatic of a (South African) society where the sense of humanity and morality seems to be deeply corrupted, and the quality of life essentially threatened. To be sure, "the state of public life mirrors the *quality of character* in the citizenry" (Birch & Rasmussen 1989:67; emphasis mine).

I instinctively began to wonder (and this became a turning point in my thinking about the integrity and relevance of biblical scholarship): Will the world still be physically and emotionally inhabitable for future generations (cf.

---

[1] These examples are isolated and rather arbitrary, and not meant to play down the seriousness of thousands of other—often anonymous—victims of various forms of crime and violence.

Bonhoeffer 1956:17–18, 134–141; Birch & Rasmussen 1989:132)? And how are Christians—individually and collectively—responding to this?

Since the Ephesians epistle was the pastoral "world", the metaphorical "home" in which I lived at the time (Lindbeck, referred to by Smit 1991b:56, 59), I challenged it with various questions arising from these and other experiences. By now I intuitively sensed that Ephesians—being an old document from within totally different socio-historical circumstances—would not necessarily provide direct answers to my and other people's (sometimes inappropriate, albeit sincere) questions (cf. Combrink 1986:214).[2] However, while aware of my own presuppositions, I nevertheless searched for consolation, hope, and rest in the pages of this ancient epistle. *Somehow* I kept on clinging to the living God to whom it testifies, realizing that it once made sense to people in need of comfort, and that it has the communicative potential to rise beyond its time and place to reach me and many others across the centuries and continents.

I chose the three situations of the murdered girl, Johan Heyns and Chris Hani as a case study for my own use of the Bible in present-day contexts. In retrospect, I may evaluate my response by asking: What did I expect from Ephesians? Why did I use the Bible *at all*—and particularly this text—to relate to my own and other people's needs? *How* did I use it? Was Ephesians, under the circumstances, supposed to relate to specific *issues* only, or was more at stake? What kind of moral discourse—with the families, members of the faith community, and society at large—would be appropriate under such devastating circumstances? And specifically: What role *did*, and *could*, or *should* the Bible play in it?[3]

Although there are times and places for different modes of moral discourse, I realized that in these particular instances neither a prophetic, nor a philosophical-ethical or policy mode would work *for me*—at least not in the initial phases of my shock and grief.[4] My questions as to who and what a moral Christian

---

[2] These *inter alia* refer to the (typical?) *"why"* questions people ask under circumstances of suffering: "Why did it happen?," "Why did *God* allow it?," "Why *our* child/mother/etc.?," "Why in such a cruel and inhuman way?," "How long before justice will prevail?" (See Allen Verhey's discussion on appropriate questions and levels of questioning with regard to the use of Scripture in Christian ethics—1984a:174–187; 1984b:220–229).

[3] These rhetorical questions form the stimulus for the discussion following in the rest of the chapter, and are not specifically dealt with here.

[4] The authoritative North American ethicist James Gustafson was once invited by the Department of Church and Society of the World Council of Churches to analyze the broad tendencies in their documents and activities, points of view, and declarations of the last twenty years (cf. Smit 1994b:17 n.5). As a result of these ideas, he developed a typology of four varieties of moral discourse or rhetoric (Gustafson 1988), namely *prophetic* discourse (characterized by indictments and utopian visions); *narrative* discourse (emphasizing issues of identity, ethos, character, vision, values, virtues, examples of martyrs and

should be, what good and moral Christian behavior should be (especially with regard to a good and moral society), were—under the circumstances—asking for *more* than a (conventional) sermon, instant solutions or ready-made answers.[5] I was actually yearning for a larger picture, for some integrating pattern or process of meaning that would allow me to understand the purpose of my life, and to define its place in the world here and now. I suppose this yearning may be phrased as a need for the comprehensive paradigm of a story—a story wherein past, present and future would somehow flow together in a coherent whole (blending also with the stories of other people), a story which would rise beyond the boundaries of my own limited insight and perspective, a truthful, comforting, healing, gripping story with trustworthy, virtuous heroines and heroes, a story which would draw me into the hopeful anticipation and security, the logic and interaction of its world—a story which would "enliven my moral imagination."[6]

---

saints); *ethical* discourse (representing philosophical, analytical, sometimes logically rigorous modes of argument); and *policy* discourse (pertaining to concrete historical matters). In the South African context the following documents could—among many others—respectively serve as examples of these four varieties of moral discourse: *The Kairos Document: Challenge to the Church*, 2nd ed. (Grand Rapids: Eerdmans, 1986), Sindiwe Magona's autobiography *To My Children's Children* (Claremont: David Philip, 1990), Vincent Brümmer's *Speaking of a personal God* (Cambridge: Cambridge University Press, 1992), and the South African *Bill of Rights* (Sections 7–39 of The Constitution of the Republic of South Africa, Act 108 of 1996).

It is important to note that all four of these varieties occurred and still occur in the different historical paradigms of (Christian) ethics—cf. 4.4.1. In fact, each of these could be important under specific circumstances, but not in itself necessarily sufficient to deal with a particular ethical challenge, whether pertaining to moral action, people or society. Religious education—and especially the Christian churches as communities of moral discourse—therefore ought to include all four varieties (cf. Gustafson 1988:53). In accordance with the Ephesians analogy (as I understand it), the study eventually focuses on the role of *narrative* in the formation of moral *people* (cf. 4.4.2.2), which is supposed to impact on *ethical* discourse in processes of decision-making (4.4.2.3).

[5] By a "conventional sermon" I mean a one-sided mode of communication (usually rendering cut and dried solutions or prescribed actions), while the audience remains fairly passive. This particular pastoral need on my side probably developed in reaction to people's sometimes insensitive albeit well-meant responses, which do not always involve the bereaved, or leave room for them to voice their real feelings, or work creatively through their grief. In the case of the murdered girl, some would say: "When your time has come, that is it." Others would try to console the parents by somehow linking the occurrence to God's will. Neither was effective. Rather, it aggravated their initial anger and rebellion—also against God.

[6] Birch and Rasmussen (1989:219 n.10, cf. 106) refer to Robert Coles, a psychiatrist who taught at Harvard University at that stage. At a seminar for business people, Coles used well-known novels as the vehicle for discussing the moral quandaries people in business frequently face. In the process, "(h)e found that 'stories enlivened (the participants') moral imagination.' Stories, he says, 'can work their magic on the heart—and help one

It is in this sense that the *narrative* of Ephesians, the old-old *story* of the gospel of Jesus Christ, indeed provided and still provides such a paradigm.... for me. Yet, why a *story*? What does "story" in particular yield for the kind of pastoral and moral needs mentioned above?[7] And how do I account for such claims? How do I render my Christian convictions morally intelligible?

At this stage, it has to suffice to say that "(w)hat narrative does is bring order to what otherwise might be a chaotic stream of events, impressions, insights, memories and emotions. *Narrative gives form to experience* in ways which tie the past to the present and anticipate the future. Or, from another angle, *narrative discloses an order* which may already be there, but which comes to expression as we tell of it" (Birch & Rasmussen 1989:105).[8] Psychologists argue that it is through story that people create their own plot lines, and establish the hermeneutic framework in which they choose to live. In this sense people's life stories become metaphors or models for laying down routes into memory, and guiding their lives. In McFague's (1982:31–54) and Ricoeur's (1980:26) terms: Stories or parables represent metaphorical processes in narrative form. They redescribe and reshape reality, present alternative worlds, and open new ways of seeing and being. In this way stories have an enormous communicative and transformative potential (cf. 3.3.3; Spohn 1984:92–102).

Such an approach would obviously have direct importance for the subject of ethics. This is especially true about *Christian* ethics which in its essence has the character of a religious story (cf. Meeks 1993:172–173, 189–210; Hays 1983:

---

resist the ever present temptation of the intellect to distance anything and everything from itself through endless generalization. Yes, we used our head in that course. But mostly we sat back and let those stories get to us, prompt us to remember past times and wonder anew about the future.'" It is in this sense I believe that stories can contribute significantly toward appropriating knowledge and experience as "an integrative act of imagination" (Hays 1990:45; cf. 4.5).

[7] The *purpose* of the case study in the broad structure of the book is to illustrate the use of the Bible in one particular mode of ethical discourse. Although it focuses on the narrative mode, it certainly does not deny the validity of different complementing modes of moral discourse under different circumstances (cf. n.4 above).

[8] This reminds of McFague's description of metaphor "as the instinctive and necessary act of the mind exploring reality and ordering experience" (1982:32; cf. 1.6.2.1–2). With reference to Hauerwas, Spohn (1984:95) explains that "(a)n adequate and effective community story encourages its adherents to face the particular challenges and tragedies of life," and then rightly adds: "Christians, however, believe the story of Jesus *not because of its functional value in ordering life but because of its truthfulness*" (emphasis mine). See in this regard the famous chapter in Niebuhr's *The meaning of Revelation*, titled 'The story of our life' (1941:32–66; 4.4.2.2). In the context of a philosophical discussion on different metaphors expressing the meaning of life, Solomon (1990:276) remarks about life as a *story*: "It is the story of our life that gives life its meaning.... and to not know one's role in one's own story—or to have too many roles or incoherent roles—is to find one's life meaningless."

225–235, 258–264).[9] It entails time, place, the implied development of different characters, and the promise that something significant is happening. The Christian narrative revolves around the story of Jesus of Nazareth (cf. Wright 1992:145–464). Like all good stories, its rhetorical aim is to *invite*, to persuade people to become part of it, and to live and participate in its alternative world. Powerful stories *"mold people's identities and their sense of the world and reality.* (They) create a *basic orientation* for those who are drawn into them.... They help form commitments and convictions. They yield insight, and inspire. They create and shape virtue, value, vision, and obligation"* (Birch & Rasmussen 1989: 106–107, cf. 21, 125; emphasis mine).[10] In sum: Stories can change people's way of looking at life, and their ways of behavior.[11] Indeed, "(a) way of life and a narrative go hand-in-hand" (Birch & Rasmussen 1989:106, cf. 137; Eph. 4:1). To illustrate the point, I retell the Ephesians story....[12]

---

[9] The potential of narrative for New Testament theology and ethics is convincingly illustrated by British scholar N. Thomas Wright in a recent monograph, *The New Testament and the People of God* (1992). In his comprehensive multi-dimensional approach toward New Testament hermeneutics—which, analogous to Rousseau's model, integrates the intellectual processes involved in literary criticism, history and theology—Wright regards the category of *story* crucial in the *enactment of knowledge* gained through such an approach. In storytelling—one of the most basic modes of human life—people constitute their perspective or world view, and by the modification and subversion of such stories alter their knowledge of the world. Wright transfers the principle of "critical realism" (cf. 1.3 n.13) to the analysis of literature as "the telling of stories which bring worldviews into articulation," and to history which inevitably involves not only selection and interpretation, but also expression in some sort of meaningful *story* (Wright 1992:65, cf. 83, 116–118). For him historical analysis therefore has to seek the *intentionality* that drives such meaning-laden stories. And it is in this notion of intentionality (thrust, direction, and perspective of a text—cf. 1.6) which Wright finds a useful link to theology and ethics (1992: 44–46, 465–476). He further sketches the Christian world view through its praxis, symbols, and sets of questions, and then considers Christianity's primary stories—*inter alia* the extended narratives of the Gospels and the narrative world of Paul (Wright 1992:38–80, 370–409; cf. Thiselton 1992:566–575).

[10] North American narrative ethicist Stanley Hauerwas—strongly influenced by Richard Niebuhr and James Gustafson—has become well-known during the past two decades for emphasizing and establishing the significance of narrative for ethical reflection, and Christian communities of character as context for moral development (cf. Hauerwas 1981:129–152; Spohn 1984:92–99; Richardson 1994; Vosloo 1994; Smit 1994c).

[11] In this context Birch and Rasmussen (1989:106, 219 n.11) quote Lindbeck: Religions are *"comprehensive interpretive schemes"* which are expressed in narrative and myth and are heavily ritualized. *Via* story, myth, and ritual, religion *structures* human experience and understanding of self and the world in ways which relate them to matters of *ultimate* significance and meaning. See Smit 1991a; 1991b:55–63 for a discussion of the process by which such "interpretive schemes" are constructed.

[12] To deal with Ephesians as "narrative" is not to discard its *genre* as an epistle. It is a matter of translating—or "transposing," to use a musical term—its content into a parti-

4.2 THE CONTINUING STORY OF EPHESIANS

The story of Ephesians is framed by remembrance, imagination, and hope. While looking back to a period "before the creation of the world," it anticipates—somewhere in future—a "day of redemption." It is about a living God, and the tremendous power of God's glory, love and mercy. It is also about previously deprived people and their worth, potential, and responsibilities. It starts with the God and father of Jesus Christ whose "pleasure and will" it is to bless his people graciously and abundantly, to give them peace, *shalom*, wholeness. God did this by choosing them to be God's own family, his children, so that they would live in God's presence, holy and blameless, praising his glory. God takes the initiative from the beginning to the end, and makes full provision for their present, past, and future. But as for them, they would only experience this in a relationship of faith and trust with God's beloved, Jesus Christ.

It all occurred in a strange way though. In order to bring God's people— who seem to have lived in enmity with each other before—together as a family, Christ paid an immeasurable price. He sacrificed his life by dying a horrible and shameful death—on a cursed tree. This took the shape of a cross, so that his outstretched arms would paradoxically become an embrace to an alienated, broken world. The outcome of the tragedy was that every barrier, every dividing wall causing conflict and strife within and among them, would be destroyed. Those who were previously separated, excluded, regarded as "others," strangers and foreigners, were brought together in a new community: God's household. They were to be God's church, God's body, a dwelling in which God would live by the Spirit. In this environment—in their relation to Christ—they would be able to become a new people with a new identity, and to grow and develop toward the full measure of their potential as human beings.

Once again, God initiated this dramatic turn in the story. In his dynamic power and love God raised Christ from the dead! And made him Lord of all by seating him at God's right hand in the heavenly realms. From this position of glory, honor and victory, Christ would nurture and sustain the quality of life of God's family with meticulous care. This was possible because what had happened to Christ, would also happen to those bound to him by faith. Like him, *they* were raised up to a new life as well, and seated with him, next to him, in the heavens! This is the climax of the story.

Yet, God seems to have had more in mind—even the *cosmos* would be influenced by God's actions. The story about the redemption and exaltation of God's family is framed by God's encompassing plan to bring *all things* in heaven and on earth under the headship of Christ. God's presence was meant to fill "the whole universe." This is the powerful, authoritative God with whom the believers could identify. It is *God's* story that gave sense to *their* stories—to her and his

---

cular mode of moral discourse appropriate for a specific situation and need.

stories. Previously they were enslaved and torn apart by hostility and tension, but now they were reconciled, with a new status as co-rulers with the Lord of the universe.... By sharing Christ's position of power, they could also share his perspective on humanity, and on life in general.

The story continues by describing how such privileged people were supposed to respond to what God was doing, how radically their attitudes, actions and behavior were meant to be changed. In a nutshell, they were created with the purpose "to be like God in true righteousness and holiness." Through *them*, God intended to make known God's manifold wisdom to the rulers and authorities. As the body of Christ, they were commissioned and authorized to represent him, his perspective, his paradoxical lifestyle. Paradoxical—for being at his right hand would simultaneously mean to be "under him," under his lordship, guidance and care, and therefore related to him in obedience, dependence and submission. To reign with him, would mean to serve with him. To bear his crown, would be to bear his cross. To share his power, would be to love as He did, to forgive as He did, and to be humble, gentle, patient, kind, compassionate....

According to the story's point of view, this would only be possible within the fellowship of God's caring community, God's body of believers. Through serving God and one another they would grow morally, and be built up to become a mature people, attaining to the whole measure of the fullness of Christ. Their new lifestyle is painted with the vivid images of *light* and *wisdom*, of *being filled with the Spirit*, of *submitting to one another out of reverence for Christ*. Concerning their role in society, they were to speak truthfully to their neighbors, and to work honestly, so that they would have something to share with those in need. They were to prevent and resist unwholesome talk and other forms of corruption, to get rid of all bitterness, rage and anger, brawling and slander, and every form of malice....

Because their struggle for what was good and moral in their community life, in their decisions and actions, was not against "flesh and blood, but against the powers of this dark world," they were not to underestimate these forces. In fact, they needed nothing less than an armor for full protection. As could be expected, God also responded to this need in a radical and imaginative way. By giving *Christ* to them in all his fullness, God provided the armor. Only by being united to *Christ*, by being *in him*, would they have the authority and power to represent him, to use his words (the "sword of the Spirit"), while putting on the belt of truth, the breastplate of righteousness, the shield of faith, the helmet of salvation.

In short: Ephesians is about the church as God's doxological community. It is about a moral people, deeply aware of their identity *in Jesus Christ*, and the vision of their full redemption in him—somewhere in future, but with radical implications for their life in the present. Indeed, theirs is a story about love and peace, about hope, about life to the fullest. For them, it was a *true* and *truthful* story, the good news of the gospel—meant to be recited and celebrated regularly, and to be passed on to every new generation....

This is the story which the church has been keeping alive—and which kept the church alive—for centuries. And it is *this* story that appeals to Christians of the early twenty-first century in our struggle to make sense of what is going on in and around us, in the church and in society. It does not necessarily answer all our questions. But, as "the Word of God," "the sword of the Spirit," it has the communicative power to stimulate and facilitate many a process. It can protect, inform and guide us in many ways: in forming our character, in affirming our vision of God and ourselves, in accepting responsibility for our decisions and actions, in asking different questions.[13] In short: It discloses a new way of looking at life. It still invites later readers to inhabit its alternative moral world. It is still meant to enliven their imagination. In this sense the story continues, and remains to be continued….

4.3 IMPLICATIONS OF THE EPHESIANS NATURE FOR CHRISTIAN ETHICS

When we undertake the journey from the ancient text of Ephesians to contemporary contexts, several *conclusions* regarding the nature of the document—as pointers toward its reappropriation—have to be borne in mind. This takes the discussion into the realm of another inter-disciplinary subject, namely Christian ethics—which has since the Enlightenment sadly become separated from biblical studies, of which it in actual fact forms an intrinsic part (cf. Furnish 1968:11, 207–241). Crossing the threshold between two often divergent academic disciplines makes me tremble, bearing in mind that Gustafson's description of biblical ethics (1984b:151) may also apply here:

> (It) is a complex task for which few are well prepared; those who are specialists in ethics generally lack the intensive and proper training in biblical studies, and those who are specialists in biblical studies often lack sophistication in ethical thought.

Some brief introductory remarks concerning the field of (Christian) ethics have, therefore, to suffice.

---

[13] In the process the *"why"* questions—which focus on the past, and which often lead nowhere—will, for example, be rephrased into *"how"* questions—which focus on the present and future, and which open up new possibilities for moral development: *"How* can God be allowed into people's lives to make God's dynamic, supportive presence felt?" *"How* can we be guided to discover and create the 'good' for which God works *in all things*, the 'good' of those who love God (cf. Rm. 8:28)?"

This shift from one set of questions to another reminds of the shift in biblical studies from *historically* oriented questions pertaining to the origins of texts, to *reader*-oriented questions. Emphasis on the creative role of readers and communication theories in the twentieth century also coincides with *responsibility ethics* as a recent trend in ethics (cf. 4.4.2.2).

4.3.1 *EPHESIANS, THE NEW TESTAMENT, CHRISTIAN ETHOS AND ETHICS*

Any comprehensive process or method relating a New Testament document or the biblical canon to ethics, has tot account for its understanding of the essential characteristics of ethics in general, and *Christian ethics* in particular. What are the origins, the range and concern, the basic elements and tasks of (Christian) ethics? What is its field of investigation? Which categories, what "canon" of methods and procedures are employed? What are the elements or dimensions of the moral life, and the resources of Christian ethics for understanding and addressing them (cf. Birch & Rasmussen 1989:15–16, 35–65)?[14]

Within the constraints of the study, it is only possible to attend to some of these questions as far as they highlight the central issue regarding the use of Scripture in Christian ethics (cf. 4.4, 4.5).

In order to answer the question "*What is Christian ethics?*," it is useful to distinguish between (Christian) *ethics* and (Christian) *ethos* (cf. 1.6.2 n.56). "In a technical sense 'ethics' is a scientific discipline, the 'science of morals,' the discipline dealing with processes of human decision-making on moral issues. 'Ethos,' however, is 'the habitual character and disposition of a group'" (Smit 1991b:52; cf. 1992:303–317).[15] Using influential arguments of Meeks, Hauerwas, and Gustafson, Smit (1991b:52–55) gives several reasons why the difference between *ethics* and *ethos* is extremely important, particularly with regard to the use of the Bible in both. Referring to the public importance of *ethics*, Smit (1991b:52) warns against its overestimation:

> (S)cholarly reflection on ethical decision-making is not that important.
> It seldom makes any difference to the way people live and act.[16] The

---

[14] This procedure once again concerns the starting point in the hermeneutical process (cf. 1.3 n.15). "At what points in the Christian moral life do biblical materials have an appropriate impact?.... What is the proper starting point? Do we begin with the biblical materials or with some issue demanding a moral decision? Or at some other point? What difference does the starting point make? Are there different starting points for different circumstances in the moral life?" (Birch & Rasmussen 1989:16). Since I found it methodologically more viable to deal with the nature of the New Testament documents *before* asking about the relation between them and Christian ethics (cf. 4.3.2; 4.4.2), the format of the book supports the notion of an exegetical analysis of the biblical documents as practical starting point. However, the continuously spiral movement between ancient texts and contemporary readers acknowledge the interwovenness of these processes.

[15] Some scholars refer to ethos in this sense as *morality*. "Morality.... names a dimension of life, a pervasive and, often, only partly conscious set of value-laden dispositions, inclinations, attitudes, and habits" (Meeks 1993:4). Birch and Rasmussen (1989:39) distinguish as follows between Christian ethics and Christian morality: "Christian ethics is (the) critical intellectual discipline *in the service of the Christian moral life*, while morality refers to the standards of character and conduct people use in living it" (emphasis mine).

[16] It is important to bear in mind that ethical formation is an integral part of all social processes. Even without using the word ethics or morality, different forces and influences

factors influencing public life, how people behave themselves, what
they think and believe, like and dislike, what they hope and fear, what
they regard as shameful or as praiseworthy, what they will do and what
they will not do.... in short, the factors influencing the 'moral world' of
people, their ethos, are quite different.

Smit (1991b:52) subsequently indicates that—from a methodological point
of view—ethos is the more comprehensive and socially influential factor:
"(E)thics seldom determines ethos. *Ethos more often determines ethics*[17].... Put
differently: the ethos of a group determines how its members live and act almost
unconsciously, unreflectively, in their everyday actions and decisions" (emphasis
mine).[18] He further considers the question as to how the Bible influences the
ethos, the moral world, the public morality of a particular society.[19] Drawing on

---

in society as a whole determine who people are and what they do. It is therefore ironical
that the impact of professional ethicists is not considered as one of the major formative influences in society.

[17] Communication theorists argue that more than 90% of all communication is
carried across by means of powerful non-verbal symbols such as attitude, respect, availability, facial expressions, tone of voice, sense of humor, lifestyle. The "success" of any
communication event is thus co-determined by the experience of the *code* of the medium
by both senders and receivers (cf. Rousseau 1986:35; Mouton 1987:52; Kelley 1977:27–
33).

[18] "The difference between ethics and ethos often has something to do with the difference between (moral) decisions and acts and (moral) human beings, between acts and
agents" (Smit 1991b:52; cf. Richardson 1994:89–96; 4.4.2). Hauerwas argues that the
emphasis ought to be on the latter, on the formation of the character, the ethos, the moral
identity of a group. His interest is, therefore, in the formation of "communities of character," and in the role the Bible can play in it. "He challenges the popular inclination to link
ethics with 'difficult decisions' and argues instead for the importance of creating contexts
more conducive to deciding one way or another. Contexts like these are found in
communities, like the church: social institutions seeking to embody a specific configuration of virtues in its members. These virtues are formed by the language, the 'grammar,'
the collective stories or narratives of the group.... Much more important, according to
Hauerwas, than looking at the role of the Bible in particular difficult decisions and acts, is
therefore to look at the role of the Bible within the social institutions where the people's
ethos is being formed" (Smit 1991b:53). Later in this chapter (4.4.2.2), Niebuhr's
contribution to the formation of moral people will be discussed briefly, as a contemporary
appropriation of the Ephesians christological-ecclesial perspective— although he himself
does not claim that explicit link.

[19] We have seen in 1.6.2 that the term "moral world" refers to the collective moral
network of a group or society (in terms of customs, rules, taboos, traditions), i.e. the world
which they construct for themselves to live in, the world which has been internalized in
their thoughts and deeds (cf. Meeks 1986b:11–17; Smit 1991b:56; 1992:303–306). The
overarching notion in the moral world is "moral agency," a technical term in (Christian)
ethics for the human capacity to choose and act responsibly, in such a way that people are
held accountable for their choices and actions. This includes moral vision, character form-

Gustafson's famous analysis of the role of the Bible in Christian ethics (1970; 1984b)[20], as well as Lindbeck's cultural-linguistic approach, Smit indicates how powerfully the Bible affected the moral language and imagination of traditionally Christian societies, and therefore also their culture and ethos, and how its role and importance change with changing socio-historical circumstances (Smit 1991b: 55–61; cf. Meeks 1986a:5).[21]

Consequently, one of the main concerns for Christian ethics can be described in terms of the following question: *How can the Bible influence the ethos, the language, the story, the culture of individual people and contemporary society?* Or, phrased differently: Are the communities, institutions and establishments who are reading the Bible (albeit in diverse ways), powerful, persuasive, convincing enough to influence the personal and public ethos in a given society? (cf. Smit 1991b:59–63).[22] For the purpose of this study, the issue becomes: How can biblical scholarship in general, and Christian ethics in particular—meaningfully, that is, in the closest possible co-operation—contribute toward the information

---

ation, decision-making and behavior, i.e. the good and moral *person, society* and *action*, moral virtues, values and obligations; in short: the ethics of being and doing (cf. Birch & Rasmussen 1989:39–65). In the language of Eph., it refers to the inseparable unity of identity and ethos (cf. Ogletree 1983:135–173). When the different elements of moral agency are being differentiated here, it is for the sake of analysis.

[20] The value of Gustafson's analysis and examples of the role of Scripture in the different stages of ethical discourse, is *inter alia* "that it shows that ethical decision-making, even so-called scientific moral argument, is never 'pure,' but ethos-laden, deeply influenced by the moral visions, the virtues, the values, the priorities, in short, taking for granted moral assumptions of the group to which the ethicist belong, however 'professional' they may be" (Smit 1991b:55). This confirms the relationality of all experience and interpretation (Van Huyssteen 1986:151–168; 1987:5, 24–31; cf. 1.3; 1.5).

[21] "In short.... biblical literacy—in Lindbeck's terms—means that the Bible influences the imagination and the language of society, the way people see, their vision, their grasp of reality, of history, of totality, and the way people talk, their language, 'the house in which they learn to live'.... One can therefore popularize these views and say that the Bible will influence the ethos, the moral world, of society to the extent that it teaches people to see and it teaches them to speak" (Smit 1991b:59; cf. 1.6.3).

[22] In this context Smit particularly addresses South African New Testament scholarship, reminding that it has not been very influential in the ethos of past and present South Africa. "In fact.... one may generalize and say that its own dominant ethos has been, for many years, the scientific ethos of detached inquiry, and that it has deliberately stayed clear from the corridors of power in both church and society, thereby influencing ecclesial and public ethos only in the negative way that it did not really contribute much" (Smit 1991b:63; cf. 1990a; 1990b; 1992:317–325; 1994d). Smit's criticism should be welcomed as a constructive contribution toward an inter-disciplinary discussion among biblical scholars and Christian ethicists, particularly by considering methodological (including philosophical-interpretive) difficulties implicit in the role of the Bible in society, and by helping to formulate more precisely the complexity of issues at stake.

and transformation of the moral identity and ethos of individuals and society? This question will be further nuanced in 4.4.2 in terms of (Christian) *responsibility*—a central notion in contemporary ethics—as the formation of moral *people* or *agency*, as informing moral *action*, and as transforming *society*.

It has been argued in 2.2 that Ephesians represents remarkable traces of the long and complex process underlying the origins of Christian morality. The document therefore does not reflect a neat, ready-made theological doctrine or ethical system (cf. Lincoln 1990:lxxxvii–xcvii; Furnish 1968:10–11, 207–224). It is, however, characterized by the dynamic processes involved in a community's *wrestling* to understand God's will for their particular situation. While various traditional materials contributed to the formation of the moral identity and ethos of the early Christians (Meeks 1986b; 1993), the unique hallmark of this process is its continuous and radical orientation and reorientation to the story of Jesus Christ. Since then, Ephesians—being one of the canonized documents witnessing to the experience and interpretation of these original events—has been stimulating an ongoing process of moral formation and development.[23]

In the following six sub-divisions (4.3.2–7) important aspects of the Ephesians nature—particularly relevant to its use in Christian ethics—are summarized as *conclusions* from the multi-dimensional analysis of the previous two chapters. During the ongoing processes underlying moral formation, decision-making and the transformation of society, the task of hermeneutic appropriation requires that all these aspects be kept in some kind of creative balance as "an integrative act of imagination" (Hays 1990:45).

4.3.2   *THE DYNAMIC NATURE OF EPHESIANS AND THE ONGOING DIALOGUE WITH ITS AUDIENCE/READERS*

It has been suggested in 1.6.3 that the interpretation of the biblical writings should—according to their dynamic nature—reflect an ongoing dialogue with later readers. The imperative of ongoing interpretation is in actual fact already implied in, and stimulated by the very nature of these texts:

> Met betrekking tot het dynamisch karakter van het Nieuwe Testament kan worden vastgesteld dat in de laatste tijd het belangrijke inzicht is ontstaan dat de bijbel zelf de kenmerken van een interpretatieproces vertoont. Zoals de bijbel de geschiedenis van Israël niet als zodanig beschrijft maar een geïnterpreteerde geschiedenis geeft, zo bevat de bijbel ook niet de wil van God zonder meer als ware het tijdloze en

---

[23] Although I am working within the parameters of the so-called Protestant canon, the argument could just as well be applied to the Roman Catholic and other canons. The point is that the Ephesians story represents but one voice in the full drama of the New Testament. A Christian ethic would therefore have to remain in dialogue with all the perspectives of the New Testament, representing different approaches, genres, styles, needs, and answers to specific questions.

afgesloten grootheid maar hij brengt deze over als een worsteling van de gelovige om tot het juiste verstaan van die wil te komen. Al in de Schrift zelf is uitlegging verondersteld (Lategan 1982:48, cf. 48–50; Fowl & Jones 1991:36–44; Hartin 1994:511–513).

This is also true of the Ephesians document. Its entire character resembles a dynamic interpretive process which seeks to understand human existence in the light of the Christ event.[24] The *in Christ* perspective therefore *orientates* not only the hermeneutic process implied within the document itself, but also the interpretive process activated and facilitated by it (cf. Rousseau 1986:51, 400–414, 431–432; 1988a:50–53; Verhey 1984a:179–187; Combrink 1986:217–218; Mouton 1987:173–175).[25] The implied author and readers' willingness and openness to be filled with the illuminating, creative Spirit of God would be the primary requisite for understanding God's will in their situation (5:10, 17–18). An ethical reading of Ephesians by subsequent readers likewise calls for a continuous *wrestling*, for imaginative, Spirit-filled and critical reflection on the active presence and will of God in different times and ever changing circumstances. According to the thrust, perspective, and transformative potential of the epistle, this process has to focus on its implied moral identity (theology) and ethos—that is, the growth of the body toward "the whole measure of the fullness of Christ" (4:13).

The dynamic nature of Ephesians is also reflected by its rich metaphorical language (cf. 2.1.3). It has been argued that the importance of metaphor for biblical hermeneutics lies in its particular ability to radically (re)describe, (re)interpret, (re)create, discover, change, transform, reverse (Ricoeur 1977:216–256; 1980:26; McFague 1982:36). We have seen that metaphors work on a pattern of orientation, disorientation, and reorientation (Ricoeur 1975:122–128; McFague 1982:46–47). The vitality of a metaphor exists in "two active thoughts which remain in permanent tension or interaction with each other" (McFague 1982:37–38). Active metaphors are therefore sufficiently surprising, unconventional and shocking. Their intention is to upset conventional, comfortable and secure interpretations and expectations of reality. When metaphors are literalized, the tension and open-endedness so critical to the communication of new insight, are lost—a

---

[24] Cf. 2.2.1 and 3.3 for the author's (re)interpretation of metaphors and traditional material within the whole of the document's discourse.

[25] Well-known New Testament scholar from Emory University, Atlanta, Luke T. Johnson, developed a model for the communication of New Testament documents in a way similar to that of Rousseau (1986). Johnson's now widely recognized book, *The Writings of the New Testament: An Interpretation* (first published in 1986 and extensively revised in 1999), focuses on the interaction between the two processes of *experience and interpretation* as stimulus not only for the formation of the early Christian communities and their writings, but also for the canonization and ongoing interpretation of these texts. N. Thomas Wright is likewise concerned to restore the present fragmentation of literary criticism, historiography and New Testament theology to a unitary enterprise which might have a certain normative force (Wright 1992:26–28, 139–144; cf. n.9 above).

danger which is ever present in religious language.

To reinterpret the metaphorical language of the Ephesians epistle, and particularly the experiences to which it refers, thus requires from later readers to respect the nature of its language. This has been characterized as *personal* and *relational*, as *indirect, radical, surprising* and *ordinary* (dealing with everyday situations). Just as the thrust of Jesus' teaching and healing was *toward people* (their relation to God and fellow-people, and their physical, spiritual, emotional, and social wholeness), the "theology" and implied ethos of Ephesians is *toward* the health and quality of *relations* among different people oriented by the same faith perspective.

In general, we can say that the Ephesians metaphors function in the play of two different orientations, modes of existence or perspectives on reality. It is within this context, within the *in Christ* divine-human relationship as interpretive framework of faith, that the communicative power of its metaphors as strategic shifting devices has to be appropriated by later readers (cf. 3.3.3).

4.3.3 *THE COMPLEX NATURE OF EPHESIANS IN CREATIVE TENSION WITH CONTEMPORARY NEEDS*

How, then, could an ancient canonized text such as the Ephesians epistle be used by subsequent readers, in totally different socio-historical circumstances, to define their self-understanding, to inform their decisions and actions, and to influence their responsibility in society?[26] In spite of vast contextual differences between "then" and "now," the Bible has through the centuries been, and is still considered by many people to be "the book of the church," and therefore the charter document for the Christian moral life (Smit 1991b:60; Fowl & Jones 1991:1; Birch & Rasmussen 1989:9–10). It has been canonized by early faith communities, and is since then considered normative for use in Christian worship, preaching, teaching, and pastoral care. It is still widely used—by individuals and institutions—in different contexts of religious education, to empower and affirm moral identity, to shape character and conduct, to provide guidance and authority.[27]

---

[26] The question "How *is* Ephesians, and the rest of the canon, *used* in ethical matters?" would ask for a different, empirical approach (cf. Lategan & Rousseau 1988). The question "How *should* the Bible *be read*?" presupposes a normative reading (cf. Lategan 1992a:9–10), whereas the question "How *could* the Bible *be read*?" leads to a more theoretical approach, which represents the hermeneutical vision and focus of this book.

[27] Contemporary Christian believers are confronted with totally different moral issues/choices and historical forces than the Christian communities of the first centuries C.E. "While there is much in human nature that binds all of us together across vast stretches of time and culture.... it is yet undeniable that Christian ethics today must find its way amidst moral questions which never appeared on the horizon of biblical ethics" (Birch & Rasmussen 1989:12; cf. Rossouw 1980:23; Combrink 1986:217–218). Although a

This brings—among numerous other related issues—a core set of questions to the fore: What kind of authority is the Bible (supposed to be) for Christian morality? At what stage, and how does Christian ethics draw upon biblical resources, and for what purposes? How authoritative are non-biblical sources of insight? What is the role of faith communities in the formation of moral people and action, as well as a moral society? Specifically, what are the manifold uses of Scripture in the church for fashioning moral character and conduct (cf. Birch & Rasmussen 1989:10, 15–16)? And in a broader context, what is the role of theological reflection, and specifically religious education, in facilitating an accountable use of Scripture in Christian ethics? How can biblical studies and ethics collaborate effectively to bridge the gap between them?

It is not possible to deal with all these questions satisfactorily within the parameters of this book. I shall therefore focus on the role of New Testament scholarship and Christian ethics in religious education at large—which implicitly includes the formal and informal training of church leadership.

Because many believers consider the Bible to be the primary source for the Christian moral life, its use in contemporary moral deliberations will necessarily have to be determined by the complex, multi-dimensional nature and intended pragmatic functions of these writings. In order to grasp something of Scripture's complex communicative nature, it was necessary to take a roundabout way before dealing with its use in Christian ethics. The ongoing process of its interpretation and appropriation can, therefore, be expected to be just as (and even more) diverse and complex as questions regarding the very nature and intention of these documents.

The network of communication processes underlying the New Testament writings has been discussed in 1.6, as an essential element of the ethics of biblical interpretation. An interrelated analysis of the Ephesians text and its communicative, rhetorical power or transformative potential (chapters two and three)

---

moral issue—such as poverty and hunger, for instance—remains much the same in its basic outline, the *context* might be so altered that the character of the biblical response no longer applies. Simultaneously, Christian ethics today does not find sound justification for accepted biblical practice concerning, for example, slavery and the treatment of women as property (cf. Fiorenza 1983:266–270). For these reasons Birch and Rasmussen (1989:11–14; cf. Verhey 1984a:159–160; Curran 1984:187–194) distinguish between *biblical ethics* and *Christian ethics*. It is precisely this difference which prompted the underlying challenge for the study. A major task of biblical scholarship and Christian ethics would, therefore, be to inform and guide Christian faith communities in relating their daily religious experiences to the Scriptures as primal documents of their faith. As a crucially important aspect of an ethics of interpretation, this obviously involves a comprehensive study into the nature of the biblical documents. We have seen that they *inter alia* claim to be *historical* documents, dealing with historical people, places, and events. They are not dealing with timeless realities or truths to be appropriated directly in different circumstances (cf. Van Huyssteen & Du Toit 1989:31–40).

served as practical illustration of that theory. In sum, it has been argued that Ephesians—like the other biblical documents—naturally functions on different levels, namely with regard to a structural, socio-historical, and faith (rhetorical or theological) level (cf. Silva 1994a). To avoid a one-sided approach, a responsible appropriation of Ephesians in Christian ethics has therefore to give account of *all* these dimensions in their entirety and interrelatedness (cf. Lategan 1982). If one dimension would be overemphasized at the expense of the other, the document could easily be misunderstood and misused (cf. Rousseau 1986:19–28).

Going hand in hand, for instance, with the over-exposure of the Bible's *theological* dimension, some scholars and ordinary Christian readers follow a prescriptive approach where biblical *imperatives*—e.g. Eph. 5:22 and 6:5 with respect to the position of women and slaves—are seen as direct commands of God, as casuistic laws with objective status, which have to be obeyed in exactly the same way at all times and under all circumstances. A one to one relationship is thus believed to exist between past and present (cf. Combrink 1986:217). This would obviously lead to an "unproblematic" and "straight-forward" ethical system, but would however negate and inhibit the dynamic, creative role of later readers.[28] From the preceding discussion it should be obvious why such an approach disregards the complex nature of a New Testament document:

> (It) fails to do justice to the New Testament in two respects. Firstly, it does not take cognizance of the historical, cultural and literary context of the time from which the Bible originates and the totally different contexts of today's world. Secondly, to view the New Testament simply as a law book, is a distortion of the dynamics of this body of literature (Botha 1991:13; cf. Hartin 1991:3).

Likewise, overemphasizing the historical or linguistic-literary facets of New Testament documents—at the expense of their theological and canonized nature—would distort and reduce them to mere historical or literary phenomena. Such an approach would also neglect or inhibit their potential to stimulate and facilitate—via biblical scholarship, systematic theology and especially Christian ethics—a lively, appreciative, and critical response to the present (cf. 1.2).

---

[28] During the history of biblical interpretation the notion of revealed morality as "timeless truths" has also taken other forms. In Liberal Protestantism, for example, the *ideals* or *principles* that lie *behind* these imperatives were upheld as binding, instead of viewing specific laws as having binding force on the believer, in a literal sense. (This was a trend in Protestant theology during the late nineteenth and early twentieth centuries. It advocated rationality and discarded those orthodox opinions which were not compatible with rationality and a scientific outlook. It also fostered an optimistic view of humankind's inherent morality—cf. Deist 1990:143). "The problem with this approach is that it tends to reduce the wealth and variety of the New Testament teaching simply to a limited number of principles. Furthermore, it does not explain why supposedly universally valid principles which can be derived from the New Testament can be in conflict with each other" (Botha 1991:14).

Recognizing the complex and multi-dimensional nature of New Testament documents, necessarily leads to the realization that these writings do not supply later readers with simple, ready-made answers to their moral questions.[29] The answers to the abovementioned and other ethical questions put to Ephesians and the rest of the New Testament canon, are diverse and complex (cf. Smit 1992: 306–317). Not every possible question or approach will fit its unique nature and intention.[30] It is, therefore, not to be regarded as a kind of encyclopaedia or ethical text- or reference-book, not even for Christians (cf. Smit 1993b:1). Easy, straightforward answers simply do not exist (cf. Birch & Rasmussen 1989:220 n.12, 141–202). All that contemporary readers do have, is the *analogy* of the early believers' *wrestling* to understand God's will for their lives (cf. Lategan 1982:48; Hartin 1994:521–523).[31] This analogy particularly applies to the use of language: "We simply have no language but analogy for speaking about God, inadequate as such language is" (McFague 1982:42).

This realization challenges both biblical scholars and Christian ethicists in several crucially important and inescapable ways.[32] They are *inter alia* challenged to encourage and guide communities of faith in reappropriating the *perspective*

---

[29] "Die tyd is verby waarin ons op 'n probleemlose wyse kan terugval op naïewe en onverantwoorde 'Skrifbewyse.' Die Bybel is nie 'n bundel kant en klaar geformuleerde geloofswaarhede nie. In die Bybel is mense aan die woord in die taal en denkwêreld van hul *eie* tyd, en hierdie 'eie tyd' is só ver terug, so ingrypend anders dat dit onmoontlik geword het om ter wille van 'n 'Bybelse' standpunt 'n bepaalde teks of teksgedeelte as towerformule na vore te haal" (Van Huyssteen & Du Toit 1989:3, cf. 36–40).

[30] In this sense the primary task of biblical scholarship can be phrased in terms of the challenge to sensitize, guide and equip (theological) students and the faith community in developing a problem awareness with regard to biblical exegesis, as well as a reading competence which would rather focus on learning to ask appropriate questions than to find the "right" answers (cf. Deist 1989b; 4.1 n.2).

[31] Tracy (1981) refers to analogy as a certain "similarity in difference" (cf. Hartin 1994:516, 521–523; Hays 1989:27–29). This confirms the metaphorical nature of the creative, imaginative human ability to relate different experiences to one another, a process which can be summarized in McFague's words (1982:15): "Thinking metaphorically means spotting a thread of similarity between two dissimilar objects, events or whatever, the one of which is better known than the other, and using the better-known one as a way of speaking about the lesser known." Robert Czerny, who was a co-translator of Ricoeur's *The Rule of Metaphor* (1977), wrote in his introduction to this formidable work: "(A) good metaphor implies an intuitive perception of the similarity in dissimilars" (1977:vii). These observations imply that "the notion of morality has no one meaning and any attempt to talk in general about morality will require analogical control. Correlatively, this means that one community's sense of moral development may be quite different from another's" (Hauerwas 1981:129).

[32] For the old debate on the urgent need for meaningful co-operation among biblical scholars and Christian ethicists, and specifically its current appeal in the South African context, see Smit 1992; Roberts 1993a.

(orientation), *thrust* (essence or direction), and *strategy* (transformative potential) of these documents—*that is, the delicate network of communication processes underlying them*—with regard to the needs of changed and changing circumstances.

To respond with sensitivity to the rhetorical functions of these texts, is to account for their communicative power or transformative potential *amid* their cultural-historical biases. For most of us, however, this means taking *one step at a time* in refocusing ourselves according to a multi-vocal biblical perspective (cf. Bosch 1976:185–186). Yet, while recognizing the limitations of our own interpretations and their ethical implications, we must not lose sight of the radical and powerful force reflected by these writings. Paradoxically, the Ephesians epistle does not bind its later readers in a rigid, legalistic way, but *liberates them toward the imaginative appropriation of the healing power of God's love.*

This necessarily needs to be done in critical dialogue and communion within the Christian faith community (cf. 4.3.5; Fowl & Jones 1991:29–134; Smit 1994d; Glanville 1994:130), but also with other disciplines such as the human and natural sciences, and especially with Christian ethics.[33] Biblical scholars and Christian ethicists have the *moral obligation* to engage in the conversation between "reading" and "accountability," that is, to involve themselves in the complexities and creative tension of the "liminal space" between the dynamics of the biblical texts and the multiple needs of contemporary readers (M. K. Taylor 1990: 199–208):

> The task of biblical studies.... is.... to make available to humanity on the brink of atomic annihilation the moral resources and ethical directives of biblical religions (Fiorenza 1988:13).

However, before we can consciously undertake the journey from the ancient document of Ephesians to its use in contemporary situations, we have to attend—by way of summary—to some major "theological" and "ethical" pointers within the text itself. These would necessarily have to be respected in the process of its appropriation by later readers. I focus on three aspects only: the Ephesians community's implied identity and ethos as centered *in Christ*; their ethos as *community* ethos; and the persuading role and function of "Scripture" in Ephesians and early Christian moral life.

---

[33] Different disciplines might operate with different sets of questions and methodologies. For example, Christian ethicists might (consciously) tend to approach the Bible from the perspective of contemporary needs and contexts, whereas biblical scholars usually take the ancient documents as their point of departure. Whatever the differences in approach, none of these should be absolutized as to blur the conversation. Different viewpoints should rather be evaluated critically, and considered as complementing, stimulating, and challenging each other in an ongoing inter-disciplinary discussion.

4.3.4 *THE EPHESIANS COMMUNITY'S IMPLIED IDENTITY AND ETHOS AS CENTERED IN CHRIST*

By now it should be clear that the Ephesians community's (communities') relation to God *in Christ* forms the pivotal point of the theology and ethics of the document (cf. 2.1.2; Jeal 1990:91–268). This is affirmed by the chiastic centre of the first main section, and the great doxology toward its end (1:22–23; 3:20–21; 2.1.2.2). We have seen that aspects of identity and ethos in the Ephesians story merge like different nuances of a watercolour painting (cf. 2.1.2; 3.3.1). Identity and ethos are defined in *relational* terms—the relation to Christ as God's gift of peace, and to the community of believers as God's *body*. *In Christ* they have been blessed with every possible blessing. In him their past, present and future flow together in a coherent whole. In the mighty presence of Christ and the Spirit lie their strength, encouragement, and consolation. In faithful obedience to God they would be able to live a daily life worthy of the calling they have received from God.

The implications of Christ's redemptive death and resurrection are so radical, that it is described in terms of the metaphorical contrast between life and death (Eph. 2:5, 6; cf. 1:19–21; 3:16, 20; 4:9, 10; 5:14–20; 6:10). The death, resurrection, and exaltation of Christ become metaphors for God's way of dealing with hostility among God's people (cf. Eph. 1:7; 2:15, 16; 5:2). By means of the author's interpretation of these metaphors, his audience is challenged toward a total reorientation and revisiting of their lives according to their faith in Christ. The early and later followers of Christ were/are therefore challenged to reflect the same attitude (cf. Ogletree 1983:146–152). Their behavior should be characterized by his metaphorical and parabolic qualities of freedom, forgiveness, righteousness, sacrificial love (cf. Eph. 4:32; 5:2, etc.).

To be *in Christ* thus means to identify with him in his power as *lord*, qualified by his humility and love as *servant*. Consequently, several relations are redescibed in terms of this paradoxical status.[34] By destroying the barriers and

---

[34] The husband, for instance, is reminded that he is the *head* of the wife "*as Christ is the head of the church*" (5:23). His position of authority is thus *also* qualified by Christ's power *as servant*. Simultaneously, the style of Christ's servitude is characterized by the power of his love—power which is paradoxically revealed in the "weakness" of his suffering. To be submitted to his wife (5:21), and to love his wife "just as Christ loved the church and gave himself up for her" (5:25), would therefore imply a transformation in the husband's self-perception, a recovery of his caring potential.

The text likewise encourages the wife to reclaim her primary identity in Christ, and be empowered by his example—as a paradoxical combination of power and weakness. It also implies submission to a husband whose identity and ethos have been redefined by his relation to Christ. A major problem in the contextualization of this text though, is that its androcentric language through the ages served to perpetuate patriarchal perspectives—in spite of suggested alternatives. Readings of Eph. 5:21–33 often over-emphasize the subdividing walls of hostility through his cross (Eph. 2:14, 16), Christ gave birth to a new creation, a new humanity. Like him, they are called to a life which always stands in criticism of the status quo, and which presses toward the full potential of the body of Christ (Eph. 4:13). From this perspective the author relativizes past traditions, and takes *one decisive step* beyond the cultural-historical norms of his time. Although structures of, for instance, patriarchy and slavery are not directly addressed, radically new attitudes are encouraged (cf. Fiorenza 1983:140–154). In this way Ephesians—in concurrence with the New Testament canon—suggests a dramatic shift in the understanding of God and humanity. Christ's role as *caring and serving head of his body* becomes the model for mutual respect and dignity, responsibility and freedom in all relations, which would implicitly replace any domination as the exploitation of power and authority.

Contemporary readers of Ephesians would therefore be challenged to allow the creative presence of the living God to redefine their relations by transcending all possible barriers:

> If, and only if, the movement from Scripture to moral claims today is coherent with the message that God has already made his eschatological power and purpose felt in the resurrection, is the use of Scripture authorized.... But loyalty to the risen Lord will not permit the simple repetition of the New Testament as normative for us without critical reflection, without passing through the prism of the resurrection, without being authorized by coherence with the eschatological power and purpose of God (Verhey 1984a:183).

By identifying with Christ in the paradoxical triumph of his resurrection and exaltation, present-day readers are challenged to grow beyond all limited views of themselves and others—in terms of traditionalism, sexism, racism, or classism.[35] To respect the transformative potential of the Ephesians document, means to

---

missive role of the wife while underemphasizing the nature of the love required by the husband. This obviously happens to the detriment of the *direction* and *essence* of the Ephesians text as a whole. This is why biblical scholars are challenged to account for the socio-cultural bias of a text and its language (in this case the social superiority of men as cultural norm). Otherwise it will lose its inherent transformative power and continue to create a *theological* problem by representing both the nature of God and the nature of humanity in terms of predominantly male references (cf. Ogletree 1983:167–168).

This implies that different aspects of Christ's nature—either his power or submission—might have to be highlighted according to the need of different situations. Applications of the text might thus vary from context to context (cf. Wessels 1989).

[35] With regard to the challenges of feminist hermeneutics and the life-giving, liberating potential of women's religious experience, see the authoritative contributions of Sandra M. Schneiders 1986; Rosemary Radford Ruether 1986; Elizabeth A. Johnson 1990: 97–127; South African systematic theologians Denise M. Ackermann (1992a; 1992b; 1993), Helena L. Glanville (1993; 1994), Piet J. Naudé (1993); and South African missiologist J. N. J. Kritzinger (1988:21–22).

dedicate oneself to accomplishing the full potential of the body of Christ. *Any-thing less would confine the God of Ephesians to the boundaries of an ancient canonized text in a way contradictory to its own nature.* This, I believe, provides later readers with an important criterion toward the reappropriation of the document.

In sum, if Christian ethics regards this document as authoritative for moral formation and decision-making, it will have to respect its particular *christological perspective and orientation*, that is, the dynamic *in Christ* relation, as central to a life lived in the presence of God. Phrased from a broader biblical viewpoint, this implies that "(t)he character and identity of people formed by the Bible can only be the character and identity of followers of Jesus Christ.[36] The vision, the values and the virtues formed by the Bible can only be shared by people committed to its message" (Smit 1991b:60; cf. Rousseau 1986:418–422, 431–432).

4.3.5 *THE IMPLIED ETHOS OF EPHESIANS AS COMMUNITY ETHOS*

Another major characteristic of Ephesians particularly significant for Christian ethics, is that it emphatically describes the religious and moral identity of its implied author and readers in terms of *communal* images. They are the living God's *family, household, body, church*—reconciled to be God's one people. Their identification with and responsibility toward God as father of the family, Christ as head of the body, the Spirit as guarantee of their full redemption, and one another as members of the body, are essential to their story, and to their moral life (cf. 2.1.3.1). A practical ethos—character and conduct—worthy of their calling would therefore have to be in keeping with who they were as *a people of God.*

In the religious and moral world of early Christian communities, *who* people were and *how* they were to behave, were indeed so intertwined, that the moral life was not even considered a separate topic (cf. 4.3.4). "Rather, morality and ethics were dimensions of community life in which the concern was how a people of God were to live with one another and with those outside the faith community. The broader interest was *faithfulness toward God as the way of life of a people*" (Birch & Rasmussen 1989:20).

The narrative of the Ephesians communities can therefore be described as a story about *community life* radically formed and transformed by the empowering experience of God, Christ, and the Spirit. Their story witnesses to the reality that

---

[36] Every Christian ethic—by implication—views the moral life as embedded within, and framed by the story of God in Jesus Christ, a story far grander and more encompassing than its own. The multi-vocal Christian story is carried by a variety of experiences and symbols—key ones being the cross, resurrection, and exaltation of Jesus. These would therefore always be of vital importance for Christian ethics (cf. Müller & Smit 1994; Birch & Rasmussen 1989:64–65).

they did not so much *have* a social ethic as that they *were* a social ethic in the process of formation (cf. Hauerwas 1985a:181–184).[37] Birch and Rasmussen confirm this by saying that

> Morality was a dimension of shared religious experience.... The ethics were.... *koinonia* ethics—community-creating human relatedness rooted in a compelling experience of God (Birch & Rasmussen 1989:31, cf. 34).[38]

The faith communities implied in Ephesians and the other New Testament writings can thus be described as *communities of moral or character formation* around a way of life centered in Jesus Christ.[39] "The *community's task* was to socialize its members into forms of life which displayed the kind of conduct befitting the experience of God in community.[40] To be a Jew was to learn the story

---

[37] This concurs with the intertwined relation between identity and ethos in the "self revelation" of God in the Bible—obviously perceived through the eyes of human beings. E.g., in Ex 3:14 (cf. 15–17) God says to Moses: אֶהְיֶה אֲשֶׁר אֶהְיֶה—"*I am who I am*," which may also be translated with "*I am what I do*." Many exegetes understand the ἐγώ εἰμί sayings in the Johannine gospel as a reappropriation of this utterance. The structure of these sayings is remarkably coherent with the discourses and miraculous signs in John's gospel, which confirms the close relation between Jesus' work and identity (cf. Du Rand, J. A. 1990. *Johannese perspektiewe: Inleiding tot die Johannese geskrifte*. Pretoria: Orion, 79–83).

[38] Meeks' recent book, *The Origins of Christian Morality*, rests on the thesis that contemporary readers of the New Testament "cannot begin to understand that process of moral formation until we see that it is inextricable from the process by which distinctive communities were taking shape. Making morals means making community" (Meeks 1993: 5). Moral formation and growth in early Christianity have, therefore, to be explored against this complex, all-encompassing sociological process of community formation.

[39] Sociologically, the process by which moral character is formed, is the interaction amongst different social communities of which individuals and groups form a part. "It occurs in a communal process of specific, changing, and continuing social relations. *'Character' is the name given to the moral being of a person or group as that is forged into a distinctive constellation....* A person 'with character' is someone with judgment to know what is right and courage to do what is good" (Birch & Rasmussen 1989:74). Within the Christian paradigm, this process is christologically oriented.

[40] Non-Christian writers often referred to Christianity as a "philosophical school." Such schools formed a lively part of ancient Greek and Roman public life (cf. Meeks 1986b:40–64). Good philosophy, according to these communities, revolved around lifestyle and ethics, which philosophy sought to embody in a life of discipline and virtue (*psychogogia*, i.e. "soulcraft"). Aristotle, for instance, understood the pursuit of philosophy to include active care for the πόλις by nurturing moral agency in community and orienting it to the practice of virtue (Birch & Rasmussen 1989:23). He in fact uses the term κοινωνία—the community or fellowship which philosophy was to promote—which would become a key word in the vocabulary of early Christianity. For the latter the process of soulcraft would entail a radically changed moral identity, a conversion, the reorientation

of Israel and the rabbinical traditions well enough to experience the world *from within these stories*, and to act in accord with that experience as a member of an ongoing faith community.[41] Similarly, to be a Christian was to learn the story of Israel and of Jesus and the ongoing church traditions well enough to experience the world *from within those stories*, and to act in keeping with that experience, as a member of that community" (Birch & Rasmussen 1989:21, cf. 66–84; emphasis mine; see also Hays 1983:218–221; Meeks 1993:172–173, 189–210; (cf. Volf 1996:99–165).[42] This means that the ethic of the community was inferred from the character of the divine presence in their midst. This was the moral vision which was meant to influence and orientate every dimension of their lives, and which had to be nurtured and developed (cf. Birch & Rasmussen 1989:61–62, 71).[43]

These observations have important implications for the ecumenical use of Scripture in Christian ethics (cf. Rossouw 1980:18–21; Roberts 1981). For subsequent readers of Ephesians and other New Testament documents, one of the major implications of its communal thrust is "that the faith community is to *remain* the reference point and the ongoing socializing agent for the moral life. In Christianity, moral deliberation and moral formation are to be tied to the shared memory, mission, and continuing life of Christian faith communities. That continuing life means that Christian ethics.... is always in process; it changes with developments in the community. Scripture itself witnesses to this" (Birch & Rasmussen 1989:33; cf. Ogletree 1983:182–187, 192–199).

---

from a new perspective, a resocialization or "relearning of another language" (Meeks 1986b:15).

[41] Cf. ancient Israel's strong sense of being a "people" as their most essential characteristic (Meeks 1986b:65–96), as well as the discussion on Old Testament traditions in Eph. (2.2.1.1–2).

[42] In the process, critical, often unique historical events such as the exodus, exile, and Jesus' crucifixion and resurrection gave rise to stories, traditions, and rituals which were remembered generation after generation for moral guidance and orientation. Worship, spirituality, and festivity helped fashion the kind of people God's community was to be.

[43] See in this regard the works of Hauerwas, especially his *A Community of Character* (1981) and the (new) introduction to his *Character and the Christian life: A Study in Theological Ethics* (1985b). Gustafson (1988:19, 20) summarizes the central thesis of Hauerwas' work in the following terms: "Narratives function to sustain the particular moral identity of a religious (or secular) community by rehearsing its history and traditional meanings.... Narratives shape and sustain the ethos of the community. Through our participation in such a community, the narratives also function to give shape to our moral characters, which in turn deeply affect the way we interpret or construe the world and events and thus affect what we determine to be appropriate action as members of the community." See also Richardson 1994, and the unpublished doctoral thesis of Robert R. Vosloo on Hauerwas' ethics, "Verhaal en Moraal: 'n Kritiese ondersoek na die narratiewe etiek van Stanley Hauerwas" (1994).

Being *community* ethics in its origins (cf. Meeks 1993:1–17), Christian ethics continues to be *communal* in nature—though the shape and function of community life may change from time to time (cf. Schneiders 1986:236–265).[44] In a broad sense, this concept refers to the wide variety of communities within which the moral lives of people are necessarily embedded, and by which they are decisively influenced (Fowl & Jones 1991:4–28; Birch & Rasmussen 1989:70–81). However, the notion of *relationality* applies with even greater force to the *Christian* moral life, and to *Christian* ethics.[45]

In 1.2 we have seen that different interpretations of the New Testament, and therefore of Christian ethics, are due to a large variety of factors which may be summarized as the readers' *point of view* (cf. also 4.4.1). What is not always recognized, however, is that differences of perspective depend on *how readers and viewers are enabled and accustomed to read and to see*. This is of crucial importance for the question regarding the formation or development of moral communities—the internalization and integration of their social, religious and moral world. Such a selective process moulds the way in which people see the world, think about it, and respond to it. To see the world, is far more than simple observation. *It is perceiving, selecting, interpreting and evaluating* (cf. Fowl & Jones 1991:29–109; Birch & Rasmussen 1989:74–79).

In their discussion of the significance of perspective, of faith and perception for the moral life, Birch and Rasmussen (1989:77–78) contend:

---

[44] It can even be said that the *most essential trait* of Christian ethics is its communal orientation (Birch & Rasmussen 1989:17–34, 70). However, it remains crucially important to note that it is *God* who consistently acts as protagonist in the Christian story. God is the one who calls, elects, and blesses the Ephesians author and readers. The goal of their lives is, therefore, to live "to the praise of *his glory*" (1:6, 12, 14). The morality of Eph.—and the other NT writings—is in the very first instance a *theocentric* morality, embodied in the form of a community (cf. Birch & Rasmussen 1989:20). Gustafson's major work on ethics, his two-volumed *Ethics from a Theocentric Perspective* (1981; 1984. Chicago: University of Chicago Press), emphasizes that the essence of, and prerequisite for Christian ethics is the perspective of faith in a sovereign God (cf. Niebuhr 1941:1–31).

Yet, *even more basic* to the early Christians' sense of community, was the dynamic process by which they gave expression and social form—in terms of worship, liturgy, human relations, day-to-day moral issues—to their collective experiences of God's mighty presence in Jesus and the Spirit (Birch & Rasmussen 1989:26–31). This process would *inter alia* be determined by their understanding of Old Testament and early Christian oral and written traditions, and would have important implications for the interpretation of Scripture by the Christian church in the centuries to follow.

[45] The term "community" can obviously be defined from numerous different— sociological, anthropological, psychological, cultural, and other—perspectives. In this context it explicitly refers to the composition (identity) and functioning (ethos) of a diverse group of people bound together by a common faith orientation.

In short, who we are and are becoming, in accord with the faith we hold, largely determines what we see. *How we come to be* heavily influences *what we come to see....* A Chinese proverb expresses it well: 'Ninety percent of what we see lies *behind* our eyes.... Our perceptions aren't mental photographs, they are highly active images. Our faith and perception 'define' our reality. They help set the direction and limits of our conduct, generating certain choices and actions rather than others, underlining some issues as more significant than others, and disposing us to some responses rather than others.... In a word, *believing is seeing*.

This process obviously has important implications for Christian ethics. *Which* objects of faith and social experiences, *which* images and stories, role models, examples, heroines and heroes have been internalized and integrated, matter immensely for morality (Fowl & Jones 1991:29–55; Müller & Smit 1994: 385–399). The Christian community is "the socializing agent for faith" (Birch & Rasmussen 1989:78), and has the task of forming perception and character in accord with its faith in Jesus Christ. This is where the relevance and integrity of the Ephesians epistle's persuasive, communicative power for contemporary readers are at stake—cf. the discussion on the deliberative use of Christ's example as rhetorical strategy in 3.3.5.3.

4.3.6 *THE RHETORICAL ROLE OF "SCRIPTURE" IN EARLY CHRISTIAN MORAL LIFE*

It has become clear that, for the early Christian communities, belonging to the people of God meant "the formation and transformation of personal moral identity in keeping with the faith identity of the community" (Birch & Rasmussen 1989:45). In this process, the "Scriptures" of the community—its authoritative oral and written traditions[46]—were a prime medium of moral formation (cf. 2.2.1; Meeks 1986b:12; 1993:91–110).[47] We have seen that this was a complex and

---

[46] "The Hebrew Scriptures, or *Tanak* (the Christian Old Testament), did not take final canonical form until near the beginning of the second century after Christ.... The Greek Scriptures (the Christian New Testament) were a selection of early church writings which received canonical sanction in the fourth century after Christ. Until that time, varied collections of these writings, together with Hebrew Scriptures, were used as Christian Scriptures" (Birch & Rasmussen 1989:31; cf. Du Toit 1989:171–272; Johnson 1999:595–603).

[47] In this process "*memory and imagination* were mixed with other human skills in charting the way" (Birch & Rasmussen 1989:28; emphasis mine). These concepts aptly rephrase the metaphorical processes of orientation and reorientation discussed in previous chapters. Later developments, however, blurred and weakened the inherently communal sense of the church considerably, especially since the Enlightenment (cf. Birch & Rasmussen 1989:27; 4.4.1.3).

comprehensive process, meant to establish a new way of life.[48]

Of particular importance for the purpose of this study, is *how* Scripture functioned in the process of early Christian moral formation—in learning and appropriating the Christian story (cf. 3.3). In this respect Birch and Rasmussen (1989:45) make an important distinction between direct and indirect processes of moral formation, ascribing an explicitly functional role to Scripture (cf. Eph. 5: 18–21):

> Scripture is used less.... for *direct* moral *exhortation* than for indirect means to achieve moral formation. Psalms sung again and again in worship or read in quiet devotion foster certain 'senses' which take the form of virtues: a sense of gratitude, dependence, responsibility, humility, and awe, for example:... Likewise, the recital of the great narrative accounts in Scripture.... create moral identity.... Scripture in the life of the Christian community has this moral vocation, to shape the personal moral identity of community members in keeping with the ways of God.

The faith communities of the New Testament inherited a high authority of "Scripture" for the moral life from preceding generations. However, the role of Scripture for them was different to what it is and can be for subsequent believers, because the Scriptures were still in a process of formation as documents of various faith communities—first in oral, then in written forms which were added to, passed along, and preserved. How their authority could function in and for later communities of faith will be discussed in the next section (4.3.7). The point at this stage is that, for the early Christians, the

> Scriptures comprised a reliable guide in matters of faith and life. Not *all* that was necessary for the living of the moral life was found in these sacred pages, however, and the faith communities made no claim that the Scriptures constituted a full ethical system. The direct moral exhortation that *is* present.... functioned more as *exemplary* guidance, rather than comprehensive instruction. Instructions in 'the Way' were more akin to strong signals than legislation.... What is signaled and exemplified is *the sort of life* expected of the community in view of the

---

[48] Paul frequently uses the phrase "to live a life worthy" (cf. Eph. 4:1; 1 Ts. 2:12), or literally translated, "to *walk* (περιπατεῖν) a way worthy." For the wider context of this expression see Meeks 1993:95, 150–173. The early followers of Jesus were *inter alia* referred to as "people of the Way" (Acts 9:2). This denoted a particular ethics, a pattern of living, the training required for Christian discipleship, the crafting of moral people. It was a new way of living which had to be learned as part of the ongoing life of the community. This learning process involved the continuous remembering and retelling of their formative stories, above all the Jesus story (cf. Dahl 1976:11–29; Meeks 1993:33–36, 96–98, 216–217). In Eph., this process is stimulated and maintained by the creative presence of the living God, and described in terms of various irreconcilable contrasts, and the growth of the body toward the fullness of Christ (2:11; 4:13).

presence of God.... (S)aid somewhat differently(:) The Scriptures were not so much a *fixed moral deposit* for these communities as they were precious community records of what it meant in varied times and places under varied conditions.... to *be*.... a Christian people of God (Birch & Rasmussen 1989:32).[49]

In the process moral wisdom came from other resources such as *non*-Jewish and *non*-Christian sources as well—a process reflected by the biblical accounts themselves (cf. 2.2.1). "In both biblical and post-biblical worlds.... resources from beyond the faith community's traditions were filtered through the community's own self-understanding and shaped in keeping with its own corporate temper. The community.... was itself altered in the process of appropriating materials from its wider world; sometimes it was dramatically altered. In turn, it frequently influenced the very world which had deeply affected it" (Birch & Rasmussen 1989:33; cf. Meeks 1986b:40–64; 1993:1–36).

Since the first centuries, the church's sense of community *in Christ*, and of Scripture as normative tradition, would "soon come to include a certain complex and living set of events, figures, and stories, rituals, beliefs, practices, rules, oral and written wisdom, and institutions. These would be shared across centuries and continents, albeit with extensive modification, additions and elaboration; they would nonetheless yield a recognizable cohesiveness amidst vast differences of custom, geography, language, culture, race, class, and national origin" (Birch & Rasmussen 1989:26).

4.3.7 *EPHESIANS (AND THE NEW TESTAMENT) AS AUTHORITY FOR CHRISTIAN TRADITION*

Since the New Testament is still considered to be a profound shaping force for the Christian moral life, in spite of socio-cultural differences between the first and twenty-first centuries of this era, the relationship between these documents and contemporary religious experience, the church and theological reflection becomes the issue.[50]

As might be anticipated against the background of the discussion so far, the

---

[49] Apart from the presence of God as stimulus for the moral life, there is an even more encompassing moral use of Scripture in these communities. This refers to their claim that the Scriptures express and promote its place and role within the overarching context of God's purposes for all creation (Meeks 1993:174–188; Birch & Rasmussen 1989:32–33)—a theme which takes a prominent place in the epistle to the Ephesians (1:10, 14, 21–22; 3:10; 4:6, 10, 30; 5:5; cf. Smit 1983a; Cloete & Smit 1988).

[50] It has been indicated that—within a wide variety of possible uses of the Bible—this study concentrates on its role in the scholarly, professional sphere, where it is used for religious education, i.e. the training of (religious) leadership for different spheres of life. However, as such it is necessarily interested in its wider use by individuals and groups in churches, schools and private devotions.

Bible's normative role has in the past been understood in many diverse ways. A good example of this is found in David H. Kelsey's *The Uses of Scripture in Recent Theology* (1975; cf. Kelsey 1968; 1980), which has been referred to in 1.1 n.6. Kelsey discusses seven case studies of particular theological proposals made by Protestant theologians "on the basis of Scripture."[51] These studies may be considered as *representative* (not typological—Kelsey 1975:16) of the diverse ways in which biblical writings are construed when taken as authority for theological proposals. Important for the purpose of this study is that Kelsey's illustration of how Scripture has been construed in *theology* in the past, *may also be used to describe the diversity in the use of Scripture among ethicists* (cf. Gustafson 1984b; Spohn 1984; Verhey 1984a:232; Rousseau 1985a). To raise the ques-tion of biblical authority with regard to Christian ethics, therefore, means to explore the nature and degree of influence given to the Bible in shaping identity, character and behavior—in the light of its continued acknowledgement by the church and other institutions as *Scripture* (cf. Kelsey 1975:89–100, 109–112; Verhey 1984a:1–5, 200; Spohn 1984:70–128).

What has been said with respect to the nature of Ephesians as *Scripture* and its implications for Christian ethics (4.3.1–.6), can now be summarized in terms of its *authority* for the Christian tradition—or phrased differently—*its epistemological status in theological and ethical thought* (Van Huyssteen 1987:2). The authority or epistemological status of Ephesians—and other New Testament documents—necessarily has to reckon with its dynamic, metaphorical, multi-dimensional, and specifically its relational, christological and communal nature.

.1   The Focus of New Testament Authority: Responding to the Presence of God, Jesus Christ, and the Spirit

In accordance with the relational nature of Ephesians, its authority for subsequent readers is first of all embedded in their faith response to the mighty presence and

---

[51] These cases are drawn from the writings of Karl Barth, Hans-Werner Bartsch, Rudolf Bultmann, L. S. Thornton, Paul Tillich, G. Ernest Wright, and B. B. Warfield. All of them (except Warfield) were active mainly between the 1920s and 1960s. Kelsey (1975: 4–155) analyzes their use of Scripture by asking the same set of four questions in each case: (1) What aspect(s) of scripture is (are) taken to be authoritative?; (2) What is it about this aspect of scripture that makes it authoritative?; (3) What sort of logical force is ascribed to the scripture to which appeal is made?; and (4) How is the scripture that is cited brought to bear on theological proposals so as to authorize them? (Kelsey 1975:2–3, 15–16). For the Warfield position, also see Dunn 1982a. Kelsey consequently discerns a certain pattern in the ways in which these scholars "construed" Scripture, namely as propositional content, as conceptual content, as a narrative of the acts of God (in which Christ is the primary agent), as images of a cosmic process, as images of a self-understanding, or the relation between the self and the world. Kelsey's description illustrates that the decision about how to construe Scripture, decisively depends on the reader's decision concerning its nature and wholeness (cf. Verhey 1984a:156–157, 232).

actions of the protagonist (God) and adjuvants (Christ and the Spirit) in its story (cf. Eph. 2:22; 3:17; 4:6, 10). The focus on the presence and activity of God is an inherent part of the biblical documents. It is evident from Ephesians and the rest of the Bible that it is the *dynamic, transformative power of God's love* which is the focus of the Christian faith—not a book. To appropriate those texts today—in continuity with their intention and direction, and in discontinuity with their first century socio-cultural setting—would therefore mean to respect them in their multi-dimensionality, and in particular the communicative power of their theological or rhetorical dimensions (cf. 3.3; Van Huyssteen 1987:44).

This has significant implications for the use of the Bible in Christian ethics. Current responses to issues of biblical authority—particularly for its use in Christian ethics—tend to focus on *the continuing presence and activity of God* here and now, and *not* on inherent qualities of the Bible itself (cf. Niebuhr 1941; 1963: 108–126, 161–178; Spohn 1984:14–17; Gustafson 1984a:140–146; Curran 1984: 180–184; Van Huyssteen & Du Toit 1989:36–40; Birch & Rasmussen 1989:149–158; Botha 1994a:40–42). This represents the welcome shift in recent Christian ethics from viewing the Bible as revealed *morality* to revealed *reality* (the reality of God's presence), from a *prescriptive* approach—via an ethics of *principles* and *ideals*—to an approach of *relationality* and individual and collective *responsibility*.

Yet, such a claim may overemphasize a basic *discontinuity* between the biblical texts and contemporary readers, and has therefore to be nuanced. Indeed, it is exactly in the focus on God—and the continuous revelation of God's will to people in and through God's activity in the world—that biblical studies and Christian ethics find significant common ground. Both seek to discern the disclosure of God's will for people of faith—biblical studies with regard to the experiences of Israel and the early church, and Christian ethics with regard to the experiences of present faith communities. "In a sense exegesis moves from the historic witness to the present witness while Christian ethics begins with a present demand to be and do, and draws on the historic witness to meet that demand. But both activities are the necessary activities of the same community, the church. *As such, it is a travesty that the work of biblical study and of ethics have been so often compartmentalized from one another*" (Birch & Rasmussen 1989:150; emphasis mine).

Kelsey's book (1975; cf. also Ogletree 1993; Verhey 1984b) is representative of work which focuses biblical authority in terms of the Bible's *function* in the life of the church, rather than its inherent character as a revelatory document. By focusing on *uses of Scripture*, he assumes an ecclesial location as necessary for understanding appeals to the Bible. He asserts that the Bible itself cannot determine the character of Christian faith. Faith communities must come to a certain commonality of perspective, an "imaginative construal", in order to make normative appeals to the Bible in matters of theology and ethics (Kelsey 1980: 400–401). For Kelsey, the Bible has authority to the extent that it functions in the church to shape new human identities and transform individual and communal life. This is an explicitly *theological* understanding of the function of Scripture—referring to God who is active in Scripture, shaping identity and using Scripture toward the actualization of God's goal with humanity (cf. Fowl & Jones 1991: 56–83; Birch & Rasmussen 1989:152; Verhey 1984a:200). This view of Scripture necessarily reinterprets the classical images of—an exclusivist, fundamentalist, uncritical, absolute, timeless—"revelation," "inspiration" and "Word of God." These are dealt with in the following section.

.2 The Location of New Testament Authority: Church, Theology, and Religious Experience

Many biblical scholars and Christian ethicists (Kelsey 1975:205–212; Hauerwas 1981; Smit 1993b:1; Bird 1994b; Hartin 1994:520–521; Birch & Rasmussen 1989:149–158, 120–140; Fowl & Jones 1991:4–28, among others) primarily locate questions of biblical authority in the *church*, which claims a unique place for the Bible as part of its own identity. For them, the Bible has no special status outside the faith community. Therefore, authority ascribed to the Bible is *community* authority. It is enacted by the church as it uses the Bible for preaching, teaching, liturgy and guidance in its life and mission.

Van Huyssteen (1987:2–3) is convinced though that the authority of the Bible is also a *trans-confessional* problem—with reference to the broader context of *religious experience*—an issue with which systematic theology can only deal responsibly by realizing that the epistemological nature of the problem also involves meta-theological criteria. Van Huyssteen (1986:177–187) consequently specifies three contexts by which systematic theology (and its use of the Bible) is necessarily influenced, and which serve as target groups for the appropriation of its scholarly results: the broad context of *religious experience*, the more specific context of the *church*, and the context of *theological reflection* (cf. Van Huyssteen & Du Toit 1989:41–63; Thiselton 1992:4–8).[52] These contexts also apply to biblical studies and Christian ethics. For all these spheres

> (t)he Bible is.... the major source of knowledge about the ultimate object of Christian moral allegiance, God in Jesus Christ, as experienced in the Spirit. Scripture is the major source of the story which is the very center of the faith community's identity (Birch & Rasmussen 1989:14, cf. 9).

According to the christological and ecclesiological nature of the Ephesians thrust, perspective and strategy, as well as its history of canonization by the early Christian church, it needs to be appreciated and respected for what it is: part of

---

[52] This corresponds with Tracy's well-known distinction of three "audiences" or "publics" within which theology operates, namely society, church, and academy (Tracy 1981:1–48).

the canon, the holy Scriptures, the Book of faith *of the Christian church*. For the Christian tradition, for those who faithfully responded and still respond to God, Christ and the Spirit, the Bible is the authoritative "Word of God" (cf. Eph. 6:17). It is the early Christian word of witness to, and celebration of God's presence and grace. By claiming continuity with the past, biblical scholars are therefore responsible to acknowledge the biblical writings and account for them as an integral part of the *Christian* tradition. The primary task of theological reflection—including biblical studies and Christian ethics—is therefore to aid the church in discerning God's will in relation to successive faith communities.

As authoritative Word of God, Ephesians (like the rest of the Bible) functions on different levels, supplies in many, many needs, and influences people's lives in numerous ways. Through the ages, and in a large variety of cultures, it fulfilled and still fulfils a profound rhetorical role in the lives of individual Christians and communities of faith (cf. Meeks 1983:140–163; 1993:91–110). It strengthens, encourages, exhorts, consoles, binds together, informs, builds up, confronts, warns.... Christians use the Bible for personal and group meditation and study. It is read and preached in church, it forms the heart of Christian religious practice, the cult, the worship service, the sacraments. In short: *For Christians*, the Ephesians document, and the Bible of which it forms a part, is "sufficient" for matters of faith and life (albeit not in an exclusivist sense).

Thus, to say that Ephesians is authoritative as part of the writings of the *Christian* canon and tradition, is to acknowledge its position as normative for the *Christian life*. This further implies that Ephesians should be read, interpreted, heard, believed and acted out *by Christian believers*, by people sharing its perspective, respecting its relational nature and intention, and not by anybody in general (cf. 4.3.4; Rousseau 1986:431–432; Smit 1991b:60; 1993b:1).[53] Although its message was from the outset meant to be all-inclusive, and to be made known even "to the rulers and authorities in the heavenly realms" (Eph. 3:10), it is *not* meant as general prescriptions, norms, principles, or guidelines for non-Christians, on how they should act, make decisions, or organize society.

In what way(s) then, is the Bible authoritative for later Christian readers? It is significant that Birch and Rasmussen (1989:141–158) deal with this issue *after*

---

[53] To paraphrase what Bultmann once said in this regard: "God's act is hidden from all eyes other than the eyes of faith." The focus of the Ephesians document is that God should continuously be praised, glorified and honored by God's redeemed children for what God has done *in Christ* (1:6, 12, 14; 5:19, 20). The substance of this praise-giving is a holy life of love and obedience before God (1:4). In affluent language the author focuses the readers' attention on God's work in Christ, and guides them toward understanding the practical implications thereof (Mouton 1987:210). Only if they (and subsequent readers) acted according to their new status in Christ, and obeyed the intentions of the text, would the implied function of the writing as a pastoral letter be fulfilled.

having discussed the role of the church and the Bible in the religious experience and moral life of people.[54] They ask (1989:141):

> What is the nature of biblical authority in shaping moral character and in the making of moral judgments? The Bible is not the only source of identity-shaping authority.... The shaping of both Christian character and conduct involve many influences and sources of insight. What is their authority in relation to one another?

They then deal with the concept of authority in the following terms:

> The word authority refers to that which an individual or a community acknowledges as a source of decisive influence in its life.... The matter of authority focuses not on some inherent quality in a source of authority but on *the process of authorization that takes place in the interaction of that source with.... individuals and communities....* Authority is not a property inherent in the Bible itself. It is the recognition of the Christian community over centuries of experience that the Scripture is a source of empowerment for its life in the world. Authority derives from acknowledgment of a source's power to influence us, not from absolute power that operates apart from the affirmation of the community (Birch & Rasmussen 1989:142; emphasis mine; cf. 4.3.5).[55]

Bearing in mind that many other sources of influence and insight apart from the Bible become authoritative in moral deliberation—e.g. historical perspectives, socio-economic and other scientific data, rational arguments, etc.—it is obvious that the authority of the Bible cannot be absolute or exclusive. The question thus becomes: What is the relevance of non-biblical sources for Christian ethics? And what is the relation between biblical authority and the authority of other sources? Or, phrased differently: Is there a distinctively Christian ethic (cf. De Villiers

---

[54] Birch and Rasmussen (1989:120–140) discuss the role of the church in the moral life of people under the following rubrics: The church as a community of moral formation, as a bearer of tradition, as a community of moral deliberation, and as an agent of action. All these aspects necessarily bring issues of authority to the fore. In summary, the format of the book witnesses to a functional and relational view on biblical authority (cf. Kelsey 1975:89–119, 147–155).

[55] The Gospels frequently say that Jesus spoke "with authority (ἐξουσία)." "It refers to Jesus' speaking in a way which related to his listeners (and by extension with us, the readers) at the deepest levels of their being.... Jesus' power is not in his words, as such, but in their ability to call forth in people power they may not have known they had, but can hardly resist because it issues from their very being.... Jesus' hearers.... are authorized, empowered to new life" (Birch & Rasmussen 1989:142, cf. 150). It is the mediated authority of the testimony from those who experienced the power of Jesus' words which constitutes the authority of the Bible. In this process both Jesus and the Bible are metaphorical expressions which point to God. This brings the important issue regarding the reference of human language about God to the fore (cf. McFague 1982:1–4; Lategan 1985b; Van Huyssteen 1987:1–7).

1980; Curran 1984:194–207; Verhey 1984a:187–197; 1984b:229–233)? The book has been dealing with this matter in terms of the unique orientation or perspective of the biblical documents.

Birch and Rasmussen (1989:143, cf. 144–149) further argue that most views of biblical authority in the past "have been too rigid to allow a dialogic relationship of biblical material with non-biblical material in moral judgments. Such traditional views have collapsed in the face of developments in modern theology and biblical studies, and this creates a new context in which questions of authority must be raised" (cf. Dunn 1982a, 1982b).[56]

It is in this sense that Van Huyssteen's contribution (1987) is noteworthy. By rephrasing the problem of the authority of the Bible in terms of its epistemological status in theological and ethical thinking, he draws it into the more comprehensive context of epistemological theories present in contemporary philosophy of science. In the light of this broader discussion, metaphors such as revelation, inspiration, and the Bible as Word of God are also reinterpreted and expanded (cf. Van Huyssteen 1987:44–51).[57] In the process, text and tradition are

---

[56] These challenges have *inter alia* been caused by the development of *historical-critical methods of biblical study*. Whereas inspiration models previously focused on the biblical text itself, the results of these and later social-scientific methods shifted some of the attention to the *processes* behind the text, and specifically the social location and role of the communities where those processes unfolded (cf. Meeks 1986a:3–4; 1986b:12–17). In recent times, reader-oriented theories strengthened the notion that the "meaning of a text is seen less as a quality which resides in the text alone than as a quality that arises out of the reader's encounter with the text" (Birch & Rasmussen 1989:146; cf. Thiselton 1992: 58–63, 515–555, 586–592).

Another area of challenge to traditional views of biblical authority has come from *liberation and feminist theologies and the hermeneutics appropriate to them*. These theologies, from the perspective of marginalized people, challenge the prevailing modes of predominantly Western, white, male interpretation of the Bible as ideologically based. They refuse to let the inevitable biases of every interpreter remain hidden and unexamined, thus allowing biblical authority to function on behalf of those hidden agendas. By means of "a hermeneutics of suspicion" biblical authority could be reclaimed out of captivity to oppressive social contexts, leading to "a hermeneutics of retrieval" (cf. Thiselton 1992: 344–358, 411–427; McDonald 1993:208–218; Berg 1991:250–300; Frye 1989; Mosala 1950). With different emphases, feminist biblical scholars took this further by reconstructing and recovering the marginalized roles of women in the biblical story, which reflects the patriarchal character of the faith communities where they were told (Fiorenza 1983; Birch & Rasmussen 1989:147–149; Schneiders 1986; West 1991a:80–103; Ackermann 1992a; Carmody 1992; Thiselton 1992:430–462; Bird 1994a, and many others).

[57] Traditionally, some views on inspiration-based concepts of biblical authority tended to invest undue sacral authority in the text of the Bible itself, its origins and character. "Christianity then becomes a book-centered religion rather that a God-centered one.... Obviously a more multifaceted view of biblical authority results in a less problematic view of the God who addresses us through the text in a dynamic way rather than a God whose

subjected to critical theological reflection—growing in part out of the experience of God's ongoing activity in contemporary situations. In this context Birch and Rasmussen (1989:148–149) quote Elisabeth Schüssler Fiorenza who suggests "the need for a move from viewing the Bible as timeless archetype to seeing it as prototype, an open-ended paradigm that sets experiences in motion and invites transformations."

.3 New Testament Authority, Theology, and Christian Ethics

In concurrence with the relational nature of Ephesians—*in Christ*, and in relation to the *community*—it has been suggested that its authority centers in the implied readers' knowledge and perception of God, and their faith response to him. Their "theology" would thus determine their "anthropology," identity and ethos. This means that questions pertaining to authority, theology, and Christian ethics necessarily belong together.

In this respect Birch and Rasmussen (1989:152–158) make four useful proposals concerning biblical authority and Christian ethics. While they allow for a *flexible* and *functional* view of biblical authority, they emphasize the necessary biblical frame for any *Christian* ethical inquiry.

Firstly, they suggest that biblical authority be viewed in terms of *primacy* rather than *self-sufficiency* (cf. Gustafson 1984b:170–176; Verhey 1984a:1–5). By this they mean that—because of its powerful and unique *function* in the church tradition—the Bible should stand out as primary source among many possible ethical insights and influences. This illustrates James Barr's view of authority (1973) as relational or hierarchical, which refers to the function or ability of authority to order or prioritize various powers and influences.

As the original documents of the early faith communities, the Scriptures contain the only written witness to the person and work of Jesus Christ, the focusing centre of the Christian faith and moral life. As such, these writings did not only establish the particular identity of the church in its origins, but continue to do so as a source of empowerment in every new generation. Through all the diverse ministries of the church (liturgy, proclamation, teaching, pastoral care), the Bible continues to shape Christian moral agency. It constantly influences the ability of the faith community to discern God's dynamic will—also in non-biblical sources of moral authority. It therefore has to be taken seriously as the single *necessary* point of reference in all Christian ethical reflection (cf. Van Huyssteen 1986:140–143; 1987:32–38; Niebuhr 1941:5–31).

Secondly, Birch and Rasmussen emphasize that, while the Bible is a

---

inspiration is statically embodied in the text itself" (Birch & Rasmussen 1989:145, cf. 149–152; McFague 1982:4–10, 43, 54–66; Ackermann 1993:8–16; Bird 1994b). If the focus is on the will of God as revealed *in Scripture* (cf. Protestantism's emphasis on *sola scriptura*), its contents can be misused in a directly prescriptive way to determine what people should be, and how they should behave.

necessary source, it is not sufficient—in an absolutistic sense—for Christian
ethical reflection. It has to be in constant dialogue with the many other sources of
ethical knowledge and insight, provided by the data in understanding contemporary issues (cf. Van Huyssteen & Du Toit 1989:38). Many of these—e.g.
nuclear weapons, organ transplantation, and computer networks—could simply
not be foreseen in biblical communities, while the contexts and complexities of
others such as poverty and marriage relations, were not anticipated (cf. Birch &
Rasmussen 1989:11–16).

What then is the authority of the Bible in relation to other moral sources?

> Biblical authority may, however, function to help us claim the autho-
> rity of nonbiblical sources. It is from the Bible that we have drawn
> models of the transforming power of encounter with God. As we come
> to understand the images, symbols, and metaphors used to describe that
> encounter in the biblical communities, we become sensitized to the
> possibilities for such encounters with God and their transforming
> power in our world. It is our knowledge of God mediated through
> Scripture which helps us to discern God acting in the present (Birch &
> Rasmussen 1989:154).

We have seen in 2.2.1 how the Ephesians author appropriated Old Testament and other traditional material to communicate his and the faith community's
understanding of their relation to God in Jesus Christ. Their new *in Christ* experience formed the perspective and orientation point from which those traditions
were to be reinterpreted and appropriated. Likewise, "(t)he Bible authorizes our
efforts to couple biblical insight with insight drawn from our own time and place
to create models appropriate to proclaim God's 'new thing' (Isa. 42:9) in continuity with God's graceful presence in our past" (Birch & Rasmussen 1989:154).

Apart from the Bible, Christian ethics is dependent on a long history of biblical interpretation and its related moral and theological tradition (cf. 1.2; 4.4.1).
Outside the primary location of the church, Christian ethics inevitably has to take
account of the socio-cultural context in which ethical issues arise, and in which
religious education seeks to shape moral agency. This implies that Christian
ethics is of necessity an inter-disciplinary endeavor. This observation is of equal
importance for the appropriation of the intended ethos of the New Testament
documents, as it is for understanding the moral world of the early Christians.
Reading a New Testament document ethically thus involves a responsible reading
of the contemporary context, the moral world within which that text is used as
normative.

In line with the emphasis of the book on understanding as a referential and
metaphorical *process* (Ricoeur 1975; McFague 1982; Lategan 1985b; 1994b;
Meeks 1986a), Birch and Rasmussen (1989:155–157) *thirdly* argue that the authority of the Bible for Christian ethics rests as much in its modeling of a *process* as
in its mediation of content. When the documents of the New Testament invite
contemporary readers to *remember* the collected testimony of persons and com-

munities to the transforming and redemptive activity of God, it is not only done for the sake of those ancient events, but also to enable them to discern the revelation of God in their own lives (cf. Niebuhr 1941:32–66). Its authority thus resides in the *transformative encounter with the living God* which the Bible mediates and stimulates (cf. Lategan 1992b:154; 1994b:131–133). To phrase it in Allen Verhey's terms, in the context of his "modest proposal" for the use of Scripture in Christian ethics (1984a:180–181):

> The task of a theological ethic.... is not to systematize and republish the content of Scripture, but *to facilitate a new revelation, a new encounter, a concrete command of God in that moment* (emphasis mine).

To focus on the underlying and continuing *processes* of New Testament texts, instead of the product as a definitive collection of timeless, unalterable, revealed truths, has important implications for the understanding and use of the concept of *canon* by later readers (cf. Kelsey 1975:100–108, 192–197). The conviction of Birch and Rasmussen in this respect (1989:156–157, cf. 175) confirms the communication processes underlying the main argument of this study:

> The canon functions not in isolation from our own experience of God but precisely *in the process of letting our own story be intersected by the biblical story* and reflecting critically and acting faithfully.... out of those intersections. The end result.... is a deabsolutized canon which allows for the honoring of ancient witness.... while at the same time honoring the power and authority of our own experience of God (emphasis mine).

Focusing on *processes* does not, however, mean that there is no continuity of biblical content to be claimed. Moral identity is obviously shaped by images, stories, and metaphors which form part of the Bible's content (referring to real experiences), and not just its witness to a process. But, these cannot be regarded as revelatory deposits functioning as divinely sanctioned doctrine (McFague 1982:54–66).[58] The content of the Bible's culturally bound, human language must be constantly tested by the processes of experience and interpretation by later readers (cf. Glanville 1993, 1994).

Fourthly, Birch and Rasmussen (1989:157–158) suggest that any view of biblical authority adequate for Christian ethics must take cognizance of the great diversity—with regard to perspective, genre, context, etc.—within the biblical tradition (cf. Verhey 1984a:6–152; Schrage 1988; Breytenbach & Lategan 1992;

---

[58] Birch and Rasmussen (1989:157) illustrate this point by asking: "Which stories and images continue to manifest the redeeming power of God? Some matters of content are reassessed by the church, e.g., the biblical acceptance of slavery, Paul's admonition for women to keep silent in the church. Some matters.... are reasserted, e.g., God's preferential option for the poor and the oppressed. Some.... remain central although our interactions with them may change, e.g., the gospel story of the life, death, and resurrection of Jesus."

Marxsen 1993; Hays 1990:46–55). There is no single way in which the Bible is authoritative in ethical matters. Different *genres*—for instance—have to be appropriated in different ways, with respect to their own nature and intentions. In fact, if the totality of the Bible's resources is to be made available to Christian ethics, a multi-faceted view of biblical authority becomes imperative.

To summarize, it needs to be emphasized that the task of an ancient text's hermeneutic appropriation in different socio-historical circumstances requires that all the above-mentioned aspects be kept in mind in a creative, imaginative, balanced and open-ended way. In the rest of this chapter, and as a final conclusion to the book, the ongoing rhetorical processes of appropriation underlying the formation of moral agency, decision-making and the transformation of society, will be viewed from the perspective of different historical paradigms in Christian ethics, with special emphasis on twentieth century contributions.

4.4 THUS, HOW DID/DO WE GET FROM "THERE" AND "THEN" TO "HERE" AND "NOW?"

Accounting for the processes involved in the interpretive acts of biblical scholarship and Christian ethics—with regard to moral formation, action and decision-making—necessarily happens within the hermeneutic grid of a long tradition of Bible reading. By way of an excursion, I now proceed with a very cursory overview of the history of (Christian) ethics. This is meant to represent the historical bridge between the New Testament and contemporary moral challenges. By way of conclusion, and as a rephrasing of 4.3, the central question concerning the use of Scripture in Christian ethics will then be dealt with in terms of the concrete needs which arose from these phases, and which still prevail today.

4.4.1 *[EXCURSION: A TYPOLOGY OF HISTORICAL PARADIGMS IN (CHRISTIAN) ETHICS]*

The long journey of biblical hermeneutics since the first centuries C.E. reveals a large variety of ways in which the Bible has been used in concrete situations (cf. 1.2). In order to understand something of our moral inheritance, of the endless number of spheres and contexts of Christian ethics within which the Bible played an important role, as well as the complexity of contemporary challenges with regard to biblical hermeneutics—especially the use of the New Testament in Christian ethics—it is necessary to remind ourselves of some of the most important historical phases in the development of ethics in general, and *Christian* moral thinking in particular.[59] Christian ethics was decisively influenced by

---

[59] A *typology* of these historical phases or paradigms is meant to simplify it in the form of a cursory overview, albeit superficially. The typology presented here corresponds to a large extent with the paradigm changes in missiology which authoritative South African theologian and missiologist David J. Bosch indicates in his epoch-making book *Transforming Mission: Paradigm Shifts in Theology of Mission* (1991a). Bosch follows the six major historico-theological subdivisions in the history of Christianity as suggested by

these developments, but, in turn, also influenced the interpretation of the Bible in many ways.

The historical phases, paradigms or positions in the development of (Christian) ethics can be described from various perspectives, and with many different emphases. Among the large number of overviews available, North American moral philosopher Alasdair MacIntyre's *A short history of ethics* (1966) is (still) particularly helpful. Smit (1994c:20–21) skillfully translates the surveys of MacIntyre and other scholars into an accessible grid by dividing the development of ethics into three major phases, namely the *classical*, *premodern* and *modern* periods, to which he adds a fourth phase of *recent trends* in ethical thought.[60] I only concentrate on major sets of problems, on dominant *questions* being asked during these phases, and not on the wide variety of *answers* given to those challenges and questions by different philosophical schools and ethical traditions. It was indeed these sets of problems and questions which gave each epoch in history its specific character.

.1 The Classical Phase

The history of (Christian) ethics actually starts with the great philosophers of the Hellenistic period—centuries before Christ. These philosophers were the first to ask ethical questions, and to produce literature on ethics (cf. Sidgwick 1967:xvii–xxi, 12–108). Together with Jewish traditions of the Old Testament, they strongly influenced the formulation of ethical notions in Christian traditions, including the writings of the New Testament (cf. Meeks 1986b; 1993; Birch & Rasmussen 1989:23).

This epoch can broadly be described as the "classical" period, with reference to the communal lifestyle of the Greeks. Smit (1994c:20) explains this lifestyle as follows: "In any pre-modern, homogeneous society, ordinary people just 'know' how to live, what to

---

Hans Küng (Bosch 1991a:181–510). Each of these periods reveals a peculiar understanding of the Christian faith, and offers a distinctive understanding of Christian mission. Consequently, Bosch (1991a:511) defines mission as "a continual process of sifting, testing, reformulating, and discarding. Transforming mission means both that mission is to be understood as an activity that transforms reality and that there is a constant need for mission itself to be transformed." Bosch further explains that this mission is performed in hope. "(I)t may be correct to label our entire, comprehensive mission in the context of our eschatological expectation as 'action in hope'.... Witnessing to the gospel of present salvation and future hope we.... identify with the awesome birthpangs of God's new creation" (1991a:510). This is also the hopeful anticipation from which the current study on Christian ethics has evolved.

[60] Many of the thoughts in this section and the rest of the chapter developed during and after a post-graduate seminar on *Contemporary trends in Christian ethics—and reading the New Testament in South Africa today*, held at the University of Port Elizabeth from 2–6 May 1994, as well as a course titled *Huidige tendense in die Christelike Etiek—Met implikasies vir die kerk in Suid-Afrika*, 6–8 June 1994, organized by the Bureau for Continuing Theological Education and Research, an institute of the University of Stellenbosch. Professor Dirkie Smit (Universities of the Western Cape and Stellenbosch), who consistently encourages and facilitates dialogue among (South African) biblical scholars and ethicists, acted as guest lecturer at both occasions.

do and what not to do, how to behave themselves." Their lives are determined by customs, rules, rituals, taboos which are accepted by all members of the community as natural, divine, holy, eternal. They live—*without reflection*, without alternatives—in a moral world which is a given to them, which they take for granted from their childhood, and which is the *only* world they know.[61] In such societies the norms of religion, morality and judicial law are one and the same thing. All aspects of life are perfectly integrated.

Within this broad classical paradigm of moral development two further distinctions can be made (MacIntyre 1966:5–13). An earlier stage is characterized by the societies described in the heroic poems of Homer, probably dating from as early as 900 B.C.E. (cf. Rogers 1979:250; Johnson 1999:36). A second phase represents the development—since the fifth century B.C.E.—of the so-called *city-states* in Greek culture (MacIntyre 1966:14; Meeks 1983). It is in this later phase that critical ethical reflection in the philosophical sense of the word occurs for the first time. Famous people who worked and wrote in this phase were *inter alia* the Sophists, Socrates, Plato, Aristotle, the Epicureans and Stoics (cf. MacIntyre 1966:5–109; Sidgwick 1967:12–108; Lohse 1976:243–252; Meeks 1986b:40–64; Solomon 1990:3, 13, 34, 37, 93–97, 299–300; Wogaman 1993:16–22).

Aristotle (384–322 B.C.E.)—Plato's student for eighteen years, but who then parted from Plato's views—was perhaps the best known and most influential person among these philosophers (cf. Solomon 1990:93–97, 309; Meeks 1993:7–8, 12–13, 37–41). He argues that ethics has to do with what is good *for society* (referring to the city-states). The fundamental ethical question for him is *What is a good or moral society?* All his writings on justice and peace revolve around this question. For him the τέλος of all good and moral life is *a moral society or community* (cf. Solomon 1990:242–263; Richardson 1994:93). Good and moral human beings are therefore people who serve the τέλος, the purpose, the well-being of this society. Because of this, the notion of *virtue* becomes extremely important for Aristotle. The good life is to develop the virtues, the moral skills that would enable people to be good citizens, i.e. to know their place in a stratified society (Meeks 1986b:32–38; 1993:40; cf. 1983:51–73), to serve the purpose of the good society, and to live according to its rules, expectations, and interests (cf. Ogletree 1983:15–22; Birch & Rasmussen 1989:43–47). For Aristotle the four important virtues needed for this purpose were wisdom (prudence), justice, courage, and temperance or modesty (cf. MacIntyre 1966:57–83; Meeks 1986b:60–64; Wadell 1989:9–69; Hauerwas 1993:251–256). One important constituent structure in the Greek πόλις was the *household*, where relationships of power, protection, submission, honor and duty were to be properly shaped if a city was to flourish morally (Meeks 1993:38–39).

An individual could not become a virtuous person by himself (*sic*) though. In order to achieve these virtues, a student had to be taught by, and to associate with a virtuous person, a respectable teacher, an authoritative exemplar. Such a teacher would then teach his student those virtues which would enable him to serve the common purposes, interests and

---

[61] Scholars sometimes refer to societies of this nature as *honor and shame cultures* (cf. 3.2.3 n.12; Domeris 1993, *inter alia* with reference to Bruce Malina). In such a society people behave according to, and are motivated by the customs, rules, taboos of their specific group. In the Greek villages or cities of the first century, "(i)dentity was a matter of family and clan, and family honor was a powerful sanction affecting every choice. To act in a way that brought shame on one's family or on a prominent member of it was dreadful" (Meeks 1986b:12, cf. 19–39, 54; 1993:37–90).

needs of the society in which he lived—almost like a craftsperson or artisan would train an apprentice to perform a specific art or skill.

Structurally, this kind of moral network would be similar to that of the Homeric societies. In a first (unreflective) phase, the way in which one should behave or not, is taken for granted. Everyone lives from a shared set of assumptions and traditions of what a good society is. In a second phase, people might become critical and reflect on the moral life, as philosophers like Plato and Aristotle did in their writings on politics and ethics. In principle however, they still think and act within this broader frame of reference, serving the common τέλος of a good society.

.2 The Premodern Phase

A second phase in the history of morality comprises the period from the development of Christianity in the first centuries B.C.E., right through the Middle Ages (500–1500) with the Dominican monk Saint Thomas Aquinas (1225–1274) as its most important exponent (cf. Wogaman 1993:82–95; Solomon 1990:66–69, 295–296; Hauerwas 1993:256–260), until the *Renaissance* (roughly the fourteenth to sixteenth centuries—cf. Sidgwick 1967: xxi–xxii, 109–157). This phase is broadly characterized by the gradual rise and development of a wide variety of powerful and authoritative *institutions* in given societies, including so-called Christian societies. These included different forms of public, state and church power (cf. MacIntyre 1966:110–120).

This means that, for the first time, different—institutionalized, authoritarian—moral claims are made with regard to the same subjects. In distinction from the Greek city-states with its common ethos, where the society was also the state—where cult, ethics, politics, and economy were almost synonymous—these institutions gradually started to prescribe to those people under their authority and control, how they should behave or not.[62] This could become *an ethics of law or duty* (Smit 1994c:20). Good and moral people are still referred to as *virtuous* people—Aristotle's influence was indeed still important in this phase—but it becomes the virtues, laws, rules and traditions of a particular institution. Generally speaking, the church or the state now determined how people should live. Thus, although there is still a link between a good society and good, moral people, a proliferation of societies occur to which people respond in different ways. After they made a choice as to which political or ecclesial tradition they should follow, their *identity* (who and what they preferred to be) and *ethos* would be characterized by their trust, respect, love, obedience to the *external* authority of that particular institution.

Often though, this loyalty was motivated by a fear of punishment, which means that, for the first time, a distance developed between people and the norms and prescriptions they lived by. Nevertheless, whether people obeyed out of love or fear, they did what they were told, they obeyed the duties and prescriptions, they fulfilled the laws and social roles expected from them by the institutions. In this sense not much room existed for critical

---

[62] Sometimes these institutions were in conflict, even in war with one another (pope versus emperor; pope versus king or governor; one church, church order or society against the other—cf. the history of the Crusades in the eleventh to thirteenth centuries, the fall of the Roman Empire, etc.).

reflection within the different institutions—a trend which *inter alia* limited the development of exegetical methods for centuries in Christian history (cf. Lategan 1982:54–55).

.3 The Modern Phase

This phase in the history of moral thinking and action was prepared by the Renaissance, which led into the Enlightenment, and then to what we today know as *modernity* (characterized by industrialization, modern political systems, etc.).

The French mathematician and philosopher René Descartes (1596–1650) was probably the major scholar who paved the way for modernity (Solomon 1990:30–31, 70–71, 98–99, 309). As a student at the Roman Catholic University of Paris, he was well-trained in the tradition of Aristotle. In his philosophical treatise he expressed a deep concern for not being able to discern between what was true or false in that tradition. All that he was sure of, was his doubt, his uncertainty. For Descartes, the certainty of the ability to doubt, meant that he could *think*, a function that also determined his humanity. From this simple logical principle emerged his famous Latin statement "*Cogito, ergo sum*": "I doubt/think, therefore I am" (cf. Niebuhr 1941:103; 1963:101–102, 109–110; Solomon 1990:131–132). Descartes was thus convinced that his reason, his ability to *think for himself* a way through the knowledge and traditions he inherited, would enable him to distinguish between right and wrong, between whom and which claims and truths to follow, and whom and what to discard.

This line of thought would already represent the notion or ideology of the Enlightenment in a nutshell. More than a century later, the great German philosopher of the Enlightenment and very influential since then, Immanuel Kant (1724–1804), wrote that the essence of the Enlightenment is *that every human being is able to think for him/herself* (cf. MacIntyre 1966:190–198; Ogletree 1983:23–34; Sidgwick 1967:270–278; Solomon 1990: 72–73, 106–109, 135–137, 204–205, 310).[63] The basic thrust of the Enlightenment was therefore that every human being is a rational subject who can think critically, *and decide* for him/herself what to believe and what to do. People are now faced with a wide variety of religious (including Christian) and secular options. Sometimes they appeal to principles, or norms, their own conscience, or attitude—obviously oriented according to their own perspectives. The central question now shifts to *What is good and moral action, activity, or behavior*—but, important, *for the individual*? Faced with particular issues or actions, the question becomes: *What* choices or decisions should an individual take; *how* should s/he take that decision; what considerations would be important (cf. MacIntyre 1966:249–269)?

---

[63] With regard to morality, this means that every human being has to decide for him/herself what is good or bad, and then do what they *ought* to do, which means that *duty* becomes the key to morality (cf. Solomon 1990:208–240; Birch & Rasmussen 1989:35–37). For Kant, the guarantee for this is that all human beings are rational, orderly and well-behaved. Therefore (and this is typical of modernity), *if* people all use their minds, their similar rational capacities, and *think* and talk about what is good or bad, they will eventually agree and come to the same conclusion (Solomon 1990:210, 291–292). Kant obviously said this from the perspective of the small, homogeneous community of his hometown, Königsberg, East Prussia, where he spent his whole life (MacIntyre 1966:191–192; Solomon 1990:13).

Thus, in the modern phase morality is—for the first time in history—faced and characterized by the appearance of the thinking, questioning *individual*, severed from the good society and its institutions. Strangely, almost paradoxically, it is more the human critical faculty that occupies centre stage than the whole, historical, living person (Richardson 1994:91). Kant's wish "is to exhibit the moral individual as being a standpoint and a criterion superior to and outside any actual social order" (MacIntyre 1966:198). Previously, it was society, or an institution, which determined how people should live. Now the rational individual, and that individual's *conscience* or inner moral voice—often in an authoritative way—becomes the moral agent who decides how to live and what to be. Authority thus shifts from *external* institutions—whether the state, church, or the Bible— to *internal* convictions, principles, attitudes, and decisions. "*Heteronomy*, laws of 'others,' laws from outside, whether the Bible, the church, or important people, duties imposed by others, were replaced by *autonomy*, by the convictions, the beliefs, the norms of the human beings themselves, the duties they decided to take on themselves. Individuals, so-called moral agents, whether Christian or not, lived, acted and decided on the basis of their own convictions, beliefs, principles and ideals" (Smit 1994c:20; emphasis mine; cf. Solomon 1990:210, 227–229).

It is significant to note that also Protestantism forms an integral part of modernity. In fact, the period of the Reformation—seen against the backdrop of other important cultural developments of the time—can be regarded as the beginning of the modern phase. Luther, Calvin, and other theologians of the Reformation, think to a large extent in terms of these individualistic questions, and supply answers to them.

A wide variety of ethical positions develops in this phase—cf. *inter alia* Pietism, Rationalism, Existentialism and the so-called "situation ethics" in Christianity, the Charismatic movement, and different forms of democracy with its emphasis on individual rights. Although these movements give different answers, they all respond to the same sets of questions. During the eighteenth and nineteenth centuries the focus was almost entirely on these issues. Hardly any attention was given to questions pertaining to the identity, character, and values of a good and moral person—issues which were only to be taken seriously in the twentieth century.

The majority of people today (including religious people), however, still—only— think about ethics in the narrower sense of issues (e.g. abortion, euthanasia, pre-marital sex, homophilia), principles, and norms. How they deal with such specific issues, how they respond to problems and crises, how they take decisions, is determined by the basic premise of the individual's authority to decide for her/himself.[64] The use of the Bible in Christian ethics has also often been, and is often still dominated by this attitude.

---

[64] Jeffrey Stout, moral philosopher at Princeton University, describes this process with both religious and secular proponents in his book *The flight from authority: Religion, morality, and the quest for autonomy*. Notre Dame: University of Notre Dame Press (1981). In the words of Max Weber, this process may be viewed as the replacement of the ethics of external law by *an ethics of principle*, of internal disposition, a *Gesinnungsethik* or "gesindheidsetiek" (Smit 1994c:20).

.4 Recent Trends in Christian Ethics

In the twentieth century, a variety of events and developments led to yet a new phase. At the beginning of the century, more and more people realized—especially with regard to the threat of a nuclear holocaust after the Second World War—that an ethics of autonomy, of personal conviction, principle and attitude (as advocated during the modern phase of the development of Christian ethics, was insufficient to deal with the complex issues of twentieth century societies, and was in fact often extremely dangerous. More people realized that by focusing on individualistic questions of moral *action*, other major questions—with regard to moral *people* and a moral *society*—are left behind, and sometimes totally ignored. It was realized that society is still being formed and reformed, but by its own momentum. Individuals no longer have the collective power to influence the morality of society.

An Ethics of Responsibility

To what extent, then, did the question of a good and moral society concern moral philosophers, and particularly Christians and the churches in the twentieth century?

In a classical form, the problem of an ethics only based on principle and convictions—the tradition characteristic of followers of Kant and a deontological approach—was formulated by Max Weber (1864–1920) in his famous distinction between a *Gesinnungsethik* and a *Verantwortungsethik*.[65] He pleads that an ethics of principle and attitude be balanced by *an ethics of responsibility*—asking about the consequences or results of every decision and act. "Since Weber, an ethics of responsibility means: Realistically considering the possible future effects of actions. It means: Seriously considering what is possible and what not. It means: Honestly listening to other people concerned, to heed their advice, to respect their opinion, to enquire with them about the best possible future, about the concrete steps to an attainable good society" (Smit 1994c:21). Since then many scholars—social scientists, ethicists, philosophers, theologians—contributed to this discussion.[66]

---

[65] Weber did this—just after the First World War—in the confused, chaotic months at the start of the reconstruction of European society. "He was asked to talk about 'the vocation of politics,' about the kind of people Europe needed to help build a new, a good society. He argued that people who decide only on the basis of principle and *gesindheid*, only on the basis of convictions, ideals and slogans, without taking account of the possible consequences, the possible outcome, the possible results of their action, were irresponsible, incapable of contributing to a good society and public life and dangerous. He specifically addressed his criticism to Protestant pastors, who had wonderful visions and moving rhetoric, but who misled and confused people, because they made them irresponsible" (Smit 1994c:20–21).

[66] I briefly mention three examples. The well-known German theologian of the Second World War, Dietrich Bonhoeffer (1906–1945), wrote moving passages on this aspect. For recent discussions of his life and work, see Fowl & Jones 1991:135–164, and Russel Botman's doctoral dissertation entitled "Discipleship as Transformation? Towards a Theology of Transformation" (1993:55–235). Drawing on the work of various scholars who made in-depth studies on Bonhoeffer's life, Botman distinguishes three phases in his life, while emphasizing the continuity of his thought. He then appropriates Bonhoeffer's

notion of *discipleship as transformative responsibility* to the contemporary context of socio-political change in South Africa. For another useful discussion on the relevance of Bonhoeffer for the South African context, see De Gruchy 1984.

As was and would be the case with theologians such as Niebuhr and Hauerwas, the "who" question is much more important for Bonhoeffer than "what" and "how" questions. People's actions follow their being, who they are. For Bonhoeffer, the most important question concerning Christ, is *Who is Christ, and who are we? Who is Jesus Christ for us today?* His conclusion is that the church is *Christ existing in the world*—the implications of which he would continuously discuss in communion with like-minded friends and disciples. In his writings on ethics—before and during his imprisonment—there is a growing awareness of the *public responsibility* of the church and (ecumenical) theologians, of the serious need that reflection should be followed by action with regard to society. This is already sensed in his published doctoral thesis *Sanctorum Communio: Eine dogmatische Untersuchung zur Soziologie der Kirche* (1969, München: Chr. Kaiser Verlag), which was originally presented to the Theological Faculty in Berlin in 1927. It places social philosophy and sociology in the service of dogmatics by explaining the structure and concrete functioning of the Christian church *as community in this world.* Bonhoeffer further developed these notions in various books, essays, meditations, letters and other writings, which were compiled and published under well-known titles such as *The Cost of Discipleship* (1959, London: SCM), *Life together* (1954, London: SCM), *Ethics* (1955, London: SCM), London: SCM), *Letters and Papers from Prison* (1956, London: SCM), *Het wezen van de kerk* (1972, Baarn: Ten Have) and *Midde-in die wêreld* (1971, Kaapstad: Tafelberg). Generally speaking, one can say that there is a very close relation between "the cost of discipleship" and "ethics" in Bonhoeffer's thinking and praxis.

After him, in 1979, "the former German theologian and philosopher, Hans Jonas, then working in New York, wrote an award-winning study called *Das Prinzip Verantwortung.* He argued that, for the first time in history, humanity has become so powerful through the development of technology, that we are capable of, and on the way to, destroy the whole world, if we do not become responsible people, for the sake of the future, and deliberately and freely restrain ourselves. He argued on the basis of what he called 'a heuristic of fear': We must become responsible now, otherwise the future will be too ghastly to contemplate. We must consider now what is going to happen if we do simply continue to live the way we are, and in responsibility to the future and to future generations, we must restrain ourselves and change our ways. This is the logic of an ethics of responsibility" (Smit 1994c:21; cf. Huber 1993; Schweiker 1993; Tanner 1993).

In this context mention has also to be made of the recent book of North American social ethicist Larry Rasmussen, *Moral Fragments and Moral Community: A Proposal for Church in Society* (1993, Minneapolis: Fortress). Rasmussen (an authority on, and follower of Bonhoeffer) challenges communities of character with regard to their eventual impact on society—communities such as Christian churches, families, schools, and Christians involved in trade unions and religious education. He indicates that Western society today lives from community fragments and moral fragments alone—fragments which are being destroyed more quickly than they are replenished. After having assessed the reasons for this situation (describing how the market society and state society have eroded the bonds of community), Rasmussen proposes forms and tasks which churches can undertake to help people see what is happening in society as *their* co-responsibility, and to mend and

During the first half of the century, many theologians followed the influential Swiss theologian Karl Barth, by emphasizing that the Bible is not "the revelation of *a morality*, but the revelation of *the living God*. Christians ethics, therefore, had to think not about morality reduced to propositions, but about God and how life ought to be rightly related to his power and his presence" (Botha 1991:14; emphasis mine; cf. Botha 1994a:40–42; Kelsey 1968:9–16; 1975:39–50). For Barth, what is required of ethics is obedience to a Person, not a proposition (Gustafson 1984a:141; cf. R. M. Naudé 1993:158–160; Spohn 1984:14–17).

In a next phase, directly building on the previous one, the approach of *relationality* and *responsibility* focuses on Christians' response to (the acts of) God, and not to rules, laws or duties. A new openness and responsiveness to the work of the living God was particularly encouraged by H. Richard Niebuhr, probably the most influential North American practical theologian of the previous century. He was convinced that "too much of Christian ethics tries to find 'Christian answers' to problems of morality instead of being open and responsive to the work of the living God. The Bible has to be used in such a way that it helps the Christian community to interpret the God whom it knows in its existential faith and not for giving a revealed morality that is to be 'translated' and 'applied'" (Botha 1991:15; cf. 1994a:41–42; Gustafson 1984a:140–143). For Niebuhr, Christian ethics requires *response* to a Person, and not a rule (Gustafson 1984a:141). Being a good example of *responsible* biblical hermeneutics in a twentieth century context, the theology and ethics of Niebuhr will be discussed further in 4.4.2.2.

Gustafson (1984a; 1984b)—in a discussion on several variations of the ethics of faith-response—argues for a *relationality and responsibility model* as a primary way to understand Christian ethics today.[67] The results of historical-critical scholarship have shown that what might have been a valid norm in the context of the biblical world does not necessarily mean that it has equal reference and validity today (Botha 1991:15; Rousseau 1985b:96–99). Gustafson's approach (followed by several other scholars) also places *the living God*—and not a specific law or norm—in the very centre of activity, while the encompassing role of believers is seen as a response to what God has done and is doing, with final responsibility and obligation to this God (cf. Curran 1984:180–184; Birch & Rasmussen 1989:57).[68]

---

improve civil society.

[67] Responsibility as criterion for ethical evaluation necessitates consideration of both the nature of the text with which one is dealing, as well as the situation in which the act of interpretation takes place. At the same time the role of readers is described in terms of their relation to that specific context or situation (cf. Botha 1992:169–170).

[68] Drawing on notions from Bonhoeffer, Emil Brunner, Sharon Welch and Richard Niebuhr, Smit (1994c:21–25) elaborates on the *nature* of moral responsibility in this sense. Firstly, to be responsible means to "deliberately, consciously, take responsibility for what is going to happen, for the results of our actions, for the implications of our present behavior, in short, for the future" (Smit 1994c:22). Secondly, "'(c)oncrete responsibility' means *taking the real-life circumstances of the present seriously*. It means asking: What must we do *now*, as responsible people, to contribute to 'a good society' in the future, one in which our children will be able to live, peacefully, in justice, happily, humanly? What must we do *now, given the situation as it is, reality as it is, conditions as they are, the options as they are limited by present realities?*" (Smit 1994c:22). A third aspect of responsibility has

The *responsibility-relationality* model for the interpretation of the New Testament in Christian ethics, is also followed by Patrick Hartin, a leading South African New Testament scholar and ethicist. He motivates this approach as follows:

> The person of Jesus remains the very centre of the life and action of the Christian. Morality is no longer limited to the narrow legalistic carrying out of stipulated laws. Instead, morality emerges from the very context of the Christian faith as a way of life which is led as a response to the gift of faith which the believer has received. In no way can the Scriptures be used as a law book of revealed morality.... What they do give us is a picture of the understanding which these people had of themselves as they lived their lives under God's covenant and in a relationship to Jesus (Hartin 1994:520; cf. 1991:3–4).

Since I find these trends analogous to the perspective and communicative power of the Ephesians epistle, I use the two notions of *relationality* and *responsibility* as the essence of my own concept of an ethics of interpretation for Ephesians in particular, and the New Testament at large. Responsibility, in the Ephesians sense, would mean to respond to what God has done and is doing in Jesus Christ—by living a life worthy of God's calling, i.e. to live *in a relationship of love and obedience to Christ*. Practically this means to act in accordance with Christ's example, to communicate a *Christ-like* ethos of loving concern, empathy, caring and empowering service in every aspect of life, including society at large (Eph. 4:32; 5:1, 2, 23, 29). These relations are described in terms of a continual and concrete process of renewal, reconstruction and growth (4:23–24).

The movement toward *responsible involvement of Christians in society*—considering the relation between moral *action* and a moral *society*—represents the first trend in contemporary Christian ethics. In this regard I shall focus on the contributions of Niebuhr and Tödt in 4.4.2—as representatives of the many twentieth century scholars who worked and still work with these concepts, and which occur to be in continuation with the Ephesians thrust and perspective (cf. Niebuhr 1941; 1956; Bonhoeffer 1956; Hauerwas 1977; 1984; 1985a; 1985b; Tödt 1977; Hauerwas & MacIntyre 1983; Verhey 1984b:214–218; Lundin, Thiselton & Walhout 1985; Smit 1990c; 1993a; 1994c; Beardslee 1990; Ackermann 1992a).

Closely related to an ethics of responsibility—with overlapping elements in its contribution toward a more humane society—is a second trend called "discourse ethics."

Discourse Ethics

The picture of recent trends in (Christian) ethics would be incomplete without referring to the extremely influential contribution of Jürgen Habermas, social philosopher of Frankfurt, Germany—particularly with regard to his deliberate attempt to bring individual rational morality and societal issues together, however still in continuation with the modernity

---

to do with "power, with ability, with possibility. When we are able to achieve something, to do something, to be something.... then we are responsible. We are responsible for the difference, however small, that we can make, and for the contribution, however insignificant, we can make" (Smit 1994c:24). The implications of these notions for *Christian* ethics in particular, will be explored further in 4.4.2.

project.[69] Although he was a social philosopher, and a neo-Marxist—with reference to the so-called *Kritische Theorie* of *Die Frankfurter Schule*, some of the most interesting appropriations of his thoughts are made by Christian theological students, and especially practical theologians (cf. Arens 1989:7–38; Botha 1993). In this sense, and specifically by bringing theology (back) into the public sphere, Habermas indirectly made a very significant contribution to contemporary ethics.[70]

The complexity of Habermas' thinking is enormous, and it is impossible to come to grips with it within the parameters of a small subsection of the book. Because of the promises his theories hold for theology and ethics, however, a very brief and rather superficial overview is nevertheless given here. In his evaluation of structural changes in the public sphere, Habermas fiercely criticizes so-called public opinion and the (false) notion of democracy, and how knowledge is always driven by interest. Instead, he pleads that the production and use of knowledge be driven by an "emancipatory interest," and be utilized in aid of a more free, humane, rational, democratic and moral society (Thiselton 1992: 379–385). Habermas wrote numerous books and essays on his vision for society, which stimulated many, many responses (cf. Rasmussen 1990:114–140). His major work, *Theorie des kommunikativen Handelns* (Frankfurt am Main: Suhrkamp, 1981), consists of two volumes (1167 pages), and respectively deals with reason and the rationalization of society, and a critique of functionalist reason. Like Kant, Habermas pleads for a more rational society, but realizes that reason means different things to different people. He tries to solve this problem by developing "a theory of communicative action" (cf. Rasmussen 1990:18–55; Thiselton 1992:385–393).

For Habermas (1988:63–104), the basic forms of human action (*Handeln/Handlungen/Interaktion*), namely doing and producing, are performed *purposefully*, in order to achieve a specific function. The purposes of these activities—according to him—are threefold: *instrumental* (dealing with impersonal objects or "things"), *strategic* (dealing with, and persuading human beings as if they are things), and *communicative* (dealing with people, but with the purpose to achieve mutual understanding). The first two are geared toward achieving results. Habermas says that modern society is essentially generated

---

[69] Habermas stands in the tradition of Kant. He can actually be considered as the last exponent of Rationalism with its emphasis on the rational abilities of the individual, but in a radically different way (cf. Rasmussen 1990:6–17). See also Thomas McCarthy's introduction to Habermas 1990 (vii–xiii).

[70] Being a student during the Second World War, Habermas was deeply troubled by the extent to which Germany—which stood in the traditions of Kant, Hegel, Marx, Goethe and others—degenerated under the Nazi regime. This formed the pathos behind his work. In his encounter with the works of Kant, Habermas realized that there was a certain dialectic in the Enlightenment—a positive and negative side—and had therefore to be assessed critically (Rasmussen 1990:1–17). Negatively, the Enlightenment brought about a great deal of *alienation*. This is *inter alia* illustrated by (what has become) the proliferation of different academic disciplines—which inhibit dialogue among scholars, with disastrous effects on the integrity and moral identity of universities and other academic institutions dealing with education. Such specialized academic knowledge is also alienated from everyday human life. Moreover, autonomous, free individuals have been alienated from society, and lost the power and ability to influence the systems at work in—industrial, economic, political—society.

toward achieving *strategic* purposes, and that people are in the process manipulated toward that goal. For a society to become humane and democratic, he argues, it must strive for a *communicative* purpose (cf. Keulartz 1992:9–26, 251–270; Hohengarten 1992:viii–xix; Botha 1993:69–78).

The prime form to achieve human understanding is to use *language*. In this broad sense language is seen as human action dealing with other human beings in order to understand and to be understood.[71] Thus, in order to bring about a more humane and moral society, Habermas suggests that people *learn to talk to one another*. This means that communication, dialogue, and public debate should be cultivated. But what kind of communication, dialogue, and public debate would be appropriate to facilitate such a change? Following John Searle, Habermas emphasizes four basic aspects involved in language which need to be borne in mind, namely clarity, truth, intention, and truthfulness (Habermas 1988:136–149; Keulartz 1992:251–265).[72] For communication to succeed, the receiver or listener has to understand and accept all four these aspects.

These aspects, Habermas continues, have to do with four different worlds: a language world, an objective world (things as they are in themselves), a social or relational world, and a subjective or personal world (cf. Habermas 1990:133–141).

In any rational communication situation where people wish to make collective decisions, where they want to persuade each other toward a new vision (e.g. public dialogue or political debate), misunderstanding can occur on any of the four levels mentioned in n.72. When people misunderstand each other on the first level, Habermas says, they must solve it by means of an *explanatory* (*explikatieve*) discourse (e.g. by explaining what is meant by concepts like reconciliation, justice, peace, etc.), on the second level with *theoretical* discourse, and on the third and crucial level with *practical* discourse—where he distinguishes between different discourses concerning the *implications* of the propositions made with regard to truth claims. The most difficult problem lies on the fourth level, when people do not trust one another, and do not accept one another's credibility. In such instances, Habermas says, the purely rational discourse of the first three levels will not be sufficient to facilitate communication. What is needed then, is "therapeutic criticism," a different kind of interaction which will cultivate friendship and mutual trust, so that rational dialogue would be able to continue again (cf. Habermas 1988:63–104; 1990:43–115; Rasmussen 1990:56–74; Keulartz 1992:251–265).

Habermas further argues that rational people have the obligation to broaden their public dialogue to include the so-called "system." He insists that society should be open to

---

[71] In his analysis of language, Habermas makes use of the work of John Searle, linguist from Berkeley, and the English language philosopher J. L. Austin, author of the famous *How To Do Things With Words* (New York: Oxford University Press, 1965). Searle was a student of Austin's, and elaborated extensively on the latter's insights in speech act theory (Habermas 1988:136–149; Rasmussen 1990:27–28, 39; Keulartz 1992: 197, 249, 252; cf. Thiselton 1992:283–307, 358–368; Ricoeur 1976:14; 1977:73).

[72] These aspects are: language as *utterance* (*Äußerungsakt*, referring to syntax and semantics, i.e. clarity, understandability), language as *propositional* (factual truth claim), the *illocutionary* aspect of language (referring to the intention or implication of the speaker's words, "*die Richtigkeit*" or correctness of the utterance), and the *perlocutionary* aspect (dealing with "*die Wahrhaftigkeit*," the truthfulness, authenticity, right of the person and claims of the speaker). See Habermas 1988:68–75; 1990:116–194, especially 133–141.

debate, in such a way that all rational people could participate in collective decision-making. Such a debate should not be manipulative, threatening, or coercive. However, it should be an *"ideal speech-situation"*—democratic and free, allowing people to listen to one another, be informed by, and understand each another. Kant said that people, when faced with moral decisions, should *think* about what other rational beings would do in the same situation. To this Habermas adds the notion of free dialogue ("machtsvrije communicatie"—Keulartz 1992:260–265), encouraging people to do what other rational beings would do if they were in a position to talk under ideal conditions, and collectively come to a decision. The problem is that there is a tension between the ideal and what is attainable. But still Habermas would say: Talk *as if* all other people were present, and in a way that would also serve their interests. That is, for him, the only way to move toward a more humane society (cf. Keulartz 1992:266–291). Although he does not give particular guidance in terms of good or bad, he makes useful proposals by encouraging training and practice in the *formal procedures* by which moral decisions can be made in as many as possible different contexts (school, university, society, church).

Although Habermas' solution could be criticized as still too idealistic or rationalistic, or in terms of other forms of dialogue which might be needed in some contexts in society, one has to agree that the basic characteristic of the church—albeit from a different perspective—is precisely that of a compassionate, humane community, a communicative body of believers who collectively function (interacting, celebrating, talking together) to serve specific goals. In this sense it should not come as a surprise that so many theologians have gained from Habermas' theories. Analogous to the Ephesians author who reinterpreted traditions from his environment from a new perspective, contemporary Christian ethics can gain a lot by utilizing and reappropriating this tradition if it wants to take its societal role seriously (cf. Botha 1993:78–84).

Why is Habermas important for the purpose of this study? Where does his argument of "coercion-free discourse" fit into a better understanding of the use of the Bible in Christian ethics? It has become clear that the popular (modernistic) use of the Bible—focusing only on contemporary *issues*—does not necessarily impact upon broader societal problems. In fact, Christians have been alienated from society, and lost the power to influence it by focusing on those issues (only). Habermas indirectly challenges all rational, moral Christians to seriously ask whether they can use the Bible in such a way that it would have an influence, and bring about significant change—especially with regard to society at large.

In this sense, Habermas indirectly challenges our discussion on the appropriation of Ephesians, and particularly its vision of a moral society. How is the Ephesians view of *community* supposed to influence contemporary—early twenty-first century, Western, male-oriented—society? What kind of values, virtues and communicative structures would prevail in such a community? How could the alternative perspective of Ephesians influence contemporary notions of moral discourse, rationality, democracy, knowledge, moral people's role in society, and particularly the power of people's ethos and words to impact on society? What kind of inclusive language would be appropriate to translate that perspective—as a vehicle to bring about effective change in society? (See Bird 1988; Glanville 1992:49–74). These questions would necessarily form part of the ethics of interpretation and appropriation of the Ephesians document in present-day circumstances.

Narrative Ethics

A third trend in contemporary (Christian) ethics, which has become known as *narrative ethics*, represents the work of scholars such as Richard Niebuhr, MacIntyre, Hauerwas, Meilaender, and others—albeit with different emphases—who have started to take seriously questions concerning the formation of moral *people* (cf. Spohn 1984:89–105; Vosloo 1994:26–46). For these scholars the major ethical question has shifted to: What is a good and moral *person*? What are the virtues in which moral people are supposed to be trained? And how and where are such people formed? The fundamental question now becomes one of *identity*: Who am I? Who are we? The assumption behind these questions is that who people are and who they want to be will determine what they see as challenges, and how they will respond to them (cf. Smit 1994c:26–29). By *starting* with these questions, and not with questions pertaining to actions or society, these scholars emphasize the formation of moral *people* who will, hopefully, be able to take good, moral *decisions*, and contribute to—the story of—a good, moral *society* (cf. Müller & Smit 1994; Mott 1982).[73]

A well-known conviction and claim of narrative theology and ethics is that *people are their stories*, since they "are what they tell of themselves (or what is told to them) in their story and what they make of this story" (Dietrich Ritschl, quoted by Müller & Smit 1994: 385). Stories further "constitute the communities of character in which we learn virtues, thereby shaping our present lives, views, convictions, opinions.... stories even inform our emotions, teaching people what to fear and what to hope for, when to become angry and when to rejoice.... such collective stories provide people with the language they use" (Müller & Smit 1994:385).

Richard Niebuhr, through his emphasis on "point of view" and "the story of our lives" has probably contributed more than anyone to make twentieth century ethicists aware of the crucial importance of these questions (Niebuhr 1941; Smit 1994c:27 n.8; cf. Müller & Smit 1994:386). I shall therefore devote more time to his contribution (see 4.2.2).

Alasdair MacIntyre's first major work, *After Virtue: A Study in Moral Theory* (2nd ed. 1984), would become one of the most important works on moral philosophy during the past decades. However in a totally different way, this phase is characterized by a renewed focus on the moral philosophy of Aristotle—especially his sense of friendship and the cultivation of virtuous people, meant to serve the τέλος of a good and moral society (cf. Wadell 1989:31–45; 4.4.1.1). This is mainly a response to the inheritance of modernity and its focus on individual morality, which caused questions of good and moral people to

---

[73] The rationale behind the work of ethicists focusing on questions pertaining to the formation of moral people is *inter alia* described by Lutheran scholar Gilbert C. Meilaender, who has been at the forefront in the movement to return virtues and character to a central place in ethics—though he still understands character and the shape of ethics in ways focused on the individual (Fowl & Jones 1991:23 n.10; cf. Vosloo 1994:67–72). Meilaender emphasizes that the moral dilemmas people perceive, depend upon the *persons* they are. Recognition of a moral dilemma depends upon *character*: what duties and even what dilemmas people perceive, will depend upon the virtues which shape their vision of the world (cf. Tödt 1977:83, step 1).

be neglected for a very long time.[74]

MacIntyre compares the severity of current moral challenges to the fifth and sixth centuries C.E.—the period in the Western world when the Roman Empire declined into the Dark Ages. At that stage, MacIntyre argues, people like Saint Benedict—who lived and worked in central Italy in the first half of the sixth century, famous for composing his Rule, which became the basis of the monastic life, since the six century—realized that it was no longer possible to salvage the so-called Christian Empire and its public order. No longer could the public order be identified with Christianity, morality, and civilization. The only way to keep Christianity and morality in tact, was to retreat from public life into monasteries, into smaller communities where people of faith, character and virtue could study, and keep Christian, moral and intellectual traditions alive *until* the day would hopefully come to make some impact on society again.

MacIntyre comes to a similarly pessimistic conclusion about contemporary Western society, and says that we again need a St. Benedict, which means new monasteries and new communities of character where the emphasis will be on virtues and a moral life style, and not on moral *issues* or the *public order*.[75] Many North American theologians took this challenge seriously, of which only a few are briefly mentioned here.[76]

Perhaps the most influential (albeit controversial) example of contemporary scholars focusing on these questions, is Stanley Hauerwas of Duke University—also a Niebuhr

---

[74] Many moral philosophers and ethicists today criticize the theories of Kant (see n.63 above). It has been indicated that the basis of modernity and democracy—the results of Kant's thinking—rests on the presupposition that, if all well-informed, rational people would think and talk together on moral issues, they would eventually agree. More ethicists are saying that such a presupposition can only be valid if all the people involved are *moral* people, formed in virtues and tradition. Modernity, however, by its one-sided nature, *rejected* and *destroyed* the institutions capable of producing the very people it needed to be a rational, *moral* society. The secularized, industrialized society of the late twentieth century is an ironic illustration hereof. Modernity ridiculed all authoritarian institutions, including many aspects of education and the church. This is the reason why ethicists such as Hauerwas started to put all the emphasis on the issue of *good and moral people*.

[75] In response to (North American social democrat) John Rawls' influential neo-Kantian *Theory of Justice*, MacIntyre wrote another important work, *Whose Justice, which Rationality?* in 1988. Contrary to Kant's view that all human beings share the same form of rationality, MacIntyre argues in this book that what (individual) people will regard as rational, will depend on who they are, and on the community of character in which they live. With regard to the issue of justice, he puts forward the view "that conceptions and theories of justice are almost without fail deeply socially and historically grounded, i.e. they are determined by the groups from which they emanate and whom they are intended to serve" (Smit 1993a:14). Moral people—with a sense of justice with respect to society— will thus have to be trained and formed in communities of justice.

[76] Cf. the broad difference between contemporary German churches which (mainly) function as "public institutions," and North American churches which (mainly) function as "worship communities." The ideal, of course, is that both these realms be acknowledged as representing the essential character of the Christian church (cf. Smit 1993a; 1994a; Müller & Smit 1994).

pupil and follower.[77] Hauerwas has popularized questions of moral identity and responsibility in his so-called "ethics of a community of character" (Hauerwas 1977; 1981; 1984;
1985a; 1985b; 1993; Vosloo 1994:47–72, 115–203; Spohn 1984:92–99; Müller & Smit
1994:385; Smit 1994c:27; Richardson 1994:93–96).[78] According to him, "we are formed
as moral human beings, as moral agents, with visions of what is good and bad, with
virtues, with life-skills, with convictions, with a certain moral character, within a particular
community. We find our identity in this community. That determines what we are going to
do. *Agere sequiter esse*. What we do is the result of who we are. Says Hauerwas: 'Prior to
the question of the kind of choices we make is the kind of person we should be. Therefore,
virtue is prior to decision, character to choice'" (Smit 1994c:27). In his entire ethical
project Hauerwas pleads for a revaluation and integration of the categories of identity,
character, vision, virtue and narrative for the moral life. Although he does not systemat-
ically indicate how these are related, they have to be seen as closely interdependent. For
Hauerwas, the value of *narrative* as relational concept is that it focuses ethical reflection
on the moral *agent* (the acting person/community), and not on isolated decisions, choices
or actions.[79] According to him, a person *is* her/his own story. Whatever s/he does, is a reflection of what s/he is, and adds to the story, or changes it. In summary, Hauerwas (1981:
144) suggests "that descriptively the self is best understood as a narrative, and normatively

---

[77] However, Niebuhr and Hauerwas represent two totally different ways of dealing
with Christian ethics. Both are not interested in questions pertaining to moral *issues*, and
both are concerned with the formation of moral *people*. The main difference between them
lies in their view on the role of moral agents with regard to *society*. For Niebuhr (1941;
[1951] 1975), the definition of moral people should be broad enough to include the transformation of society. Whereas for Hauerwas, the social ethics of the church is more limited
to *simply being the church*, a caring community which practices Christian values and
virtues. For Hauerwas, "(t)he church is a social ethic.... the first social ethical task of the
church is to be the church—the servant community" (quoted by Richardson 1994:95). For
this emphasis Hauerwas has been criticized of "sociological sectarianism" (cf. Smit 1993a:
9; Spohn 1984:93; Müller & Smit 1994:385).
[78] See the bibliographies of Smit 1994c and Vosloo 1994 for major works by
Hauerwas.
[79] Hauerwas (1981:131, 151) also uses narrative to explain the process of *moral
growth* (of becoming one's potential), which is so central to Ephesians and other New
Testament documents. These writings do not primarily provide principles to be used with
regard to *issues*, but witness of, and encourage a dynamic relation with God the Father,
Jesus Christ and the Spirit. According to Ephesians, the Spirit wants to open the believers'
eyes to see Christ and his liberating power and love (1:18), to renew their mind (4:24), to
facilitate growth toward their full potential (4:13). Christian moral growth, the learning
and practising of the Christian story and its virtues and values, would thus be growth in the
awareness of who/what they are *in Christ*, and the willingness to imitate and follow him.
This leaves room for a reclaiming of the Christian story, and a new appreciation of
spirituality, community and saints (as heroines/ heroes or role models)—through worship,
prayer, liturgy, ritual, discipleship (cf. Botman 1993:128–235; Spohn 1984:89–105;
Müller & Smit 1994:399–406). It is in this sense that Hauerwas' project counteracts the
liberal tradition of the Enlightenment, in which people were taught to see themselves as
contextless, story-less individuals, as autonomous subjects protected by individual rights.

we require a narrative that will provide the skills appropriate to the conflicting loyalties and roles we necessarily confront in our existence" (cf. Vosloo 1994:73–115).

The *relevance* of this shift in emphasis regarding moral theory, and particularly Christian ethics, should be obvious. "The crisis of morality, in many societies, is at heart a crisis of identity. The corrupt societies we produce are the result of the corrupt people we are" (Smit 1994c:27; cf. Birch & Rasmussen 1989:67). It is at *this point*, I believe, that an analysis of the orienting perspective and transforming power of the Ephesians story can contribute meaningfully to the discussion (see further 4.4.2). Smit (1994c:27) summarizes the radical implications of this shift from the broad perspective of the New Testament: "For Christians, our ultimate responsibility is to be Christians.... To live, daily, consciously, according to the biblical narratives we celebrate in Christian worship, before the face of God the father, according to the salvation in Jesus Christ, through the renewing power of the Spirit, in such a way that we contribute to a good society, a better future, for all our children, in such a way that we witness to the coming of the kingdom of the Triune God. That is our identity. That is who we want to be. That is who we claim we are. That is the story of our lives. That is the point of view from which we should look at society. That is our responsibility. This makes *integrity* so important. Too often, we are not what we claim to be and even who we think we are. This is why many ethicists, like Hauerwas, stress *truthfulness* as the only way to demonstrate the truth of the claims we make, about ourselves, about God and about the world. We must truthfully live the Christian story. We must be the Christian story. We must be transformed according to the Christian story. We must truthfully be a community of Christian character" (cf. Hauerwas 1977:15–143; 1981: 149–152; 1985a; Richardson 1994:94–96).

Another example of this trend is North American sociologist Robert Bellah who—with colleagues from other disciplines—co-edited the widely read and discussed *Habits of the Heart: Individualism and Commitment in American Life* (1985, Berkeley: University of California Press). It analyzed a vast number of interviews with white upper class young people in California, USA, geared toward understanding how they think about different aspects of their lives. The result was the realization that all these people were completely individualistically oriented. The morals engraved in their lives—the habits of their hearts—were all morals that served their own personal good, not that of other people, including their spouses, family members, and society. The argument of the book is more or less that liberal Western democracy has dug its own grave by emphasizing individual rights and individual moral agents, to such an extent that these people are no longer involved in communities, and no longer interested in society.

A few years later—in 1991—the same group of authors published another book, *The Good Society* (New York: Vintage Books), which was meant to offer a solution to the analysis of *Habits of the heart* (cf. Rasmussen 1993:21, 88, 99, 108–109, 154). They showed how the different institutions in society—family, neighborhood, centres of education: schools, colleges, universities, churches, etc.—should work together in training and forming people in order to serve the public good, and to contribute to a moral, civil society. Democracy, they conclude, means "paying attention," being involved, accepting one's responsibility (cf. Smit 1993a:19; 1994c:28).

Postmodern Thinking

A fourth trend in contemporary (Christian) ethics has become known as *postmodern thinking*—a development which takes the current proliferation of moral discourses seriously. Although it is not possible, and not always necessary, to relate all the diverse aspects of moral thinking with each other, contemporary readers of the Bible somehow have to live and cope with plurality—the co-existence of distinct but different socio-religious groups, and the recognition of their different moral languages. From a postmodern perspective, reality—including textual reality—is regarded as "a differential network, a process rather than a completed product, whose meaning cannot be closed off in a definitive rendering" (Lategan 1994b:123 with reference to a postmodern perspective of history). This creates various inescapable challenges for biblical scholars and contemporary Christian ethics.[80]

Yet, even the context of the reader should not be absolutized. "Subsequent developments in the form of deconstruction and post-modernism have made clear that even the reader does not represent a fixed point in the process of interpretation. It has forced us, however, to acknowledge and face up to the reader-mediated nature of all our pronouncements on the author, structure, audience and meaning of texts and to accept interpretation as the ongoing challenge that it will remain" (Lategan 1991c:5).

In this regard Mark Kline Taylor, systematic theologian from Princeton Theological Seminary, made a useful contribution in his thought-provoking book *Remembering Esperanza: A Cultural-Political Theology for North American Praxis* (1990). By following a "cultural-political" approach, he works with the basic premise that sexism forms the web which holds all other forms of discrimination in place. This leads him to address at least three aspects of postmodern thinking, namely *domination* (of one sex over all other groups), *traditions* (decided on by one sex and enforced on all other groups), and *pluralism* (the co-existence of different moral convictions). While Taylor deals with these aspects specifically within a North American context, his work opens a meaningful way beyond the impasse of modernity, so as to empower all people to new ways of thinking and behaving (cf. Glanville 1992:91–100; Vosloo 1994:10–16).

Taylor (1990:40–45) suggests that, in every situation under review, the abovementioned three aspects be kept together in a creative "trilemmic" tension. He calls this "*a post-modern trilemma*," that is, the trilemma of keeping all three demands in focus at any one time. This challenge involves the simultaneous *acknowledgement of tradition, the*

---

[80] For the many challenges involved in an ethically responsible reading of the Bible and moral discourse within a postmodern context, see Tracy 1981; Hutcheon 1986; McKnight 1988; Stout 1988; Levin 1988; Phillips 1990; Burnett 1990; De Villiers 1991; Glanville 1992; 1993; Cloete & Smit 1994; Deist 1994; as well as a series of four papers by Dirkie Smit read at consecutive meetings of the Western Cape branch of the Theological Society of South Africa during April and May 1993. These were respectively titled "Etiek na Babel? Vrae rondom moraliteit en die openbare gesprek in Suid-Afrika vandag;" "Etiese spraakverwarring in Suid-Afrika vandag;" "Is 'n gemeenskaplike morele taal nodig?"; and "Oor die skepping van 'n grammatika van saamleef" (Smit 1994a; 1995a; 1995b; 1995c). "The plurality of audiences and readings underline the need to do theology in an ecumenical context, to create a space where these readings can interact in a dialectical, critical and creative way" (Lategan 1991c:5).

celebration of plurality, and resistance to any form of domination. To emphasize one of these aspects at the cost of the other, would—according to Taylor—be highly problematical. It is not so much a matter of keeping them in balance, but rather that

> (t)he various kinds of tension experienced in this trilemma provide an important way to view the situation in which contemporary theologians work.... If the trilemmic character of the three traits means anything, it is that taking seriously the demands of each trait requires radical revisioning, not just a modest balancing act among all three (M. K. Taylor 1990:23, 43).

In conclusion, Taylor's suggestions with respect to the postmodern trilemma challenge contemporary ethicists to revision all the existential questions inherited from the past (whether pertaining to society, people or issues), and take them seriously in their interrelatedness as they are still alive today—albeit in varied forms.

.5 Implications from the Historical Overview

It has been argued in 1.4 that the final test for an ethically accountable reading of a New Testament document, is its continuous translation in terms of everyday practical—personal, family, institutional and societal—needs and realities (Fiorenza 1988). Indeed, the processes of interpretation and re-interpretation already form an integral part of the biblical documents, and as such, these documents continue to stimulate and facilitate further discussion and interpretation (Lategan 1982). The brief overview of important phases in the development of (Christian) moral thinking illustrated these ongoing processes during the past twenty centuries.

A major implication from the historical overview is that the Bible has been used in many different ways in Christian ethics in the past—*depending on the particular question(s) being put to it* (cf. 1.2). We have seen that the methodology to be followed, as well as the ethical answers to be found in the Bible, depend to a large extent on the point of view of the researcher, and the question(s) being put to the Bible (Kelsey 1968; 1975; Lategan 1982; Rousseau 1985a). If people want to use it in making decisions with regard to particular moral *issues*, they will use it in a specific way. If they wish to use the Bible in *forming communities of character* where people learn to become wise readers of Scripture and truthful disciples, they will use it in other ways. If they want to use the Bible to accomplish their vision of the *world and society*, they will use it in yet another way. People thus approach the Bible from radically different historical paradigms, and consequently come to different conclusions.

The typology of historical paradigms in (Christian) ethics was also meant to define more concretely some of the many challenges for an ethically responsible interpretation of the Bible today. These challenges will—in continuation with the results of a multi-faceted reading of the Ephesians text (cf. 4.3)—briefly be dealt with in the rest of this chapter. The issue now becomes: How can, and how is

Ephesians, and the New Testament at large, supposed to impact on the different dimensions of Christian ethics?

4.4.2 *EPHESIANS RESPONDING TO DIFFERENT MORAL PARADIGMS*

Contemporary trends in (Christian) ethics tell the story of how ethicists of this century have been, and are taking seriously the moral challenges of our time, and particularly those inherited from the Enlightenment (4.4.1.4). A *major challenge* underlying these trends, is *where to start*, and where to put the *emphasis* within a given situation or under given circumstances. In short: What would be the most influential force(s) to stimulate, facilitate, and maintain good and moral *action*, to empower and form good and moral *people*, to bring about a good and moral *society*?

The answer to these questions will consciously or unconsciously be influenced by all possible aspects involved in the hermeneutical process: the self-understanding of the moral agent, the historical paradigm from which s/he operates, the ability to read the situation or context, the interpreters' critical awareness of their own personal, socio-cultural and religious presuppositions, academic background, personality structure, commitments, preferences, interests, *et cetera*. For Christians, the answer to these questions will also be influenced by their particular understanding of the biblical vision of God and God's involvement with humanity. Recognizing these elements as potentially either creative or restrictive, I shall now summarize possible roles and functions of—my understanding of—the implied alternative world and perspective of the Ephesians story with regard to recent trends in Christian ethics (cf. 4.2).

In order to define the challenges for the use of Ephesians (and the rest of the Bible) in Christian ethics, for translating its communicative power in terms of current personal and societal needs, I start by highlighting three major questions or needs which have been identified during the different historical phases of (Christian) ethics (4.4.1).[81] In essence, the different paradigms brought three major sets of moral questions to the fore, which are all still widely influential

---

[81] It has been noted that a variety of moral discourses, modes or styles of speaking, teaching, preaching, and behaving, different forms of rhetoric, can occur in each of these phases or paradigms (cf. Gustafson 1988; 4.1 n.4). In fact, each paradigm has its own discourse. Of utmost importance for the purpose of the book, is the realization that the Bible has been playing, and is still playing a significant role on different levels and in various (sometimes diverse and conflicting) ways within this network of moral processes. This happens everywhere—at home, in church, in the class room, and in society—whether formally or informally, consciously or unconsciously, directly or indirectly (cf. Smit 1992: 303–317). *This makes the use of Scripture in the wide spectrum of what we collectively call Christian ethics, a moral or an ethical issue, which means that the essence, the identity, the integrity of what Christians are and want to be, is at stake in their interpretation of the Bible* (cf. 1.1).

today. This means that the subject of (Christian) ethics may be approached from several different angles, or that the ethical question can be phrased in different ways (cf. Smit 1993b:2–5).[82]

Firstly, it may be asked: What is good and moral *action*? For Christians, the question is: What is the Ephesians, the New Testament, the biblical, the Christian view of good and moral decisions, actions and conduct—under specific circumstances, and in the face of specific challenges?[83]

Secondly, it may be asked: Who are good and moral *people*? What constitutes a good and moral *person*? And, for Christians: What is the Ephesians, the New Testament, the biblical, the Christian view of a good and moral person? What is her/his character supposed to be like, and where are such people formed?[84]

Thirdly, one may ask: What is a good and moral *society*, a good and *moral world*? For Christians, the question is: What is the Ephesians, the New Testament, the biblical, the Christian view of a good, happy and moral society?

The first question, *What is good and moral action?*, concentrates on specific *issues*, activities, concrete decisions or choices with regard to particular circumstances and moral dilemmas (cf. Furnish 1968:227–241; Birch & Rasmussen 1989:41–42, 52–58).[85] In the second question, *Who is a good and moral person*

---

[82] In so far as the different trends in ethics claim to be *Christian*—i.e. in continuation with the Christian canon and tradition, they are directly relevant to our discussion, and need to be challenged and evaluated from the perspective of the Ephesians epistle and the other documents of the Christian canon.

[83] Cf. Hays (1990:43–45), step 2.

[84] Narrative ethics locates the answer to these questions in people's sense of identity with regard to their life stories, naturally embedded in the functioning of Christian communities of character.

[85] This is sometimes referred to as a *deontological* approach to (Christian) ethics (from the impersonal Greek verb δεῖ, referring to the way people *are supposed to* behave, according to specific rules, norms, principles, duties, obligations, prescribed by "divine" laws, regardless of the consequences—cf. Deist 1990:68; Ogletree 1983:24–28; Layman 1991:85–119; Birch & Rasmussen 1989:52–58; Hartin 1991:2–3; 1994:517; Richardson 1994:91). "*Deontological* theories of ethics interpret the moral life in terms of *timeless rules and strict compliance*. Morality is fundamentally a matter of principled obedience or legal conformity" (Smit 1990c:18; cf. 1992:316). Because the words of the Bible are taken quite literally in this approach, as an expression of the moral life required from Christian believers, the Bible—as the revelation of God's will by means of particular laws or commandments—is basically treated in a fundamentalist way. "The most obvious criticism directed against such an approach is its failure to appreciate that the writings of the Bible emerge from a particular historical and cultural situation and are determined by their own specific worldview" (Hartin 1994:517).

The first two questions pertain to the so-called *teleological* approach—where good/bad action, people, society are goal-oriented, and judged by their τέλος, aim, consequences. "*Teleological* theories of ethics interpret the moral life in terms of the *goals of*

or Christian?, the emphasis is on *virtues*—e.g. wisdom, humility, honesty, trust-worthiness, integrity). What is considered to be *moral*, is determined by the type of human beings people want or choose to be—by their character, or identity (cf. Birch & Rasmussen 1989:40–47). Thirdly, the question *What is a good and moral society?* focuses on *values* (e.g. peace, justice, equality, liberty, liberation), which are normally communicated via symbols, slogans and banners (cf. Birch & Rasmussen 1989:47–52).[86] For people living in this frame of mind, that which is considered to be *moral*, is determined by the kind of value or cause they live and strive for.[87] Christian ethos and ethics invariably involves all these dimensions.[88]

To summarize, the question concerning good/moral action can also be

---

human behavior and the *consequences* of human choice. Morality is fundamentally a matter of purposive shaping of life toward future and final goals" (Smit 1990c:18; cf. Deist 1990:254; Birch & Rasmussen 1989:52; Hartin 1991:3; 1994:518). With reference to the selective way in which Roman Catholic and Protestant theology have often chosen one or other scriptural ideal or theme as the end to which Christian life works, such as *love* or *the Kingdom of God*, Hartin (1994:518) criticizes such an approach because "it tends to lift one particular theme out of the biblical witness and gives it an authority and importance it never had within the context of the biblical writings themselves." The use of Scripture in Christian ethics thus calls for an integrated, multi-dimensional approach to the biblical writings and contemporary reality.

[86] Good refers to "*prized qualities of being* or *desirable traits of moral character*.... The reference is to *the kinds of persons* the moral agents are" (Birch & Rasmussen 1989: 40). "Character" refers to the internal moral elements of a person or group: motives, dispositions, attitudes, intentions, perceptions. These belong to moral "being," as aspects of moral identity. Moral judgments about character and moral identity are judgments about *virtue*, which does not only concern the qualities of good people, but also includes that of good communities—the sort of world that must exist so as to foster the desired qualities. The focus of concrete choices and deeds, on the other hand, is on moral values and obligations as qualities of overt behavior or "doing." "Being" and "doing" are thus in a constant reciprocal relation of shaping and informing one another. It also emphasizes the fact that the Christian life is more than virtue (cf. Birch & Rasmussen 1989:40–47).

[87] "Value ethics generally emphasize the possibilities for human growth and development. There is a strong sense of human agency in value ethics (unfinished agents acting in an unfinished world)" (Birch & Rasmussen 1989:52, cf. 57).

[88] Each of the different aspects of moral agency—virtue, value, duty, vision—illumines *an* aspect of the moral life, and none is adequate to serve as *the* organizing concept for the whole. The brief history of (Christian) ethics showed how each of these has been elaborated as *the* form of Christian ethics and as *the* focus of the moral life. Any adequate Christian ethic, therefore, cannot be reduced to one facet of the moral life. It has to include all these elements, and be oriented by "an overarching moral vision that encompasses all creation.... Wise use of Scripture is sensitive to the varied dimensions of the moral life embedded in the biblical texts themselves, and in our own lives" (cf. Birch & Rasmussen 1989:63, 64, cf. 62–65, as well as the important discussion on character formation and social structure in 85–99. It emphasizes the importance of an adequate Christian ethic to promote both effective social action, a moral society, *and* good character).

phrased as a *how* question: HOW should we behave in particular circumstances?; the question of good/moral people as a *who* question: WHO should I/we be?; and the question of a good/moral society as a *what* question: WHAT should we strive for? The first question (How should we behave?) represents an ethics of *Doing* (*Sollen*), whereas the second and third questions (Who should we be? and What should we strive for?) represent an ethics of *Being* (*Sein*). In the first paradigm the moral *act* is important, while the moral *agent* is central in the second position, and the moral *ideal* or *vision* in the third (cf. Birch & Rasmussen 1989:39–62).[89]

The Bible deals with all these questions in an extraordinary variety of ways (cf. Ogletree 1983:47–173; Verhey 1984a:6–152; Birch & Rasmussen 1989:64; Schrage 1988; Wright 1992:145–464; Smit 1993b:3–5; Marxsen 1993; Mott 1982). Similarly, the Ephesians author seems to be deeply aware of all three these matters (see—with different emphases—Baker 1979; Frerichs 1988; Garland 1979; Simmons 1979; Story 1984; Strauss 1986).

Good, morally responsible Christian *conduct* is described in the Bible, in a variety of ways. The advice of the Ephesians author on how Christians should

---

[89] It has been argued that the Bible has been interpreted during the past twenty centuries, and continues to be used, in many different ways (cf. 1.2; 4.4.1). Often without realizing it, people (including Christians) can approach the Bible from radically different— sometimes incommensurable—paradigms and sets of questions, and therefore get different answers, and come to different, even divergent conclusions. Consequently, contemporary religious and philosophical ethicists are faced with enormous moral dilemmas.

Due to the emphasis on individualistic actions and decisions during the past two centuries, other important sets of questions have been ignored. This often meant that the moral *people* behind the actions and issues were neglected, while *society* was allowed to develop on its own—determined by impersonal forces, structures and systems. The problem was that such faceless structures and systems could hardly be criticized by moral people, including philosophers and theologians. We realize today that, as individuals, we do *not* have the collective or institutional power to influence what is happening in society. For this reason, more and more ethicists ask what can be done to impact on society in order to make it more moral and human. This, *inter alia*, contributed to the development of *an ethics of responsibility* and *discourse ethics* (cf. 4.4.1.4). Both these concerns still attempt to relate questions of good/moral action to questions of a moral society, and ask: How can we, *together* (no more as autonomous individuals), take responsibility for what is happening in society, and how can we influence it?

Proponents of *narrative ethics* likewise attempt to relate questions of good and moral people to that of a moral society. These ethicists concentrate on the formation of moral people in communities of character and virtue, with the hope that such formed and informed people will eventually contribute toward a better and moral society (cf. Fowl & Jones 1991:84–134). Others have rejected (aspects of) this trend as "sectarian"—the retreat to small communities with no real discussion with wider circles pertaining to science and society at large. For a balanced discussion of the criticism on a so-called subjectivistic, relativistic, agent-centered position versus a more "non-arbitrary" ethics of principle, see Vosloo 1994:116, 204–277.

behave, on which norms and principles should determine their actions, the priorities according to which they should make decisions, point to *Christ-like* ways of conduct. Christians love and forgive one another, because they have been loved and forgiven a thousand times more (4:32). They accept, with loving compassion, people different from them—foreigners, strangers, outsiders, people excluded by social biases—and care for them. They submit willingly to one another, out of reverence for Christ (5:21). Their ethos (in terms of marital, family, and socioeconomical relations—always within the ethical context of the church) is characterized by worship and praise-giving to God. All this implies a radical renewal in the attitude of their minds (4:23).

On the other hand, amid human possibilities and capacities for good, the Ephesians epistle also reckons with the fragile realities of human limitations and fallibility, and its inclination toward evil impulses. This gives pause to all hopes that character and virtue can be created instantly so as to guarantee good. In this struggle God provides Jesus Christ as the full armor of God's protection against the "powers and principalities."[90]

Secondly, good, moral, responsible, Christian *people* are also portrayed in Ephesians, in these positive terms. They are created with the potential to know God, to become wise and mature people, attaining to the whole measure of the fullness of Christ (4:13). They are created to be like God in true righteousness and holiness (4:24). They are called children of God, the body in which God lives by God's Spirit, and are chosen to be holy and blameless in God's sight (cf. 2.1.3.1). They can only be like that, because Jesus Christ is their role model. They know and follow him, live according to his example, are filled with his Spirit (5:18). They are therefore characterized by virtues such as love, patience, humility, honesty, truth, wisdom, mutual submission, and values such as peace and righteousness. These are also pictured in terms of the complete absence of enmity, strife, jealousy, (sinful) anger (4:26), selfishness, dissension, sexual immorality, greed, obscenity, foolish talk or coarse joking (5:3–5). Such practices—or the attitudes causing them—are considered as *idols* (cf. 5:5; Niebuhr 1941:54–59), which destroy the unity among them, which are not honorable, which do not fit a life worthy of their calling.

The answer to the third question is exactly the same. The good *society*, God's alternative moral world, is described in Ephesians as a place, a home, where traditional enemies are reconciled in peace. It is characterized by the "rule" of Jesus Christ, by his radical love, forgiveness, *shalom,* wholeness, righteousness and holiness. It is a world where all things—all stories—in heaven and on earth are brought together and united under Christ's headship (1:10, 22), and where the whole universe is filled with his presence (4:10). It is a world where

---

[90] This means that attention must be given with the greatest care "to the complex interplay of character and social structure so that virtue is not only cultivated, but far more important, that virtue and right action converge" (Birch & Rasmussen 1989:99).

God is represented by the church, the embodiment of God's fullness (1:23), a dwelling in which God lives by his Spirit (2:22). Because of the dynamic, creative presence of God, Jesus Christ and the Spirit in and through the church, the world and society is implicitly marked by love, grace and compassion, peace and unity, dignity and respect, gentleness, kindness, patience and forgiveness, hope and salvation, righteousness and holiness.... (cf. Combrink 1986:230–234). Put differently, it is characterized by a total absence of barriers, of conflict, hostility and strife, violence and jealousy, exclusivism and domination.[91] If the church and

---

[91] This vision of a moral society implicitly results from a Christian community which truthfully lives up to its calling within a particular socio-historical context (cf. Bosch 1976; 1982a; 1982b; Barnard 1971; Honig 1978; Bakker 1978; Theron 1982; 1985; Pieterse 1985; Nolan 1986; 1988; Kritzinger 1988; Robinson 1990; Wessels 1990c; Venter 1991; Kruger 1991; Yoder 1991; Fowl & Jones 1991:44–50). In a discussion of the relation between "the two stories" of Christianity and society, and with reference to Niebuhr's *Christ and Culture*, Müller and Smit (1994:389) describe this ongoing hermeneutical process as follows: "In terms of the story-approach, the institutionalized church, as 'a story-telling and -celebrating community'.... always exists within the more comprehensive community of a particular society, with its own collective stories and histories, celebrations and hopes, institutions and social practices. The institutional church finds its own identity and fulfills its own calling, in every society anew, somewhere in the tension between complete adaptation to the public story and complete isolation from the public story, between total legitimisation and blessing and total escape and rejection." And, in terms of the very fragile metaphorical network involved in such a process, they add: "The church tells its own story in ways between the extremes of becoming merely a repetition of the public stories already at hand, or of being so radically different from the public stories that no meaningful connection is possible" (cf. Lategan 1992c:627; 1994b:131–133).

In concurrence with the Ephesians perspective, Müller and Smit (1994:399–406) further argue that the basic identity and character of the church ought to be visible when sharing its story in public worship. If the church acknowledges God's sovereignty in every sphere of life, and wishes to represent a truthful voice in society, it first needs to communicate its message as *one, united, inclusive, ecumenical church*. In South Africa there is an urgent need for the Christian church "to be the place where other voices, including those from the bottom and the edges, and especially those from the marginalized and the victims, the voiceless and the downtrodden, should be heard" (Müller & Smit 1994:401–402). This implies a second characteristic of the church, namely "its *catholicity or fullness*", which has had a variety of meanings in history. The thrust of the Ephesians epistle is an invitation to the rich diversity of society, races, sexes, classes and cultures—all to be included in the one church, under the fullness of the lordship of Christ (cf. Ogletree 1983:152–168). This already leads to a third characteristic of the church, namely its *holiness*, reminding of its strange, alien, paradoxical story, "witnessing to the Other, the Completely Other, the Holy One.... Telling and celebrating the Christian story means listening to a 'different' story, a story of challenge and calling, of conversion and change" (Müller & Smit 1994:403). A fourth characteristic is that the church should be *Christian, apostolic, prophetic, truthful*— true to the Bible as Word of God, and in continuation with the first Christians and the Christian tradition (cf. Hauerwas 1985a). The church has the obligation to proclaim, cele-

theological education at large do not take this strange, alternative vision seriously as its very essence, identity or character, its integrity within a broken and needy society is likely to be in serious jeopardy (cf. Du Toit 1981; Müller & Smit 1994: 399–406).

However, the Ephesians author is also deeply aware of the paradoxical "not yet" of God's work of redemption. That the implied readers' involvement in the document's alternative world was not considered to be an easy task, is illustrated by the provision of God's full armor for the struggle—the war which is not against flesh and blood, but against the rulers, the authorities, and the powers of this dark world, the spiritual forces of evil in the heavenly realms (6:12). Once again, God's provision is embodied in the gift of God's Beloved (6:10; 1:3, 6). Contemporary readers of the document—albeit in totally different socio-historical situations—can identify with its implied struggle in numerous ways (cf. 4.1). Yet, *amid* the moral challenges of our time, the Ephesians vision of a new moral world, of God's new society[92], of new moral people, of God's body, and of good, moral action, inspires later readers to appropriate the communicative power of the document, and to collectively pray and work toward the radical renewal of all three the abovementioned spheres.

.1 Preliminary Conclusions: Ephesians and Moral Identity, Vision, Agency, and Decision-Making

Although Ephesians is concerned with all three sets of questions referred to above, an ethical reading of the document—against the full scope of its linguistic-literariness, socio-historicity and rhetoricity—strongly affirms the shift in emphasis reflected by recent trends in Christian ethics (4.4.1.4). The shape of this document—with its strong sense of *identity* in relation to God and other Christian believers, with its *vision* of the church's full potential in Christ—seems to directly link on to the question concerning good and moral *people*. From this perspective, questions pertaining to ethos, moral action or decisions, and a moral *society*, would be intrinsically embedded in, and determined by the formation of good and moral people (cf. Carmody 1992:147–152). The latter is, therefore, suggested as a *starting and focal point* in the discussion on the use of Ephesians in Christian ethics today. From that orientation—*and as a result thereof*—attention may be given to the other two equally important sets of moral questions.

The question remains, however: How and where is all this supposed to

---

brate and live the *one, strange, full, and true story* of God the Father of Jesus Christ, of Christ as parable of God's radical and unconditional grace and care for sinners, strangers and sufferers, and the life-giving and life-enabling Spirit of Christ; and to wrestle with its implications for a needy society (cf. Durand 1982; Schneiders 1986:266–284; Bosch 1976: 179–186; 1982b:138–142; Richardson 1994:96–100; Pieterse 1991; Du Toit 1981; Smit 1989; R. A. Culpepper 1979; Van Engen 1984).

[92] Subtitle of J. R. W. Stott's *The Message of Ephesians* (1979).

happen in practice? Where are readers of the Bible formed and informed to become moral people who would be sensitive to contemporary moral issues, who would understand who they are in relation to God, Christ, and the Spirit, who would take responsible decisions and actions, who would accept responsibility for what is happening in society?

In order to provide a context from wherein these questions may be dealt with, I draw on notions from two major trends in contemporary Christian ethics, namely those which focus on *responsibility* and *narrative ethics*—particularly with regard to the formation of Christian believers as moral agents. This emphasis should not, however, exclude the complementary potential of discourse ethics and postmodern thinking. By means of an excursion, I shall briefly discuss elements from the work of H. Richard Niebuhr as major proponent of these trends, and as an example of how creatively the New Testament can be used in Christian ethics. Although Niebuhr does not use the particular language of Ephesians, his work represents the crucially important shift in ethics from "doing" to "being," with the concepts of moral identity and a corresponding ethos being central to it.[93] Ultimately, his intertwining of theology and ethics, and of several aspects mentioned in 4.3, offers an accountable example of biblical hermeneutics as "an integrative act of imagination" (Hays 1990:45–46; cf. Kelsey 1975:159–163, 166–175, 212–216).

.2 Responsibility as the Formation of Moral *People*, and the Transformation of *Society*

[*Excursion:* The Theology and Ethics of H. Richard Niebuhr]

Helmut Richard Niebuhr (1894–1962)—together with his brother Reinhold (1892–1971)—is presently regarded by many as one of the most influential (North American) theologians of the twentieth century (cf. Smit 1990c; Vosloo 1994:28–36; Hartin 1994: 519–520). Reinhold Niebuhr, however, considered himself more of a political philosopher, whereas Richard Niebuhr mainly operated as a practical theologian. Almost all leading contemporary ethicists—such as MacIntyre, Gustafson, and Hauerwas—were influenced by Richard Niebuhr, albeit with different consequences. A closer look at his ethical thought may, therefore, be instructive and helpful.

---

[93] According to Gustafson (1984a:137, 143–144), the shift in emphasis in Christian ethics from the *imperative* (What does God command?) to the *indicative* mode (What does God do?), represented by Niebuhr, is even stronger in the work of Paul Lehmann. Gustafson (1984a:143–144) quotes Lehmann: "'Christian ethics.... is oriented toward revelation and not toward morality;' and 'Christian ethics aims, not at morality, but at maturity. The *mature* life is the fruit of Christian faith. Morality is a by-product of maturity.'" Instead of dealing with biblical morality, Lehman focuses on Christian maturity, anticipating and assuming that the mature person would be able to discern through her/his transformed motivation and sensitive imagination what God is doing. This focus seems to echo the thrust of Eph. 4:11–16.

Niebuhr and the Meaning of Revelation

One of Richard Niebuhr's most important works is his classic *The meaning of revelation*, which was published in 1941, during the Second World War. Several of the concepts coined in this study became extremely popular and influential. Especially its first and second chapters—respectively called "The point of view," and "The story of our life"—have become seminal as the first documents to put into motion the broad trend of responsibility and narrative ethics in the twentieth century.

In the period of reconstruction after the war, Niebuhr wrote another important book, *Christ and Culture* ([1951] 1975). It deals with the crucially important question of the relation between Christianity and society or public life, between church and state, between Christ and culture, between religion and "world" (cf. Müller & Smit 1994:388–389). In this book Niebuhr distinguishes five typical positions which marked the relation between Christ and culture through the history of the church since New Testament times: Christ (and Christians) against culture, and directly opposite to that, the Christ of culture (e.g. when Christianity is equated with culture), Christ above culture (cf. Roman Catholic tradition), Christ and culture in paradox (where the two worlds are irreconcilable—cf. the so-called "two kingdom theory"), and Christ the Transformer of culture, as a middle position. In the latter, Christians take culture and society seriously by affirming it—yet, not as it is. Because they believe that it is God's world, and that Christ is Lord of all and everything, including the whole of public life, they want to recognize, proclaim and obey him in every sphere of life. According to Niebuhr, this has been typically exemplified by the Methodist and Reformed Calvinist traditions, with their emphasis on the sanctification of human life, church and society (cf. Vosloo 1994:187–193; Müller & Smit 1994:403–404).

In the relatively peaceful period after the war, Niebuhr defended this last position of "transformation," or "conversionism" which seems to be the position he favored (at least under those circumstances). In fact, he would argue "for the legitimacy of all five types, in different socio-historical situations, and even at the same period in time, for they complement one another, and one without the criticism of the other would be a mistake" (Smit 1990c:22). By the term "conversionism" Niebuhr emphasized the responsibility of the church, Christianity and theology to be continuously transformed, converted, changed—in the words of Eph. 4:23: "to be made new in the attitude of your minds"—in response to what God is doing under differing circumstances.

While it seems as if Niebuhr favors the notion of "Christ the Transformer of Culture" ([1951] 1975:190–229), it is clear that his vision of the role of Christianity, the church, and theology with regard to the transformation of society and culture, can only be understood against the backdrop of his previous thinking and development, and his (social) ethics in general.

"In general, one can say that for Niebuhr, *(systematic) theology precedes ethics*" (Smit 1990c:9). According to him, theological reflection has a certain priority in the work of the moral theologian. This is the recurring theme of all the scholars who focus on questions pertaining to moral people: who they are, and what they believe to form the basis of moral action. From a Christian perspective, whether ethics is regarded as theocentric (Gustafson), or embodied in one's life story (Hauerwas), one's faith precedes the ethical question. According to Niebuhr, this means that, "(b)efore asking: what must we do?, we must ask: *What is happening? What is God doing?* Only then, understanding what is going on and what God is doing, can we ask: *How must we respond?*" (Smit 1990c:9).[94]

Niebuhr himself answers the question of how to find out what God is doing in *The meaning of revelation*. In the first chapter he emphasizes the relativity of all knowledge and, therefore, of history (Niebuhr 1941:1–31; cf. Müller & Smit 1994:386–387). All people are conditioned by their socio-cultural situation. This also applies to their notion of revelation. People can think and speak about God only from the point of view of their faith in God. Niebuhr thus realized that, to utilize Scripture convincingly in Christian ethics, would entail much more than a mere "reading" of biblical information and "appropriating" it to contemporary situations.[95] And yet, in spite of the relativism of history and revelation, Christians still have the need to confess their faith and practise theology (cf. Niebuhr 1941: 35–40). The problem, however, is how one can confess if you cannot prove anything? How can one be certain of anything, and speak of revelation, if everything is relational? (This would later become the typical challenge of postmodern thinking.)

Because of the relativity of all knowledge, including religious language and experience, Niebuhr argues that Christian theology has no other option but to be "confessional," i.e. to start "by stating in simple, confessional form what has happened *to us in our community*, how *we* came to believe, how *we* reason about things and what *we* see *from our point of view*," or: "by recalling the story of Christian life and by analyzing what Christians see from their limited point of view in history and in faith" (Niebuhr 1941:29, 31; emphasis mine; cf. Smit 1990c:10). This brings him to the discussion of "The story of our life" in the famous second chapter.

In this chapter Niebuhr (1941:32–66) develops the tools for answering the questions posed in the first chapter. He deals with that under four sub-titles: The historical method of Christian faith, History as lived and as seen, Faith in our history, and Relations of internal and external history. Under the first rubric (1941:32–43), Niebuhr explains how people express the certainty of their faith in different ways. Some say they know God from nature, others by experience, and others from Scripture. He refutes all these possibilities (as "objective" knowledge), because people necessarily view all aspects of life, including nature and Scripture, from their historically determined perspectives. According to Niebuhr, there is only one method for analyzing and understanding Christian faith, and that is to appeal to its essence, namely its history. Its basic claim is that God revealed Godself *in history*, namely in Jesus Christ who died on a cross and who was resurrected and exalted. Therefore, "(t)he church has no other way of stating its faith than by telling its own story" (Smit 1990c:10).

In the second section of "The story of our life," Niebuhr (1941:44–54) deals with the

---

[94] This obviously implies further (directly related) questions like: *Who is God?* And who are we? What is our primary identity—in relation to God, and God's involvement in history? I suggest that this approach also be followed in response to the questions being raised in the case study in 4.1 ("Where do we find hope?").

[95] Niebuhr articulated these thoughts after a study tour to Germany where he *inter alia* came into contact with the well-known historical-critical scholar Ernst Troeltsch, on whose work he wrote his doctoral dissertation at Yale. Troeltsch himself gradually came under the impression of the relativity of the historical-critical paradigm. This also had a lasting influence on Niebuhr's thinking, and led to his acceptance of the historical and cultural relativity of all knowledge (cf. Smit 1990c:23). It also determined his notion of *responsibility*, as being exercised *in society, and in time and history*.

relativity of (Christian) history, by making the important distinction between "history as seen" and "history as lived," or "external" and "internal" history:

> (T)he history to which we point when we speak of revelation is not the succession of events which an uninterested spectator can see from the outside but our own history.... When we speak of revelation in the Christian church we refer to *our* history, to the history of selves or to history as it is lived and apprehended from within (Niebuhr 1941:44).

It is important to note why Niebuhr makes this distinction between personal, normative history "as lived" and impersonal, descriptive history "as seen" from the outside. The history to which historical criticism referred by saying that God cannot be found in history, is *external* history. The tools they used, says Niebuhr, pertained to the method of an outsider-spectator. But there is another history, *our* history, the "subjective" history in which we participate, and it is that history within which Christians confess that God revealed and is still revealing Godself.

He uses this distinction between two histories for his next argument, and says that it is now possible to base our faith in history—not as seen, but as lived. He then explains the relation and mutual influence between the two (Niebuhr 1941:54–66). With regard to the so-called truth claims of this "subjectively" described story of Christianity, Niebuhr (1941: 46–47) argues that

> (t)he distinctions between the two types of history cannot be made by applying the value-judgment of true and false, but must be made by reference to differences of perspective. There are true and false appeals to memory as well as true and false external descriptions.... Events may be regarded from the outside by a non-participating observer; then they belong to the history of things. They may be apprehended from within as items in the destiny of persons and communities; then they belong to a life-time and must be interpreted in a context of persons with their resolutions and devotions.

Niebuhr (1941:49–52) illustrates the distinction between lived and seen—internal and external history—with reference to different conceptions of value, time, and human association employed in the two contexts. With regard to *value*, he remarks:

> In external history value means valency or strength. The objective historian must measure the importance of an event or factor by the effect it has on other events or factors in the series.... Looking upon events in the manner of an impartial spectator, he seeks to suppress every response of love or repugnance and to apply a more or less quantative measure of strength in determining the importance of persons or events. In internal history, however, value means worth for selves; whatever cannot be so valued is unimportant and may be dropped from memory.... this history calls for joy and sorrow, for days of rededication and of shriving, for tragic participation and for jubilees. The valuable here is that which bears on the destiny of selves; not what is strongest is most important but what is most relevant to the lives of 'I's' and 'Thou's.' Value here means quality, not power.... In this context we do

not measure the worth of even our own desires by their strength but by their relevance to the destiny of the self (Niebuhr 1941:49–50).

With regard to *time*, Niebuhr (1941:50–51) explains:

> (I)n external history.... time is quantitative.... numbered.... always serial. In the series, past events are gone and future happenings are not yet. In internal history, on the other hand, our time is our duration. What is passed is not gone; it abides in us as our memory; what is future is not non-existent but present in us as our potentiality.... Time in our history is.... a dimension of our life and of our community's being. We are not in this time, but it is in us.... (as) our remembered past.

Likewise, with regard to *human association*:

> The external knower must see societies as made up of atomic individuals related to each other by external bonds. Yet even the human individuals are depersonalized, since they are understood as complexes of psychological and biological factors. Society, to his view, is a vast and intricate organization of interests, drives or instincts, beliefs, customs, laws, constitutions, inventions.... In internal history, on the other hand, society is *a community of selves*. Here we do not only live among other selves but they live in us and we in them. Relations here are not external but internal *so that we are our relations and cannot be selves save as we are members of each other*. When there is strife in this community there is strife and pain in us and when it is at peace we have peace in ourselves. Here social memory is not what is written in books and preserved in libraries, but what—not without the mediation of books and monuments, to be sure—is our own past, living in every self. When we become members of such a community of selves we adopt its past as our own *and thereby are changed in our present existence*.... what has become a part of our own lives as selves—is the important thing in this internal view. *In our history association means community, the participation of each living self in a common memory and common hope* (Niebuhr 1941:51–52; emphasis mine).

Accordingly, who people are, is decisively influenced and shaped by the memory of their internal histories (cf. Durand 1993:291–292, 298–303; Volf 1996:131–140). In order to understand any community, to understand people in any socio-cultural situation, including the Ephesians community, one has to look *with* them and not *at* them, and understand the full story of their lives (cf. Meeks 1986a; Tödt 1977:83, step 2). For it is from within this collective life-story that people "interpret what is going on, that they believe, that they choose ultimate values, that they search for ultimate meaning, that they follow ultimate loyalties" (Smit 1990c:10).

The Ephesians author reminds both his implied Gentile and Jewish recipients of their past and inherited traditions—which endured in them as their memory, and which made them the people they used to be. However, their unification with Christ and each other introduced a radically new chapter in their stories. Who they used to be (Eph. 2:11–22), and how they used to behave (2:1–4; 4:17–19, etc.), belonged to a previous period of separation and alienation from God and one another. Christ translated those different stories into one new story, into *a common memory*, and this new common memory was to become their *common hope*. No wonder that the author relates this story by often referring to the God and Father of "*our*" Lord Jesus Christ" (1:3, cf. 1:17), to what has happened to "*us*" (1:3–4; 2:6, etc.), and to the blessings "*we*" possess (1:7, etc.).[96]

Niebuhr and the Problem of Idolatry

In his preface to *The meaning of revelation*, Niebuhr (1941:x) states that "the great source of evil in life is the absolutizing of the relative, which in Christianity takes the form of substituting religion, revelation, church or Christian morality for God." This conviction forms the heart of his argument in the book, and is the second of three fundamental convictions mentioned in the preface. He returns to the problem of "idolatry" (i.e. taking something relative for the living God) in the last chapter, entitled "The Deity of God" (Niebuhr 1941: 101–139; cf. Smit 1990c:10).[97]

For Niebuhr, the problem of idolatry is a continuous temptation facing Christianity. In fact, people can live for several gods at the same time: "For the most part they make gods out of themselves or out of the work of their own hands, living for their own glory as persons and as communities" (Niebuhr 1941:57). The reason why people make idols for themselves is because they need coherence and unity in their life-stories, "ultimate centers of value and meaning" (Niebuhr 1941:56–57):

> Such faith in gods or in values for which men (*sic*) live is inseparable from internal history. It is the gods that give unity to the events of personal life. A nation has an internal history so far as its members have some common center of reference, some good for which they live together, whether that be an abstract value, such as equality or democracy which unites them in common devotion, or whether it be the personalized community itself, such as Athena, or Brittania or Columbia.... A man has one internal history so far as he is devoted to one value (Niebuhr 1941:57).

Normally, Niebuhr (1941:57–59) continues, this can take the form of many gods in the lives of people and communities. By means of their god(s) or God, people connect events in a meaningful pattern, and integrate their histories and social memories. He therefore concludes: "To be a self is to have a god; to have a god is to have history.... to have one god is to have one history. God and the history of selves in community belong together in inseparable union" (Niebuhr 1941:59). For people to have many gods—whether particular self-interests, pleasures, persons, closed societies, nations, institutions or sociopolitical movements—is to be divided against and within themselves, and to be estranged

---

[96] The potentially persuasive power of the author's alternative use of "we" and "you" in 1:3–14; 2:1–19 has been discussed in 3.3.4.

[97] According to Smit (1990c:10), one should understand this against the backdrop of Niebuhr's development during the twenties and early thirties, when he became deeply under the impression of the sovereignty of God. Niebuhr's dealing with the one sovereign God, who decisively revealed Godself in Jesus Christ, reflects the thrust, perspective, and strategy of the Ephesians epistle in a remarkable way (cf. 2.1.2).

from, and in conflict with their fellow human beings and other living creatures.[98] Commenting on these notions of Niebuhr, Smit (1990c:13) concludes: "It is from these sinful, divisive and destructive interpretations of society and culture that the revelation of the One God in Christ can liberate us."

Niebuhr and the Interpretation of History: The Story of Our Life

The crucial question is how contemporary Christians could or should use this internal, relational view of revelation in interpreting history *theologically*. *How should we use the Bible* to understand concrete, present-day events, to understand what the one God is doing in history, so that we can respond to God's Person and actions? (cf. Smit 1990c:13). This is also the basic interest of the present study.

Niebuhr (1941:67–100) explains this by emphasizing the role of imagination and reason in chapter three of *The meaning of Revelation*, called "Reasons of the heart." For him, imagination can play an important role in seeking patterns for interpretation (cf. Hays 1990:45–46), but *only if* it is informed by "revelation"—which is not opposed to, or a substitute for reason. In this process, Niebuhr says, Christians have a moral choice: They can either use the revelation of God in Jesus Christ—particularly his cross and suffering—as key to unlock history, or they can view it from the "evil imaginations of the heart," i.e. from the perspective of their own self-centred and idolatrous interpretations (Niebuhr 1941:79–80).[99] They can either interpret history in terms of the one, sovereign, living God (as the unifying core of their lives), or in terms of their idols (resulting in the self-destructive sin of division and fragmentation), which deprive them from their identity and character. For Christians, the unity in their life-story is given in the revelation and exper-

---

[98] These can take the form of national or cultural idols which have indeed often been the case in Christian history. In *Christ and Culture* Niebuhr deals with this issue under the rubric of the "Christ of Culture" position ([1951] 1975:83–115). The basic problem, Niebuhr says, is that Christ is identified with what people conceive to be their noblest institutions, and their best philosophy. All tensions between their (new) faith and (old) world are eased. The result thereof is that their loyalty to contemporary culture qualifies their loyalty to Christ (cf. Müller & Smit 1994:388–389). This is what Niebuhr elsewhere refers to as "henotheism," which he calls "the first major pathological form of natural faith" (quoted by Smit 1990c:12).

Language obviously plays an important role in this regard. Sallie McFague warns against the idolatry of familiar metaphors for God which have lost their relational and unconventional power, and pleads for alive religious metaphors which would redescribe reality, also the reality of a sovereign, living God, in an open-ended way, and with affective power (McFague 1982:41–43).

[99] Niebuhr calls these "evil imaginations of the heart" *egotism* (referring to individuals or groups): "The group also thinks of itself as in the center. So all nations tend to regard themselves as chosen peoples. Defeated or victorious they only become more aware of themselves, using both pain and pleasure to fortify themselves in the conviction that all the world is centered in their destiny. Such imagination can never enter into the knowledge of another self; it is always the 'I' that is known and never the 'Thou.' The self lives in a real isolation in which others serve only as mirrors in which the ego is reflected" (Niebuhr 1941:74).

ience of the one, personal, living God in the Christ-event. They must therefore reject all attempts to absolutize or "idolize" relative values (Niebuhr 1941:63).[100]

The destructive consequences of such an isolated self-centred perspective, devoid of criticism of other selves, says Niebuhr (1941:75), necessarily leads to the impoverishment and alienation of the self, as well as the destruction of others. Christians therefore have no other choice than to interpret history, life, culture—in short: to interpret what is happening, what the one, living God is doing. "Revelation.... requires of those to whom it has come that they begin the never-ending pilgrim's progress of the reasoning Christian heart" (Niebuhr 1941:100). But how?

Therefore, says Niebuhr, Christians *should* find the real story—the revelation of God in Jesus Christ—which constitute their subjective lives, and confess it as truthful and reliable. That should become our point of view, the paradigm according to which we evaluate and imaginatively interpret the stories of our lives, including the "evil imaginations" of our worst individual and collective memories—those interpretations of the world and ourselves done from the perspective of our own interests (which could be true from our own experience, but false according to the paradigm of the revelation of God). Christians should therefore be prepared to have their life stories evaluated by this paradigm, and be converted, so that their story could take on the shape and the power of the *real* story of the revelation of God in Jesus Christ.

According to the basic faith commitment of Christians, Niebuhr says, the Christian story should become their dominant perspective, determining all other aspects of their story. This would be the only thing for them to be absolutized, while anything else should be considered as relative, and not be misused as an idol.

Niebuhr and Solidarity, Suffering and Memory

In his explanation of how this happens, Niebuhr (1941:80–96) employs three important notions, namely *solidarity*, *suffering* and *memory*. How to understand suffering, and how to respond to it—in view of his fundamental conviction with respect to the sovereignty of God—became *the* core issue of Niebuhr's religious reflection. He shows how the revelation of God in Jesus Christ, and particularly his suffering, can help Christians to interpret the present, past and future (Niebuhr 1941:80–100).

(i) With regard to the *past*, revelation functions in three ways. "First of all, the revelatory moment is one which makes our past intelligible. Through it we understand what we remember, remember what we have forgotten and appropriate as our own past much that seemed alien to us" (Niebuhr 1941:81). It that sense revelation can help us to appropriate the past history of our fellow human beings as well. In the Christian church revelation thus provides the image or paradigm by means of which the reasoning imagination can unite, in a dramatic way, all the disparate elements of the past into a coherent, meaningful unity (cf. Smit 1990c:14). Of special significance is the potential that the seemingly meaningless

---

[100] Obviously, these observations would have crucially important consequences for the interpretation of the New Testament, and its use in Christian ethics. If what is considered to be morally right or wrong, *only* centers around institutions, issues, particular individuals or activities, the thrust and perspective of a document like Ephesians would be distorted. Cf. 2.1.2.3; 3.3.5.4 and 4.3.5 with regard to the Ephesians emphasis on the unity of the faith community.

suffering of the past, "the nameless sufferings of untold generations, the groaning and trav-
ailing of creation until now—all that otherwise is remembered only with despair" (Niebuhr
1941:82), can also be included in this dramatic unity:

> There is no part of that past that can be ignored or regarded as beyond
> possibility of redemption from meaninglessness. And it is the ability of
> the revelation to save all the past from senselessness that is one of the
> marks of its revelatory character (Niebuhr 1941:82–83).

Secondly, revelation makes it possible for Christians to bring back to memory those
sufferings which they have tried to suppress:

> By reasoning on the basis of revelation the heart not only understands
> what it remembers but is enabled and driven to remember what it had
> forgotten. When we use insufficient and evil images of the personal or
> social self we drop out of our consciousness or suppress those mem-
> ories which do not fit in with the picture of the self we cherish. We
> bury our follies and our transgressions of our own law, our departures
> from our own ideal, in the depths of our unconsciousness. We also for-
> get much that seems to us trivial, since it does not make sense when in-
> terpreted by means of the idolatrous image. We do not destroy this past
> of ours; it is indestructible. We carry it with us; its record is written
> deep into our lives. We only refuse to acknowledge it as our true past
> and try to make it an alien thing—something that did not happen to our
> real selves. So our national histories do not recall to the consciousness
> of citizens the crimes and absurdities of past social conduct, as our
> written and unwritten autobiographies fail to mention our shame. But
> this unremembered past endures.... (Niebuhr 1941:83).

From this it is clear that people—including Christians—never succeed in suppressing
their painful past memories completely. These memories have powerful, destructive
effects on our lives (cf. Smit 1990c:14; Durand 1993; Volf 1996:57–98). For outsiders,
when they look at the church and Christian individuals and groups, "these effects are obvious, they see how we are determined, constrained, enslaved by these suppressed memories of our previous idolatrous thought and action" (Smit 1990c:15). As Niebuhr warns:

> When we live and act in accordance with our inward social constitution
> in which there are class and race divisions, prejudices, assumptions
> about the things we can and cannot do, we are constrained by the un-
> conscious past. Our buried past is mighty; the ghosts of our fathers and
> of the selves that we have been haunt our days and nights though we
> refuse to acknowledge their presence (Niebuhr 1941:83).

It is exactly because of this reality that the communicative power of the all-embracing
revelation of God in Jesus Christ has to be taken seriously by the Christian church. For
Niebuhr, as for the Ephesians author, this revelatory moment marks the turning point for
individuals and communities—the putting into motion of a continuous process of persuasion, association and disassociation. This consequently makes confession of sin an essential element of the very life of the Christian church:

The revelatory event resurrects this buried past. It demands and permits that we bring into the light of attention our betrayals and denials, our follies and sins. There is nothing in our lives, in our autobiographies and our social histories, that does not fit in. In the personal inner life revelation requires the heart to recall the sins of the self and to confess fully what it shuddered to remember. Every great confession, such as Augustine's or St. Paul's, indicates how this rationalizing of the past takes place. And every social history, not least that of the church itself, when recollected in the light of revelation, becomes a confession of sin.... (F)or Christians critical history of self and community, wherein the forgotten past is recollected, is the possible and necessary consequence of revelation (Niebuhr 1941:83–84).

Although the issue regarding the confession of sin is not explicitly dealt with in Ephesians, its accountable use in the Christian church and ethics today will necessarily lead to the confession of repressed memories of individual and collective sin—the self-critical remembrance of the idolatrous past (cf. Eph. 4:32).

Niebuhr (1941:84–86) refers to a *third* function of revelation with respect to the past, as the "appropriation" of the past (sins) of other groups from whom the church used to be alienated:

When men (*sic*) enter into a new community they not only share the present life of their new companions but also adopt as their own the past history of their fellows.... *Where common memory is lacking, where men (sic) do not share in the same past there can be no real community, and where community is to be formed common memory must be created....* To Christians the revelatory moment is not only something they can all remember as having happened in their common past, be they Hebrews or Greeks, slaves or free, Europeans or Africans.... It becomes an occasion for appropriating as their own the past of all human groups (emphasis mine).

Interpreting the aspect of "common memory" in Niebuhr's thinking, Smit (1990c:15; cf. 1993a:8, 17–19) remarks: "It means that, in order for *solidarity* to become possible—which is imperative for people believing in the *one* God—human beings must be willing to appropriate those elements of the past which seem alien to themselves, the past histories, the idolatries and sins, of their fellow human beings with whom they now want to be united in a new-found solidarity and community. *A common memory is necessary for real community....* The important point is that this whole process of interpretation, remembering and appropriating is for Christians "*a moral event*," "*a conversion of the memory.*" *Remembering the suffering of the past, both caused and suffered by one's own group, and appropriating the suffering of others is the only way to real solidarity, and the only proper response to the revelation of the one, living God in Christ.*"

This seems to be analogous to the Ephesians author's identification with his audience in 2:3: "*All of us* also lived among them (the disobedient) at one time.... *Like the rest, we were by nature objects of wrath*" (see also 1:13; 2:11; Meeks 1993:33–36 with regard to the role of memory).

Niebuhr further emphasizes that this "conversion of the memory" is never completed,

but is "a permanent revolutionary movement." "The conversion of the past must be continuous because the problems of reconciliation arise in every present" (Niebuhr 1941:86–87).
He illustrates this in the following pages (1941:87–91) by referring to the complexities involved in uniting not only the Christian church, but human societies and cultures at large:

> The measure of our distance from each other in our nations and groups
> can be taken by noting the divergence, the separateness and lack of
> sympathy in our social memories. Conversely the measure of our unity
> is the extent of our common memory (Niebuhr 1941:88).

Like Niebuhr, the Ephesians author was also convinced that only the revelation of
God in Jesus Christ could help people to overcome their separate and idolatrous historical
constructions of the past. While reminding his (mainly) Gentile readers of their separated
past in relation to the Jews, he emphasized their newly created status in Christ (Eph. 2). In
the process it was necessary to reinterpret those previously divisive traditions and past
memories—brought about by the absolutization of, e.g., the Mosaic law—and to develop a
new *common memory* by reminding them of what God had done for them (both Jewish and
Gentile Christians) in their past and pre-past *in Christ* (Eph. 1:3–14). We have seen that
the *berakah* of Ephesians 1–3 is essentially an act of remembrance, meant to make the past
active in the present (cf. 2.1.2.2). On the one hand, the communicative power of the document is the implied readers' continuous association with Christ, and on the other, disassociation with their divisive past (cf. 3.3).

(ii) With regard to the *present*, Niebuhr likewise argues that Christians need "revelation"
to understand what God is doing, and what they are doing—also to one another:

> If our past in inner history is everything we carry with us, or what we
> are, our present is our action, our doing and our suffering of deeds done
> to us. As an evil imagination hides from us what we are so it also ob-
> scures what we are doing (Niebuhr 1941:89).

Once again, Christ's suffering and forgiveness is needed to expose the evil imaginations of people's hearts—those self-centred interpretations which prevent them from seeing what they are doing and not doing, and what the moral *effects* of their actions and in-
actions really are. Niebuhr (1941:89–90) illustrates this by demonstrating how easily
Christians lose perspective of what is happening and of what they are doing, especially in
times of social and family crisis:

> We are particularly aware of this in times of great social crisis when
> our complacent dogmatism is shattered and we realize that what is go-
> ing on.... is too great for our imagination or interpretation. We have no
> pattern of personal thought inclusive and clear enough to allow us to
> discern any orderly connections between the wild and disturbed actions
> of men and nations. We do not know what we are doing by our
> aggressions and participations, our inactions and isolations from con-
> flict. We move from day to day, from moment to moment, and are
> often blown about by many winds of political and social doctrine.
> What the sources and what the issues of our deeds and sufferings may
> be remains obscure (Niebuhr 1941:89).

At the root of these insufficient patterns of interpretation—of these evil imagina-tions—lies, again, people's selfishness:

> In all this effort to understand or at least to justify our actions the self is likely to remain the central figure (Niebuhr 1941:90; cf. Smit 1990c: 16–17).

(iii) With regard to the *future*, "revelation" again provides the pattern of understanding for the reasoning imagination:

> We reason in our hearts in order that we may know the whither as well as the whence and where of our personal lives. If the past in inner his-tory is what we are and the present what we do, our future is our poten-tiality. Through revelation we seek to discover what is implicit in our lives and will become explicit (Niebuhr 1941:95).

Again suffering plays an important role. Since revelation brings our sin and idolatry to the fore, "(w)e discover that our egotistic attempts at safeguarding and securing our own future, will lead to suffering, destruction—for ourselves and others.... Therefore, all reas-oning of the heart with the aid of revelation is painful and none more so than that which leads to knowledge of the self" (Smit 1990c:17; cf. Niebuhr 1941:96).

What then is the proper image, the pattern provided by the revelation in Christ? For Niebuhr, the cross of Jesus Christ becomes the basic paradigm by which to interpret and to respond to suffering (cf. Niebuhr 1941:91; Smit 1990c:17). If Christians understand what God is doing in history in and through Christ, the most important ethical question be-comes: How do we respond? With reference to the suffering caused by war, Niebuhr suggests that the proper response for Christians in such times of crisis would be repent-ance, radical conversion, a total revolution of their minds and hearts (cf. Smit 1990c:18 n.49). This is, once again, in concurrence with the communicative power of the Ephesians text (cf. 3.4).

Niebuhr and an Ethics of Responsibility

After having discussed the basis of Niebuhr's thoughts as developed in *The meaning of revelation*, Smit (1990c:18) concludes: "By now it is obvious why *responsibility* became *the* single term by which Niebuhr could describe the proper moral conduct of Christians. They must *respond to the living God*, revealing Godself in history according to the pattern of Jesus Christ." Niebuhr summarizes this in a famous motto in his posthumously published *The Responsible Self: An Essay in Christian Moral Philosophy* (1963:126): "Responsibility affirms: 'God is acting in all actions upon you. So respond to all actions upon you as to respond to his action.'" He elaborated more fully on the notion of respon-sibility in his *Christ and Culture*, especially with regard to the role of Christians in society.

Acknowledging the value of *teleological* and *deontological* theories of ethics (cf. 4.4.2 n.85), "Niebuhr wants to complement them with a theory of moral *responsibility*, using the image or root metaphor of '*human-beings-as-answerers*.' He sees moral action as more a matter of situational response to challenges than as pursuing ideals or adhering to laws" (Smit 1990c:18). Niebuhr explains this further in *The Responsible Self* (1963:61): "(F)or the ethics of responsibility the *fitting* action, the one that fits into a total interaction as response and as anticipation of further response, is alone conducive to the good and alone is right." Along these lines he develops his ethics of responsibility as *a response to God's revelation in Jesus Christ*. During his time, this emphasis represented a fundamentally new approach to Christian ethics (cf. Spohn 1984:70–88, 129–136).

It now becomes clear why—in Niebuhr's thinking—theology is so important for ethics, why revelation is important for the interpretation of history, why God has to be distinguished from the idols, and the absolute from the relative:

> All forms of natural faith respond to the final context in suspicion and hostility, while radical faith responds in trust and loyalty. Natural faith leads to *defensive* forms of responsibility and ethics, giving loyalty to relative centers of value, responding 'fittingly' to partial interpretations of reality.... finally resulting in distrust, fear, division and destruction.... It leads to an *ethics of death*, expressed on personal level in self-preservation and socially in the closed society.... Radical faith leads to *faithful* forms of responsibility and ethics, responding 'fittingly' to total interpretations of reality and within a universal community of solidarity, resulting in trust, an ethics of life, replacing self-preservation with self-giving and the closed society with an open society. Only a radical conversion to *monotheistic faith* can, however, accomplish this (Smit 1990c:19).

Niebuhr would argue that the only morality which can liberate people from the necessity of establishing their own worth, and of favoring their own group, would be a morality grounded in one steadfast Other, whose love and loyalty to *all* creatures never wavers—a morality exercised in one beloved community embracing *all* those creatures. Niebuhr develops these thoughts more fully in *The Responsible Self*. Once again, suffering plays a special role in understanding how people (should) respond:

> (I)t is in the response to suffering that many and perhaps all men (*sic*), individually and in their groups, *define themselves, take on character, develop their ethos*. And their responses are functions of their interpretation of what is happening to them as well as of the action upon them (Niebuhr 1963:60; emphasis mine).

Again, I believe, Niebuhr's pattern of thought concurs with the perspective and intention of the Ephesians author. According to the latter, God responded to the multi-faceted suffering of people *in Christ* (cf. the contrasts in 2:4, 13). As God's chosen people (1:4), children (1:5), heirs (1:11), household (2:19; cf. 2.1.3.1.2), they were destined to live worthy the example of God and Christ (4:20, 32; 5:1–2, 22, 25, 29). The recipients of Ephesians were supposed *to define themselves, to take on character and to develop their ethos* by serving God and other human beings after the example of Christ. Consistently responding to what God is doing in Christ would—for Niebuhr—result in a society and a world without walls. This would however not be possible for a divided church, carrying in itself the characteristics of ethical irresponsibility.

For this reason, Niebuhr considered the reformation of *church and society* as the continuing imperative of the Christian faith (Smit 1990c:19). Yet, *how* would Christians—responding to the living God—be able to transform society? In his preface to *The meaning of Revelation*, Niebuhr (1941:x) states as a third of three basic convictions underlying this book, "that Christianity is 'permanent revolution' or *metanoia* which does not come to an end in this world, this life, or this time." Through the years Niebuhr used many synon-ymous expressions for this ongoing process, *inter alia* a change of mind, redemption, re-interpretation, transformation. It is *this* conviction which underlies the fifth type in *Christ and Culture*, namely "Christ the Transformer of Culture" (Niebuhr [1951] 1975:190–229). He consequently calls this position *conversionism*—referring to the continuous, radical conversion of Christians as response to what the living God is doing in particular, con-crete, ever-changing socio-historical situations (cf. Smit 1990c:19–23).

These convictions of Niebuhr obviously have important implications for how Christians could use the Bible in Christian ethics:

> The conversion, the proper transformation of self, church and society, does not take place in terms of timeless, abstract and never-changing principles, ideas or slogans, but in terms of the concrete and very par-ticular life-situations, the historical contexts, and what the sovereign God, known in Jesus Christ, is doing there and then. This, of course, makes a *theological* analysis of the situation or historical context a pre-requisite for moral response (Smit 1990c:20).

However, to *know* what God is doing in concrete life-situations, is—according to the Ephesians perspective—only possible for people who have "the Spirit of wisdom and revelation" to enlighten their hearts (1:17, 18).

Niebuhr was always acutely aware of the context, both of time and place, in which he and others practised theology—a sensitivity which marked all his works.[101] "He never simply looked at ideas, principles or motifs, but also discussed theologians as concrete, living people, within particular historical contexts and movements" (Smit 1990c:20). What Niebuhr would consider to be a proper response under given circumstances, would there-fore differ from context to context.[102]

---

[101] In his first book, *The Social Sources of Denominationalism*, published in 1929 (New York: New American Library), Niebuhr made a socio-historical and ethical analysis of the American churches and their denominational differences. Contrary to previous efforts which distinguished churches primarily by reference to their doctrine, Niebuhr's approach to the problem of church unity introduced a new way of doing situational theol-ogy, and would have major influences in American theology in the twentieth century. In 1937, he complemented the sociological approach with a theological interpretation of the American churches, *The Kingdom of God in America* (referred to by Smit 1990c:20). This was followed by another penetrating study, *The Purpose of the Church and Its Ministry: Reflections on the Aims of Theological Education* (New York: Harper & Row, 1956), which revaluated the role of the churches and their leaders in American life, while em-phasizing the aims, development, and future of theological education.

[102] According to Smit (1990c:20–23), this explains why the proper response ex-pected of the church differs so fundamentally in Niebuhr's own publications, and why he uses different images or paradigms—e.g. crucifixion, resurrection—to interpret the task of the church under different circumstances. In 1929 he was concerned with the reformation and unification of the churches in order that they might play their proper role in society. In his later years he numbered himself among those particularly concerned with the re-formation of the church itself, so that it could ultimately contribute, by its service, toward a better society.

In the end, Niebuhr opts for a midway between egoistic authoritarianism and the skepticism of historical relativism, a way which he calls "a critical historical theology." "In his view such a critical historical theology must be aware of its own contextuality, its socio-historical and cultural relativity, and the particularity of its concepts and language. Nevertheless, it must also be willing to be a *confessional theology*, and not fall into scepticism" (Smit 1990c:23). This has crucially important implications for the functioning of the Bible in Christian ethics:

> A critical historical theology cannot, to be sure, prescribe what form religious life must take in all places and all times beyond the limits of its own historical system. But it can seek within the history of which it is a part for an intelligible pattern.... Such theology can attempt to state the grammar, not of a universal religious language, but of a particular language, in order that those who use it may be kept in true communication with each other and with the realities to which the language refers.... Such theology in the Christian church cannot, it is evident, be an offensive or defensive enterprise which undertakes to prove the superiority of Christian faith to all other faiths; but it can be a confessional theology which carries on the work of self-criticism and self-knowledge in the church (Niebuhr 1941:13).

For the church to remain self-critical, means for Niebuhr to be willing to listen to other voices—an approach which has often been emphasized in this study (cf. 4.3.5). The theology of the church should therefore be an *ecumenical theology*, which makes it—according to Niebuhr (1941:62–63, cf. 15)—"a moral experience":

> To see ourselves as others see us, or to have others communicate to us what they see when they regard our lives from the outside is to have a moral experience. Every external history of ourselves, communicated to us, becomes an event in inner history.... Such external histories have helped to keep the church from exalting itself as though its inner life rather than the God of that inner life were the center of its attention and the ground of its faith. They have reminded the church of the earthen nature of the vessel in which the treasure of faith existed.

In this regard Smit (1990c:23) summarizes the heart of Niebuhr's ethics as follows:

> For Niebuhr, therefore, in our interpretation of what is going on in society and culture, in our reading of revelation in history, in our interpretation of God's actions in events and movements and in our decisions as to what is responsible praxis within our situation, we must realize our relativity and limitations. That should not make us afraid of confessing and acting, instead, it should encourage us to listen to others, especially to those 'on the underside of history,' those suffering under a cross, and we should be willing to be converted in a fundamental and a radical way.

In sum, I believe, that the thrust of Niebuhr's thinking is analogous to the direction and perspective of the Ephesians document. This brings me to taking stock of Niebuhr's relevance for this study.

Summary: Challenges Arising from Niebuhr's Theology and Ethics

Niebuhr thus leaves us with several important challenges regarding the imaginative appropriation of the theology and ethics of an ancient document such as the Ephesians epistle:[103]

- Niebuhr challenges us to see culture—and therefore the possibility of *transforming* culture—as having to do with *people*, and not with rules, objects, practices, or products of human behavior.[104]

- Niebuhr emphasized the importance and implications of the *contextual* or local nature of theology and ethics. In order to do this, it is also necessary to give *theological* analyses of our context(s)—complementing sociological, political, economic and cultural analyses. By accounting for the different stories (including non-biblical stories) which inevitably shape the beliefs and character, values, virtues and actions of Christian communities, Niebuhr developed what is still regarded as a most helpful typology of possible relationships between Christ and culture (cf. Müller & Smit 1994:385–387).

- Niebuhr—like many others since him—underlined the need *to listen to others*, especially to their suffering, and to discuss ethics *in communion* (cf. Fowl & Jones 1991:110–134; Van Huyssteen & Du Toit 1989:38; Bosch 1991c; Smit 1993a). How that should be done, will necessarily have to be part of churches' agendas for reflection and action in the transformation of an "ethics of death" (arising out of fear and self-defensiveness) to an "ethics of life"—given the contextuality, confessionality, and limited points of view of all theologies, and the complex psychological processes involved in the conversion of (suppressed) memories.

- Niebuhr's *starting point* in the process of reflection on the transformative role of the church in society, is noteworthy. According to him, we have to start by responding to what the one living God is doing, and then be *converted* to this God, asking ourselves to whom we are responding, and for what we are responsible, and in which community of human solidarity we really find ourselves.

- Niebuhr often refers to the role of *imagination*, especially with regard to the

---

[103] Smit's article (1990c) is an edited version of a paper originally presented at a meeting of the Theological Society of South Africa in Bloemfontein, 31 Aug.–1 Sept. 1989. In the original paper conclusions with a view to the South African context were made, some of which are presented here in a generalized form.

[104] This perspective is also reflected in the description of culture by the World Council of Churches (Vancouver Assembly, 1983—referred to by Smit in the original version of his paper mentioned in the previous note): "Culture is what holds a community together, and what constitutes the *collective memory* of the people and the *collective heritage* which will be handed down to generations still to come."

interpretation of history and what is happening. First of all, if we want to transform culture, we need people who—through the power of human imagination—are able to hope for, and to see that which now still seems impossible, and who will continuously be willing to be converted to such a new imagination, to be made new in the attitude of their minds, and be liberated to respond, to act accordingly (Eph. 4:1, 23). Niebuhr refers to the freedom of Christian ethics as *the freedom to act now* (cf. Gustafson 1984a:141–143). Put differently, ethics is about human creativity unleashed in response to divine creativity, which cannot be seen by the suspicious, unenlightened eye (cf. Eph. 1:18).

.3 Responsibility as the Information of Moral *Action*

Probably the most popular way of dealing with the Bible in relation to Christian ethics, is to ask questions of how answers can be inferred from the Bible to help people in making decisions on specific moral issues. In this way the Bible is often seen—in a fundamentalist sense—as a kind of recipe, reference or textbook, an encyclopaedia containing norms, principles and directives for all times and places in exactly the same way. Accordingly, the popular question is how to read the Bible in a legitimate and responsible way so as to help people solve those problems.

It has become clear that such a selective use of the Bible only represents a small fraction of possible functions of the Bible in Christian ethics. Some contemporary ethicists hold that these are not even the most important questions in Christian ethics today. Christian ethics actually involves much more—it involves *every part* of our lives: when we pray, when we go to church, when we teach and educate our children, when we reflect on our lives, our visions, identities, values.... This means that the Bible has to be related to a much broader ethical context—indeed to our entire lives—and not merely to solving particular issues. This challenge has been confirmed particularly by the history of the development of Christian ethics (cf. 4.4.1).

This does not wish to negate or underestimate the process of ethical decision-making as indeed a crucially important aspect of the moral life and ethical discourse (cf. Glanville 1991). The point of this study, however, is that the information of such *actions* should be considered as *following* the formation of moral *people*. *Agere sequiter esse*. What and who people are and want to be, will determine how they behave. However, it cannot be taken for granted that good character and sound social arrangements will necessarily result in responsible and ethically accountable decisions. The reason for this being that decisions entail questions and require information which character and social structure do not supply (Birch & Rasmussen 1989:101). Analogous to processes of community and character formation, ethical decision-making entails several processes which have to be *learned*.

Within this context, the question becomes: What kind of information and tools do Christians need to take good and responsible decisions, when faced with ethical dilemmas? How does one argue in such a situation, or convince others toward responsible decision-making? What constitutes good and moral behavior when faced with a dilemma? What role does the moral agent's *ethos* play in this regard? And most important for our purpose: What rhetorical or communicative role does the Bible play, and do we expect it to play, in the process of ethical decision-making? What role is it *supposed to* play, and *supposed not to* play?

To consider the possible role of the Ephesians perspective in matters concerning good and moral action, behavior and decisions, can therefore be helpful in order to get a better understanding of the way in which moral judgments are made, and moral decisions are taken.

The process of ethical decision-making mainly represents the more formal, philosophical, abstract, theoretical and technical mode of moral discourse as referred to by Gustafson (1988:31–44; cf. Smit 1994b:8–9, 13–14; De Villiers & Smit 1994:236–239; Birch & Rasmussen 1989:100–119). An analysis of this process may help to understand how individuals and groups view their own and other people's context, how they make ethical decisions, what range of factors (could) play a role, and therefore help to understand why people—including Christians—so often differ from, and misunderstand each other in the handling of conflict, and the taking of decisions.[105] It is in this sense—and particularly with regard to the usually unconscious role of identity and self-understanding during the different phases of decision-making—that the contribution of Heinz Eduard Tödt, former professor in Social Ethics from Heidelberg, Germany, is significant.[106]

[*Excursion:* H.E. Tödt and the Process of Ethical Decision-Making]

Tödt has probably done more than anyone else to analyze—in a philosophical sense—how people's minds work in the process of ethical decision-making, and to put these issues on the agenda of (German) Protestant ethicists. His theory is considered to be one of the most provocative and well thought through contributions to the cumulative discussion on ethical decision-making (Tödt 1977; cf. De Villiers & Smit 1996). This makes him one of the best (recent) examples of the paradigm which focuses on *moral action*.

Disillusioned by the failure of the collective conscience and decisions which led to the Second World War—during which he fought as a soldier—Tödt became very interested in the formation of theologians and Christians as moral human beings. Since 1977, through several publications, he continued to contribute to the discussion on ethical

---

[105] Generally, Protestant ethicists have to a large extent ignored these questions, while giving the impression that—assisted by the Bible and the Holy Spirit—they have all the answers, and know what to do. But it gradually became clear that this process is much more complex and problematic, especially in the light of vast differences among Christian ethicists.

[106] For other useful discussions in this regard, see Childs 1991 and Kilner 1989.

decision-making—often by revising his original position (cf. De Villiers & Smit 1996:n.3). I shall briefly analyze the six most important aspects of his theory, and comment on how the Ephesians perspective could impact on these.

Tödt (1977:83) distinguished six major aspects in the process of ethical decision-making, while some of his students—*inter alia* Wolfgang Huber, his successor at Heidelberg, and prominent German social ethicist and ecclesiologist at the moment—added a seventh one, namely a further reassessment of the whole procedure. These aspects are not seen as chronological steps in the process of decision-making. Rather, they represent (usually unconscious) facets of a continuous process which (only) become clear when one looks back and inquires about possible considerations which played a role, and factors which have been taken into account, which eventually contributed to the final decision. Tödt's distinction is, therefore, an ideal-typical analysis of opinion forming and decision-making (1977:84).

Seeing, Accepting, and Describing the Problem

For Tödt the processes of seeing, accepting, and describing a problem play a key role in the entire process of decision-making—whether it be an unresolved past conflict, an anticipated problem in future, or a personal, church or societal challenge. To *identify* a problem—to *see* it as a problem—is the *first* step in forming an opinion about it.[107]

Secondly, a problem has to be *accepted* as one's *own* problem, and therefore as an *ethical* problem. Often people consider family, social, global and other challenges to be the responsibility of "others." Even if they consider a problem to be theirs as well, it is often viewed as a mere technical, administrative, political or economical problem, and not necessarily as something which has to do with *their Christianity, their morality, identity, character and integrity as human beings* (cf. Birch & Rasmussen 1989:101–108). Obviously, says Tödt, all people cannot accept all problems as their own. As human beings we are constrained by numerous factors. We, therefore, have to make selections. Yet, already *in these choices*—e.g. in accepting a problem which is situated far away, while neglecting people and situations closer to you—an element of guilt can be involved, which makes it a moral issue.

Thirdly, before people can come to a collective decision on any problem, they have to (provisionally) agree on its *precise nature* ("*das eigentliche Problem*"—Tödt 1977:83). People can easily think that they are talking about the same thing, while they may perceive it from totally different view points.[108] This often becomes clear when people are asked to formulate the exact problem for themselves. The challenge would then be to find a

---

[107] In Germany the famous *Kirchentag, Akademien* and *FEST* (research institute of the *Evangelische Kirche*) were all formed and developed with the purpose of bringing people together—in meetings, conferences, etc.—to provide them with the opportunity to reflect on urgent moral issues in society, and to be sensitized and informed on those issues, so that they would be able to *recognize* them, and *act* responsibly. Georg Picht, a former director of FEST, often challenged people to think of the kind of— still unforeseen— problems Germany would face within ten years' time, as the most important issues for research.

[108] See, e.g., Smit's discussion on homophilia as moral issue in the Reformed tradition (1992:306–317).

common description of the particular issue *through dialogue with others*. This responsibility, Tödt argues, forms an integral part of the process of ethical decision-making (cf. De Villiers & Smit 1996:33–36).

Analyzing the Situation

With reference to the previous aspect, Tödt (1977:83) emphasizes the importance of a proper analysis of the situation within which the particular ethical problem is embedded. An all-encompassing, objective and final construction of any context is of course impossible, because those who analyze in context are part of the situation and therefore influenced and biased by it.[109] A *selection* from the larger picture would thus be inevitable. Such a reduction, Tödt says, will necessarily be determined by the life and world view, the intentions and interests of the moral agent(s), and therefore be part of the ethical responsibility of decision-makers.[110]

Because of this, Tödt considers a *second* aspect under this rubric of crucial importance, namely the contribution of other sciences—other "interpretive frameworks," other sources of information, other statistics, etc. (De Villiers & Smit 1996:36). This immediately complicates the process in other ways. The human, social and natural sciences, for instance, occupy themselves with different—often strictly demarcated—aspects of reality, and can therefore only offer limited categories and methods for obtaining and evaluating knowledge. Their claims can also be divergent and even incommensurable. The mere choice of scientific voice(s) to be included in, or excluded from the dialogue, of which sciences and which representatives of those sciences are listened to or not, therefore becomes part of the responsibility of ethical decision-making.

A *third* aspect is closely related to the foregoing. For a situation analysis to be relevant, it must be simple and accessible. Simplification and generalization would, therefore, be unavoidable.[111] Obviously the choice for such a simplified interpretation, for the reduction of the problem to its essence, to what is regarded as really at stake, is in itself a deed of moral responsibility—with far-reaching consequences for the rest of the process of decision-making.

In this regard Tödt discusses a *fourth* aspect, which ties in with Niebuhr's notions (1941:32–54) on the interpretation of history and the story of our life. An indispensable part of such a schematizing analysis, Tödt says, would be to gain insight into the *genesis* or history of the problem, including forces from the past which have a lasting effect in the present situation. If this aspect would be ignored or underestimated, the true nature of the

---

[109] This has been illustrated by the discussion on the multi-facetedness and complexities involved in human communication (chapter 1).

[110] Compare, e.g., different readings or situation analyses of the South African context in *The Kairos Document: Challenge to the Church—A Theological Comment on the Political Crisis in South Africa* (Grand Rapids: Eerdmans, Revised 2nd ed. 1986), and the Dutch Reformed Church's testimony *Church and Society* (Bloemfontein: Pro Christo, Oct. 1986). For a critical assessment of the latter's social analysis, see Maimela 1990.

[111] This will obviously be dealt with differently in homogeneous and pluralistic societies. In a homogeneous society where the ethos of the group is taken for granted, people would spontaneously act according to such a collective scheme. In a heterogeneous society, however, reality is viewed as much more complex and obscure, and therefore in need of some kind of simplification.

problem might be misjudged, and a responsible decision and reaction be impossible (cf. De Villiers & Smit 1996:37–38).

By pleading for an accountable situation analysis, Tödt firmly rejects presuppositions of intuitive, uninformed, so-called "practical" moral judgment by people who claim that they simply know what to do by following their own consciences and wisdom.

Considering Possible Available Responses

The third facet in Tödt's analysis (1977:83) is the consideration of different *options or responses* available to solve or alleviate the problem, and the assessment of applicable, appropriate action. This phase would necessarily *follow* the *acceptance* of a problem as moral responsibility, and a proper *analysis* of the situation. Christian ethics is indeed concerned with appropriate responses to various challenges.

Of crucial importance for the purpose of this study, is that such a response or reaction—i.e. what is to be considered as good and moral action or behavior, which would lead to a good and moral decision—will essentially be determined by how the people involved *understand themselves as human beings* (cf. Richardson 1994:89–92). This is naturally so because people involve themselves in problem-solving *as human beings*. "Für die in Betracht gezogenen Handlungsalternativen und ihre voraussehbaren Folgen stellt sich die Frage, ob 'gut' sei, sich so oder so zu verhalten (Kontroll-funktion des Gewissens, Frage nach der Identität oder Integrität des oder der Handelnden)" (Tödt 1977:83). This means that they actually devise themselves, their own lives, characters and moral identity in the way they design solutions to the challenges they have seen and accepted as their own (cf. De Villiers & Smit 1996:38–39). Their behavior cannot be separated from who they are and what they want to be (Tödt 1977:86). It is possible to make pragmatic decisions which might seem viable for the moment, yet with disastrous effects to one's own being.

It is therefore important, says Tödt, that people should remain truthful to themselves and to their consciences in their moral responses. He therefore disregards any form of so-called value-free, technical and pragmatic solutions to ethical problems, where the role of the moral agent's identity and perspective is ignored. That would be typical of the modernistic fragmentation of life into isolated segments, each with its own laws and canons, which in turn would determine how people should act and behave. Because these decisions might have dramatic effects on the quality of people's future lives, Tödt insists that such decisions be accountable to ethical evaluation.

A *second* aspect has to be seen in connection with this. Because the future (long term) consequences of our present (short term) pragmatic decisions are unforeseen, and therefore not transparent, our moral judgment is constrained by our inability to see and to know (cf. Bonhoeffer 1956:17–18). That implies that we are more than often not in a position to discern between what is simply good or bad, but rather between what is better and worse—between what is morally more accountable and intelligible and what not.

That leads to a *third* aspect. The complexities of human communication and interpretation in general, and ethical decision-making in a pluralistic society in particular, can easily lead to hesitancy and indecision. Not taking a decision is also taking a decision, and would in itself be an immoral choice.[112] For that reason, guilt—and the way it is dealt

---

[112] In his well-known *Letters and Papers from Prison* Bonhoeffer often deals with this issue. In the paper "Who stands his ground?", he writes: "What then of the man (*sic*)

with—forms an integral part of the ethical process, and a fundamental problem of the moral life. Already in the analysis of a problem (which we are compelled to do), we take the risk of making mistakes. Thus, *not* to consider all the possible responses and actions, and *not* to bear the possible future consequences in mind, would be irresponsible and negligent (cf. De Villiers & Smit 1996:39–40).

Evaluating Applicable Norms and Criteria

After having obtained the best possible picture of the situation, and after having considered possible responses, the next (obvious) phase in the process of ethical decision-making is the *selection* and *evaluation* of these responses. To be able to do that, one needs what Tödt refers to as "norms, goods and perspectives" (cf. De Villiers & Smit 1996:40).

Firstly, it is commonplace in (Protestant) ethical discourse that people talk about "norms" when they have to make such choices. "Eine *Norm* ist das, *wodurch man im Urteil ein(e) Situation(sschema) mit einer Handlung (Verhaltensweise) verknüpft. Sittliche* Normen intendieren, diese Verknüpfung in sittlich vertretbarer (das heißt die Integrität der Handelnden durchhaltenden) Weise geschehen zu lassen" (Tödt 1977:83). Norms are considered as morally relevant rules which claim to be followed in social relationships. They dictate or prohibit certain forms of behavior. In Protestantism, Tödt says, this issue has usually been treated in terms of the so-called "biblical norm" (singular), and, in line with that, confessional norms—which underlines the importance of an accountable use of Scripture in ethical decision-making. Concepts like "moral" and "social norms" have been introduced into theology by later moral philosophers and sociologists. According to Tödt, these have not been evaluated critically enough by theologians, out of fear that evangelical ethics may become "casuistic." The result was often a hesitancy to concretize these norms altogether (cf. De Villiers & Smit 1996:40–41).

About the functioning and authority of such norms De Villiers and Smit (1996:41) write: "Norme ontleen hulle sterkste krag uit mense se kennis van en herinnering aan hoe dit vroeër was, uit die verwagting dat dié verlede ononderbroke gekontinueer sal word en uit die oortuiging dat die lewe 'n betroubare strukturering benodig" (cf. Tödt 1977:86–90; Fowl & Jones 1991:4–21). The problem is, however, that even under the most favorable circumstances, such norms are not sufficient to explain why people make specific choices in the light of various possible responses and forms of behavior in different situations. What is more, is that—apart from norms—people's decisions and actions are intuitively co-determined by the social *institutions* of which they form a part, and by their *status* and position in society, and the expectations of their public *roles* at a specific time and place.

A *second* point under this rubric is that, in addition to norms, institutions and roles, the consideration of available "goods" (*Güter*)—i.e. material goods, abilities, capabilities and interests—plays a significant role in the solving of ethical challenges. By this Tödt means the basic needs and desires of people which are in conflict and competition with

---

of *freedom*? He is the man who aspires to stand his ground in the world, who values the necessary deed more highly than a clear conscience or the duties of his calling, who is ready to sacrifice a barren principle for a fruitful compromise or a barren mediocrity for a fruitful radicalism.... Only at the cost of self-deception can they keep themselves pure from the defilement incurred by responsible action. *For all that they achieve, that which they leave undone will torment their peace of mind*" (Bonhoeffer 1956:15; emphasis mine).

real deficits and limited physical means in society. The availability of goods can thus inhibit and constrain the process of ethical decision-making.

This leads to a *third* aspect. The claims made by different norms, and the restriction of available goods, can easily lead to conflict and divergent opinions. What people need in such a situation, Tödt suggests, are "perspectives," interpretive frameworks, an overview of the context, which would help them to (re)consider all the conflicting norms and goods in one moment. He warns against the ideal in morality of always wanting to "do" something, to achieve, to be successful. An important part of moral life, says Tödt, is simply to suffer with people because of the fact that one cannot also do or achieve what you want to. In Christian ethics it becomes extremely important not always to look for success options, but also to be willing to undergo and to suffer with those who taste defeat in what we attempt to solve—e.g. with respect to different forms of discrimination.

It is at this point that De Villiers and Smit (1996:33, 41–42) draw attention to Tödt's creative thinking and particular contribution to the discussion. Tödt namely argues that the *cognitive*—i.e. the active seeing, knowing, understanding, doing—side of decision-making has often been emphasized in Christian ethics. That gives the impression that people are always able and in control, that they can choose how they want to act and how to put their decisions into effect. Tödt, however, considers it of utmost importance that Christian ethics should also reckon with the *affective* or *emotional* side of people's judgments and responses (cf. Cuthbertson 1992). What and how we experience, and why we want to act or behave in a specific way, are also issues of moral concern, and should be taken into account in the analysis of decision-making processes (Tödt 1977:90–93).

In the end, people's choices—in the light of a variety of conflicting norms and insufficient goods—will be determined by their perspectives, their life and world views, their identities, character and visions. What they want, how they feel, which norms and goods they will give preference to in discerning between different forms of behavior and action, will all be determined by *who they are*. This concurs with what has been identified as the Ephesians thrust and perspective, which implies that every aspect of the ethos of Christian believers is meant to be determined and informed by their position *in Christ* (cf. Heyns 1992:365–367).

Listening to the Opinion of Others

This leads to a fifth major aspect, namely evaluation and control of the acceptability of those forms of action which have been decided upon, through dialogue with other moral agents (cf. Rossouw 1980:18–21; Combrink 1986:217, 234; Fowl & Jones 1991:110–134; Bosch 1991c; Heyns 1992:371; Meeks 1993:216–217; Müller & Smit 1994:399–406). The reason why this is of utmost necessity, Tödt continues, is that the presumed unity and harmony of humanity is obscured by the historical reality of alienation in, as well as among people. This is caused by deformation, tension and conflict, by what the Christian faith refers to as *sin*. We have seen how individualistic action and interests have been overemphasized in the modern paradigm—to the detriment of what is today known as *collective responsibility*. In spite of this reality of alienation, Tödt wants to cling to the presumed responsibility of all (Christian) moral agents, and to the expectation that all will, in the end, act worthy of their responsibility to God and one another as human beings (cf. De Villiers & Smit 1996:43–44). However, he does not base the importance of evaluation and control in dialogue on an idealistic ethics, but on *an ethics of responsibility*. As people

who share the world and history with other human beings, we have the concrete responsibility to act in such ways that would also meet with the approval of other moral people.
We should, therefore, be careful to generalize our own viewpoints.

For Tödt this leads to another essential aspect in the process of ethical decision-
making, namely "communicative freedom." Contrary to the typical ethos of modernity,
this means that individuals should not experience the freedom of others as a restriction of
their own freedom, but as the potential to real freedom.[113] "Juis daarin dat ons nie op ons-
self aangewys is nie, maar vry is om saam met andere, in kommunikasie en gesamentlik-
heid, te soek na die regte besluite, die regte reaksies en die regte gedrag, ontvang ons die
vryheid om te leef en te doen (De Villiers & Smit 1996:44; cf. Birch & Rasmussen 1989:
108–119).

This aspect has often been emphasized with reference to Ephesians—among other
New Testament documents—as basis for ecumenical, co-operative decision-making (cf.
Roberts 1978, 1981). This document defines moral identity and ethos *only* in terms of the
community of believers (cf. 4.3.5). While responding to the creative presence of God,
Christ and the Spirit, it is *only* in communion with other believers that the Christian church
discovers what its identity is. And it is *only* in dialogue and communion that they can
collectively decide on the best response to the unique socio-historical challenges of their
time (cf. Fowl & Jones 1991).

Taking the Decision and Acting

In a sixth phase Tödt elaborates on the ethical *decision* itself (which again includes questions of knowledge, will and identity), followed by the concrete *action* and *behavior* which
are regarded as appropriate in the particular situation (cf. Furnish 1968:237–241).

Summary: Challenges Arising from Tödt's Approach

By focusing on the decisive role of the self-awareness and identity of moral
agents in processes of decision-making, Tödt's analysis has confirmed the basic
emphasis of the study with regard to the formation of *good and moral people* as a
prerequisite for the information of *good and moral action*. Tödt's approach may
also help biblical scholars and Christian ethicists to analyze or read a contemporary situation in an ethically accountable way—an inability of which (South
African) New Testament scholars have been accused in the past (cf. Smit 1992:
317–325). For Christian ethicists, Tödt's theory may encourage and stimulate

---

[113] Kant has already been dealt with as the best example of modern ethical thought
(cf. n.63 above). Faced with ethical problems, Kant says, human beings basically ask three
questions: What may I *know*, what can I *do*, what may I *hope* for? With regard to the second, Kant's advice would be not to pay heed to external authority, but to obey one's own
conscience. He suggests that one asks oneself what would happen if all rational people in
the world, given the same situation, with the same interests, would do what you as an individual are doing. In that sense individualism is also seen in terms of its universal consequences. Tödt, on the other hand, does not use the unity of humankind in this rational,
metaphysical sense.

new dimensions in their public moral discourse—not only in understanding their past and present differences, but also in giving future direction.

These observations bring us to some final conclusions.

4.5 Hermeneutics as "An Integrative Act of Imagination": Revisionary Criteria for an Ethical Reading of the New Testament

In the end, "reading the Bible ethically" challenges scholarly and "ordinary" readers to develop a multi-focal or stereoscopic vision on various perspectives. While respecting the authority of the ancient canonized biblical texts in their complete "otherness" and textuality, biblical scholars and Christian ethicists have the collective obligation to adequately account for the dynamic, yet complex relation between these documents and their appropriation and actualization in present-day contexts. It has been emphasized that this responsibility requires an attitude of *openness* to both the text and the needs, fears, suffering, hopes, and convictions of subsequent readers, as well as an *open-endedness* which would humbly recognize the relational and provisional nature of all faith experiences and utterances. The latter leads to the liberating insight that what is considered as "the truth" at some stage, may change under different circumstances, which does not mean however that we are doomed to a paralyzing subjectivism (cf. Deist 1986). The hard work and creative tension involved in an ethics of interpretation do not guarantee final answers and certainties, yet open up the possibility to come to better or the best conclusions in specific situations. The book focused on, and was meant to foster a sensitivity for the network of processes, challenges, relations, responsibilities and skills underlying such an endeavor.

In this regard, Lategan (1984a:13; cf. 1992c:627) rightly remarks: "By far the most serious challenge is how to handle (methodologically speaking) the discovery of the creative dimensions of reception. If we allow for the creative input of the reader, how are we going to control it? Have we not put our foot on the path of destabilizing the text which in the end must lead to its abolishment?.... Where does reading end and association begin? Is understanding really possible?" Put differently: How does the free, imaginative role of readers and their contexts relate to the inherent nature and constraints of the biblical texts (while the interpretive community is accountable to both)? This has been the essence of the discussion on the ethics of interpretation in chapter one.

In concurrence with Lategan's response to these questions (1984a:13–14), it would seem that biblical scholars and Christian ethicists—if they still wish to warrant their scholarly work with biblical authority—are faced with some basic moral *choices*, which have been implied or emphasized in the discourse of the book (emphasis mine):

> Firstly, the option is either resignation concerning the possibility of understanding or *the positive acceptance of the communicative potential of biblical texts*. A 'hermeneutics of suspicion,' a critical and self-

reflective approach to texts can only be constructive within the wider parameters of a 'hermeneutics of trust.' Secondly, the interpreter of biblical texts (like his colleague in the Faculty of Law) must be clear about the *nature of the literature* with which he (*sic*) is dealing. This has to do not only with the inherent characteristics of the text, but also with the way they function in pragmatic contexts. Thirdly, the exegete should accept the limits of his own interpretative activity. This means first of all constantly reminding himself that he is not the first reader of the text.... (I)t was Fish who reminded us.... that signals function only within the conventions of an interpretative community.... In the case of biblical material, a community of faith is presupposed and in a new reading we have to take these readers seriously. But to suggest—as Fish would imply—that the text exists by virtue of these communities and their conventions, is to ignore *the role of the text as counterfoil and denies the possibility of the text breaking through conventions or estab-lishing the conventions in the first place.*[114] It is at this point that under-standing shows its character as a free, creative event.

It has been argued in 3.3.3 that the persuasive power of Ephesians is essen-tially embedded in the delicate referential or metaphorical processes of *orienta-tion, disorientation* and *reorientation* (cf. Ricoeur 1975; 1976; 1977; McFague 1982; Lategan 1985b; 1992b; 1994b). In practical terms, this means that its shift-ing, transformative potential lies in its ability to continuously reorient its recip-ients in accordance with the radical example of Christ during the process of (re)-reading. During his earthly ministry, Christ—as a living parable in his moral world—reversed, reordered and upset the familiar, conventional preconceptions of God and humanity by consistently practising an ethos of *love*. The Ephesians author translates this shift in a different context—not in terms of a new *law* or an ethics of *duty*, but in terms of *new relations* and responsibilities-in-relation, facil-itated by *a new Spirit*—the Spirit of wisdom and revelation (πνεῦμα σοφίας καὶ ἀποκαλύψεως ἐν ἐπιγνώσει αὐτοῦ—1:17), *a new mind* (ἀνανεοῦσθαι δὲ τῷ πνεύματι τοῦ νοὸς ὑμῶν) and *a new person* (ὁ καινὸς ἄνθρωπος—4:23–24). This implies a new identity and ethos—not defined by ethnicity, gender or social status, but by a relationship of trust in the living God, Christ and the Spirit.

To accept the communicative potential of such a text, to inhabit its altern-ative moral world, implies a lifelong process of learning and reorientation, which also involves the *unlearning* of old habits, dispositions and judgments (cf. Fowl & Jones 1991:29, 31; Hauerwas 1981:57; Rousseau 1986:415–416). Reading Ephesians ethically today thus asks for an openness to be constantly *persuaded* and *encouraged* by its christological and communal orientation. This implies that present-day readers of this document are challenged to reinterpret their moral worlds, symbols and traditions in accordance with, that is in a way that would be

---

[114] For a discussion of the socio-pragmatic, context-relative reader-response theory of Stanley Fish, see Thiselton 1992:515–523, 535–550, 586–592.

analogous to, its perspective.[115]

For Lategan (1984a:14), this leads to the logical consequence of two further aspects:

> Fourthly.... theological hermeneutics will have to live with the contingent nature of interpretation.... Because of the dynamic nature of textual communication, it remains an open-ended affair. Finally, theological hermeneutics does have the ability to deal with the creative dimension of understanding. When the text is neither understood as an *imitatio* of reality, nor as a fossilization of the original situation, its instructions, its *Leserangebot* can be seen as a redescription of reality, which opens up new possibilities of understanding for the reader. In this way, the text serves both as constraint and stimulus, providing both continuation and innovation.... Creative interpretation, in the best sense of the word, should not be a problem for theological hermeneutics, but its ultimate aim.

Having accepted the implied potential of the Ephesians document, the final test remains: *How* is the *in Christ* confession supposed to *realign, redefine* or *reorientate* (Ricoeur 1975:122–128) contemporary Christians' understanding of God and their existence in the world? The question, Is understanding really possible?, presupposes another question: Is hope—in the formation of new, moral people and the transformation of a new, moral society—an attainable dream? We know from experience that it is extremely difficult to change our own and other people's patterns of thinking and behaving:

> Change is always difficult and painful. It challenges what is closest and dearest to us: our ideas, our habits, our attitudes. Change means giving up survival strategies nurtured over time; it means leaving closely guarded comfort zones and venturing into the unknown.[116]

The process of ethical reading and the corresponding process of individual or societal transformation is at its best a complex psychological, sociological, intellectual and emotional matter (cf. Jeanrond 1991:105–111).

From a Christian faith perspective, the process of personal and communal change or moral growth, which includes all the abovementioned elements, con-

---

[115] The concept "analogous" here pertains to an appropriation of the christological and communal thrust and perspective, as well as the processes of interpretation underlying the document, and not necessarily the cultural-historically bound expressions of that perspective—e.g. the institutions of patriarchy and slavery. To read Eph. ethically, is to acknowledge and appropriate the *direction* of the document and its communicative processes in honest dependence on God's creative presence in ever changing situations.

[116] From an address to staff on 23 February 1995 by Professor J. M. Kirsten, vice-chancellor of the University of Port Elizabeth, in the context of institutional and organizational transformation at this university. It was titled: "The real challenge facing UPE: Building a learning organization (or The 'low road' to the new UPE)."

sists—in its simplest form—of numerous moments of interaction between the biblical texts and their readers. This process represents the dialectic relation between the ongoing revelation and loving appeal of God, Christ and the Spirit (via these texts—cf. Rossouw 1980:16–18) on the one hand, and the human response of faith, trust, reverence, and service on the other—which is simultaneously a gift and a moral choice. In Gadamerian terms, this implies a continuous fusion of the horizons of contemporary readers and ancient texts, which—according to their nature as *canonized* texts—are meant to stimulate an ongoing fusion (in terms of a relation of mutual love) between their readers and God. Consequently, moral identity and ethos are shaped by these ongoing "moments of interaction" between texts and readers—a process which involves Christ's healing presence on the one hand, and the readers' moral choices—whether large or trivial in scope and consequence—and imaginative responses to what God is doing on the other (cf. Niebuhr 1941:67–100; 1963), in a way similar to the identity and moral formation of the early Christians (cf. Meeks 1993:8, 109–110, 172–173, 189–210). Collectively, these individual moments of ethical reading would form the essential stepping stones toward attaining the Ephesians vision of "the whole measure of the fullness of Christ" (4:13). Such an approach would embrace the many dimensions of the full hermeneutical circle. In this way, the potential of the new life—as the substance of Christian hope—becomes a reality (cf. Burrell 1985).

In Ephesians, the process of moral growth is described by means of different metaphors. The most prominent among these are the church as the body of Christ and the household of God. Being a redescription of reality, and by presenting an alternative moral world, the Ephesians epistle as a whole may for that matter be considered a metaphorical expression. Without diminishing the communicative potential of an epistle, it has been suggested in 4.2 that—among other forms of moral discourse—the *genre* of *narrative* be utilized to translate the contents of Ephesians as shifting device for today. The reason being that the gospel of Jesus Christ—as reflected by the multi-vocal chorus of the New Testament—has the essential character of a *story*. It invites its readers to participate in God's continuous revelation in Jesus Christ, to be drawn into it and become part of it, to share in its blessings and responsibilities (cf. Müller & Smit 1994).

Via rituals of public worship such as baptism, eucharist, hymns, confessions, and prayers, participants in the Christian story are continuously reminded of, and encouraged by what God has done in the past, while they hopefully anticipate the fulfillment of the redemption in Christ (cf. Eph. 1:13–14; 2:11). In the unfolding of the Christian story, collective *memory* thus plays a crucial role, and because the story is unfulfilled, *hope* becomes critical (cf. Durand 1993; Meeks 1993:33–36, 216–217; Hauerwas 1984; Hartin 1992:67–72; Müller & Smit 1994:386, 390–396, 399–406; Volf 1996:193–306). In fact, "Christians become part of this story through *remembrance* and *hope*" (Smit 1994e:51; emphasis mine). In this way, the Ephesians story of moral transformation is framed by, and functions in the creative tension between the two notions of remembrance and hope. This confirms Niebuhr's sense of community as an essential element of the Christian story (1941:52): "In our history association means *community*, the participation of each living self in a *common memory* and *common hope*" (emphasis mine). As Christians we find hope in remembering what God has done and is doing, and in responding to that memory—faithfully and imaginatively (cf. Niebuhr 1963:165–166; Bosch 1976:182–184).

Therefore, despite the cultural and social chasm between the biblical world and us, "we establish a bond with those ancients: we, no less than they, are fragile social creatures, not as much in control as we sometimes fancy but much more graced with possibilities for personal and social transformation than we often dare accept" (Gottwald 1993:22). Subsequent readers of the New Testament may thus celebrate the creative tension of their ongoing dialogue with Ephesians as the *remembrance of their identity and potential in Christ.*

Because there is no other way by which later readers can interpret and integrate new insights, than by means of human, metaphorical language, entrenched within a specific socio-cultural context (cf. Combrink 1986:215), the "task of hermeneutic appropriation requires *an integrative act of imagination.*[117] This is always so, even for those who would like to deny it: With fear and trembling we must work out a life of faithfulness to God through responsive and creative reappropriation of the New Testament in a world far removed from the world of the original writers and readers. Thus, whenever we appeal to the authority of the New Testament, we are necessarily engaged in metaphor-making, placing our community's life imaginatively within the world articulated by the texts" (Hays 1990:45–46; cf. Lategan 1994b:134).

At the same time, we have to take the limitations of these texts' language in terms of their time and culture seriously. The essence of the Bible's authority is that it contains the words and deeds of a living God—who constantly reveals Godself in new and surprising ways—in the fragile vessel of human language and interpretation, which is bound to time and place (cf. Hays 1989:32–33; Meeks 1993:217–219). Later readers might, therefore, have to change the culturally-bound language of the biblical canon to allow for new explanations and experiences in their time (cf. P Naudé 1993:11–13).[118] To do this, is not to discard the

---

[117] The concept of "integration" has gradually been nuanced during the course of this study. It does not refer to some kind of grand umbrella or system or model, which—by all means—wishes to hold together every aspect of this complex reality, irrespective of its underlying presuppositions and perspectives. Rather, it refers to the willingness and openness to keep different aspects—in this case the ancient biblical texts and present-day contexts—in critical dialogue and creative tension with each other.

[118] I illustrate this by means of a controversial example (cf. Fiorenza 1983:266–270). Drawing on Virginia Mollenkott's notion of "godding" as the recovery of the "God within," Glanville (1991:43) provides a dynamic translation of the essence of Eph. 5:21–33:

canonized text, but to account for its referential power—that is the typically human *process of redescription* in the light of new knowledge and experience which underlies it.

Thus, respecting Ephesians in its otherness (*inter alia* as the product of a patriarchal society), and translating it in terms of the needs of a critical, postmodern society (which resists any form of domination and stereotyping), asks for a double ethics of (historical) reading and accountability (Fiorenza 1988)—accountability to God, to the biblical texts, to contemporary readers and their contexts, and to that which we hope for. Travelling within the liminal space between text and context is characterized by a never-ending movement between remembrance and hope (Smit 1994e:51), between the "already" and the "not yet," between history and eschatology, between a cross and a crown....

It should be clear that a hermeneutics of ethical responsibility challenges biblical scholars and Christian ethicists in many ways. To summarize, I wish to propose (in line with Verhey's "modest proposal"—1984a:169–197; 1984b) the following revisionary criteria for an ethical reading of Ephesians in particular, and the Old and New Testaments in general. According to this perspective, the process of hermeneutic appropriation does not allow—in a modernistic, fundamentalistic way—for final, unalterable answers, decisions and certainties. It is suggested, rather, that the *essence* of the cumulative discussion on the use of Scripture in Christian ethics be recognized as an ongoing *revisioning* of the relation between a distinctive self-awareness in Jesus Christ, and its practical implications for church and society. "The 're' presupposes a certain measure of familiarity, of known territory from which to push off into the unknown. What is described, is an alternative view of reality—consistent in itself, but different from what precedes" (Lategan 1994c:14).

It is suggested that this "re"-programming at least involves the following aspects:

Let your 'godding' towards one another be done out of reverence for Christ, who is your example. Wives, be committed to your husbands, as you are to the Lord. For just as Christ is committed to his church, so too, should you reflect this commitment in your relationship to your husband. Husbands, in Christ love your wives. For as the church is one with Christ, so too, must you be one with your wife. Respect the varied gifts, without prejudice, present within this relationship. Nourish and care for them so that all 'in Christ' may benefit from your example. Christ came that all might share in his life, so let mutual respect, love, encouragement and commitment motivate you towards this goal. Foster understanding by listening to one another, for this is the thrill and the mystery of your 'goddedness' and 'oneness' in Christ.

- a continuous acceptance and celebration—within the parameters of a "hermeneutics of trust"—of both the transformative potential of the biblical texts in accordance with their dynamic, multi-faceted nature and intended pragmatic effect, and the creative, imaginative role of readers/listeners in processes of understanding;

- a re-discovery and re-appropriation of the living God's presence *in Christ* and *the Spirit*, and this God's paradoxical, liberating love and power in novel situations—amid the tension of contradictions and ambiguities;

- a re-cital, a re-membering and re-vitalizing of the full, strange, truthful Christian *story*, as a continual re-actualization of the events which constitute and orientate Christian moral identity, vision and ethos, memory, imagination and hope;

- an acknowledgement of, and appreciation for the complex network of relations and interpretive processes underlying, and stimulated by the biblical texts—with special emphasis on notions such as "orienting perspective" and "shifting devices" toward new ways of thinking and behavior;

- a re-vitalization of the art of "Bible reading," coupled with a re-evaluation of the implications of the theological and ethical thrust and direction of the Ephesians and other biblical documents—in terms of the formation and empowerment of moral *people*, who would collectively take as their responsibility the transformation of a moral *society*, as well as the information of moral *action*;

- phrased differently, this means a re-focusing on the "post-modern trilemma" (M. K. Taylor 1990:40–45) which acknowledges—and, where necessary, creatively reinterprets—tradition, celebrates plurality, and resists any form of domination toward the realization of the full potential of the body of Christ.

This chapter started with the question: *Where do we find hope?* The perspectives developed in it, as a response to that question, did not—and were not supposed to—supply easy, straightforward answers. Rather, through a process of reorientation, these perspectives were meant to stimulate and open up new possibilities of hopeful, qualitative life.

Yet, to appropriate such a vision as "an integrative act," to consistently live in God's presence and know God's will, is—according to the Ephesians perspective—a *gift* of God's grace, even as a choice of faith (Eph. 1:17; 2:5, 8). However, this does not diminish human responsibility, but enhances the awesome wonder of co-responsibility-in-relation between unequals—the almighty, living God and fragile, limited human beings (though graced with enormous potential).

In the final analysis, it is the transformative power of God's love which *precedes and exceeds* all our hermeneutic endeavors—even the most imaginative ones. This allows for moral *confidence* instead of *certainty*—a reality to which the Ephesians author bears witness when he pictures God as the One "who by the power at work within us is able to accomplish abundantly far more than all we can ask *or imagine*...." (Eph. 3:20—NRSV).

Reading a New Testament document ethically has turned out to be much more than a matter of *reading*. It is actually a way of *constituting* oneself (as individual or interpretive community) in the process of reading—a manner of defining who we are and who we want to be. Simultaneously, the choice for an ethical reading of the Bible and a corresponding distinctive Christian identity, *per se* includes reflection on the particular ethos that would fit and characterize such an identity. It has become clear that the course of this symbiotic process—as well as its relevance for society—depends to a large extent on the hermeneutic *choices* readers are prepared to make. In this sense, reading a New Testament document ethically, ironically implies that readers are also *being read* by both the texts and contexts to which they are responsible and accountable. I have been convinced that the openness *to be read*, and *to be persuaded* by the strange, alternative world of the New Testament, is the most decisive of all the moral choices readers have to make. Ethical reading is therefore more than a collection of information, more than a mere description of reality as it is. It reflects the essentially critical character of Christian theology as that which offers *a critique of life*. For this reason, regular encounter with these texts has the potential to transform and to surprise.

During the final weeks of writing this book, I was privileged to visit the mighty Swiss Alps for a short retreat. To me this sublime experience became very close to reading and being read by a text. As with reading, it is a gift *and* a choice to behold and absorb, to be overwhelmed by the splendor of these mountains; to allow them to penetrate one's senses in their multi-dimensionality: to *see* the marvelous detail of shape and colour, to *feel* the chill on one's face, to *smell* the cows and the wakening spring-field, to *hear* the birds, the wind, the silence.... To appreciate the *thrust* of these mountains—their depth, width, length and height—would expect from the "reader" to rise beyond them, to look from a distance, to gain some *perspective*, but also to go back often, to walk the mountain paths and to spend the night there, to expose oneself to all their moods and challenges. Only then would it probably be possible to be persuaded by their inherent non-verbal *strategy*.

However, how far is this metaphor applicable to our subject? Can a mountain be read *ethically*? Does a mountain have an implied pragmatic function? From an aesthetic and ecological point of view, certainly. Yet, while "reading" a mountain may be very much *like* reading a canonized text, it is also very much *unlike* it. The function of a "text," whether visual (a mountain), audible (a radio speech), or both (an opera), will always depend on its particular *genre*. Though the basic principles of any communication event may be more or less the same, the rules of the game, the "chemistry" of the process, will vary according to the *genre* of the medium or text involved.

From this angle, the implied pragmatic effect of the Ephesians document may be considered as its *most unique* characteristic. Its alternative world, its vision of excellence and holiness, of power and victory, of love and service, challenges its readers with a moral choice. This choice holds the key to its transformative potential. It was Aristotle who once said: "You are what you repeatedly *do*," which may be rephrased in terms of the enormous power of the Ephesians world: "We are what we repeatedly *choose to be*."

Like Ephesians, the rhetorical, transformative potential of this study lies in its *referential power*, in its ability to point beyond itself to a reality which it could only describe in a limited and provisional way: the full, comprehensive, truthful Christian story. In this sense, it is an invitation to the larger interpretive community to join the ongoing discussion.

For me as a reformist feminist reader, the ethical reading of a New Testament document has become a liberating *and* frightening experience—liberating, because of the Christian story's potential to enable *everyone* to become a mature person *in Christ*. Moreover, it is also frightening because of the power of our ideologically based interpretive frameworks and presuppositions, and the reality of our moral world which in many, many respects seems to be so far removed from the Christian vision. However, the complexities involved in reading should neither paralyze us nor prevent us from taking decisions and acting. Appropriating the perspective of the New Testament in terms of the formation of moral people, the transformation of a moral society, and the information of moral action is a slow, continuous, lifelong, more often than not cumbersome process. There is no instant way toward accomplishing it. Like mountaineering, it is a narrow road which calls for a *hermeneutic of trust, hope and commitment*.

WORKS CITED

Ackermann, D. 1992a. Defining Our Humanity: Thoughts on a Feminist Anthropology. *Journal of Theology for Southern Africa (JTSA)* 79, 13–23.

―――. 1992b. A Time to Hope. *JTSA* 81, 66–70.

―――. 1993. Liberating the word: Some thoughts on feminist hermeneutics. *Scriptura* 44, 1–18.

Akinnaso, F. N. 1982. On the differences between spoken and written language. *Language and Speech* 25/2, 97–125.

―――. 1985. On the similarities between spoken and written language. *Language and Speech* 28/4, 323–359.

Aland, K. *et al.* (eds.) 1983. *The Greek New Testament.* 3rd ed. New York: United Bible Societies.

Arens, E. (ed.) 1989. *Habermas und die Theologie: Beiträge zur theologischen Rezeption, Discussion und Kritik der Theorie kommunikativen Handelns.* Düsseldorf: Patmos.

Arnold, C. E. 1989. *Ephesians: Power and Magic: The Concept of Power in Ephesians in Light of its Historical Setting.* Cambridge: Cambridge University. (Society for New Testament Studies [SNTS] Monograph Series 63.)

Baker, N. L. 1979. Living the Dream: Ethics in Ephesians. *Southwestern Journal of Theology* 22/1, 39–55.

Bakker, J. T. 1978. In Christus: Verzoening als levensvorm, in *De knechtsgestalte van Christus* 1978:34–46.

Barkhuizen, J. H. 1990. The strophic structure of the eulogy of Ephesians 1:3–14. *Hervormde Teologiese Studies (HTS)* 46/3, 390–413.

Barnard, A. C. 1971. Die lewende kerk volgens die Skrif. *Nederduitse Gereformeerde Teologiese Tydskrif (NGTT)* 12/4, 261–266.

―――. 1983. Efesiërs 5:21–33, in Burger, Müller & Smit 1983:181–192.

Barr, J. 1973. *The Bible in the Modern World.* New York: Harper & Row.

Barth, M. 1959a. *The Broken Wall: A Study of the Epistle to the Ephesians.* Chicago: Judson.

―――. 1959b. *Israel und die Kirche im Brief des Paulus an die Epheser.* München: Chr. Kaiser.

―――. 1974a. *Ephesians 1–3.* New York: Doubleday. (The Anchor Bible.)

―――. 1974b. *Ephesians 4–6.* New York: Doubleday. (The Anchor Bible.)

―――. 1984. Traditions in Ephesians. *New Testament Studies (NTS)* 30/1, 3–25.

Beardslee, W. A. 1990. Ethics and Hermeneutics, in Jennings, T. W., Jr. (ed.), *Text and Logos: The Humanistic Interpretation of the New Testament*, 15–32. Atlanta: Scholars Press.

Berg, H. K. 1991. *Ein Wort wie Feuer*. München: Kösel. (Wege lebendiger Bibel-auslegung.)

Berger, K. 1988. *Hermeneutik des Neuen Testaments*. Gütersloh: Gerd Mohn.

Best, E. 1981. Dead in trespasses and sins (Eph. 2.1). *JSNT* 13, 9–25.

———. 1993. Two Types of Existence. *Interpretation* XLVII/1, 39–51.

Birch, B. C. & Rasmussen, L. L. 1989. *Bible and Ethics in the Christian life*. Revised & expanded ed. Minneapolis: Augsburg.

Bird, P. A. 1988. Translating Sexist Language as a Theological and Cultural Problem. *Union Seminary Quarterly Review (USQR)* 42, 89–95.

———. 1994a. *Feminism and the Bible: A Critical and Constructive Encounter*. Winnipeg, Manitoba: Canadian Mennonite Bible College. (The 1993 J. J. Thiessen lectures.)

———. 1994b. Authority and context in the interpretation of Biblical texts. *Neotestamentica* 28/2, 323–337.

Bitzer, L. F. 1968. The rhetorical situation. *Philosophy and Rhetoric* 1, 1–14.

Black, D. A. 1981. The peculiarities of Ephesians and the Ephesian address. *Grace Theological Journal* 2/1, 59–73.

Black, M. 1962. *Models and Metaphors*. Ithaca: Cornell University.

Blass, F. & Debrunner, A. 1961. *A Greek Grammar of the New Testament and Other Early Cristian* Literature. Chicago: University of Chicago.

Blevins, J. L. 1979. The Church's Great Ministry: Ephesians 3. *Review and Expositor* 76/4, 507–516.

Bonhoeffer, D. 1956. *Letters and Papers from Prison*, ed. by E. Bethge, tr. by R. H. Fuller. 2nd ed. London: SCM.

Bosch, D. J. 1976. The Church in South Africa—Tomorrow. *Theologia Evangelica (ThEv)* IX/2 & 3, 171–186.

———. 1980. *Witness to the world: The Christian Mission in Theological Perspective*. Atlanta: John Knox.

———. 1982a. Church Unity amidst Cultural Diversity. *Missionalia* 10/1, 16–28.

———. 1982a. In gesprek met dr. P. F. Theron, in Bosch, König & Nicol 1982:134–142.

———. 1991a. *Transforming Mission: Paradigm Shifts in Theology of Mission*. New York: Maryknoll.

———. 1991b. Towards a new South Africa: The role of the church. Paper presented at DRC Ecumenical meeting, Port Elizabeth, 9 March 1991.

———. 1991c. The Church-with-others. Paper presented at Theological Study Group University of Port Elizabeth (UPE), 11 March 1991.

Bosch, D. J., König, A. & Nicol, W. D. (reds.) 1982. *Perspektief op die Ope Brief.* Kaap-stad: Human & Rousseau.

Bosman, H. L. 1986. The growth and the interpretation of the Old Testament, in Deist, F. E. & Vorster, W. S., *Words from afar,* 1–16. Cape Town: Tafelberg.

Botha, E. 1993. Habermas, critical theory and teaching biblical texts with integrity. *Scriptura* S11, 69–87.

Botha, J. 1989. Sosio-historiese en sosiologiese interpretasie van die Nuwe Testament. *Koers* 54/4, 480–508.

———. 1991. Reading Romans 13: Aspects of the ethics of interpretation in a controver-sial text. D.Th. thesis, University of Stellenbosch.

———. 1992. The ethics of New Testament interpretation. *Neotestamentica* 26(1), 169–194.

———. 1994a. The Bible and Ethics, in Villa-Vicencio & De Gruchy 1994:36–45.

———. 1994b. *Subject to Whose Authority? Multiple readings of Romans.* Atlanta: Scholars Press.

———. 1994c. How do we "read the context?" *Neotestamentica* 28/2, 291–307.

Botha, P. J. J. 1992. Folklore, social values and life as a woman in early Christianity. *S.A. Jnl. Folklore Studies* 3, 1–14.

Botman, H. R. 1993. Discipleship as Transformation? Towards a Theology of Trans-formation. D.Th. thesis, University of the Western Cape, Bellville.

Breytenbach, C. 1990. Paul's proclamation and God's "thriambos" (Notes on 2 Corinthians 2:14–16b). *Neotestamentica* 24/2, 257–271.

Breytenbach, C. & Lategan, B. (reds.) 1992. Geloof en Opdrag: Perspektiewe op die etiek van die Nuwe Testament. *Scriptura* S9a.

Bruce, F. F. 1967. St Paul in Rome 4: The Epistle to the Ephesians. *Bulletin of the John Rylands Library* 49/2, 303–322.

———. 1977. The History of New Testament Study, in Marshall 1977:21–59.

Burger, C. W., Müller, B. A. & Smit, D. J. (reds.) 1983. *Riglyne vir Doopprediking. Woord teen die Lig* 5 (*WtL*). Kaapstad: NG Kerk-Uitgewers.

Burger, C. W., Müller, B. A. & Smit, D. J. (reds.) 1990. *Riglyne vir prediking oor vrede. WtL* III/1. Kaapstad: Lux Verbi.

Burnett, F. W. 1990. Postmodern biblical exegesis: The eve of Historical Criticism. *Semeia* 51, 51–80.

Burrell, D. B. 1985. The Spirit and the Christian Life, in Hodgson, P. C. & King, R. H. (eds.), *Christian Theology: An Introduction to its Traditions and Tasks,* 302–327. Philadelphia: Fortress.

Burrows, M. S. & Roren, P. (eds.) 1991. *Biblical Hermeneutics in Historical Perspective: Studies in Honor of Karlfried Froehlich on His Sixtieth Birthday*. Grand Rapids: Wm B. Eerdmans.

Carmody, D. L. 1992. *Virtuous Women: Reflections on Christian Feminist Ethics*. Maryknoll: Orbis Books.

Childs, J. R., Jr. 1991. *Faith, Formation, and Decision: Ethics in the Community of Promise*. Minneapolis: Fortress.

Classen, C. J. 1991. Paulus und die antike Rhetorik. *Zeitschrift für die Neutestamentliche Wissenschaft (ZNW)* 82/1–2, 1–33.

———. 1993. St Paul's epistles and ancient Greek and Roman rhetoric, in Porter & Olbricht 1993:265–291.

Cloete, G. D. & Smit, D. J. 1988. Preaching from the Lectionary: Eph. 1:20–23. *JTSA* 63, 59–67.

Cloete, G. D. & Smit, D. J. 1994. "Its Name was Called Babel...." (Gen. 11:9; Acts 2:8, 11–12). *JTSA* 86, 81–87.

Combrink, H. J. B. 1986. Perspektiewe uit die Skrif, in Kinghorn, J. (red), *Die NG Kerk en Apartheid*, 211–234. Johannesburg: Macmillan Suid-Afrika.

———. 1988. Readings, readers and authors: an orientation. *Neotestamentica* 22, 189–203.

———. 1993. 'n Retoriese benadering tot die Nuwe Testament. *Skrif en Kerk* 14/2, 146–162.

Corbett, E. P. J. 1990. *Classical Rhetoric for the Modern Student*. 3rd ed. New York: Oxford University.

Corley, B. 1979. The Theology of Ephesians. *Southwestern Journal of Theology* 22/1, 24–38.

Couch, B. M. 1988. Blessed be He who has blessed: Ephesians 1:3–14. *International Review of Mission* 77/306, 213–220.

Craffert, P. F. 1991. Towards an interdisciplinary definition of the social-scientific interpretation of the New Testament. *Neotestamentica* 25(1), 123–145.

———. 1996. Reading and Divine Sanction: The Ethics of interpreting the New Testament in the New South Africa, in Porter, S. *et al.* (eds.): *Rhetoric, Scripture and theology—Essays from the 1994 Pretoria. Conference*, 54–71. Sheffield: Sheffield Academic Press.

Culpepper, H. H. 1979. Ephesians—A Manifesto for the Mission of the Church. *Review and Expositor* 76/4, 553–558.

Culpepper, R. A. 1979. Ethical Dualism and Church Discipline: Ephesian 4:25–5:20. *Review and Expositor* 76/4, 529–539.

Cunningham, D. S. 1990. Faithful persuasion: Prolegomena to a rhetoric of Christian theology. Ph.D. thesis, Duke University.

———. 1991. Theology as Rhetoric. *Theological Studies* 52/3, 407–430.

Curran, C. E. 1984. The Role and Function of the Scriptures in Moral Theology, in Curran & McCormick 1984:178–212.

Curran, C. E. & McCormick, R. A. (eds.) 1984. *The Use of Scripture in Moral Theology.* New York: Paulist Press. (Readings in Moral Theology No 4.)

Cuthbertson, J. 1992. Neurobiology and the Science Theology debate. Paper presented at Theology and Science seminar, Princeton Theological Seminary, NJ, 10 Jan. 1992.

Dahl, N. A. 1965. Bibelstudie über den Epheserbrief, in Schmidt-Clausen, K. (ed.), *Kurze Auslegung des Epheserbriefes*, 7–83. Göttingen: Vandenhoeck & Ruprecht.

———. 1976. *Jesus in the Memory of the Early Church.* Minneapolis: Augsburg.

De Gruchy, J. W. 1979. *The Church Struggle in South Africa.* Cape Town: David Philip.

———. 1984. *Bonhoeffer and South Africa: Theology in Dialogue.* Grand Rapids: Wm B. Eerdmans.

De Gruchy, J. & Villa-Vicencio, C. (eds.) 1983. *Apartheid is a Heresy.* Cape Town: David Philip.

Deist, F. 1986. *Kan ons die Bybel dan nog glo? Onderweg na 'n Gereformeerde Skrifbeskouing.* Pretoria: J. L. van Schaik.

Deist, F. E. 1989a. Die kerk: 'n Verenigende of verdelende faktor in die ontwikkeling van Suid-Afrika? *HTS* 45/4, 894–913.

———. 1989b. Eksegese as "leeskompetensie:" Oor onderrig in Skrifuitleg. *NGTT* 30, 56–63.

———. 1989c. Fundamentalisme—'n Gereformeerde beoordeling. *ThEv* 22/2, 2–8.

———. 1990. *A Concise Dictionary of Theological and Related terms.* 2nd revised and enlarged ed. Pretoria: J. L. van Schaik.

———. 1994. Post-modernism and the use of Scripture in theological argument: Footnotes to the Apartheid theology debate. *Neotestamentica* 28/3, 253–263.

De knechtsgestalte van Christus: Studies door collega's en oud-leerlingen aangeboden aan Prof. Dr. H. N. Ridderbos 1978. Kampen: J. H. Kok.

Denton, D. R. 1982. Inheritance in Paul and Ephesians. *The Evangelical Quarterly* 54/3, 157–162.

De Villiers, D. E. 1980. Het die christelike moraal 'n eiesoortige inhoud? *NGTT* XXI/4, 346–361.

De Villiers, D. E. & Smit, D. J. 1994. Hoe Christene in Suid-Afrika by mekaar verby praat. Oor vier morele spreekwyses in die Suid-Afrikaanse kerklike konteks. *Skrif en Kerk* 15/2, 228–247.

De Villiers, D. E. & Smit, D. J. 1996. Waarom verskil ons so oor wat die wil van God is? Opmerkings oor Christelike morele oordeelsvorming. *Skrif en Kerk* 17/1:31–47.

De Villiers, P. G. R. 1984. The interpretation of a text in the light of its social setting. *Neotestamentica* 18, 66–79.

—————. 1991. The end of hermeneutics? On New Testament studies and postmodernism. *Neotestamentica* 25(1), 145–156.

Domeris, W. R. 1993. Honour and shame in the New Testament. *Neotestamentica* 27/2, 283–297.

Dunn, J. D. G. 1982a. The Authority of Scripture According to Scripture. *Churchman* 96/2, 104–122.

—————. 1982b. The Authority of Scripture According to Scripture (continued). *Churchman* 96/3, 201–225.

Du Plessis, I. J. 1981. The use and meaning of the title Christ in the New Testament, in Deist, F. E. & Du Plessis, I. J., *God and his Kingdom*, 120–125. Pretoria: J. L. van Schaik.

—————. 1983. Introduction to the book of Acts, in Du Toit, A. B. (ed.), *Guide to the New Testament* Vol IV, 194–210. Pretoria: NG Kerkboekhandel Tvl.

Durand, J. J. F. 1982. Die kerk se profetiese roeping: Kommentaar op deel 2 van die Ope Brief, in Bosch, König & Nicol 1982:66–75.

Durand, J. 1993. In bewuste herinnering, in Van Niekerk, A., Esterhuyse, W. & Hattingh, J. (reds.), *Intellektueel in Konteks: Opstelle vir Hennie Rossouw*, 289–304. Pretoria: RGN.

Du Toit, A. B. 1981. Die geloofwaardigheid van die kerk en sy boodskap—Enkele Nuwe-Testamentiese perspektiewe. *NGTT* XXII/3, 166–178.

—————. 1984a. Oriënterende opmerkings oor die Pauliniese briefliteratuur, in Du Toit 1984b:1–22.

—————. (red.) 1984b. *Handleiding by die Nuwe Testament* Vol V. Pretoria: NG Kerkboekhandel Tvl.

—————. 1989. The Canon of the New Testament, in Roberts, J. H. & Du Toit, A. B., *Guide to the New Testament* Vol I, 75–272. Pretoria: NG Kerkboekhandel Tvl.

—————. 1992. Alienation and re-identification as pragmatic strategies in Galatians. *Neotestamentica* 26/2, 279–295.

—————. 1994. Enkele Nuwe-Testamentiese vertrekpunte vir die vestiging van 'n Christelike lewenstyl in die nuwe Suid-Afrika. *NGTT* XXXV/4, 480–481.

Eagleton, T. 1983. *Literary Theory: An Introduction*. Oxford: Basil Blackwell.

Elliott, J. H. 1986. Social-scientific criticism of the New Testament: More on methods and models. *Semeia* 35, 1–33.

Fiorenza, E. S. 1976. Cultic Language in Qumran and in the NT. *The Catholic Biblical Quarterly* 38, 159–177.

———. 1983. *In Memory of Her: A Feminist Theological Reconstruction of Christian Origins*. London: SCM.

———. 1988. The ethics of Biblical interpretation: Decentering Biblical Scholarship. *Journal of Biblical Literature (JBL)* 107/1, 3–17.

———. 1999. *Rhetoric and Ethic: The Politics of Biblical Studies*. Minneapolis: Fortress.

Foerster, W. 1968. *Neutestamentliche Zeitgeschichte*. Hamburg: Furche-Verlag.

Foulkes, F. 1956. *Ephesians*. Leicester: Inter-Varsity Press. (Tyndale New Testament Commentaries.)

Fowl, S. 1988. The Ethics of Interpretation or What's Left Over After the Elimination of Meaning, in Lull, D. J. (ed.), *Society of Biblical Literature 1988 Seminar Papers*, 69–81. Atlanta: Scholars Press.

Fowl, S. E. & Jones, L. G. 1991. *Reading in Communion: Scripture and Ethics in Christian Life*. London: SPCK.

Frerichs, W. W. 1988. Reconciled in Christ: Ministry in Light of Ephesians. *Word & World* VIII/3, 293–300.

Freyne, S. 1980. *The World of the New Testament*. Wilmington: Michael Glazier.

Frye, R. M. 1989. Language for God and Feminist Language: A Literary and Rhetorical Analysis. *Interpretation* XLIII/1, 45–57.

Furnish, V. P. 1968. *Theology and Ethics in Paul*. Nashville: Abingdon.

———. 1993. "He Gave Himself [Was Given] Up...:" Paul's Use of a Christological Assertion, in Malherbe, A. J. & Meeks, W. A. (eds.), *The Future of Christology: Essays in Honor of Leander E. Keck*, 109–121. Minneapolis: Fortress.

Garland, D. E. 1979. A Life Worthy of the Calling: Unity and Holiness—Ephesians 4:1–24. *Review and Expositor* 76/4, 517–527.

Glanville, H. L. 1991. Ephesians and the "schlepp" of marriage in a post-modern world. Paper presented at post-graduate seminar on "The communication of the NT as humankind's search for, and creation of meaning in our every-day world." UPE, 9–10 October 1991.

———. 1992. Theory-forming in Ethics: A Critical Realist Perspective. M.A. thesis, University of Port Elizabeth.

———. 1993. Post-modern thought in the light of women's religious experience. *Scriptura* 44, 34–50.

———. 1994. Theology in conversation with female religious experience, in Mouton & Lategan 1994:123–136.

Gottwald, N. K. 1993. Social Class as an Analytic and Hermeneutical Category in Biblical Studies. *JBL* 112/1, 3–22.

Gräbe, I. 1984. *Aspekte van Poëtiese Taalgebruik: Teoretiese verkenning en toepassing.* Potchefstroom: Dept. Sentrale Publikasies PU vir CHO. (Wetenskaplike Bydraes van die PU vir CHO, Reeks A/46.)

Gräbe, P. J. 1990. Die verhouding tussen indikatief en imperatief in die Pauliniese etiek: enkele aksente uit die diskussie sedert 1924. *Scriptura* 32, 55–67.

Grant, R. M. & Tracy, D. 1984. *A Short History of the Interpretation of The Bible.* 2nd ed. London: SCM.

Gustafson, J. M. 1970. The Place of Scripture in Christian Ethics: A Methodological Study. *Interpretation* 24, 430–455.

———. 1984a. The Changing Use of the Bible in Christian Ethics, in Curran & McCormick 1984:133–150.

———. 1984b. The Place of Scripture in Christian Ethics: A Methodological Study, in Curran & McCormick 1984:151–177.

———. 1988. *Varieties of Moral Discourse: Prophetic, Narrative, Ethical, and Policy.* Grand Rapids: Calvin College and Seminary.

Guthrie, D. 1977. *New Testament Introduction.* London: Inter-Varsity Press.

———. 1981. *New Testament Theology.* Leicester: Inter-Varsity Press.

Habermas, J. 1988. *Nachmetaphysisches Denken: Philosophische Aufsätze.* Frankfurt am Main: Suhrkamp.

———. 1990. *Moral Consciousness and Communicative Action*, tr. by C. Lenhardt & S. W. Nicholsen; introduction by T. McCarthy. Cambridge: Polity Press.

Hartin, P. J. 1986. ἀνακεφαλαιώσασθαι τὰ πάντα ἐν τῷ Χριστῷ, in Petzer & Hartin 1986:228–237.

———. 1987. New Testament ethics: some trends in more recent research. *JTSA* 59, 35–41.

———. 1991. Methodological principles in interpreting the relevance of the New Testament in a new South Africa. *Scriptura* 37, 1–16.

———. 1992. Towards a Christian vision as the basis for ethical decisions. *Scriptura* 42, 65–73.

———. 1994. Ethics and the New Testament: How do we get from there to here?, in Mouton & Lategan 1994:511–525.

Hauerwas, S. 1977. *Truthfulness and Tragedy: Further Investigations in Christian Ethics.* Notre Dame: University of Notre Dame.

———. 1981. *A Community of Character: Toward a Constructive Social Ethic.* Notre Dame: University of Notre Dame.

————. 1984. The Moral Authority of Scripture: The Politics and Ethics of Remembering, in Curran & McCormick 1984:242–275.

————. 1985a. The gesture of a truthful story. *Theology Today* 42/2, 181–189.

————. 1985b. *Character and the Christian Life: A Study in Theological Ethics.* 3rd printing, with a new introduction. San Antonio: Trinity University.

————. 1993. The difference of virtue and the difference it makes: Courage exemplified. *Modern Theology* 9/3, 249–264.

Hauerwas, S. & MacIntyre, A. 1983. *Revisions: Changing Perspectives in Moral Philosophy.* Notre Dame: University of Notre Dame.

Havemann, J. C. T. 1976. Eulogieë en Doksologieë in die Pauliniese briewe. M.Th.-verhandeling, Universiteit van Stellenbosch.

Hays, R. B. 1983. *The Faith of Jesus Christ: An Investigation of the Narrative Substructure of Galatians 3:1–4:11.* Chicago: Scholars Press. (SBL Dissertation series 56.)

————. 1989. *Echoes of Scripture in the letters of Paul.* New Haven: Yale University.

————. 1990. Scripture-Shaped Community: The Problem of Method in New Testament Ethics. *Interpretation* XLIV/1, 42–55.

————. 1996. *The Moral Vision of the NewTestament: Community, Cross, New Creation. A Contemporary Introduction to New Testament Ethics.* New York: Harper-SanFrancisco.

Hendrix, H. 1988. On the form and ethos of Ephesians. *USQR* 42/4, 3–15.

Hermans, R. & Geysels, L. 1967. Efesiërs 1, 23: Het Pleroma van Gods Heilswerk. *Tijdschrift voor Filosofie en Theologie* 28/3, 279–293.

Hester, J. 1994. Re-discovering and re-inventing rhetoric. *Scriptura* 50, 1–22.

Heyns, J. A. 1992. Enkele opmerkings oor die proses van kontemporêre etiese beslissinge. *NGTT* 33/3, 364–372.

Hoch, C. B., Jr. 1982. The significance of the *syn*-compounds for Jew-Gentile relationships in the body of Christ. *Journal of the Evangelical Theological Society* 25/2, 175–183.

Hohengarten, W. M. 1992. Translator's Introduction, in Habermas, J., *Postmetaphysical Thinking: Philosophical Essays*, vii–xx. Cambridge: Polity Press.

Honig, A. G. 1978. De kerk als lichaam van Christus voor de wereld, in *De knechtsgestalte van Christus* 1978:65–75.

Howard, F. D. 1979. An Introduction to Ephesians. *Southwestern Journal of Theology* 22/1, 7–23.

Howard, G. 1974. The head/body metaphors of Ephesians. *NTS* 20, 350–6.

Huber, W. 1993. Toward an Ethics of Responsibility. *The Journal of Religion* 73/4, 573–591.

Hutcheon, L. 1986. *A Poetics of Postmodernism*. London: Routledge.

Jayne, D. 1974. "We" and "You" in Ephesians 1:3–14. *The Expository Times* 85/5, 151–152.

Jeal, R. R. 1990. The Relationship between Theology and Ethics in the Letter to the Ephesians. Ph.D. thesis, Sheffield University.

Jeanrond, W. G. 1991. *Theological Hermeneutics: Development and Significance*. New York: Crossroad.

Johnson, E. A. 1990. *Consider Jesus: Waves of Renewal in Christology*. New York: Crossroad.

Johnson, L. T. 1999. *The writings of the New Testament: An Interpretation*. Rev. ed. Minneapolis: Fortress.

Jonker, L. C. 1991. Eksegese sonder grense? Gedagtes rondom meerdimensionele Skrifuitleg. *NGTT* XXXII/4, 552–560.

Jonker, L. 1993. "Text" in a multidimensional exegetical approach. *Scriptura* 46, 100–115.

Jordaan, G. J. C. 1990. Die verhouding tussen indikatief en paraklese in die brief aan die Efesiërs. *In die Skriflig* 24/1, 49–69.

Kaiser, W. C., Jr. 1994. A Short History of Interpretation, in Kaiser & Silva 1994:210–227.

Kaiser, W. C., Jr. & Silva, M. 1994. *An Introduction to Biblical Hermeneutics: The Search for Meaning*. Grand Rapids: Zondervan Publishing House.

Käsemann, E. 1966. Ephesians and Acts, in Keck, L. E. & Martyn, J. L. (eds.), *Studies in Luke-Acts* (Festschrift P. Schubert), 288–297. Nashville: Abingdon.

Kaye, B. N. 1984. Cultural Interaction in the New Testament. *Theologische Zeitschrift* 40/4, 341–358.

Keathley, N. H. 1979. To The Praise of His Glory: Ephesians 1. *Review and Expositor* 76/4, 485–493.

Kee, H. C. 1989. *Knowing the truth: A sociological approach to New Testament interpretation*. Minneapolis: Fortress.

Keener, C. S. 1992. *Paul, Women & Wives: Marriage and Women's Ministry in the Letters of Paul*. Peabody: Hendrickson Publishers.

Kelber, W. H. 1987. Biblical hermeneutics and the ancient art of communication: A response. *Semeia* 39, 97–105.

Kelley, R. L. 1977. *Introduction to communication*. California: Cummings.

Kelsey, D. H. 1968. Appeals to Scripture in Theology. *The Journal of Religion* 48, 1–21.

———. 1975. *The Uses of Scripture in Recent Theology*. London: SCM.

———. 1980. The Bible and Christian Theology. *Journal of the American Academy of Religion* 48, 385–402.

Kennedy, G. A. 1984. *New Testament Interpretation through Rhetorical Criticism*. Chapel Hill: University of North Carolina.

Keulartz, J. 1992. *De verkeerde wereld van Jürgen Habermas*. Amsterdam: Boom Meppel.

Kilian, J. 1985. *Form and Style in Theological Texts: A Guide for the use of the Harvard reference system*. Pretoria: UNISA.

Kilner, J. F. 1989. A Pauline Approach to Ethical Decision-Making. *Interpretation* XLIII/4, 366–379.

Kinghorn, J. (red.) 1986. *Die NG Kerk en Apartheid*. Braamfontein: Macmillan.

Kirby, J. C. 1968. *Ephesians: Baptism and Pentecost. An inquiry into the structure and purpose of the epistle to the Ephesians*. London: SPCK.

Kittredge, C. B. 1998. *Community and Authority: The Rhetoric of Obedience in the Pauline Tradition*. Harrisburg: Trinity. (Harvard Theological Studies 45.)

Kourie, C. E. T. 1980. "En Christo" in Ephesians. M.A. thesis, UNISA, Pretoria.

———. 1987. In Christ and related expressions in Paul. *ThEv* XX/2, 33–43.

Kraemer, R. S. 1992. *Her Share of the Blessings: Women's Religions among Pagans, Jews, and Christians in the Greco-Roman World*. New York: Oxford University.

Kritzinger, J. N. J. 1988. Context and Holy Spirit. *ThEv* XXI/1, 19–23.

Kruger, M. A. 1991. Een in Christus: Die ekklesiologie van Efesiërs, in Roberts, J. H., Vorster, W. S., Vorster, J. N., Van der Watt, J. G. (reds.), *Teologie in Konteks*, 248–265. Johannesburg: Orion.

Lategan, B. C. 1970. Hermeneutiek en Geskiedenis. *Neotestamentica* 4, 19–40.

———. 1978. Directions in Contemporary Exegesis: Between historicism and structuralism. *JTSA* 25, 18–30.

———. 1982. Inleiding tot de Uitlegging van het Nieuwe Testament, in Klijn, A. F. J. (red.), *Inleiding tot de studie van het Nieuwe Testament*, 47–70. Kampen: J. H. Kok.

———. 1983. Die prediker Paulus, in Du Plessis, P. J. & Lategan, B. C., *Agtergrond en geskiedenis van die Nuwe Testament*, 213–222. Pretoria: Academica.

———. 1984a. Current issues in the hermeneutical debate. *Neotestamentica* 18, 1–17.

———. 1984b. Die Pauliniese etiek, in Du Toit 1984b:320–331.

———. 1985a. Some Unresolved Methodological Issues in New Testament Hermeneutics, in Lategan & Vorster 1985:3–25.

———. 1985b. Reference: Reception, Redescription and Reality, in Lategan & Vorster 1985:67–93.

———. 1986a. Godsdiens en tussengroepverhoudinge in Suid-Afrika. *NGTT* 27/1, 94–100.

————. 1986b. Bevriesde beweging: Statiese en dinamiese aspekte van die leesproses, in Du Toit, A. (red.), *In Gesprek: Opstelle vir Johan Degenaar*, 86–96. Stellenbosch: Voorbrand-Publikasies.

————. 1987. Inleidende opmerkings oor resepsieteorie en die uitleg van Bybelse materiaal. *NGTT* XXVIII/2, 112–118.

————. 1988. Why so few converts to new paradigms in theology? in Mouton, Van Aarde & Vorster 1988:65–78.

————. 1989a. Introduction: Coming to grips with the reader. *Semeia* 48, 3–17.

————. 1989b. Intertextuality and Social Transformation: Some Implications of the Family Concept in New Testament Texts, in Draisma, S. (ed.) 1989, *Intertextuality in Biblical Writings: Essays in honour of Bas van Iersel*, 105–116. Kampen: J. H. Kok.

————. 1990. Some Implications of Hebrews 2:5–18 for a Contextual Anthropology, in Jennings, T. W., Jr. (ed.), *Text and Logos: The Humanistic Interpretation of the New Testament*, 149–161. Atlanta: Scholars Press.

————. 1991a. Reception: Theory and Practice in Reading Romans 13, in Hartin, P. J. & Petzer, J. H. (eds.), *Text and Interpretation: New Approaches in the Criticism of the New Testament*, 145–169. Leiden: E. J. Brill.

————. 1991b. Die gevare wat 'n leser loop. *Vrye Weekblad*, 11–17 Oktober 1991, 21.

————. 1991c. The challenge of contextuality. *Scriptura* S9, 1–6.

————. 1992a. The reception of reception theory in South Africa, in Lategan, B. (ed.) 1992, *The reader and beyond: Theory and practice in South African reception studies*, 1–11. Pretoria: UNISA.

————. 1992b. Hermeneutics, in Freedman, D. N. (ed.-in-chief) 1992, *The Anchor Bible Dictionary* Vol 3, 149–154. New York: Doubleday.

————. 1992c. Reader Response Theory, in Freedman, D. N. (ed.-in-chief) 1992, *The Anchor Bible Dictionary* Vol 5, 625–628. New York: Doubleday.

————. 1993. Textual Space as Rhetorical Device, in Porter & Olbricht 1993:397–408.

————. 1994a. Aspects of a Contextual Hermeneutics for South Africa, in Mouton & Lategan 1994:17–30.

————..1994b. Revisiting *Text and Reality*. *Neotestamentica* 28/3, 121–135.

————. 1996. Imagination and Transformation: Ricoeur and the Role of Imagination. *Scriptura* 3, 213–232.

Lategan, B. C. & Rousseau, J. 1988. Reading Luke 12:35–48: An empirical study. *Neotestamentica* 22, 235–252.

Lategan, B. C. & Vorster, W. S. 1985. *Text and Reality: Aspects of Reference in Biblical Texts*. Philadelphia: Fortress. (SBL Semeia studies.)

Layman, C. S. 1991. *The Shape of the Good: Christian Reflections on the Foundation of Ethics*. Notre Dame: University of Notre Dame.

Lemmer, H. R. 1988. Pneumatology and Eschatology in Ephesians—The role of the eschatological Spirit in the church. D.Th. thesis, UNISA, Pretoria.

Levin, D. M. 1988. *The Opening of Vision*. London: Routledge.

Lincoln, A. T. 1973. A Re-examination of "the Heavenlies" in Ephesians. *NTS* 19, 468–483.

———. 1981. *Paradise Now and Not Yet: Studies in the Role of the Heavenly Dimension in Paul's Thought with Special Reference to His Eschatology*. Grand Rapids: Baker Book House.

———. 1982. The use of the OT in Ephesians. *JSNT* 14, 16–57.

———. 1983. Ephesians 2:8–10: A Summary of Paul's Gospel? *The Catholic Biblical Quarterly* 45, 617–630.

———. 1987. The Church and Israel in Ephesians 2. *The Catholic Biblical Quarterly* 49, 605–524.

———. 1990. *Ephesians*. Dallas: Word Books. (Word Biblical Commentary.)

Lindemann, A. 1975. *Die Aufhebung der Zeit: Geschichtsverständnis und Eschatologie im Epheserbrief*. Gütersloh: Gerd Mohn.

Lohse, E. 1976. *The New Testament Environment*. London: SCM.

Loubser, J. A. 1986. Die belang van die konteks in die lees van 'n teks. *NGTT* XXVII/2, 146–157.

———. 1987. *The Apartheid Bible: A Critical Review of Racial Theology in South Africa*. Cape Town: Maskew Miller Longman.

Louw, J. P. & Nida, E. A. (eds.) 1989. *Greek-English Lexicon of the New Testament based on semantic domains* Vol 1. Cape Town: Bible Society of South Africa.

Lundin, R., Thiselton, A. C. & Walhout, C. 1985. *The Responsibility of Hermeneutics*. Grand Rapids: Wm B. Eerdmans.

MacIntyre, A. 1966. *A short history of Ethics*. London: Routledge & Kegan Paul.

———. 1984. *After Virtue: A Study in Moral Theory*. 2nd ed. Notre Dame: University of Notre Dame.

———. 1988. *Whose Justice, which Rationality?* Notre Dame: University of Notre Dame.

Mack, B. L. 1990. *Rhetoric and the New Testament*. Minneapolis: Fortress.

Maimela, S. S. 1990. A critical assessment of Church and Society's social analysis. *ThEv* XXIII/1, 30–37.

Malherbe, A. J. 1983. *Social Aspects of Early Christianity*. 2nd ed. Philadelphia: Fortress.

———. 1986. *Moral Exhortation, A Greco-Roman Sourcebook*. Philadelphia: Westminster.

Malina, B. J. 1981. *The New Testament World: Insights from Cultural Anthropology.* London: SCM.

———. 1994a. Early Christian Groups: Using Small Group Formation Theory to explain Christian organizations. Paper presented at SBL subgroup meeting, Edinburgh, July 1994.

———. 1994b. Religion in the Imagined New Testament World: More Social Science lenses. *Scriptura* 51, 1–26.

Marshall, I. H. (ed.) 1977. *New Testament Interpretation: Essays on Principles and Methods.* Exeter: Paternoster.

———. 1989. Church and Temple in the New Testament. *Tyndale Bulletin* 40/2, 203–222.

Martin, R. P. 1967–68. An Epistle in Search of a Life-Setting. *The Expository Times* 79/10, 296–302.

Marxsen, W. 1993. *New Testament Foundations for Christian Ethics*, tr. by O. C. Dean, Jr. Minneapolis: Fortress.

McDonald, J. I. H. 1993. *Biblical Interpretation and Christian Ethics.* Cambridge: Cambridge University.

McFague, S. 1982. *Metaphorical Theology: Models of God in religious language.* London: Fortress.

McKnight, E. V. 1988. *Post-modern use of the Bible: The Emergence of Reader-Oriented Criticism.* Nashville: Abingdon.

Meeks, W. A. 1975. The Social World of Early Christianity. *Bulletin of the Council on the Study of Religion* 6/1, 1, 4–5.

———. 1977. In one Body: The Unity of Humankind in Colossians and Ephesians, in Jervell, J. & Meeks, W. A. (eds.), *God's Christ and His People: Studies in Honour of Nils Alstrup Dahl*, 209–221. Oslo: Universitetsforlaget.

———. 1982. The social context of Pauline theology. *Interpretation* 36/3, 266–277.

———. 1983. *The first urban Christians: The Social World of the Apostle Paul.* New Haven: Yale University.

———. 1986a. Understanding early Christian Ethics. *JBL* 105/1, 3–11.

———. 1986b. *The moral world of the first Christians.* Philadelphia: Westminster.

———. (ed.) 1986c. *The New Testament in Its Social Environment.* Philadelphia: Westminster.

———. 1990. The Circle of Reference in Pauline Morality, in Balch, D. L., Ferguson, E. & Meeks, W. A. (eds.), *Greeks, Romans, and Christians: Essays in Honor of Abraham J. Malherbe*, 305–317. Minneapolis: Fortress.

———. 1993. *The Origins of Christian Morality: The First Two Centuries.* New Haven: Yale University.

Merklein, H. 1973a. *Christus und die Kirche: Die theologische Grundstruktur des Epheserbriefes nach Eph. 2, 11–18.* Stuttgart: KBW Verlag. (Stuttgarter Bibelstudien 66.)

————. 1973b. Zur Tradition und Komposition von Eph. 2, 14–18. *Biblische Zeitschrift* 17/1, 79–102.

Mickelsen, B. & A. 1981. The "Head" of the Epistles. *Christianity Today*, February 20, 20–23.

Miller, J. H. 1987a. *The Ethics of reading: Kant, de Man, Eliot, Trollope, James and Benjamin.* New York: Columbia University. (Wellek Library Lectures at the University of California in Irvine.)

————. 1987b. Presidential Address 1986: The Triumph of Theory, the Resistance to Reading, and the Question of the Material Base. *Publications of the Modern Language Association of America (PMLA)* 102/3, 281–291.

————. 1989. Is There an Ethics of Reading? in Phelan, J. (ed.), *Reading narrative: Form, Ethics, Ideology*, 78–101. Columbus: Ohio State University.

Mitchell, M. M. 1991. *Paul and the Rhetoric of Reconciliation: An Exegetical Investigation of the Language and Composition of 1 Corinthians.* Louisville: Westminster/John Knox.

Mitton, C. L. [1973] 1981. *Ephesians.* Paperback. Grand Rapids: Wm B. Eerdmans. (The New Century Bible Commentary.)

Moore, M. S. 1982. Ephesians 2:14–16: A history of recent interpretation. *The Evangelical Quarterly* 54/3, 163–168.

Mosala, I. J. 1950. *Biblical hermeneutics and black theology in South Africa.* Grand Rapids: Wm B. Eerdmans.

Mott, S. C. 1982. *Biblical Ethics and Social Change.* New York: Oxford University Press.

Mouton, A. E. J. 1987. 'n Eksegeties-hermeneutiese verkenning van die ἐν Χριστῷ-kernbelydenis by Paulus na aanleiding van Efesiërs 1:3–14. M.A.-verhandeling, UPE.

Mouton, E. 1993. Preaching from the Lectionary: Ascension. *JTSA* 82, 78–87.

————. 1994. Reading Ephesians ethically: Criteria towards a renewed identity awareness? *Neotestamentica 28/2, 359–377.*

Mouton, J. & Lategan, B. (eds.) 1994. *The relevance of theology for the 1990s.* Pretoria: HSRC.

Mouton, J., Van Aarde, A. G., Vorster, W. S. (eds.) 1988. *Paradigms and progress in theology.* Pretoria: HSRC.

Moxnes, H. 1989. Social Integration and the problem of Gender in St. Paul's Letters. *Studia Theologia* 43, 99–113.

Müller, B. A. & Smit, D. J. 1994. Public worship: A tale of two stories, in Mouton & Lategan 1994:385–408.

Naudé, P. 1993. The "pregnant Christ:" Re-reading the Scriptures from a feminist perspective, in Van Wyk, A. (ed.), *The Role of Women in the 1990s*, 8–14. Port Elizabeth: UPE Institute for Planning Research.

Naudé, R. M. 1993. Metodes in die Christelike etiek. *HTS* 49/1 & 2, 145–165.

Neyrey, J. H. 1990. *Paul, in other words: A cultural reading of his letters*. Louisville: Westminster.

Nida, E. A. 1964. *Toward a science of translating*. Leiden: E. J. Brill.

Niebuhr, H. R. 1941. *The meaning of revelation*. New York: MacMillan Publishing Co.

———. 1963. The *Responsible Self: An Essay in Christian Moral Philosophy*. New York: Harper & Row.

———. [1951] 1975. *Christ and Culture*. Reprint. New York: Harper Colophon Books.

Nolan, A. 1986. *Jesus before Christianity: The Gospel of Liberation*. 2nd ed. Cape Town: David Philip.

———. 1988. *God in South Africa: The Challenge of the Gospel*. Cape Town: David Philip.

O'Brien, P. T. 1977. *Introductory Thanksgivings in the letters of Paul*. Leiden: E. J. Brill.

———. 1979. Ephesians 1: An Unusual Introduction to a New Testament Letter. *NTS* 25/4, 504–516.

———. 1984. Principalities and Powers: Opponents of the Church, in Carson, D. A. (ed.), *Biblical Interpretation and the Church*, 110–150. Exeter: Paternoster.

Ogletree, T. W. 1983. *The use of the Bible in Christian ethics*. Philadelphia: Fortress.

O'Hagan, A. P. 1976. The Wife According to Eph. 5:22–33. *Australasian Catholic Record* 53/1, 17–26.

Old, H. O. 1985. The Psalms of Praise in the Worship of the New Testament Church. *Interpretation* XXXIX/1, 20–33.

Oosthuizen, M. J. 1988. Scripture and context. The use of the exodus theme in the hermeneutics of liberation theology. *Scriptura* 25, 7–22.

———. 1993. Towards an ethics of interpretation: The use of scripture in three recent Christian documents. *HTS* 49/1 & 2, 167–187.

Patte, D. 1976. *What is structural exegesis?* Philadelphia: Fortress.

———. 1988. Speech act theory and biblical exegesis. *Semeia* 41, 85–102.

Perdue, L. G. 1990. The social character of paraenesis and paraenetic literature. *Semeia* 50, 5–39.

Perelman, C. H. & Olbrechts-Tyteca, L. 1969. *The New Rhetoric: A Treatise on Argumentation*, tr. by J. Wilkenson & P. Weaver. Notre Dame: University of Notre Dame.

Perkins, P. 1988. *Reading the New Testament.* 2nd ed. New York: Paulist Press.

Perriman, A. 1990. "His body, which is the church...." Coming to Terms with Metaphor. *The Evangelical Quarterly* 62/2, 123–142.

Petzer, J. H. & Hartin, P. J. (eds.) 1986. *A South African perspective on the New Testament: Essays by South African New Testament scholars presented to B.M. Metzger during his visit to South Africa in 1985.* Leiden: E. J. Brill.

Pfitzner, V. C. 1978. Good Songs in Bad Times: An Exegetical and Homiletical Study of Ephesians 5:15–21. *Lutheran Theological Journal* 12/2, 45–53.

Phillips, G. A. 1990. Exegesis as critical praxis: Reclaiming history and text from a postmodern perspective. *Semeia* 51, 7–49.

Pieterse, H. J. C. 1985. The Church in the World. Singing the Lord's Song in a Strange Land: Ministry and the Communication of the Gospel. *Theology Today*, XLII/1, 84–87.

———. 1991. Credibility and the communicative power of the church in South Africa. *Scriptura* 38, 1–9.

Polhill, J. B. 1973. The Relationship Between Ephesians and Colossians. *Review and Expositor* 70/4, 439–450.

Porter, S. E. 1990. ἴστε γινώσκοντες in Ephesians 5, 5: Does Chiasm Solve a Problem? *Zeitschrift für die Neutestamentliche Wissenschaft und die Kunde der Älteren Kirche* 81/3–4, 270–276.

———. 1993. The theoretical justification for application of rhetorical categories to Pauline epistolary literature, in Porter & Olbricht 1993:100–122.

Porter, S. E. & Olbricht, T. H. (eds.) 1993. *Rhetoric and the New Testament: Essays from the 1992 Heidelberg Conference.* Sheffield: JSOT. (Journal for the Study of the New Testament Supplement Series 90.)

Purvis, S. B. 1993. *The Power of the Cross: Foundations for a Christian Feminist Ethic of Community.* Nashville: Abingdon.

Rader, W. 1978. *The Church and Racial Hostility: A History of Interpretation of Ephesians 2:11–22.* Tübingen: J. C. B. Mohr (Paul Siebeck).

Ramsey, P. 1993. *Basic Christian Ethics.* Louisville: Westminster/John Knox.

Rasmussen, D. M. 1990. *Reading Habermas.* Massachusetts: Basil Blackwell.

Rasmussen, L. L. 1993. *Moral Fragments and Moral Community: A Proposal for Church in Society.* Minneapolis: Fortress.

Reed, J. T. 1993. Using ancient rhetorical categories to interpret Paul's letters: A question of genre, in Porter & Olbricht 1993:292–324.

Reicke, B. 1968. *The New Testament Era: The World of the Bible from 500 B.C. to A.D. 100,* tr. by D. E. Green. London: Adam & Charles Black.

————. 1970. Caesarea, Rome, and the Captivity Epistles, in Gasque, W. W. & Martin, R. P. (eds.), *Apostolic History and the Gospel: Biblical and Historical essays presented to F. F. Bruce on his 60th Birthday*, 277–286. Grand Rapids: Wm B. Eerdmans.

Richardson, N. 1994. Ethics of Character and Community, in Villa-Vicencio & De Gruchy 1994:89–101.

Ricoeur, P. 1975. Biblical Hermeneutics. *Semeia* 4, 29–148.

————. 1976. *Interpretation Theory: Discourse and the Surplus of Meaning*. Fort Worth: Texas Christian University.

————. 1977. *The Rule of Metaphor: Multi-disciplinary studies of the creation of meaning in language*, tr. by R. Czerny, K. McLaughlin & J. Costello. Toronto: University of Toronto.

————. 1980. *Essays on Biblical Interpretation*, ed. by L. S. Mudge. Philadelphia: Fortress.

Rienecker, F. 1961. *Der Brief des Paulus an die Epheser*. Wuppertal: R. Brockhaus.

Robbins, C. J. 1986. The Composition of Eph. 1:3–14. *JBL* 105/4, 677–687.

Robbins, V. K. 1990. A Socio-Rhetorical Response: Contexts of Interaction and Forms of Exhortation. *Semeia* 261–271.

————. 1996a. *The Tapestry of Early Christian Discourse: Rhetoric, scoiety and ideology*. London and New York: Routledge.

————. 1996b. *Exploring the Texture of Texts: A Guide to Socio-Rhetorical Interpretation*. Valley Forge: Trinity.

Roberts, J. H. 1963. *Die opbou van die kerk volgens die Efese-brief*. Groningen: VRB.

————. 1978. De knechtsgestalte van de kerk in de brief aan de Efeziërs, in *De knechts-gestalte van Christus* 1978:166–178.

————. 1981. Skriftuurlike grondslae vir die ekumenie. *NGTT* XXII/3, 188–200.

————. 1983. Die Pauliniese beeld van die kerk as bouwerk van God. *Scriptura* 10, 1–18.

————. 1984a. Die gevangenskapsbriewe, in Du Toit 1984b:114–157.

————. 1984b. Die kerk by Paulus, in Du Toit 1984b:282–319.

————. 1986a. Pauline Transitions to the letter body. *Bibliotheca Ephemeridum Theologicarum Lovaniensium* 73, 93–99.

————. 1986b. Die eenheid van die kerk volgens die Efesebrief, in Breytenbach, J. C. (red.) 1986, *Eenheid en konflik: Eerste beslissinge in die geskiedenis van die Christendom*, 75–88. Pretoria: NG Kerkboekhandel.

————. 1986c. Transitional techniques to the letter body in the *corpus Paulinum*, in Petzer & Hartin 1986:187–201.

————. 1988. Belydenisuitsprake as Pauliniese briefoorgange. *HTS* 44/1, 81–97.

————. 1990. Die vraagstuk van 'n Nuwe-Testamentiese etiek: Enkele blikrigtings in die gang van die ondersoek. *Scriptura* 32, 36–54.

————. 1991. *The Letter to the Ephesians*. Cape Town: Lux Verbi.

————. 1993a. Teologie en etiek in die brief aan Filemon: 'n Poging tot verantwoording. *Skrif en Kerk* 14/1, 105–115.

————. 1993b. The enigma of Ephesians—Rethinking some positions on the basis of Schnackenburg and Arnold. *Neotestamentica* 17/1, 93–106.

Robinson, P. J. 1990. Mission as ethos/Ethos as mission, in Kritzinger, J. N. J. and Saayman, W. A., *Mission in creative tension: A dialogue with David Bosch*. Pretoria: SA Missiological Society.

Roetzel, C. J. 1983. Jewish Christian—Gentile Christians Relations. A Discussion of Ephesians 2:15a. *ZNW* 74/2, 81–89.

————. 1987. *The world that shaped the New Testament*. London: SCM.

Rogers, C. L., Jr. 1979. The Dionysian Background of Ephesians 5:18. *Bibliotheca Sacra* 136/543, 249–257.

Rossouw, H. W. 1980. Hoe moet 'n mens die Bybel lees? Die hermeneutiese probleem. *Scriptura* 1, 7–28.

Rousseau, J. 1984. Die Nuwe Testament—Gesagsbron vir 'n Christelike Veelgodedom?— Enkele gedagtes rondom die verstaan van die Nuwe Testament vir vandag. *Scriptura* 11, 50–78.

————. 1985a. Die Woord, waarheid en (Nuwe Testamentiese) wetenskap. *Scriptura* 16, 1–16.

————. 1985b. The communication of ancient canonized texts. *Neotestamentica* 19, 92–101.

————. 1986. A multidimensional approach towards the communication of an ancient canonized text: Towards determining the thrust, perspective and strategy of 1 Peter. D.D. thesis, University of Pretoria.

————. 1988a. 'n Multidimensionele benadering tot die kommunikasie van gekanoniseerde tekste. *Skrif en Kerk* 9/1, 33–56.

————. 1988b. The bible, communication and reality: Paradigms and our struggle for a cosmological perspective, in Mouton, Van Aarde & Vorster 1988:409–422.

————. 1988c. *Meestersimbole van God: Die kosmologiese perspektief en meestersimbole van die Nuwe Testament* (Deel 1). Port Elizabeth: Woord & Wêreld.

————. 1989a. New Testament exegesis: Theory and methodology, in Rousseau, J, *Understanding the New Testament* Vol I. Port Elizabeth: Woord & Wêreld.

———. 1989b. Beyond exegesis and theology: Communication theory and biblical interpretation, in Rousseau, J., *Understanding the New Testament* Vol 2. Port Elizabeth: Woord & Wêreld.

Rowston, D. J. 1979. Changes in Biblical Interpretation Today: The Example of Ephesians. *Biblical Theology Bulletin* 9/3, 121–125.

Ruether, R. R. 1986. Re-contextualizing Theology. *Theology Today* XLIII/1, 22–27.

Ryrie, C. C. 1966. The Mystery in Ephesians 3. *Bibliotheca Sacra* 123/489, 24–31.

Sampley, J. P. 1971. *"And the two shall become one flesh": A study of traditions in Ephesians 5:21–33*. Cambridge: Cambridge University. (SNTS Monograph series 16.)

———. 1972. Scripture and Tradition in the Community as seen in Ephesians 4:25ff. *Studia Theologica* 26/2, 101–109.

Sanders, J. T. 1965. Hymnic Elements in Ephesians 1–3. *ZNW* 56/4, 214–232.

Santer, M. 1969. The text of Ephesians I.1. *NTS* 15/2, 247–248.

Scheffler, E. 1991. What does God's word refer to? Historical-grammatical exegesis, in Bosman, H. L., Gous, I. G. P., & Spangenberg, I. J. J. (eds.), *Plutocrats and Paupers: Wealth and poverty in the Old Testament*, 52–65. Pretoria: J. L. van Schaik.

Schlier, H. 1957. *Der Brief an die Epheser: Ein Kommentar*. 6. Aufl. Düsseldorf: Patmos.

Schmidt, W. H. 1983. *The Faith of the Old Testament*. Oxford: Basil Blackwell.

Schnackenburg, R. 1977. Die grosse Eulogie Eph. 1, 3–14: Analyse unter text-linguistischen Aspekten. *Biblische Zeitschrift* 21/1, 67–87.

———. 1991. *The Epistle to the Ephesians*, tr. by Helen Heron. Edinburgh: T. & T. Clark.

Schneiders, S. M. 1986. *New Wineskins: Re-imagining Religious Life Today*. New York: Paulist Press.

Schrage, W. 1988. *The Ethics of the New Testament*, tr. by D. E. Green. Philadelphia: Fortress.

Schweiker, W. 1993. Radical Interpretation and Moral Responsibility: A Proposal for Theological Ethics. *The Journal of Religion* 73/4, 613–637.

Seeley, D. 1989. *The noble death: Graeco-Roman martyrology and Paul's concept of salvation*. Sheffield: JSOT. (JSNT Supplement Series 28.)

Sidgwick, H. 1967. *Outlines of the History of Ethics*. 6th enlarged ed. London: MacMillan.

Silva, M. 1987. *Has the church misread the Bible? The history of interpretation in the light of current issues*. Grand Rapids: Academie.

———. 1994a. How to read a letter: The meaning of the epistles, in Kaiser & Silva 1994:120–137.

————. 1994b. Contemporary Approaches to Biblical Interpretation, in Kaiser & Silva 1994:228–248.

Simmons, P. D. 1979. The Grace of God and The Life of the Church: Ephesians 2. *Review and Expositor* 76/4, 495–506.

Smit, D. J. 1983a. Hemelvaart: Efesiërs 1:20–23, in Burger, C. W. Müller, B. A. & Smit, D. J. (reds.) 1983, *Riglyne vir Paas-, Hemelvaarts- en Pinksterprediking. WtL* 3, 141–148. Kaapstad: NG Kerk-Uitgewers.

————. 1983b. Efesiërs 4:30, in Burger, Müller & Smit 1983:172–180.

————. 1986. The symbol of reconciliation and ideological conflict in South Africa, in Vorster, W. S. (ed.), *Reconciliation and Construction: Creative options for a rapidly changing South Africa*, 79–112. Pretoria: UNISA. (Miscellanea Congregalia 27.)

————. 1987. *Hoe verstaan ons wat ons lees? 'n Dink- en werkboek oor die hermeneutiek vir predikers en studente. WtL* B/1. Kaapstad: N G Kerk-Uitgewers.

————. 1988. Responsible hermeneutics: A systematic theologian's response to the readings and readers of Luke 12:35–48. *Neotestamentica* 22, 441–484.

————. 1989. Those were the critics, what about the real readers? An analysis of 65 published sermons and sermon guidelines on Luke 12:35–48. *Neotestamentica* 23/1, 61–82.

————. 1990a. The ethics of interpretation—new voices from the USA. *Scriptura* 33, 16–28.

————. 1990b. The ethics of interpretation—and South Africa. *Scriptura* 33, 29–43.

————. 1990c. Theology and the Transformation of Culture—Niebuhr Revisited. *JTSA* 72, 9–23.

————. 1991a. Wat beteken "die Bybel sê?" 'n Tipologie van leserkonstrukte. *HTS* 47/1, 167–185.

————. 1991b. The Bible and ethos in a New South Africa. *Scriptura* 37, 51–67.

————. 1992. Oor "Nuwe-Testamentiese etiek," die Christelike lewe en Suid-Afrika vandag, in Breytenbach & Lategan 1992:303–325.

————. 1993a. Revisioning during reconstruction? Contemporary challenges for the churches in South Africa. *Apologia* 8/1 & 2, 5–20.

————. 1993b. The Bible and violence. Paper presented at conference on "The Church and Violence." Pretoria, 4 Dec. 1993.

————. 1993c. What makes theological education theological? Overhearing two conversations. *Scriptura* S11, 147–166.

————. 1994a. Etiek na Babel? Vrae rondom moraliteit en die openbare gesprek in Suid-Afrika vandag. *NGTT* XXXV/1, 82–92.

———. 1994b. What did ,we do with our moral discourses? On the responsibility of Christian ethicists in South Africa. Paper presented at "Remembering for the future II" conference. Berlin, 13–17 March 1994.

———. 1994c. Morality and Individual Responsibility. *JTSA* 89, 19–30.

———. 1994d. A story of contextual hermeneutics and the integrity of New Testament interpretation in South Africa. *Neotestamentica* 28/2, 265–289.

———. 1994e. The Self-Disclosure of God, in De Gruchy, J. & Villa-Vicencio, C. (eds.) 1994, *Doing Theology in Context: South African Perspectives*, 4–54. Cape Town: David Philip. (Theology and Praxis Vol I.)

———. 1994f. Reading the Bible and the "(un)official interpretive culture." *Neotestamentica* 28/2, 309–321.

———. 1995a. Etiese spraakverwarring in Suid-Afrika vandag. *NGTT* XXXVI/1, 87–98.

———. 1995b. Het Suid-Afrika 'n gemeenskaplike morele taal nodig?/ Does South Africa need a common moral language? *HTS* 51/1, 65–84.

———. 1995c. Oor die skepping van 'n grammatika van saamleef./On creating a grammar for living together. *HTS* 51/1, 85–107.

Smith, D. C. 1989. Cultic Language in Ephesians 2:19–22: A Test Case. *Restoration Quarterly* 31/4, 207–217.

Smith, G. V. 1975. Paul's use of Psalm 68:18 in Ephesians 4:8. *Journal of the Evangelical Theological Society* 18/3, 181–189.

Solomon, R. C. 1990. *The Big Questions: A Short Introduction to Philosophy*. 3rd ed. San Diego: Harcourt Brace Jovanovich.

Spohn, W. C. 1984. *What Are They Saying About Scripture and Ethics?* New York: Paulist Press.

Stagg, F. 1979. The Domestic Code and Final Appeal: Ephesians 5:21–6:24. *Review and Expositor* 76/4, 541–552.

Stambaugh, J. E. & Balch, D. L. 1986. *The New Testament in Its Social Environment*. Philadelphia: Westminster.

Story, C. I. K. 1984. Bible Study on Peace: Ephesians 2:11–3:21. *The Princeton Seminary Bulletin* 5/1, 59–66.

Stott, J. R. W. 1982. *God's new society: The message of Ephesians*. Leicester: Inter-Varsity Press.

Stout, J. 1988. *Ethics After Babel: The Languages of Morals and Their Discontents*. Boston: Beacon.

Stowers, S. K. 1984. Social status, public speaking and private teaching: The circumstances of Paul's preaching activity. *Novum Testamentum* XXVI/1, 59–82.

————. 1986. *Letter writing in Greco-Roman Antiquity*. Philadelphia: Westminster.

Strauss, R. L. 1986. Like Christ: An Exposition of Ephesians 4:13. *Bibliotheca Sacra*, July–Sept., 260–265.

Swanepoel, F. A. 1989. *The Old Testament and its interpretation*. Port Elizabeth: s.n.

Tanner, K. 1993. A Theological Case for Human Responsibility in Moral Choice. *The Journal of Religion* 73/4, 592–612.

Taylor, M. K. 1990. *Remembering Esperanza—A Cultural-Political Theology for North American Praxis*. New York: Orbis.

The Holy Bible: New Revised Standard Version 1989. Nashville: Thomas Nelson.

The New Testament and Psalms: New International Version 1989. 3rd South African ed. Roggebaai: Bible Society of South Africa.

Theissen, G. 1987. *Psychological aspects of Pauline Theology*. Philadelphia: Fortress.

Theron, P. F. 1973. Christus, die Gees, Kerk en kosmos volgens Efesiërs 4:7–10. *NGTT* 14/3, 214–223.

————. 1982. Die vreemdheid van die kerk: 'n Reaksie van op die Ope Brief, in Bosch, König & Nicol 1982:123–133.

————. 1985. Breuk of brug? Enkele opmerkings rondom die tema: Kerk en wêreld, in Louw, D. J. (red.), *Op die breuklyn*, 43–54. Kaapstad: N G Kerk-Uitgewers.

Thiselton, A. C. 1977. The new hermeneutic, in Marshall 1977:308–333.

————. 1980. *The Two Horizons: New Testament Hermeneutics and Philosophical Description with Special Reference to Heidegger, Bultmann, Gadamer, and Wittgenstein*. Exeter: Paternoster.

————. 1992. *New Horizons in Hermeneutics: The Theory and Practice of Transforming Biblical Reading*. Grand Rapids: Zondervan Publishing House.

Thurston, B. 1993. *Spiritual life in the early church: The Witness of Acts and Ephesians*. Minneapolis: Fortress.

Tödt, H. E. 1977. Versuch zu einer Theorie ethischer Urteilsfindung. *Zeitschrift für Evangelische Ethik* 21, 81–93.

Tracy, D. 1981. *The Analogical Imagination: Christian Theology and the Culture of Pluralism*. London: SCM.

————. 1991. God, dialogue and solidarity: A theologian's refrain, in Wall, J. & Heim, D. (eds.), *How my mind has changed*, 88–99. Grand Rapids: Eerdmans.

Van der Horst, P. W. 1992. Notities bij het thema: vrouwen in het vroege jodendom. *Kerk en Theologie* 43/2, 113–129.

Van der Watt, J. G. 1989. Die verhouding tussen die Ou Testament en Nuwe Testament heilshistories oorweeg. *Skrif en Kerk* 10/1, 61–79.

Van Engen, C. 1984. The Holy Catholic Church—on the Road through Ephesians. *Reformed Review* 37/3, 187–201.

Van Huyssteen, W. 1986. *Teologie as kritiese geloofsverantwoording*. Pretoria: RGN.

———. 1987. *The realism of the text: A perspective on biblical authority*. Pretoria: UNISA. (Miscellanea Congregalia 28.)

Van Huyssteen, W. & Du Toit, B. 1989. *Geloof en Skrifgesag*. Pretoria: NGKB.

Vatz, R. E. 1973. The Myth of the Rhetorical Situation. *Philosophy & Rhetoric* 6/3, 154–161.

Venter, A. F. 1991. Biblical ethics and Christian response to violence. *ThEv* XXIV/2, 25–39.

Verhey, A. 1984a. *The Great Reversal: Ethics and the New Testament*. Grand Rapids: Wm B. Eerdmans.

———. 1984b. The Use of Scripture in Ethics, in Curran & McCormick 1984:213–241.

Villa-Vicencio, C. & De Gruchy, J. (eds.) 1994. *Doing Ethics in Context: South African Perspectives*. Cape Town: David Philip. (Theology and Praxis, Vol 2.)

Volf, M. 1996. *Exclusion and Embrace: A Theological Exploration of Identity, Otherness, and Reconciliation*. Nashville: Abingdon.

Vorster, J. N. 1990. Toward an interactional model for the analysis of letters. *Neotestamentica* 24/1, 107–130.

———. 1991. The rhetorical situation of the letter to the Romans—An interactional approach. D.D. thesis, University of Pretoria.

———. 1992a. The epistemic status of rhetoric. Paper presented at post-graduate seminar. UPE, 21–24 April 1992.

———. 1992b. The rhetorical situation. Paper presented at post-graduate seminar. UPE, 21–24 April 1992.

———. 1992c. Pauline τόποι. Paper presented at post-graduate seminar. UPE, 21–24 April 1992.

———. 1992d. Techniques of argumentation in the letter to the Ephesians. Paper presented at post-graduate seminar. UPE, 21–24 April 1992.

Vorster, W. S. 1977. *'n Ou Boek in 'n nuwe wêreld—gedagtes rondom die interpretasie van die Nuwe Testament*. Pretoria: UNISA.

———. (ed.) 1979. *Scripture and the Use of Scripture*. Pretoria: UNISA. (Miscellanea Congregalia 9.)

———. 1984. The historical paradigm—Its possibilities and limitations. *Neotestamentica* 18, 104–123.

———. 1989. The Reader in the Text: Narrative Material. *Semeia* 48, 21–39.

————. 1991. A reader-response approach to Matthew 24:3–28. *HTS* 47/4, 1099–1108.

Vosloo, R. R. 1994. Verhaal en Moraal: 'n Kritiese Ondersoek na die Narratiewe Etiek van Stanley Hauerwas. D.Th.-tesis, Universiteit van Wes-Kaapland, Bellville.

Wadell, P. J. 1989. *Friendship and the Moral Life*. Notre Dame: University of Notre Dame.

Wall, R. W. 1988. Wifely Submission in the Context of Ephesians. *Christian Scholar's Review* 17/3, 272–285.

Wedderburn, A. J. M. 1985. Some observations on Paul's use of the phrases "in Christ" and "with Christ." *Journal for the Study of the New Testament* 25, 83–97.

Wessels, F. 1989. Ephesians 5:21–33 "Wives, be subject to your husbands.... Husbands, love your wives...." *JTSA* 67, 67–76.

Wessels, G. F. 1990a. Efesiërs 2:11–22, in Burger, Müller & Smit 1990:50–60.

————. 1990b. Efesiërs 3:1–11, in Burger, Müller & Smit 1990:61–69.

————. 1990c. Efesiërs 4:1–16, in Burger, Müller & Smit 1990:70–83.

————. 1990d. Efesiërs 5:21–33, in Burger, Müller & Smit 1990:84–94.

West, G. O. 1991a. *Biblical hermeneutics of liberation: Modes of reading the Bible in the South African context*. Pietermaritzburg: Cluster.

————. 1991b. The relationship between different modes of reading (the Bible) and the ordinary reader. *Scriptura* S9, 87–110.

Wild, R. A. 1984. The Warrior and the Prisoner: Some Reflections on Ephesians 6:10–20. *The Catholic Biblical Quarterly* 46, 284–298.

Wogaman, J. P. 1993. *Christian Ethics: A Historical Introduction*. Louisville: Westminster/ John Knox.

Wright, N. T. 1992. *The New Testament and the People of God*. Minneapolis: Fortress.

Wuellner, W. 1987. Where is Rhetorical Criticism Taking Us? *The Catholic Biblical Quarterly* 49/3, 448–463.

————. 1989a. Hermeneutics and Rhetorics: From "Truth and Method" to "Truth and Power." *Scriptura* S3, 1–54.

————. 1989b. Is there an encoded reader fallacy? *Semeia* 48, 41–54.

Yates, R. 1972. A Re-examination of Ephesians 1:23. *The Expository Times* 83/5, 146–151.

————. 1977. Principalities and Powers in Ephesians. *New Blackfriars* 58/690, 615–521.

Yoder, J. H. 1991. Sacrament as social process: Christ the transformer of culture. *Theology Today* XLVIII/1, 33–44.

SUMMARY

This study is primarily concerned with the *integrity* and *relevance* of biblical studies, and specifically with reference to its influence on the public *ethos*, and its functioning in Christian *ethics*. Readers of the Bible explicitly appeal to, or implicitly presuppose, the continuing *authority* of these writings when using them to explain and justify their moral arguments and behavior. The book argues for an authority derived from an ethically responsible reading of the Bible which would be legitimized by a corresponding publicly accountable morality. By encouraging an ongoing critical dialogue between the often compartmentalized fields of New Testament Science and Christian Ethics, the book joins the urgent and cumulative discussion on "the ethics of interpretation," which aims at bridging the methodological gap between these and other theological sub-disciplines. As such, it hopes to foster a sensitivity for the network of relations, responsibilities and skills involved in the art and science of reading.

Several hermeneutic journeys are undertaken—with varying emphases: from the moral world of contemporary readers, to (the researcher's understanding of) the biblical texts and their contexts, and eventually back from *there* and *then* to *here* and *now*. *Chapter one* maps the methodological contours of the study by inquiring into the interpretive processes of which readers necessarily form a part. Because biblical scholars approach their subject from different angles, they are obliged to give proper account of their interpretive acts, especially with regard to the pragmatic effect of those acts.

An analysis of the *nature* and *purpose* of the biblical documents leads to the recognition of their dynamic yet complex, multi-faceted character. Typical of any communication event, they reflect the linguistic-literary, socio-historical, and rhetorical dimensions of reality. All these aspects are interwoven and interdependent, and essentially reveal the delicate hermeneutic *processes* underlying, and stimulated by these documents. It is particularly by investigating an author's methods of persuasion in the rhetorical phase, that the *transformative potential* of textual communication comes to the fore.

To illustrate this on a practical level, the *Ephesians epistle* is analyzed by reading it from three different textual perspectives (*chapter two*). The thrust of the document emerges as the author's focus on the mainly Gentile readers' new identity *in Christ*, and their corresponding ethos of love, compassion, righteousness and holiness. These are intrinsically related to the paradoxical power of Christ's sacrificial death, resurrection and exaltation. In the end, all the syntactic, dynamic and dialectic elements of the document converge in its christological and ecclesial orientation.

By focusing on strategic rhetorical devices in Ephesians, *chapter three* explores its transformative potential in more detail. It concludes by saying that the communicative power of the document is—in Ricoeurian terms—its ability to disclose (through the metaphorical processes of identification, estrangement and reorientation) *an alternative moral world, a new perspective on reality*. In this way Ephesians *invites* subsequent audiences and readers via the textual construct of its "implied readers" to appropriate its christological and ecclesial vision in ever changing circumstances.

Chapter four travels the long road from the Ephesians text to the present-day needs and contexts of Christian ethos and ethics. It first relates important implications of the Ephesians nature to its authority for Christian ethics. Secondly, it investigates the Ephesians response to different moral paradigms through inquiring into its potential role in the formation of moral *people*, the transformation of a moral *society*, and the information of moral *decision-making* and *action*. The book concludes by suggesting revisionary criteria for an ethical reading of the New Testament, which collectively characterize hermeneutic appropriation as "an integrative act of imagination" (Hays).

OPSOMMING

Hierdie studie is primêr gemoeid met die *integriteit* en *aktualiteit* van Bybel-kunde, en veral met betrekking tot die invloed daarvan op die openbare *etos*, en die bruikbaarheid daarvan vir die Christelike *etiek*. Bybellesers veronderstel indirek, óf beroep hul direk op die blywende gesag van hierdie ou gekanoniseerde tekste wanneer hulle hul morele argumente en gedrag daarmee sanksioneer. Die boek bepleit 'n verstaan van Bybelse gesag wat gegrond is op 'n eties verant-woordelike lees van die Bybel, gerugsteun deur 'n ooreenstemmende verant-woordbare lewenstyl. Deur voortdurende kritiese gesprek tussen die dikwels gesegmenteerde vakgebiede van die Nuwe Testamentiese Wetenskap en Christe-like Etiek aan te moedig, sluit die projek aan by die dringende en groeiende gesprek oor die "etiek van interpretasie," wat sigself ten doel stel om die metodo-logiese gaping tussen verskillende teologiese subdissiplines te vernou. Op hierdie wyse hoop die studie om 'n gevoeligheid te help vestig vir die netwerk van ver-houdinge, verantwoordelikhede en vaardighede wat in die verstaansproses ver-vleg is.

Verskeie hermeneutiese reise word—met wisselende klem—onderneem: vanaf die morele wêreld van hedendaagse lesers, na (die navorser se begrip van) die Bybelse geskrifte en hul kontekste, en uiteindelik terug vanaf die *daar* en *dan* na die *hier* en *nou*. *Hoofstuk een* baken die metodologiese kontoere van die boek af deur die verstaansprosesse waarvan lesers noodwendig deel uitmaak, krities te ondersoek. Aangesien Bybelwetenskaplikes hul vak vanuit verskillende hoeke benader, is dit noodsaaklik dat hul behoorlik verantwoording sal doen van hul verstaanshandelinge, en veral met betrekking tot die pragmatiese effek daarvan.

Wanneer die *aard* en *doel* van die Bybelse dokumente ontleed word, lei dit tot die besef van hul dinamiese en ingewikkelde aard. Kenmerkend van enige kommunikasie-gebeure, weerspieël die Bybelse tekste die linguisties-literêre, sosio-historiese en retoriese dimensies van die veelfasettige alledaagse werklik-heid. Al hierdie aspekte is ten nouste verweef en van mekaar afhanklik, en ver-teenwoordig in werklikheid die delikate hermeneutiese *prosesse* wat onder-liggend is aan, en gestimuleer word deur die tekste van die Bybel. Vir die doel van die studie is dit belangrik dat die *transformerende potensiaal* van tekstuele kommunikasie veral in die ontleding van oorredingstrategieë (hoofsaaklik in die retoriese fase) na vore kom.

Ten einde hierdie proses prakties te illustreer, word die *Efesiërbrief* van naderby belig deur dit vanuit drie verskillende perspektiewe te lees (*hoofstuk twee*). Die gerigtheid of dwang van die brief kristaliseer as die skrywer se klem op die hoofsaaklik Grieks-Romeinse gehoor se identiteit *in Christus*, asook hul ooreenstemmende lewenstyl van liefde, deernis, geregtigheid en heiligheid. Hul nuwe identiteit en etos hou direk verband met die paradoksale krag van Christus se kruisdood, opstanding en verheerliking. Uiteindelik word al Efesiërs se sin-taktiese, dinamiese en dialektiese elemente saamgetrek in die christologies-gemeentelike oriëntasie van die dokument.

Hoofstuk drie bekyk die oorredingsaspek of transformerende potensiaal van die Efesiërbrief van naderby. Die gevolgtrekking is dat die kommunikatiewe krag van dié teks—in Ricoeur se taal—geleë is in die vermoë daarvan om (via die metaforiese prosesse van identifikasie, vervreemding en heroriëntasie) *'n alternatiewe morele wêreld, 'n nuwe perspektief op die werklikheid* te onthul. Sodoende nooi Efesiërs latere gehore en lesers om deur middel van die tekstuele konstruk van die "bedoelde lesers" haar Christologies-gemeentelike visie in voortdurend veranderende omstandighede toe te eien.

Hoofstuk vier volg die lang pad vanaf die Efesiërbrief na die behoeftes en lewensverbande van die Christelike etos en etiek vandag. Eerstens word die verhouding tussen die aard van die brief en belangrike implikasies vir die gesag daarvan ten opsigte van die Christelike etiek onderstreep. Tweedens word gevra na die wyse waarop Efesiërs op verskillende morele paradigmas en vrae wat tydens die geskiedenis van die (Christelike) etiek na vore gekom het, sou reageer. Dit word gedoen deur die potensiële rol van die brief te ondersoek in die vorming van morele *mense*, die verandering tot 'n morele *samelewing*, en die begeleiding tot morele *besluitneming* en *gedrag*. Ten slotte word enkele kriteria voorgestel met die oog op 'n verantwoorde lees van die Nuwe Testament, wat gesamentlik die voortdurende proses van hermeneutiese toe-eiening as 'n "geïntegreerde verbeeldingshandeling" beskryf (Hays).